THE SPACE OF RELIGION

Sheng Yen Series in Chinese Buddhist Studies

THE SHENG YEN SERIES IN CHINESE BUDDHIST STUDIES
Edited by Daniel B. Stevenson and Jimmy Yu

Funded jointly by the Sheng Yen Education Foundation and the Chung Hua Institute of Buddhist Studies in Taiwan, the Sheng Yen Series in Chinese Buddhist Studies is dedicated to the interdisciplinary study of Chinese language resources that bear on the history of Buddhism in premodern and modern China. Through the publication of pioneering scholarship on Chinese Buddhist thought, practice, social life, and institutional life in China—including interactions with indigenous traditions of religion in China, as well as Buddhist developments in South, East, and Inner/Central Asia—the series aspires to bring new and groundbreaking perspectives to one of the most historically enduring and influential traditions of Buddhism, past and present.

For complete list see page 417

The Space of Religion

*Temple, State, and
Buddhist Communities
in Modern China*

YOSHIKO ASHIWA AND
DAVID L. WANK

Columbia University Press
New York

Columbia University Press
Publishers Since 1893
New York   Chichester, West Sussex
cup.columbia.edu
Copyright © 2023 Columbia University Press
All rights reserved

Library of Congress Cataloging-in-Publication Data
Names: Ashiwa, Yoshiko, 1957– author. | Wank, David L., 1957– author.
Title: The space of religion : temple, state, and Buddhist communities in modern China / Yoshiko Ashiwa and David L. Wank.
Description: New York : Columbia University Press, 2023. | Series: The Sheng Yen series in Chinese Buddhist studies | Includes bibliographical references and index.
Identifiers: LCCN 2022057089 (print) | LCCN 2022057090 (ebook) |
  ISBN 9780231197342 (hardback) | ISBN 9780231197359 (trade paperback) |
  ISBN 9780231552127 (ebook)
Subjects: LCSH: Nan pu tuo si (Xiamen, Xiamen Shi, China) | Buddhist temples—China—Xiamen Shi. | Buddhist monasteries—Reconstruction—China—History.
Classification: LCC BQ6345.X5352 A74 2023 (print) | LCC BQ6345.X5352 (ebook) |
  DDC 294.3/6570951245—dc23/eng/20221215
LC record available at https://lccn.loc.gov/202205708
LC ebook record available at https://lccn.loc.gov/2022057090

COVER DESIGN: Milenda Nan Ok Lee
COVER IMAGE: In 1989, Miaozhan, the abbot of Nanputuo Temple, led an ordination ceremony in Guanghua Temple, Putian, Fujian Province. It was one of the largest since the Cultural Revolution.

To Venerable Miaozhan 妙湛 (1910–1995), eighth abbot of Nanputuo Temple

CONTENTS

Acknowledgments ix

Conventions xiii

Glossary of Temple Names in Xiamen City xv

Introduction 1

PART I: Concept, Space, History

1 Themes and Concepts of the Study 19

2 Physical and Semiotic Spaces of Nanputuo Temple 40

3 Institutional Space and Nanputuo Temple's Historical Capital 70

PART II: Recovery and Development of Nanputuo Temple

4 Revival of Buddhist Practice and Education, 1982–1989 111

5 Expansion and Conflict in the Space of Religion, 1989–1995 147

6 Aligning with the Central State, 1996–2004 196

PART III: Nanputuo Temple and Local Buddhist Communities

7 Dynamism of Local Temples 237

8 Devotees and Lay Nuns 262

CONTENTS

9	The Guanyin Festival: Being Buddhist the Chinese Way	290
	Conclusion	337
	Appendix 1: Leaders of Nanputuo Temple, 1684–	349
	Appendix 2: Nanputuo Temple, a Millennium of Construction and Renewal	351
	Appendix 3: Buddhist College of Minnan Curriculum, 1989	355
	Appendix 4: Ordination Ceremony Schedule, October 13–29, 1989, Guanghua Temple	357
	Notes	359
	References	381
	Index	399

ACKNOWLEDGMENTS

THIS PROJECT BEGAN BY SERENDIPITY. After class one day, Yoshiko picked up *The Practice of Chinese Buddhism* by Holmes Welch in a pile of free books for students in Tozzer Library at Harvard University, not knowing the author. She was impressed by its excellent ethnographic details that evoked some parallels with modernization processes in Sri Lanka, where she had done her dissertation fieldwork. She showed it to David, who found it a fascinating perspective on the state and society in China, which he had experienced working in China several years earlier. This occurred in 1986 when we were both graduate students.

Three years later, we found ourselves conducting research in Nanputuo Temple in Xiamen City. Yoshiko was teaching at Xiamen University on a one-year contract while David was conducting fieldwork on the business community for his doctoral dissertation. The Tiananmen Square protest in spring 1989 temporarily halted our teaching and research. So, we started visiting Nanputuo Temple, next door to the university. The temple was alive with clerics, worshipers, and tourists. Soon, we met Miaozhan, the elderly abbot. In response to our questions about the temple, he encouraged us to talk to as many people in and out of the temple as possible. He was correct. Talking with people—shopkeepers, state officials, devotees, workers at the temple, and of course clerics, novices, lay nuns, and students—and listening to their stories drove us, for over thirty

ACKNOWLEDGMENTS

years, to learn more and more about the temple, people's lives, and Buddhism. We also conducted research at temples and their communities in Southeast Asia and North America that had historical links with Nanputuo. As clerics flow like clouds and water, we did our best to follow them accordingly. To write what we learned became another life journey for us. All the while, China's state and society changed tremendously, and so did Nanputuo Temple and Buddhist practice.

This book would not have been possible without the kindness and generosity of many people in the Buddhist communities in Xiamen and various locations around the world who shared their knowledge and experiences with us. Many elderly clerics we met have since passed away, while some younger clerics and lay nuns are now leaders of temples in China and abroad. Their devotion to Buddhism taught us what Buddhism means to them and other people. This is also how we came to understand Buddhism in practice.

Our special thanks go to Pan Hongli, with whom we started our field research in 1989 full of excitement. We thank Deng Xiaohua, Zhang Xianqing, and their colleagues and students in the Anthropology Department of Xiamen University for supporting our fieldwork. We are especially grateful to Wu Shaoren and two lay nuns whose friendship over three decades always made us feel at home in Xiamen. Their devotion to promoting Buddhism in the city greatly encouraged us to continue our study. We learned a lot from those we met on our journey, not only about Buddhism but how people continue turning the wheel of life regardless of the ups and downs.

The book has been improved by discussions with other scholars following our presentations at public lectures, conferences, and workshops. Some of these took place at Aoyama Gakuin University, Chinese University of Hong Kong, Columbia University, Free University of Berlin, Fudan University, Harvard University, Hitotsubashi University, Institut national des langues et civilisations orientales (INALCO), National University of Singapore, Pompeu Fabra University, Sophia University, Stanford University, University of Auckland, and Xiamen University. Our special thanks go to Kenneth Dean, Huang Weishan, Ji Zhe, Mark Mullins, Yasemin Soysal, Ezra Vogel, Nur Yalman, and others who gave us these opportunities for fruitful discussions. We thank our enthusiastic research assistants Gao Yang, Jiang Chengli, Yang Wenhao, and others. At Columbia

University Press, the insightful comments of series editors Daniel Stevenson and Jimmy Yu and three anonymous reviewers, the poetic translations of the couplets at Nanputuo Temple by Allison Bernard, and the efforts of our copyeditor, Mary Bagg, significantly improved the manuscript. We were most fortunate to have Lowell Frye as our editor, whose cheerful and patient accompaniment helped to produce this book. We are deeply grateful for the encouragement and support of all these individuals.

We acknowledge the generous support of the multiple agencies that have funded our research, including two Scientific Grant-in-Aid awards by the Ministry of Education, Sports, Science and Culture of Japan (1996–1998, 2016–2018); a John D. and Catherine T. MacArthur Foundation Peace and International Cooperation Research and Writing Grant (1999–2001); a Henry Luce Foundation Initiative on Religion in International Affairs Grant (2020–2025); and a Special Grant for Academic Research (2020–2023), and a publication subsidy (2019) from Sophia University. Additionally, we were supported by a Fulbright Fellowship, a Nitobe Fellowship of the International House of Japan and the Japan Foundation, and a Harvard Academy for International and Area Studies Fellowship.

The works of Holmes Welch have inspired us to weave observations and narratives by people with broader frameworks of Buddhism and modernizing processes in China. And if this book successfully appeals beyond China specialists to general issues of state and Buddhism, we owe it to the works of Richard Gombrich, S. J. Tambiah, and Gananath Obeyesekere and our conversations with them.

Finally, we acknowledge our children, Alice Kiwako and Tobias Yujin, who played in the courtyards of many temples during our research. We hope they had a good time.

CONVENTIONS

1. All Chinese transliterations follow the pinyin system. For clerics and temples outside the People's Republic of China whose names are widely known by other transliteration systems, spellings are provided at the first appearance of their names in the text.
2. The rendering of Buddhist terminology regarding Nanputuo Temple draws on publications by the temple and Buddhist Association of Xiamen, including *Qiannian gusha Nanputuo* (2013), which describes the temple in both Chinese and English.
3. Monks are referred to by their "first" names, typically consisting of two characters.
4. Chinese characters are provided at the first appearance of a name or term and may be repeated later for technical discussion and easy reference.
5. Sanskrit transliterations are provided for the names of selected deities, texts, and rituals.
6. Months and days for rituals and assemblies are given in the lunar calendar when describing it in general terms, while the solar calendar is used for a specific occurrence.
7. The major shifts in politics that affected the temple during the years of our research and fieldwork caused shifts in the value of the yuan.

CONVENTIONS

We list them to provide context for three periods that roughly correspond to the years we cover in part III (chapters 4, 5, and 6).

Exchange rates (average):
1981–1988: 1 U.S. dollar = 2.7 yuan
1990–1994: 1 U.S. dollar = 6.7 yuan
1995–2005: 1 U.S. dollar = 8.4 yuan

8. The following abbreviations are used in the text for frequently cited sources, with full information in the bibliography:

NSZ	*Nanputuo si zhi*
QGN	*Qiannian gusha Nanputuo*
XFZ	*Xiamen fojiao zhi*

9. The following acronyms are used in the text and notes:

BAX	Buddhist Association of Xiamen
BCM	Buddhist College of Minnan
CPC	Communist Party of China
PRC	People's Republic of China
ROC	Republic of China
SEZ	Special Economic Zone
XRAB	Xiamen Religious Affairs Bureau

GLOSSARY OF TEMPLE NAMES IN XIAMEN CITY

NAME IN TEXT	CHINESE	ENGLISH TRANSLATION
Bailudong Temple	白鹿洞	White Deer Grotto
Danxia Temple	丹霞宮	Red Cloud Temple
Ganlu Temple	甘露寺	Sweet Dew Temple
Guanyin Temple	觀音寺	Guanyin Temple
Hongshan Temple	鴻山寺	Swan Mountain Temple
Huxiyan Temple	虎溪岩寺	Tiger Creek Crag
Jinglian Temple	淨蓮堂	Pure Lotus Hall
Miaofalin Temple	妙法林	Exquisite Dharma Forest
Miaohui Temple	妙慧寺	Subtle Wisdom Temple
Miaoqing Temple	妙清寺	Exquisite Clarity Temple
Miaoshi Temple	妙釋寺	Wonderful Elucidation Temple
Nanputuo Temple	南普陀寺	South Potalaka Temple
Neiwu Temple	內武廟	Inner Guandi Temple
Nengren Temple	能仁寺	Capacious Benevolence Temple
Puguang Temple	普光寺	Universal Illumination Temple
Qingfu Temple	慶福寺	Auspicious Blessings Temple
Riguangyan Temple	日光岩寺	Sunlight Crag Temple
Sizhou Yard	泗洲院	River Islet Yard
Tianzhuyan Temple	天竺岩寺	India Crag Temple

GLOSSARY OF TEMPLE NAMES

Wanshilian Temple	萬石蓮寺	Ten Thousand Stones and Lotuses Temple
Wujin Crag	無盡岩	Boundless Crag
Xuefeng Temple	雪峰寺	Snow Peak Temple
Yangzhen Temple	養真宮	Nourishing Truth Temple
Zizhulin Temple	紫竹林寺	Purple Bamboo Forest Temple

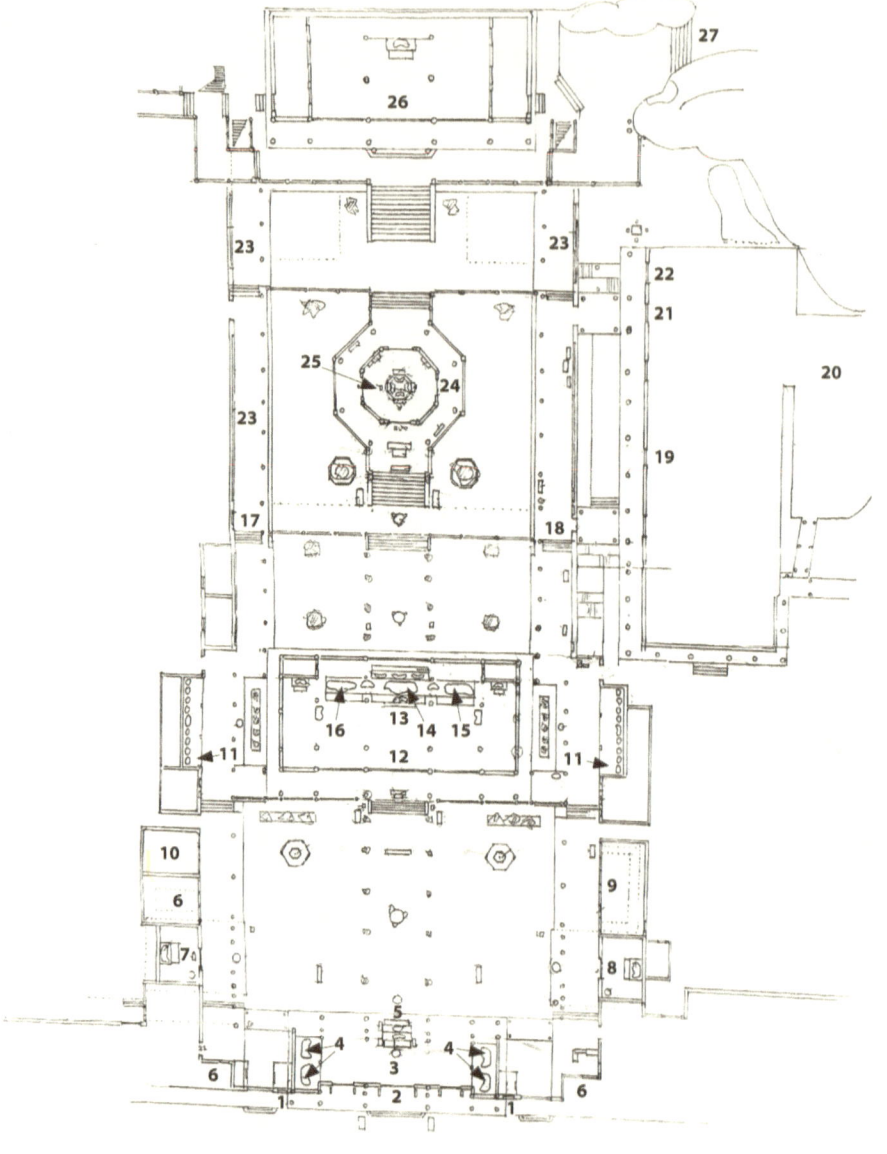

Nanputuo Temple Main Square in 1999

1. Ticket Window 售票處 (to pay fee to enter main square)
2. Heavenly Kings Hall 天王殿
3. Laughing Buddha 彌勒菩薩
4. Four Great Heavenly Kings 四大天王
5. Weituo 韋馱
6. Buddhist Scriptures and Artifacts Gift Shop 佛經法務流通處
7. Qielan Hall 伽藍殿 and Drum Tower 鼓樓
8. Dizang Hall 地藏殿 and Bell Tower 鐘樓
9. Art Gift Shop 藝術品店
10. Temple Ancestral Hall 祖堂
11. Eighteen Arhats 十八羅漢
12. Great Buddha Hall 大雄寶殿
13. Thousand-Handed Guanyin 千手觀音菩薩
14. Sakyamuni Buddha 釋迦摩尼佛
15. Medicine Buddha 東方藥師佛
16. Amitabha Buddha 西方阿彌陀佛
17. Tablet of "Following Karma" 隨緣
18. Tablet of "No Ego" 無我
19. Monastics' Dining Hall 五觀堂
20. Kitchen 廚房
21. Guest Prefect Office 客堂
22. Temple Affairs Office 寺務辦理處
23. Public Announcement Bulletin Board 宣傳欄
24. Great Compassion Hall 大悲殿
25. Thousand-Handed and Thousand-Eyed Guanyin 千手觀音菩薩
26. Dharma Hall 法堂 (1st floor) and Sutra Library 藏經樓 (2nd floor)
27. Path to the Buddha Rock 佛字石 and Back Hills (五老峰)

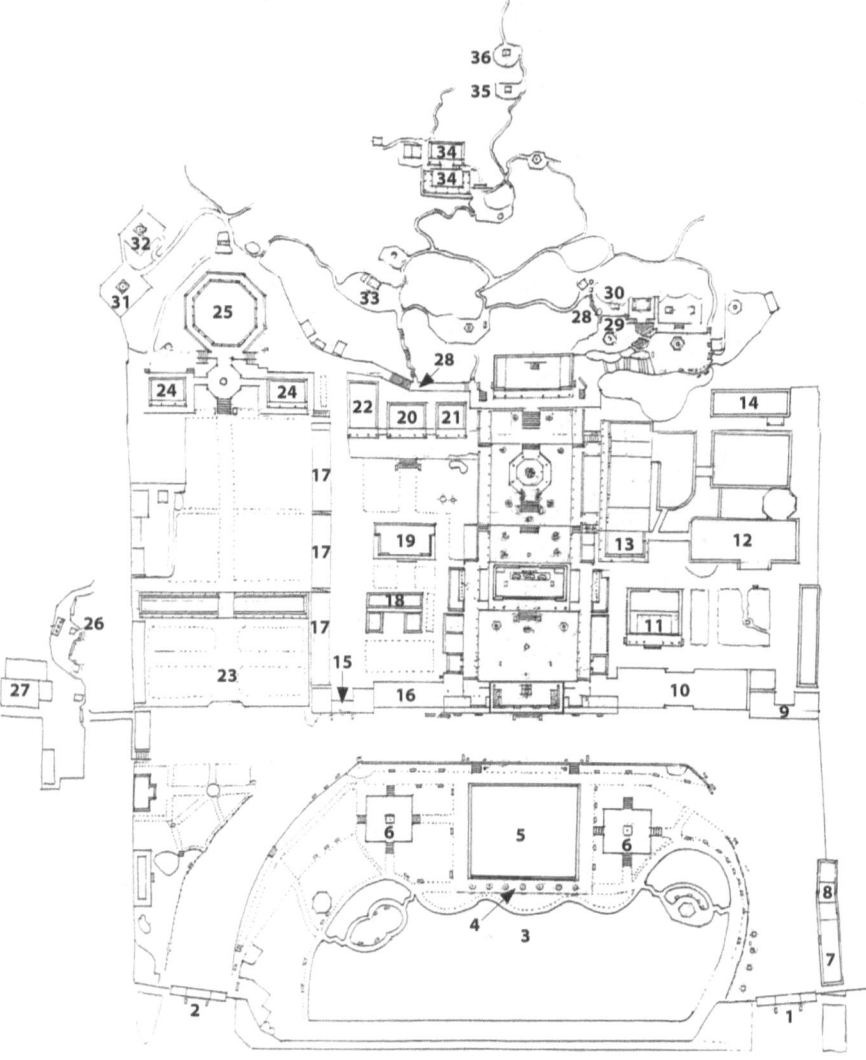

Nanputuo Temple Compound in 1999

1. East Mountain Gate 東山門
2. West Mountain Gate 西山門
3. Lotus Pond 荷花池
4. Seven Previous Buddha Pagodas 七佛塔
5. Releasing Life Pond 放生池
6. Longevity Pagodas 萬壽塔
7. Commercial Store 服務部
8. Tea House 茶店
9. East Gate 東門
10. Sutra Chanting Hall 唸佛堂
11. Merit Hall 功德樓
12. Puzhaolou Restaurant 普照樓
13. Haihuilou Restaurant 海會樓
14. Zhengming Building 正命樓
15. West Gate 西門
16. BAX Office 廈門佛教協會
17. BCM Dormitories 學生宿舍
18. BCM Classrooms 閩南佛學院
19. Taixu Library 太虛圖書館
20. Abbot's Residence 方丈樓
21. Acolyte Building 侍者樓
22. Senior Clerics' Residence 法師樓
23. Nanputuo Temple Charity Foundation 南普陀寺基金會
24. Clerics' Dormitory 寮
25. Meditation Hall 禪堂
26. Spirit Money Furnace 金紙爐
27. Guest House 上客堂
28. Paths up Wulao Peak 五老峰
29. Reverend Zhuanfeng Pagoda 轉逢和尚塔
30. Buddha Rock 佛字石
31. Reverend Miaozhan Pagoda 妙湛和尚塔
32. Reverend Huiquan Pagoda 會泉和尚塔
33. Puzhao Temple 普照寺
34. Tushita Courtyard 兜率陀院
35. Taixu Pavilion 太虛亭
36. Reverend Taixu Pagoda 太虛和尚塔

THE SPACE OF RELIGION

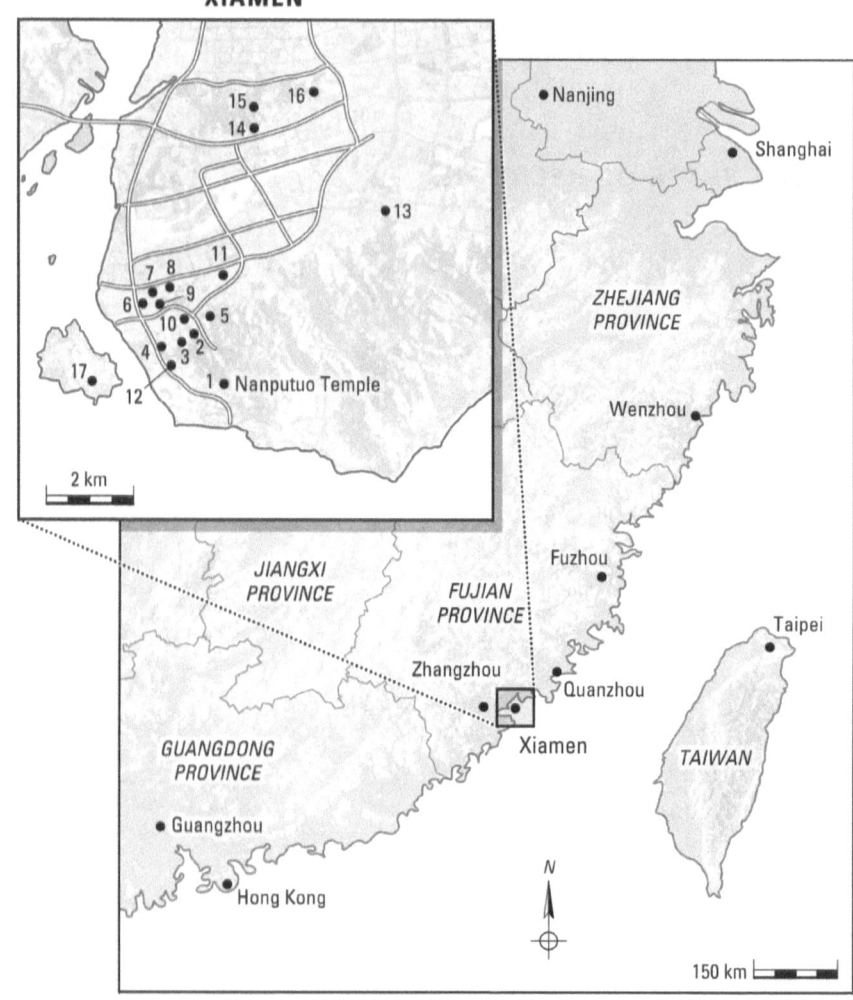

Xiamen City and Selected Temples

1. Nanputuo Temple
2. Huxiyan Temple
3. Bailudong Temple
4. Hongshan Temple
5. Wanshilian Temple
6. Yangzhen Temple
7. Neiwu Temple
8. Danxia Temple
9. Miaoqing Temple
10. Miaofalin Temple
11. Jinglian Temple
12. Qingfu Temple
13. Puguang Temple
14. Xuefeng Temple
15. Tianzhuyan Temple
16. Guanyin Temple
17. Riguangyan Temple

Introduction

FOR MORE THAN THREE HUNDRED years a Buddhist temple in Xiamen (Amoy 廈門), a port city on China's southeast coast, has been a popular site of folk belief regarding Guanyin 觀音菩薩 (Skt. Avalokiteśvara), the bodhisattva of compassion. Since the early twentieth century, the temple has been a center of the modern reform movement of Buddhism and among the first to recover after the Cultural Revolution. Its name, Nanputuo 南普陀, means "South Putuo," and refers to its location in relation to Putuoshan 普陀山, a mountain at the center of Guanyin worship in China, on an island in the East China Sea. In *The Space of Religion* we tell the story of the temple, drawing from our research of it for over thirty years.

When we first began our research in 1989, Nanputuo Temple sat at the outskirts of Xiamen. The city, located in Fujian Province 福建省, was a state-designated special economic zone intended to spearhead the reopening of the market economy in China. Its streets were dusty with construction as the old downtown was being restored, and outlying agricultural fields were being paved over to accommodate a new business district, residential areas, and export-oriented factories. Private businesses had restarted, and commodities were plentiful, but electricity shortages kept the streets dark at night, buildings remained in disrepair, and many people still wore "Mao" tunics, a reminder of harsher times. In general, residents were optimistic and ambitious even if everything seemed unstable and unpredictable.

In March 1989 we attended our first Guanyin festival (Guanyin jie 觀音節), an annual event at Nanputuo Temple to celebrate the bodhisattva's "birthday." Tens of thousands of people—young and middle-aged, male and female—came to pray to Guanyin for their prosperity and well-being. They started to arrive in late afternoon, traveling by public bus or on foot. Many stopped to buy incense, food, and paper spirit money (traditional offerings made to dead souls) from hawkers lined up along the dried-out Lotus Pond in the temple's front yard. As the evening deepened, the noise of the swelling crowd drowned out the chanting of monks in the Great Buddha Hall (Ch. Daxiong bao dian 大雄寶殿, Skt. Mahāvīra prasāda). Excitement peaked at midnight as people surged into the temple, believing that Guanyin's magical efficacy (*ling* 靈) for divine assistance was greatest at the onset of her birthday. With animated expressions, they held burning incense sticks above their heads to keep them from breaking and burning others. Young monks labored nonstop, dousing piles of discarded incense into buckets of water and gathering the bundles of spirit money that worshipers handed over for burning. A haze of smoke and dust, tinged yellow by the dim lights, burned people's eyes and illuminated the faces of the deity statues gazing down on the scene. Among the crowd, we spotted businesspersons we knew and students from Xiamen University, located next door. At the same time, other students were meeting at the university to discuss the hunger strike that had just begun among students in Beijing's Tiananmen Square. No one anticipated the massacre of the students three months later.

We had heard that Buddhism was recovering from state suppression during the Cultural Revolution (1966–1976) but were surprised by the large number of worshipers and their intense emotions. Like other temples in China, Nanputuo had been shut down during the Cultural Revolution. Now the new wood and fresh paint in the temple were signs of the rebuilding underway since 1979, when the state once again recognized religion. Piles of stones, tiles, and other construction materials created hazards for unwary worshipers, even though the renovation of the wall paintings, Lotus Pond, and monuments on the back hills had yet to begin. But people were enthusiastically participating in Buddhism, happy that the temple was open for worship. Many had come in their best clothes to pray to Guanyin for her compassion and protection, and to other buddhas and deities for wealth and prosperity in the new era of economic liberalization. With this impressive spectacle we witnessed the space of religion emerging rapidly in China and decided to sharpen our research on the recovery of Buddhism by focusing on Nanputuo Temple.

The recovery of the temple itself was part of the long transformation of Buddhism that had proceeded in tandem with modern state formation since the late nineteenth century. The idea to confiscate Buddhist temples and lands to establish public schools and hospitals came about in the final years of the Qing dynasty (1644–1912). Then, in 1912, the newly founded Republic of China (ROC) established China's first modern state constitution, which guaranteed freedom of religious belief. Although Buddhism had been much weakened by the turmoil at the end of the Qing, as well as by the invasion of foreign powers, a movement emerged to preserve and protect Buddhist teachings and institutions through their modern reform.

Since 1949 the much stronger state in the People's Republic of China (PRC), governed by the Communist Party of China (CPC), has alternated between two approaches that appear radically different. One, reflecting the Marxist-Maoist view of religion as the "opium of the people" and "feudal thinking," sought to eradicate religion, especially during the Cultural Revolution. The other approach, to cooperate with religion, was adopted in the 1950s, abandoned during the Cultural Revolution, and revived in 1979. The manner by which Buddhists survived this turmoil reflected the choices individuals made around the time of the founding of the PRC: some remained in China, living with the new state regulations and cooperating with the CPC to the extent possible; others left the country. Then, after 1979, China became economically strong and Buddhism flourished anew. We have considered how all these approaches and actions contributed to the process of constituting the state and Buddhism in modernity (Ashiwa and Wank 2009a).

Although our perspective in this book extends back to the late nineteenth century when modernizing movements began, our main narrative starts in 1979, when the state launched "reform and opening up" (*gaige kaifang* 改革開放) policies in an effort to create a new market economy through sweeping institutional and social changes. This administrative liberalization was favorable for Buddhism and other state-recognized

INTRODUCTION

religions. By the early 2000s, thousands of temples had recovered, surpassing their previous glory and attracting greater numbers of worshipers. Surveys in the early twenty-first century estimate that 20 percent of China's population, over 250 million people, are Buddhists (Chinese Academy of Social Sciences 2010), making it the largest religion in China and accounting for about half of all Buddhists globally (Pew-Templeton Foundation 2012, 32). Yet these numbers may be too low if compared to how populations of other religious groups are measured. For example, we observed many people who bowed and offered incense in temples but did not acknowledge being Buddhists (*fojiao tu* 佛教徒) when we asked them. In Christianity and Islam, however, believers are more clearly defined by their baptism or conversion, and other practices. Therefore, the number of people practicing Buddhism in China could be larger.

By 2004, the year that marks the end of our Nanputuo narrative in this book, the temple fully recovered and was changing to meet the state's growing emphasis on Buddhism as a culture and on the "Chineseness" of Buddhism in the PRC. This trend has further intensified since 2013, when Xi Jinping introduced the slogan "Chinese Dream" (Zhongguo meng 中國夢), an idea suited to promoting Buddhism as a foundation of traditional Chinese culture and increasing CPC control over the religion globally. We mention these changes in state policy and their effects on Nanputuo Temple (and Buddhism in general) in this book's conclusion and plan to examine them more broadly in future publications.

The Space of Religion combines our perspective of modern Buddhism from the late nineteenth century to the present with our decades of fieldwork-based observations of Nanputuo Temple and its relation to the state. We have already published various works that address related themes, including the politics of Buddhism in modernity (Ashiwa 2009; Wank 2009), the local politics of the temple's recovery (Ashiwa 1991; Ashiwa and Wank 2006; Wank 2000), transnational networks (Ashiwa 2000, 2001; Ashiwa and Wank 2005, 2016), and local Buddhist traditions in Xiamen (Ashiwa and Wank 2019). In our edited volume *Making Religion, Making the State* (Ashiwa and Wank 2009b), we introduced an institutional analysis to explain the mutual constitution of state and religion in modern China. In that analysis we reject dualistic assumptions of the state as a power that seeks to control or suppress religions struggling to be autonomous, independent, and free. Instead, we consider the relations of state and religion as constituted by multiple actors, values, and agendas in processes and interactions of conflict, cooperation, and competition. This book brings these insights together with unpublished data and our concept of religion as a space to explain Buddhism in the modern transformation of the state.

Reform, Recovery, and Religion as Space

As we began to assess the results of our long-term fieldwork and observations of Nanputuo Temple, three themes emerged regarding Buddhism in China. One concerns the importance of connecting the recovery of the temple, beginning in 1979, to the movement for the modern reform of Buddhism that originated in the early twentieth century. In particular, the temple's leadership in the 1920s and 1930s by the monk Taixu 太虛 (1890–1947), famous for his ideas to modernize Buddhism, created historical capital that furthered the temple's rapid recovery after the Cultural Revolution. We show how the events we observed are part of processes in the modernization of Buddhism that began in the early twentieth century, and we trace how the reactivation of other forms of capital are linked to the recovery and expansion of the temple after 1979.

The second theme occupies most of the book, in which we explain how the recovery of Nanputuo Temple from 1979 until 2004 has proceeded in networks of actors that extend to local communities in Xiamen, overseas Chinese, and the state administration of religion. We analyze several phases of the temple's recovery during our field research. Although each phase lacks a clear demarcation, we consider certain national events and institutions that signal a shift to the next phase. In 1979, the state reopened the institutional space of religion, but for the next three years, the revival of Buddhism proceeded slowly due to the CPC's equivocal stance. The first phase of the temple's recovery lasted roughly from 1982 to 1989, when the state clarified its institutional space of religion. This enabled the temple to reactivate links to overseas Chinese communities, rebuild the temple compound, and restart clerical education. The second phase began after the 1989 Tiananmen Square protests when the state demanded that religions adapt to state needs. During the next six years Nanputuo Temple expanded by establishing a charity foundation and meditation hall while sending clerics to serve in temples in overseas

Chinese communities. But the growing power and prominence of the temple increased conflict with the local state administration. In the final phase, from 1996 to 2004, a new abbot sent by the central authorities in Beijing required the temple and its teachings to adhere to new state standards, stabilizing it as a Buddhist temple in the state system of modern religious administration.

The third theme to emerge from our combined work involves our concept of religion as a space. We view the temple as a physical space (a compound of buildings, land, and statuary), a semiotic space (a place for Buddhist teachings and practices), and an institutional space (with a focus on state rules for religion through laws, policies, and constitutional principles). This view of religion, we argue, enables a more realistic explanation of multiple aspects of the recovery of the temple, including its positioning in the state system. In devising the framework, we have been inspired by the ideas of several social theorists who sought to avoid reductionist analyses, binary frameworks, and essentialist concepts. Our claim that religion is a space is not a theory of religion per se but rather a way to conduct fieldwork on a social phenomenon and provide an explanation of its transformation that integrates complexities into a realistic social science narrative.

Given our pursuit of these intertwined issues through fieldwork, the analysis in this book bridges two distinct bodies of literature in the empirical study of Buddhism. One includes historical studies of the social and organizational transformation of Buddhism from the nineteenth century in colonial and semicolonial contexts (Blackburn 2010; Bond 1988; Jones 1999; Welch 1968). Some of these studies foreground the importation of the European political ideology of secularism to Asian contexts. They trace the complex refiguring at multiple levels of Buddhist teachings, practices, and beliefs to fit attempts to form a state that includes "religion" as a necessary administered category to be considered modern (Asad 2003; Nedostup 2010; Van der Veer 2001). The other body includes fieldwork approaches to understanding the daily lived experience of Buddhists as they adjusted to the contemporary social and political contexts in Asia (Buswell 1992; Gombrich 1971; Gombrich and Obeyesekere 1988; LeVine and Gellner 2007; McLaughlin 2019; Southwold 1983; Spiro 1982), North America and Europe (Bao 2015; Wilson 2012), and transnational and global movements (Berstein 2013; Geary 2017; Learman

2005). We examine these concerns in the adjustments and transformations of the monastic order and Buddhist communities within the modern state in the PRC. Since its founding in 1949, the PRC has been ruled by a communist party that has fluctuated between trying to eliminate religion and using it for political purposes. Fieldwork has fostered our understanding of how Buddhist communities linked in various ways to a major Buddhist temple have maintained and adjusted Buddhist teachings and practices in the context of shifting CPC expectations, state enforcement of religious policies, and the growing wealth of society.

Xiamen's Place in the "Land of Buddhism"

Fujian Province is known as the "Land of Buddhism" (*fo guo* 佛國), a place where Buddhism has flourished since the Tang dynasty (618–907). This long history is embodied in the thousands of Buddhist temples that, even today, account for the largest number of temples of any province (Ji 2004). Although many scholars argue that Buddhism was introduced to China through the northern Silk Road traversing central Asia (cf. Rong 2004), its path into China can also be traced via the southern seas from India, Sri Lanka, and Southeast Asian countries. Buddhism came to Fujian on the winds and waves of the Maritime Silk Road that brought trade goods, as well as Buddhist teachings and clerics from South and Southeast Asia, while the province's mountainous boundaries helped protect Buddhism from periodic attempts by imperial states to suppress it.

Much of Fujian's maritime history has been centered in Minnan 閩南, a region with its own dialect, on the province's southeastern seaboard. From the eleventh to fourteenth centuries, China's international sea trade centered on a Minnan port city called Quanzhou 泉州, which connected China to Southeast Asia, India, and routes to the Middle East, Africa, and Europe. People from many parts of the world came to Minnan, and Chinese travelers from Minnan who settled along trade routes in Thailand, Indonesia, and the Philippines established early overseas Chinese communities (Schottenhammer 2001). These movements brought commodities as well as technologies, ideas, and religions (including Buddhism, Islam, and Jainism) to China. Chinese monks like Faxian 法顯 (337–422) and Yijing 義淨 (635–713), who traveled by land from China to India and then to Sri Lanka, returned to China along these sea routes, passing

INTRODUCTION

through Southeast Asia. Such exchanges by Chinese and non-Chinese clerics brought Buddhism—"authentic," "transformed," "indigenized"—to China, along with teachings, arts, and sutras from Thailand, Burma, Sri Lanka, and other countries with Buddhist traditions.

The fishing village of Xiamen became an increasingly important port over the centuries. In the mid-fourteenth century, the Ming dynasty's (1368–1644) ban on international trade (Clark 2002) precipitated the rise of Xiamen, whose remoteness and excellent natural harbor had made it an ideal center for smuggling. In the late fourteenth century, the Ming built a fort to fight smuggling and prevent Portuguese sailors from landing. With the defeat of the Ming dynasty by the Qing in the mid-seventeenth century, Xiamen became a base for Ming supporters until the late seventeenth century, when the Qing armies vanquished these Ming holdouts and opened up a dozen ports for trade, including Xiamen. Then, in a policy reversal in the mid-eighteenth century, the Qing restricted all international trade to the port of Guangzhou, Guangdong Province 廣東省廣州市 (Ng 1983; Schottenhammer 2007). This led to fighting between the British and Chinese, known as the Opium War (1839–1842). China was defeated and forced to reopen Xiamen and four other ports—Guangzhou, Shanghai 上海, Ningbo 寧波, Fuzhou 福州—to Europeans.

By the mid-1800s, Xiamen ranked among China's top cities in terms of international connections and exposure to modernity. It was the leading exporter of Chinese tea and porcelain. Many Chinese farmers migrated through its port to labor in British and Dutch plantations in Southeast Asia, giving rise to a sizeable overseas Chinese population of Minnan-speakers. Xiamen merchants imported significant amounts of opium and sugar, and the city acquired accouterments of modern systems and infrastructures, such as schools and electrical grids. Protestant missionaries in Xiamen, who became fluent in the Minnan dialect while serving in overseas Chinese communities in Southeast Asia, founded the New Street Church (Xinjie libaitang 新街禮拜堂) in 1848, the first church to preach to the Chinese people in Chinese. The missionaries also operated mission schools and hospitals. The most famous were in an international settlement located on Gulangyu 鼓浪嶼, a small island in Xiamen's harbor, and thus outside Chinese sovereignty, as were treaty port cities in general. Newly wealthy Chinese business families and the growing middle class sent their children to the settlement's missionary schools, where they learned Western music, art, and sports. These schools also exposed them to Christianity, which became popular in Xiamen (White 2018).

The period from the 1910s until the Empire of Japan's invasions of China in the 1930s was a high point for the region's economy. While World War I distracted European powers, the city deepened its trading relations with overseas Chinese communities in Southeast Asia. Xiamen's status as a treaty port had already increased the financial and personnel resources of Nanputuo, eventually transforming the locally popular temple devoted to Guanyin worship into an ecumenical one with a wide-ranging reputation and network. The temple became renowned in China as a center of the modern reform of Buddhism associated with the monk Taixu, who came in 1927 to serve as abbot and rector of its newly founded Buddhist academy for the modern education of clerics.

A decade and a half of political and economic turmoil began with the Japanese military invasion that sparked the Second Sino-Japanese War in 1937 and continued with the civil war (1945–1949) between the armies of the CPC and the Republic of China (ROC). Facing the prospect of living under communist rule, many businesspersons, intellectuals, clerics, and others emigrated to Southeast Asia, Taiwan, and Hong Kong. In 1949, one of the last battles in the civil war was fought around Xiamen. The defeated ROC army retreated to Taiwan but held on to several small islands just off Xiamen's coast. For several decades, Xiamen was on the frontlines of intermittent hostilities that discouraged state economic investment and thus impoverished the city. During the Cultural Revolution, the remaining monks in Xiamen were forced to disrobe, and many laicized. At the same time, during the mid-twentieth century, clerics who had emigrated from Xiamen became part of increasingly prosperous Chinese communities in Taiwan, Hong Kong, and Southeast Asian countries.

The reform and opening-up policies profoundly affected Xiamen. In 1980, the city was designated as one of the PRC's four special economic zones, along with Shantou 汕頭, Shenzhen 深圳, and Zhuhai 珠海 in Guangdong Province, that were intended to entice foreign investment. The central state also gave autonomy to the local state administration, which invited investment in the local economy, especially from businesspersons of Chinese descent in Taiwan, Hong Kong, and Southeast Asia. In

INTRODUCTION

the 1980s these monies flowed in, boosting the city's economic growth to 20 percent annually, double the national average. Xiamen became a model in the PRC for economic reform and prosperity. Its liberal administration encouraged the recovery of religions. Nanputuo Temple was among the first Buddhist temples to recover, with much support from overseas Chinese. In the 1990s, the city faced corruption scandals but became more administratively organized. In the early 2000s, its economy began diversifying from export processing to service and cultural industries, such as tea culture, modern Chinese fashion, and tourism (including Buddhism). Xiamen became one of China's most livable cities due to its wealth, low pollution, cultural industries, excellent schools, public transportation, and scenic sites, including its colonial architecture and Nanputuo Temple.

By 2004, the conclusion of our narrative, Xiamen was the smallest, wealthiest, and most urbanized of the Minnan region's three major cities, the other two being Quanzhou and Zhangzhou 漳州. Its 1,700-square-kilometer area included the city districts on Xiamen Island and suburban and rural districts lying across a narrow bay in Tongan County 同安縣 on the mainland. The population of two million people (quadruple that of 1979) mostly lived in the city districts. Xiamen also housed the international airport that connected the Minnan region to the fifty million Minnan speakers in Taiwan, overseas Chinese communities in Southeast Asia, and in global cities, including Melbourne, Seoul, Tokyo, and Los Angeles. In 2003, Xiamen pioneered direct passenger flights between the PRC and Taiwan. It became more common to see Buddhist monks and nuns at the Xiamen airport traveling to far-flung destinations.

Fieldwork and Data

We have based our account of Nanputuo Temple's recovery, and the transformation of Buddhism and the state, on fieldwork we conducted for a total of twenty-six months spread over the years from 1989 to 2018; although our narrative of Nanputuo Temple ends in 2004, the subsequent fieldwork we conducted during the following fourteen years let us conclude the book with our observations of Nanputuo entering a new phase. Our discussion of the fieldwork begins with a description of our positions

INTRODUCTION

in relation to the research and the field site, and then we consider issues of location, timing, sources, and data.

We acquired the guiding insights and main data during two main periods of fieldwork and numerous smaller field trips in the PRC and places outside the country connected to Nanputuo Temple. The first period extended from spring 1989 to spring 1990. During this time, we gained an overview of the operation and activities of the temple, its relations with the local state administration, and smaller temples and devotee activities in Xiamen in the decade since the temple reopened in 1979. The second period occurred during the summers of 1999 and 2000. Each summer we spent two months in Xiamen, updating and deepening our understanding of the temple and its relations with other Buddhist communities. In addition, we conducted shorter periods of research in the country, lasting from one week to over a month (1995, 2007, 2014, 2015, 2016, 2017, 2018). While in Xiamen, we stayed in university guesthouses and dormitories at Xiamen University 廈門大學, a national university, and Lujiang Industrial University 鷺江職業大學, a city-level institution, both of which were a few minutes' walk from Nanputuo Temple. We could easily go to the temple to conduct interviews, observe rituals, and socialize, and then return to our living quarters to record our findings. We invited clerics, lay nuns, devotees, and Buddhist Association of Xiamen (BAX) officers to our quarters for extended conversations. Most of our fieldwork in Xiamen occurred in the urban Kaiyuan and Siming districts on Xiamen Island. Outside of the PRC, we conducted fieldwork at many places with connections to Nanputuo Temple, including in Taiwan (1992, 2011), Hong Kong and Macao (1989, 1990, 2017), Malaysia (2015, 2018), Singapore (2001, 2015), Sri Lanka (2002, 2015), Philippines (2001), Canada (2017), France (2015), and the United States (2002–2003, 2008, 2017). These research periods, ranging from days to months, deepened our understanding of the transnational links and interactions of Nanputuo Temple with temples and Buddhist communities outside the PRC.

We used multiple methods. One was interviewing. We conducted hundreds of interviews with a wide range of people with some connection to Nanputuo Temple. We conducted most interviews ourselves in Mandarin and a few in Japanese, with some conducted in Minnan dialect through an interpreter. At Nanputuo Temple, interviewees included monks and nuns in administrative, teaching, and work positions; and students and laypersons holding administrative positions. Several key informants have been interviewed repeatedly over the years, mostly face-to-face in Xiamen but also via telephone. We were exceptionally fortunate to have met and conversed with the three abbots serving the temple since the Cultural Revolution. Many interviews were with clerics connected to Nanputuo Temple but not residing there; others were with nuns and monks at dozens of local temples in Xiamen and other major Buddhist temples in Fujian and China; and others still with teachers and students in Buddhist academies, including the Buddhist College of Minnan (BCM), the China Buddhist Academy, and the Fujian Buddhist Academy. Outside the PRC, we interviewed overseas Chinese clerics in Singapore, Malaysia (Penang), Philippines (Manila), Taiwan (Taipei and Gaoxiong), Hong Kong, the United States (mainly Los Angeles and New York), Canada (Toronto, Vancouver), France, Sri Lanka (Colombo), and Tokyo. We interviewed directors, secretaries, and other officers of state-approved Buddhist associations at the local, provincial, and national levels, including Dao Shuren 刀述仁 (in 1990), vice president of the Buddhist Association of China (Zhongguo fojiao xiehui 中國佛教協會). Other Buddhist interviewees were devotees (*jushi* 居士) and believers (*xintu* 信徒) (including some active before 1949), lay nuns, chanting group participants, wealthy donors, persons commissioning on-demand rituals, and members of overseas Chinese Buddhist communities in Singapore, Malaysia, and the Philippines. Interviewees who were state officials included persons in the religious affairs bureaus of Xiamen and Fujian Province and other branches of the local state administration, including the Xiamen Municipal United Front Work Department (Xiamen shi tongyi zhanxian gongzuo bu 廈門市統一戰線工作部).

The second method was observation, allowing us to describe in detail Buddhist rituals, including morning and evening services at Nanputuo Temple and other temples and shrine halls, ceremonies for clerical ordination and abbatial ascension, Guanyin festivals, and on-demand rituals commissioned by laypersons. A third method was survey, the basis of data we collected at all local temples in Xiamen and from participants in the Guanyin festival in 1989 and 1999. We conducted these surveys with the assistance of graduate and undergraduate students from the anthropology and international journalism departments at Xiamen

INTRODUCTION

University. A fourth method was archival research. During the 1980s and 1990s, most of the documents we acquired were unpublished. Gazetteers of Buddhism in Xiamen and Nanputuo Temple did not appear until 2007 and 2012, respectively, and the temple website came online in the early 2000s. Therefore, practically all of the primary documents cited in this book, including prepublication drafts of gazetteers, were given to us during fieldwork. This had the advantage of letting us learn from those providing the documents as to how the documents had been created, used, and interpreted in the local contexts.

Through the fieldwork and archival research, we acquired nine types of documents. First, commemorative volumes published upon the death of a master monk, the ascension of a new abbot, and anniversaries of temples, academies, and associations provided details of clerical careers and organizational histories. Second, administrative documents from Nanputuo Temple, such as charters, schedules, curriculums, and protocols, gave insight into its internal organization and administration. Third, gazetteers, including the *Gazetteer of Nanputuo Temple* (*Nanputuo si zhi* 南普陀寺誌), and multiple drafts of the *Gazetteer of Xiamen Buddhism* (*Xiamen fojiao zhi* 廈門佛教誌), provided historical insight. Fourth, publicly posted documents on bulletin boards and temple walls, such as ritual announcements, tourist information, and temple reports, provided insight into temple activities and the face of the temple that the clerics wanted to show the public. Fifth, correspondence among Nanputuo Temple monks, officers of Buddhist associations, and state officials at local, provincial, and central levels gave rich insight into relations between the temple and state. Sixth, state media reportage on the temple and related events, such as the campaign against Falun Gong (法輪功), revealed what the state wanted the public to know about Buddhism and religion. Seventh, diaries, letters, and an unpublished memoir of a BAX official provided firsthand accounts by persons who participated in events described in this book. Eighth, schedules of rituals and ceremonies, such as the ordination and abbot's ascension, and participant lists helped us understand these events. Ninth, epigraphs, including couplets, stories of the temple, and Buddhist teachings, whether carved on stone walls, pillars, and steles or painted on lacquered boards on temple walls, revealed the semiotic spaces of Nanputuo Temple and local temples.

INTRODUCTION

We cite the sources of these materials in several ways. Key interviews are cited in the notes. Over the years, the state's attitude to field research by international scholars on religion in the PRC has shifted considerably. Therefore, to protect our informants, we provide the month and year of an interview but not the specific date, and we refer to most informants by pseudonyms or occupational titles. We only name abbots and priors of temples who were publicly identifiable at the time of the interviews. The documents are listed in the references section for primary sources, except for the ninth type, mostly epigraphs, which are described in the text.

The richness of the data constitutes the strength of the ethnography of Nanputuo Temple, which is our social science narrative. Nothing presented in this book relies on a single source. All information we learned from an interviewee was corroborated by at least one other interviewee or document. Therefore, this book provides an accurate and realistic account of the situation of Buddhism in the PRC during its recovery from 1979 to 2004, as seen through one temple and in the broader context of modern China.

Précis of *The Space of Religion*

We have organized this book in three parts, each containing three chapters. In part I we present the themes and concepts for studying the space of religion. Chapter 1 establishes our guiding concept of religion as a space with physical, institutional, and semiotic dimensions to analyze the data. Chapter 2 introduces the main subject, Nanputuo Temple, by describing its physical and semiotic spaces as they appeared during our fieldwork. Chapter 3 examines the institutional space of religion when it reopened from 1979 to 1982, as the CPC renounced the Cultural Revolution ideology that had denied religion to instead reacknowledge it as an administrative category in the state. At the same time, Nanputuo Temple reactivated its historical capital, including its legacy of Taixu, transnational ties, and the leadership of the old-generation monk Miaozhan 妙湛 (1910–1995).

In part II we chronologically narrate Nanputuo Temple's recovery. Chapter 4 addresses the first phase of its recovery in the context of the religious policies from 1982 to 1989. Various forms of support from

INTRODUCTION

overseas Chinese helped revitalize the temple by rebuilding the compound and restarting its Buddhist academy, ordinations, rituals, and administration. But the growing power of the temple created tension with the local state administration. Chapter 5 traces events from 1989 to 1995, the second phase of the temple's recovery and expansion. It started with the ascension of Miaozhan as abbot, in a ceremony postponed by the Tiananmen Square protest, which nevertheless symbolized the rapid revival of the temple. Until his death in 1995, Miaozhan led the temple in facing new central state demands for internal changes in Buddhism and growing conflict with the local state over the temple's wealth and development. The central state, which attached much importance to Nanputuo Temple, sent representatives to the temple to try to solve the conflict, which even disrupted the semiotic space of Miaozhan's funeral. Chapter 6, which covers the third phase, from 1996 to 2004, looks at the growing alignment of the temple with the central state. In 1996, the central state sent a new abbot, Shenghui 聖輝 (1952–), to instill conformity with Buddhist discipline and national standards and handle the conflict with the local state administration. Shenghui was a "new-generation" monk who understood the communist ideology and how to get along with the state religious policy, including the campaign against Falun Gong and the Buddhist diplomacy of the state. As the temple aligned with central state initiatives, it became more detached from local communities in Xiamen.

In part III we examine Nanputuo Temple's connections to Buddhism in Xiamen, where the temple is located. Chapter 7 describes the local temples, increasingly staffed by clerics who had graduated from the BCM. It illustrates how relations with Nanputuo were crucial in recovering the lineages of these temples and the flexibilities in the space of religion. Chapter 8 looks beyond ordained clerics to examine two communities of Buddhists. One is devotees, including elderly ones in the state-approved devotee association as well as new groups of intellectual youth creating their own activities. The other community is lay nuns (*caigu* 菜姑), a Minnan custom recognized as a distinct local category of Buddhist. Chapter 9 focuses on those who participate in mass worship at the Guanyin festival. This extends our argument about the space of religion to the folk beliefs of the masses who worshiped the temple's exquisite statues of Thousand-Handed and Thousand-Eyed Guanyin (Qianshou qianyan Guanyin 千手千眼觀音). The passion and enthusiasm of these

INTRODUCTION

worshipers were most heated at the festivals occurring three times a year. In describing their activities and perceptions during the October 1999 festival, we view these attendees as a social body that creates a living space of religion in temples as a part of modern Chinese society. The festival was the moment when the temple's semiotic, institutional, and physical spaces functioned for the largest number of people as they worshiped Guanyin. In the book's conclusion, we identify a new phase of Nanputuo Temple from the early twenty-first century as Buddhism increasingly came to be seen as "culture" by the CPC and clerics in the context of China's growing wealth and global economic and political power.

In these chapters we weave a narrative encompassing the history of the temple and Buddhism, networks extending from the local to the global, and an analysis of religion that simultaneously embraces beliefs, art, laws, and modern ideas of the sacred and secular. Our extended time frame for researching and writing the book, while prolonging its completion, allowed us to acquire rich data, deepen our analysis, and impart sharpened perspectives to our narrative. The result is a realistic and accurate account of a Buddhist temple as it recovered from the state's suppression of Buddhism.

PART I
Concept, Space, History

1

Themes and Concepts of the Study

A TEMPLE IS THE CORE of Buddhist practice as a religion and the core of Buddhism that can be controlled by the state. It is a sacred space representing the cosmology of Buddhism and containing images of the Buddha, bodhisattvas, and other deities for worship. A temple has a monastery, small or large, where monks or nuns live and practice Buddhist discipline.[1] Temples are connected to other temples by lineages of Buddhist teachings, master-disciple and dharma brother relations, and in other ways, but there is no overarching ecclesiastical organization as in Roman Catholicism. Generally speaking, Buddhist teachings prohibit clerics from laboring and allow them to possess only minimal belongings, such as a begging bowl, clothes, and a fan, so they can devote themselves to Buddhist practice. Therefore, temples rely on the laity and secular authorities for support while profiting at times from landholdings. Regarding state control, especially in China, Buddhism has been variously tolerated, patronized, and crushed by emperors since Buddhism first reached China. Especially now in the PRC, a country ruled by a communist party, the state permits religious activity only in the physical space of temples, administratively defined as "religious activity sites" (*zongjiao huodong changsuo* 宗教活動場所). Buddhist practices are prohibited, in principle, outside of temples if conducted as the propagation of religion.

By centering our study of Buddhism in China on a temple, namely Nanputuo Temple, we were able to focus on the complex and diverse practices of Buddhist communities as they faced state efforts to control Buddhism as an administered category of modern religion. In *The Space of Religion* we explain how multiple aspects of a temple—landscape, architecture, personnel, religious disciplines, state rules—presented and represented, and produced and reproduced Buddhism as it recovered from suppression in the Cultural Revolution. In this chapter, we first locate our study in the literature as an ethnography focusing on a Buddhist temple in the PRC. Second, we give an overview of modern state formation and modern Buddhist reform in China. Here we introduce Nanputuo Temple, a famous Guanyin temple, an especially active center of modern Buddhism, a leader in the recovery of Buddhism after the Cultural Revolution, and a hub for connecting Buddhism in China with overseas Chinese. Third, we elaborate on our analytic framework constituted by the concepts of space, network, and episode.

Positioning Our Study

Most scholarship on Buddhism in China addresses the tradition of Buddhist studies and history. It consists of textual and iconographic analyses of sutras, disciplines, Buddhist art, philosophy, history, and rituals (e.g., Carter 2010; Pittman 2001; Schlutter 2010; Wu 2015; Yü 2001), and historical studies of the economic and political organization of temples and their contexts in the imperial era, Republican period (1912–1949), and early years of the PRC until the Cultural Revolution (Brook 1994; Gernet 1998; Kieschnick 2003; Scott 2020; Welch 1967, 1968, 1972; Yu 2015a). Recently more scholars have been conducting anthropological and sociological fieldwork-based studies of Buddhism in the PRC.[2] They have published monographs on Vajrayana and Theravada Buddhism, illuminating the particular contexts of the Tibetan, Mongolian, Dai, and other ethnic minorities that practice them (Barstow 2017; Borchert and Rowe 2017; Buffetrille 2012; Goldstein and Kapstein 1998; Humphrey and Ujeed 2013; Kojima 2012; Liang 2018; Powers 2016; Tan 2005), and the interactions of Tibetan Buddhism and Han Chinese (Bianchi 2001; Esler 2020; Yü 2014).[3] Despite the much larger number of Han Chinese practitioners of Mahayana Buddhism, however, there are only two ethnographic monographs;

one about the Kaiyuan Temple 開元寺 in Quanzhou, Fujian (Nichols 2022), and the other on Buddhist lay practice (Fisher 2014).[4]

Our book is the first ethnography to focus on one Buddhist temple and its relations to other Buddhist temples and communities in the locale, and its dynamics with the state in the political, social, and global contexts of modern China.[5] Political turmoil and the sensitivity of the topic in the PRC prevented the publication of book-length studies of monastic Buddhism in the PRC after the trilogy written by Holmes Welch (1967, 1968, 1972). In the final volume, *Buddhism Under Mao*, he examined Buddhism from 1949 until 1967 (encompassing the first two years of the Cultural Revolution), based on state media reports and accounts of monks who left China and were interviewed in Hong Kong and Taiwan. Welch wove information from these sources into a comprehensive account of Buddhist practices and their transformation during the turbulent politics in the first decade and a half of the PRC. Our research occurred in different circumstances when it became possible to do fieldwork in the country. We had the opportunity to stay in Xiamen City, Fujian Province, and observe the transformation of Buddhism and the state that occurred in tandem with rapid economic growth.[6]

Our research strategy to carefully observe one temple over a long period allowed us access to interactions, activities, and events that occurred there or were linked to it. As we describe in this book's introduction, this approach made it possible to assess the reality of how the temple's management, strategies, and contents of rituals could exist and develop in the PRC. We came to understand the local and central state policies of Buddhism and religion, and the situation of Buddhist communities in Xiamen—and in particular how Nanputuo Temple, a center for modernizing Buddhism with extensive ties to overseas Chinese, spearheaded the recovery and transformation of Buddhism. Through fieldwork in the temple we observed the contradictions, confrontations, cooperation, and creative interactions that formed as Buddhist practice met state administration. Long-term observation let us understand the process of reopening the space of religion and recovery of a Buddhist temple, not as abstract categories of "religion" and "state," but as the lived experiences of people in a modern state under a communist party. Although freedom of religion is an emblematic right granted by a modern state, such freedom is delimited by the CPC, whose ideology denies religion. Our focus on one temple highlights aspects of Buddhism that changed to meet state demands when drawn into the institutional category of religion in the state system. Although Nanputuo Temple has particular attributes, as does any Buddhist temple, the understanding we gained by observing the transformation of Buddhism and the state may illuminate the situation of other temples, as well as Buddhism in China and globally.

Buddhism as a Project of Modernity, Nineteenth to Twenty-First Centuries

As a result of Western influences, Chinese elites in the late nineteenth century began to pursue multiple projects of modernity in such areas as science, citizenship, sanitation, democracy, education, and religion (Duara 1995; Garrett 1970; Harrison 2000; Rogaski 2014). A master project among these pursuits was the making of a modern secular state that included the administrative category of "religion," and modern reform movements of religions (Ashiwa and Wank 2009b; Nedostup 2009; Yang 2008). Modern state-making has been ongoing ever since, compelling innovations in Buddhism to fit the category of "modern" religion (Ashiwa 2009; Ji 2008; Wank 2009).

Modern State Formation with the Category of Religion

The ROC, founded in 1912 as China's first modern state, gave constitutional protection to religious belief for Buddhism, Catholicism, Daoism, Islam, and Protestantism. "Religion" (*zongjiao* 宗教), along with its antithesis of "superstition" (*mixin* 迷信), was an imported category of modernity (Ashiwa 2009). To political elites, religion embodied doctrinal, spiritual, and ethical systems that depended on social organization and contributed to the public good, whereas superstition was concerned with this-worldly material gain, practiced by charlatans, lacked a social organization, and harmed the public good (Goossaert and Palmer 2012, 58). The status of Buddhism and Daoism as "religion" was ambiguous because some of their beliefs and practices in local society could be difficult to distinguish from "superstition." Consequently, many Buddhist temples were destroyed or converted for public use as schools and local state offices during "smashing superstition" campaigns. Buddhist elites worked to increase recognition of Buddhism as a "religion" by modernizing some practices and creating a national association in 1929 to represent Buddhists in the polity.

The PRC, established in 1949 as the second modern Chinese state, was headed by the CPC, which held two different ideological views of religion. One view, which combined the Marxist idea of religion as an "opium" used by the exploiting classes to control the masses, viewed all religions as akin to superstition with no place in the modern order. Another view reflected the CPC's efforts prior to 1949 to project a "united front" by cooperating with nonparty groups (see chapter 3). During the fight against the ROC in the 1930s, for example, the CPC gained support from minority ethnic populations during the Long March (1934–1935) by cultivating relations with their leaders, including religious ones. Then, during war with Japan from 1937 until 1945, the CPC forged an anti-Japanese alliance with various groups, including religions.

In the first PRC constitution, adopted in 1954, the CPC took a tolerant approach toward religion. The constitution declared that "citizens . . . enjoy freedom of belief" (People's Republic of China 1954, art. 88). The rationale for protecting religious beliefs in a state led by a communist party was expressed in an editorial published four years earlier in the *People's Daily* (*Renmin ribao* 人民日報), the official newspaper of the CPC.

> Until that time, so long as a part of humankind is technologically backward and hence continuing to be dependent on natural forces and so long as part of humankind has been unable to win its release from capitalist and feudal slavery, it will be impossible to bring about the universal elimination of religious phenomenon from human society. Therefore, with regard to the problem of religious belief as such, any idea about taking coercive action is useless and positively harmful. This is the reason why we advocate protecting freedom of religious belief, just as we advocate protecting freedom to reject religious belief. (*Remin ribao*, quoted in Welch 1972, 4)

This editorial showed that even as the CPC was committed to the Marxist view of religion, it foreswore state efforts to eliminate religion as divisive and disruptive. Nevertheless, while protecting religious beliefs, the constitution did not recognize the establishment or practice of religion, and the editorial characterized the existence of religious beliefs in the PRC as a "problem." To handle it, the CPC created a state administrative apparatus, described in chapter 3, for the five religions it recognized—Buddhism, Daoism, Catholicism, Islam, and Protestantism.

From 1957, the state became increasingly hostile toward religion. This antagonism was linked to new CPC security concerns, including the diplomatic break with the Soviet Union, problems in the state-planned economy, and ideological disagreements among the CPC leadership over the direction of the revolution. The Anti-Rightest Campaign was launched that year to expose domestic enemies, mainly those with nonconformist ideas, including religious believers. The following year, the CPC launched the Great Leap Forward (Da yuejin 大躍進) (1958–1962) to rapidly make China a communist society by establishing people's communes (renmin gongshe 人民公社). At the same time, the CPC declared that religion had lost the basis for its existence in the new communist society (Luo 1991, 144). During the Great Leap Forward, many temples were converted into "productive" factories, communal canteens, and community centers. During the Cultural Revolution, the attack on religion became a mass movement in the campaign called Shatter the Four Olds (Po sijiu 破四舊)—old customs, culture, habits, and ideas.[7] Many temples were destroyed or defaced, clerics were forced to laicize, and devotees and believers were persecuted. The state apparatus of religious control was shuttered, accused of harboring religious sympathizers.

In 1979, the CPC began to denounce the Cultural Revolution and launched the Four Modernizations (Sige xiandaihua 四個現代化), a master project to make China a modern, powerful socialist state through an internationally integrated market economy. The "opening-up" policies to restructure the state and society for a market economy included a favorable social and cultural liberalization for religion. The CPC once again acknowledged religion, restarted the state administration of religion, and permitted Buddhists to reclaim and restore Buddhist temples and practices. During the 1980s and 1990s, Buddhism recovered within this administration. Then, in the early 2000s, the CPC began to increasingly emphasize Buddhism as Chinese culture and part of a Sinocentric view of global economic, political, and cultural order.

Movement for Modernizing Buddhism

In the early twentieth century, a movement for the modern reform of Buddhism took shape in the face of growing competition from Christianity and expectations of modern "religion" by the new ROC state. Some Buddhists began to adopt practices from Christianity, such as establishing seminaries for the professional education of clerics, encouraging clerics to preach to the people, sanctioning charitable activities, emphasizing spiritual and ethical cultivation, and performing choral music. The first reformers included educated devotees with deep understandings of Buddhism who lived in treaty ports or had been abroad in places exposing them to modern ideas. In particular, Yang Wenhui 楊文會 (1837–1911) was a state official whose service in the Chinese embassy in England introduced him to the new scientific study of religion (Welch 1968, 2–10). His interaction with the Sri Lankan Buddhist reformer Anagarika Dharmapala inspired him to propagate Buddhism globally (Ashiwa 2001). In 1908, he opened the Jetavana Hermitage (Qiyuan jingshe 祇園精舍) in the port city of Tianjin 天津 to teach Buddhism through innovative methods, such as teaching clerics and devotees in the same classroom. In 1919, the May Fourth Movement (Wu si yundong 五四運動) inspired nationalistic Chinese youth to see Buddhism as a "Chinese religion" that could oppose foreign Christianity. They advocated an "orthodox Buddhism" (*zhengxin fojiao* 正信佛教) that emphasized scriptural study and was purged of "superstitious" practices, such as burning spirit money for ancestors and worshipping deities not originally found in Buddhism.

The monk Taixu, who had studied in the Jetavana Hermitage, became the most radical reformer among the clerics. He integrated Buddhist teachings and practices with everyday life in the modern world by proposing a Buddhism for the Human Realm (Renjian fojiao 人間佛教). It refocused Buddhism from a concern with ritual and better reincarnation toward worldly concerns to realize the Pure Land in society. He modernized Buddhism by creating Buddhist academies (*foxue yuan* 佛學院) that taught clerics both Buddhist teachings and secular subjects. He broke new ground by using cultural translation, such as metaphors from Western science, to illustrate key concepts. He advocated for a national Buddhist association of clerics to replace the many local associations formed after 1912 to represent Buddhist interests as a "religion" in the modern state polity. And uncharacteristically for a cleric, he developed ties with politicians and apparently held political views (Pittman 2001; Welch 1968, 51–71).

From 1927 to 1937, the movement for the modern reform of Buddhism accelerated. It coincided with the greater centralization of the ROC state following the defeat of provincial warlords who had seized power after the collapse of the Qing dynasty. In 1929, clerics founded the China Buddhist Association (Zhongguo fojiao xiehui 中國佛教會), a national platform to negotiate with the authorities to reduce the confiscation and destruction of Buddhist temples. This period saw the proliferation of new Buddhist organizations, such as publishing houses that reprinted sutras and issued vernacular translations of scholarship on Buddhist history and lectures by famous monks, or Buddhist academies inspired by the model that Taixu established in 1922 at his Wuchang Buddhist Studies Academy (Wuchang foxue yuan 武昌佛學院). These schools adopted modern pedagogical techniques, including graded evaluations, blackboards in classrooms, and encouraging students to answer in their own words. A national survey by the Chinese Buddhist Association in the 1930s estimated that there were 738,000 clerics in 297,000 Buddhist temples (Welch 1967, 411). But most were small, local temples whose resident clerics were outside the stream of modern Buddhist reform. Then, from 1937 to 1949, Buddhism was disrupted by the social, political, and economic turmoil of the Japanese invasion of China and the ensuing occupation and civil war.

Following the founding of the PRC in 1949, some Buddhists sought to gain CPC recognition for Buddhism. A key figure was Taixu's disciple Juzan 巨贊 (1908–1984), who proposed a Buddhist-Marxist synthesis emphasizing manual labor and self-sufficiency (Li 2017; Tymick 2014).[8] In 1952, Buddhists founded the Buddhist Association of China as a state-controlled organization. But the situation for Buddhism deteriorated as temples lost their economic base. The land reform movement (1949–1952) confiscated temples' agricultural land that provided rental income, while patrons lost their wealth with the nationalization and collectivization of private business. From the mid-1950s, increasing state hostility toward religion threatened the existence of Buddhism for the next two decades (Welch 1968; Yu 2015a). Military and local state administrations requisitioned temples as observation posts, storehouses, factories, and schools, while clerics were forced to laicize. The onset of the Cultural Revolution in 1966 intensified the attack on religion. Young communist activists known as Red Guards destroyed many Buddhist temples and confiscated Buddhist publications from the homes of devotees. This situation expressed a view of religion in the CPC's communist ideology. By 1970, violent attacks on temples had stopped, but religious practices remained suppressed. When the Cultural Revolution ended in 1976, several dozen prominent temples were reopened as parks and museums but not for worship, because the CPC had not reacknowledged religion.

In 1979, the start of the opening-up policies marked another turning point for Buddhism in the PRC when temples could be open for Buddhist practice and worship. Buddhists began a two-decade-long effort to reclaim and repair destroyed, abandoned, and damaged temples and replenish the ranks of the clergy. By the early 2000s, Buddhism had largely recovered and entered a new stage in the PRC. The rise of a powerful Chinese state and wealthy society spurred the unprecedented development in the scale of temples, numbers of academies, new practices of Buddhism as religion and culture, and the globalization of Chinese Buddhism.

Historical Sketch of Nanputuo Temple

Since the tenth century Buddhist temples have existed at the foot of the south side of Wulao Peak (Wulao feng 五老峰), a 185-meter-tall, steeply sloped hill on Xiamen Island. They have been repaired, destroyed, rebuilt, and reconsecrated. The first temple, Sizhou Yard 泗洲院, was affiliated with the Linji school (*linji zong* 臨濟宗) of Chan Buddhism.[9] In the Northern Song dynasty (960–1127), the temple was renamed Wujin Crag 無盡岩. At the start of the Ming dynasty (1368–1644), it was rebuilt on a larger scale with hundreds of monks in residence and renamed Puzhao Temple 普照寺. In the early seventeenth century, Puzhao Temple was destroyed during fighting between supporters of the Ming dynasty and the invading Manchu army, which founded the Qing dynasty (1644–1912).

Consecrating Nanputuo Temple to Guanyin

In 1685, the Qing admiral Shi Lang 施琅 rebuilt the temple at the foot of Wulao Peak after vanquishing the last supporters of the deposed Ming dynasty. He consecrated it to Guanyin to console the souls of soldiers killed on both sides of the fighting and built a Great Compassion Hall (Dabei dian 大悲殿) housing a statue of Guanyin, sometimes called the Goddess of Mercy in English. The temple was named Nanputuo after Putuoshan 普陀山, a mountain island 750 kilometers to the north, said to be the home of Guanyin; we refer to it as Mount Putuo in this book.[10] Since then, Nanputuo Temple has been a prominent focus of people's worship, especially during the Guanyin festival, held three times a year. Around 1730, the temple became associated with the Heyun 喝雲 religious lineage of the Linji school based at Nanshan Temple 南山寺 in Zhangzhou 漳州, an urban settlement near Xiamen.[11] For the next two centuries, the priors of Nanputuo Temple belonged to the Heyun lineage.

The temple's dedication to the popular bodhisattva Guanyin gave it close ties to local communities, especially fishermen and merchants who prayed for protection on dangerous sea voyages. In 1764, a folk belief temple (*miao* 廟) for the Dragon King (Long wang 龍王), popularly worshiped as the water deity, was erected on the west side of Nanputuo's Great Buddha Hall (Daxiong bao dian 大雄寶殿). It was likely built by seafaring merchants who held meetings in the temple (Lin 2015) until moving it in the mid-nineteenth century to the harbor to be closer to worshipers (*QGN*, 3). In 1866, a large character for "Buddha" (*fo* 佛) was engraved on a boulder at the foot of Wulao Peak behind the temple; this addition reflected the passion of people's worship at the temple. In 1904, a Releasing Life Pond (Fangsheng chi 放生池) was dug in front of the temple for the popular ritual of freeing caught fish and turtles. These three places, the Great Compassion Hall, the Buddha Rock, and the Releasing Life Pond, have been the most popular places for visitors to the temple.

Opening Nanputuo to the Stream of Modernity

In the early twentieth century, Nanputuo Temple became a center of the movement for Buddhism's modern reform. This was possible because, as a popular temple for Guanyin worship, Nanputuo had less religious status in Buddhism than other temples in Minnan, such as Guanghua Temple 廣化寺 in Putian 莆田 and Nanshan Temple, which appeared much earlier in historical records. Therefore, Nanputuo Temple was more flexible and open to the stream of modernity. This openness was seen in efforts to establish a new school for Buddhist education at Nanputuo Temple beginning in 1913 with the Sandalwood Academy 旃檀學林, followed in 1920 by the Jingfeng Buddhist School 景峰佛學社 (*XFZ*, 7). These initiatives paved the way for establishing the Buddhist College of Minnan (BCM) in 1925, which was open to modern pedagogy.

In 1924, Zhuanfeng 轉逢 (1879–1952), the ambitious prior of Nanputuo, ecumenicized the temple by implementing the *shifang conglin* system 十方叢林.[12] This opened Nanputuo to clerics without regard to their affiliations with a Buddhist lineage or school.[13] Clerics were invited to become abbots based on their merit and prestige, which, in turn, raised the religious standing of the temple in Buddhism.[14] First to be invited was the prominent monk Huiquan 會泉 (1874–1943), who was prior of Xiamen's Huxiyan Temple 虎溪岩, a Buddhist temple within the Huangbo 黃檗 lineage of the Linji school.[15] Although the temple was smaller than Nanputuo, it had a higher religious status as a site of Buddhist teachings, evident in its history of holding large, triple-platform ordination ceremonies for monks (*san tan chuanjie dafa hui* 三壇傳戒大法會) (*XFG*, 78). Therefore, Huiquan's assumption of the Nanputuo abbotship in 1925 raised the temple's status. Concurrently, Huiquan became rector of the BCM.

The status of Nanputuo increased further in 1927 when Taixu agreed to serve as the temple's second abbot and rector of the BCM. Taixu was already well-known for his ideas on the modern training of clerics, which he introduced four years earlier at his Wuchang Buddhist Academy.[16] Yet his willingness to become abbot of the still little-known Nanputuo Temple indicated that his ideas were far outside mainstream Buddhism. His presence attracted other prominent Buddhist monks interested in the modern reform of Buddhism. Most notable was Hongyi 弘一 (1860–1942), recognized for his contributions to Buddhist arts, who came to Xiamen in 1932. Two years later, he established the Buddhist Instruction School (Yangzheng yuan 養正院) to teach Buddhism to local Minnan clerics who lacked the educational background to enter the BCM (*NSZ* vol. 2, 254).[17] The presence of Taixu and other prominent monks attracted young clerics to Nanputuo, eager to learn the new modern Buddhism. By the mid-1930s, two hundred clerics, including BCM students, resided at the temple. In 1947, the temple's religious status rose ever further when it held its own large, triple-platform ordination ceremony. The ordination masters were the prominent clerics Xuyun 虛雲 (1840–1959) and Yuanying 圓瑛

(1878–1953) (*NSZ*, 25), who gave the precepts to a thousand clerics and laypersons coming from around China and overseas (*XFZ*, 50).

Reformist monks at the temple worked with young devotees in Xiamen to found a Buddhist association, Buddhist publishing house, and Buddhist education for the laity. The devotees were the young and idealistic sons of newly rich, entrepreneur-merchant families in the treaty port searching for their own identities in the turbulent times. Stimulated by the "enlightened" modernism and nationalism of the May Fourth Movement in 1919, they took an interest in Buddhism, which they saw as the essence of the "authentic" tradition and long history of China. The closeness of Nanputuo Temple to the people through Guanyin worship made it open to devotees. Together, the Nanputuo clerics and young devotees were full of energy for reforming Buddhism to face modern times and place it at the core of Chinese identity.

Nanputuo Temple attracted much funding from devotees and worshippers for restoration and expansion in the decade following its ecumenicization. The Great Compassion Hall and Great Buddha Hall were rebuilt. New construction included the east and west arhat arcades, bell and drum towers, a two-story Dharma Hall (Fa tang 法堂), a four-story dormitory for elderly monks, a classroom and dormitories for the BCM, and a sutra chanting hall used by devotees. On Wulao Peak, a retreat was built for Taixu called the Tushita Hall (Dou lütuo yuan 兜率陀院). The hall's name expressed Taixu's devotion to the Pure Land of Maitreya as the basis of social engagement propounded in his Buddhism for the Human Realm (Jones 2021; Ritzinger 2017). A cave on Wulao Peak was also fashioned into a meditation retreat for Hongyi.

Japanese Occupation to End of Cultural Revolution

Japan's military invasion of China in 1937 ended the flourishing decade of Nanputuo's prosperity and reform. A bomb from a Japanese airplane destroyed the BCM classroom building and dormitory, and the following year the Japanese military occupied Xiamen. Some monks sought refuge in the international settlement on Gulangyu Island, while others fled, either inland to areas still under Chinese government control or abroad to Singapore, the Philippines, and Malaysia, countries Japan soon occupied. Given the defeat of Japan in 1945 and the following four years of civil war between communists and nationalists, Nanputuo Temple, now largely empty of monks, fell into disrepair.

With the founding of the PRC, Nanputuo Temple's situation deteriorated further through loss of revenue and the declining number of worshipers. CPC antipathy toward religion made some people afraid to come to the temple, while others, especially youth, were attracted to communist ideology rather than Buddhism. Parts of the temple were repurposed, such as the establishment in the 1950s of a primary school for secular public education. Yet some religious construction did occur during this period. Overseas Chinese paid for renovating the Great Buddha Hall in 1959 and building memorial pagodas to Zhuanfeng in 1954, Taixu in 1959, and Huiquan in 1963. In 1962, the Xiamen Municipal People's Government granted cultural preservation status to the temple and renovated the Great Compassion Hall the next year. But the number of clerics declined as there were no young novices, and many ordained clerics had to disrobe and return to their rural villages. By the start of the Cultural Revolution, only ten middle-aged and elderly monks remained.

During the campaign to Shatter the Four Olds in 1966, temples in Xiamen, as elsewhere in China, were attacked by Red Guards. Many smaller, local temples were reduced to rubble, but Nanputuo Temple suffered relatively minor damage. Red Guards toppled one of the statues of the Four Heavenly Kings (Ch. Sida tianwang 四大天王, Skt. Catvāro mahā-rājāḥ) in the Heavenly Kings Hall (Tianwang dian 天王殿), smashed arhat statues, and burned ancestor tablets in the Merit Hall (Gongde lou 功德樓).[18] The following year, the local revolutionary committee turned the arhat arcades into a textile workshop for weaving and drying cloth, while the BCM classrooms became a kindergarten.[19] Even though the temple was closed for worship, some Xiamen residents told us they continued to go to Wulao Peak behind the temple to worship. When a son or daughter was sent off to the countryside, they prayed for their health and safe return.[20] Some people claimed to have seen lights in the Great Compassion Hall on the evenings of the Guanyin festival. In 1976, the Cultural Revolution ended, and the temple reopened as a park named Wulao Peak Scenic Area (Wulao feng fengjing qu 五老峰風景區).

CONCEPT, SPACE, HISTORY

Recovery and Expansion

In 1979, CPC ideology began to reacknowledge the existence of religion within regulatory delimits, enabling Nanputuo to reopen as a Buddhist temple. The following year, the Xiamen government shut down the primary school at Nanputuo but gave the temple's remaining agricultural land to Xiamen University for faculty dormitories (Wu 2014, vol. 7, book 1, 23, 163–164). Over the next two decades, the temple recovered and expanded its activities and built area. By the late 1990s, there were 541 clerics at Nanputuo Temple and the BCM, possibly the largest number of any temple in the PRC at that time (Huiran et al. 1998). By then, Nanputuo Temple had a modern and cosmopolitan reputation for its excellent Buddhist academy, Buddhist charity foundation, international ties, and exquisite southern-style architecture.

During the two decades, buildings and functions were restored. New granite mountain gates and pavilions on the mountainside were constructed in 1980. In 1981, the Heavenly Kings Hall was rebuilt, and repairs were made to the Bell Tower (Zhong lou 鐘樓) and Drum Tower (Gu lou 鼓樓). In 1982, the Great Buddha Hall and Great Compassion Hall were renovated. The education of Buddhist clerics resumed with the reopening of the Buddhist Instruction School in 1982 and the BCM in 1985. New educational facilities included a student dormitory in 1983 and a classroom and library in 1990. Two hostels for pilgrims and visitors to the temple were opened in 1989. In the early 1990s, the Releasing Life Pond and Lotus Pond were refilled with water, pagodas were erected in front of the temple compound, and new buildings were constructed for the Meditation Hall, the Nanputuo Temple Charity Foundation, and temple administration. In 1997, a nuns' campus of the BCM opened in Zizhulin Temple 紫竹林 at another location in Xiamen. Other construction included two vegetarian restaurants and a two-story department store.

The recovery and development of Buddhism was reflected in the lives and activities of its three abbots since 1979. Miaozhan, born at the end of the Qing dynasty, led the recovery of the temple until his death in 1995. A survivor of much political turmoil, he worked hard to regain the beauty and glory of the temple and propagate Buddhist teachings in new ways. The next abbot was Shenghui, who served from 1996 until 2005. Raised and educated in the PRC, he was dispatched in 1996 by the

Buddhist Association of China to tighten administration and religious discipline in the temple. His efforts moved it closer to the central state, making it almost a national temple. The abbot Zewu 則無 (1974–), who succeeded Shenghui and was still in office in 2023, was a member of the post–Cultural Revolution generation and the first abbot to have graduated from the BCM. Since assuming office in 2005, he has propagated Buddhism in terms of "culture" and "ethics," deepening the temple's connection to local Buddhist communities. (See appendix 1 for all priors and abbots of the temple.) For this book we focus on the recovery period of Nanputuo Temple under the first two abbots from 1979 to 2004, and we briefly update its situation since then in the conclusion.

Framing Our Analysis

Through our research, we have been observing and following changes in a single temple while reflecting on the concept of space.[21] We focus on Nanputuo as a space where: the heterogeneous practices of Buddhism meet state efforts to define and control Buddhism as the category of "religion" in modern state administration; the temple collaborates with the state while making efforts to preserve its independence as a religious site; and the expectations of believers and their folk beliefs are manifested. To understand these complexities, we needed a framework for viewing a Buddhist temple as multiple and continuous interactions of ideas, actors, power, resources, and other entities. The framework should also reduce nomothetic bias in explaining the interactions in a single case by eschewing a categorical definition of religion. Hence, we propose a framework built around the concepts of space, network, and episode that constitute, respectively, our view of religion, method of analysis, and narrative technique.

The framework builds upon our earlier critique of essentialist approaches to religion and state (Ashiwa and Wank 2009a). It advances an integrated analysis and explanation of a multidimensional phenomenon that avoids categorical definition of phenomena in question. We seek to avoid frameworks premised on "state" and "religion" as binary interactions, such as hegemony/subjugation, control/autonomy, and authority/resistance. We do not deny insights stemming from such frameworks, but we do supplant them by explaining a more complex reality of actions and commitments by diverse agents (persons, organizations, policies, resources) and levels (local, regional, transnational, global) that generate the space of religion. Our framework draws on ideas of social theorists about social organization and transformation.

Space

Henri Lefebvre premised that human society consists of the appropriation and assignment of spaces to social relations (2009b, 186–187). Spaces are not "natural" but produced and reproduced in social relations. Although he has been recognized for opening the analysis of how large-scale systems operate through the lived experiences of people, his discussion remains abstract. In particular, the rhetorical fluidity of his argument, unaccompanied by empirical examples applying his concept of an integrated space, can make his ideas challenging to use. Nevertheless he presents a powerful argument of social transformations: not as a theory of history or in terms of essentialist categories, but rather as a contrivance of human activities in making and reproducing space (Lefebvre 1991). In particular, his theory of space to explain the reproduction of capitalism without basing it on the contradictions of capital and labor suggests how we can go beyond conceiving "religion" and "state" as oppositional categories.

We view the transformation of religion as an integrated space constituted by three dimensions.[22] This space has a physical existence that is subject to rules and regulations and can generate semiotic meanings. Elaborating on Lefebvre's idea, space consists of three dimensions or kinds of space: physical space, institutional space, and semiotic space. Physical space has a tangible presence experienced by people through their senses, such as buildings, landscapes, and monuments. Institutional space is constituted by rules and systems through policies, constitutions, laws, regulations, and guidelines. Semiotic space exists through the imaginations of persons and groups in their emotions, perceptions, and knowledge, while its meanings, such as cosmology, values, and morality, are produced, consumed, and spread in social interactions. We now apply this theory of space to the empirical study of religion.

First, the physical space of religion is the geography of the land and landscape. It includes memorial sites, halls, hidden buildings, graveyards, and such items inside buildings as shrines, statues, icons, ornaments, and secret treasures, as well as small items people possess, such as prayer beads. For Buddhism, a temple with its compound of halls and courtyards is the center of religious cosmology and authority and, especially in China, the physical space where the state delimits the practice of Buddhism as religion. The physical space creates sensual experiences for people, is laid out in specific arrangements, and exists over time as it is built, maintained, expanded, destroyed, neglected, and rebuilt. Since the end of the nineteenth century, in the movements of multiple projects of modernity, the physical space of temples has been the object of confiscation by the state to make public facilities.

Second, the institutional space of the modern state is shaped by its values conveyed as rules through national constitutions, policies, laws, regulations, and guidelines (Meyer et al. 1987; Shore and Wright 1997). While private or semipublic associations can create regulations, these should conform to state rules. In the PRC, the state institutions reflect the CPC ideology regarding the definition of religion and the manner of its existence in society. These rules are discourses that format practices in religious communities. Religious practices that adapt or incorporate this formatting gain state recognition for their existence. In this way, the institutional space makes Buddhism part of the state system as the administered category of religion. Of course, according to Buddhist tradition, a temple is an autonomous organization with internal regulations based on Buddhist teachings that have nothing to do with rules outside the temple, even those created by state power. Once even a criminal is ordained as a cleric, they can stay in the temple, and the state cannot, in principle, arrest them. But states have historically had administrative sections in charge of religions, and in modern states, all people and their actions, including clerics, reference state rules. They observe the laws or face resistance from the state if they challenge the rules or fail to observe them. Therefore, the rules, including local state laws and regulations, are part of the space of religion.

Third, semiotic space is created by the imagination. As shared meanings and values, semiotic space is constituted by morals, norms, ideologies, idealism, history, ethnicity, memory, aesthetics, knowledge, and technology. The semiotic space of religion is often represented by symbols and actions, such as rituals, that produce and convey meanings. For example, a sacred site is a semiotic space for those who share the meaning of its sacredness, but for others who believe in different religions or have no religion, this semiotic space may not exist. For them, it is just a physical space or a different semiotic space, such as a political ideology or paganism. Semiotic space does not necessarily adhere to boundaries of physical space or institutional space. But institutional space can induce the production of semiotic space as a result of politics, policies, and education, and cause changes in the physical space through destruction, building, and other actions.

In Buddhism, the core of semiotic space is the teaching of Buddha, represented by sutras, rituals, architecture, statues, lifestyles of clerics, ornaments, art, and inscriptions, which are symbols or symbolic actions. In a temple, Buddhist teachings and cosmology are expressed in every item, producing the semiotic space of religion that turns a temple's physical and institutional spaces into Buddhism. For example, a Buddhist academy transmits the teaching of Buddha, and the everyday lives of the clerics following the Vinaya are the living teachings of the Buddha. Even though visitors and tourists who come to the temple to make offerings and look around may lack textual knowledge of Buddhist teachings and understanding of the symbolic meanings, their sensual experiences—the sounds of sutra chanting, scents of burning incense, sights of red and gold engravings, beautiful gardens, and magnificent halls—stimulate their imaginations. This shapes the semiotic space of Buddhism, which includes folk beliefs of cosmology and mythology as the basis of popular Buddhist practices. In this sense, festivals and rituals at a temple are opportunities to create a semiotic space through the collaboration of clerics and visitors to the temple. The physical and institutional space cannot exist as the space of religion if the semiotic space is deficient.

There is duplication and overlap among these spaces. Physical space continuously produces semiotic space. Institutional space seeks to format the array of the physical space. Semiotic space may fully or partially adapt to the institutional space, or not at all, while giving meaning to physical space. The three spaces overlap and interact in ways that can be mutually reinforcing, cause conflict, resolve tension, and so forth. The semiotic space can be embodied in the physical space in ways that contradict the institutional space, causing the semiotic space to shift by contracting, expanding, or creating new meanings to reduce conflict, thus securing and maintaining the semiotic space. Nanputuo Temple has recovered through the gaps, overlaps, and tensions in the three spaces constituting the space of religion in the PRC.

Network

The space of religion is activated by networks that, in Buddhism, are concentrated in temples.[23] A piece of rock carved by an artisan is infused with semiotic meaning by worshipers who come to the temple. A state policy document issued in the capital institutionally may delimit whether people can burn incense in front of the statues. The semiotic importance of a building may lead people to donate money to restore it. For these reasons, we view the temple as continuous interactions that replenish the semiotic, physical, and institutional spaces of religion. Viewing a temple as a confluence of networks draws our attention to how various entities, including people, rules, materials, and meanings interacting at the temple, animate the space of religion.

A network methodology typically involves both description and analysis of actors and their interactions. The premise of this study is well expressed by the admonition of Bruno Latour (2007, 11–12) to "follow the actors."[24] Our first step was to identify the various actors and their functions at the temple, including clerics, devotees, and officers, and their connections to those outside the temple, including in Xiamen's society, different levels of the state, and transnationally to overseas Chinese communities. The second step was to view the effects of actors. This requires establishing connections between actors in their decisions and actions. The third step was understanding the agency of actors. For this, we paid attention not only to what actors did but how they justified their decisions and actions by reference to teachings, ideologies, procedures, norms, and policies. These three steps illuminate how networks activate and format the space of religion.

The analysis is "flat." It avoids positing actors at different levels of abstraction and the corollary assumption that higher levels have greater causality (Latour 2007). Thus, in our analysis, the state is not merely hegemonic power but an organizational hierarchy with agentic possibilities at each level. The top of the hierarchy—the CPC Central Committee—establishes a controlling ideology to create rules conveyed through networks between higher and lower levels, among offices at the same level, and to societal groups. Likewise, the core of Buddhism in the PRC consists of temples constituted by internal networks and external interactions with other Buddhist temples, devotees, believers, overseas Buddhists, and state officials in multiple offices and levels. Communications and actions proceed in networks via negotiations, interpretations, judgments, and so on. These interactions can create local changes that may constitute systemic transformations.

Episode

The final aspect of our framework involves the concept of "episode," which we use to narrate interactions of networks that constitute the temple's recovery and the changing state system of religion. Niklas Luhmann, in his influential social systems theory, posited the concept of episode as the process of change in systems structures, which we summarize here. An episode is an interaction of communication among actors within an organization in a society. An episode has a beginning and an end in its time sequence. During an episode, communication among actors may reference organizational rules and societal values in innovative ways. Therefore, an episode may be part of the transformation within organizations and in society from one phase to another (Luhmann 1995, 405–436).

In our framework, to be specific, an episode is a configuration of actors and interactions that may affect changes in the temple, state, and society.[25] We selected the episodes from among those we compiled to best illustrate the recovery and operation of the temple and its positioning in the state administration. The beginning and the end of episodes are often vague. In some cases, they have a clear beginning and end, such as a sudden change in state policy or a natural disaster. The end may not be definite, as it survives as a memory in people's minds. Whether vague or definite, the systems and values are clearly changed. In part II of the book, we have placed multiple episodes occurring at about the same time in Nanputuo Temple into a single chapter. Therefore, each of this part's three chapters narrates a phase of the temple's recovery as part of transformations of Buddhism, the state, and society. These transformations are then reflected in the chapters on Buddhist communities in part III.

Each episode compiles multiple stories and cuts. A story is an account by one agent but lacks an overview of the entire phenomenon. It can be expressed orally by a person or in writing via a newspaper article, gazetteer, or policy paper. Some stories were told to us by one actor, while others were recounted by diverse actors, each contributing an aspect. A cut is the smallest action that, unlike a story, lacks context or plot, such as a comment, anecdote, or inscription. Some stories and cuts refer to events openly observed by many people, such as the funeral of the abbot, whereas others had unseen internal issues, such as the struggle over the ownership of temple property between Nanputuo monks and the local state officials. Among the stream of stories and cuts, some appear linked and can be brought together as an episode. In each episode, we describe the manifold aspects—the trigger, actors, negotiations, and outcomes—that constitute the episode.

Conclusion

The Space of Religion is a study of the recovery and development of Nanputuo Temple from 1979 until 2004. During this period, the temple was among the first Buddhist temples in the PRC to fully recover after the Cultural Revolution. By focusing on the temple and related issues and phenomena from the levels of individuals, levels of state administration, the monastic system, and Buddhist communities in Xiamen and their transnational ties, we trace the recovery process of a Buddhist temple as the interaction of religion and the modern state. To do so, we introduce a theoretical concept of religion as space and use a network approach to narrate multiple episodes in the recovery of a temple and its connections to local communities of Buddhism.

2

Physical and Semiotic Spaces of Nanputuo Temple

NANPUTUO TEMPLE LIES THREE KILOMETERS from the center of Xiamen City at the end of an old thoroughfare called Siming Road (Siming lu 思明路). The temple is surrounded by green trees and somewhat removed from the noisy downtown. It is said to have exceptional feng shui, lying at the foot of Wulao Peak's southern exposure facing the nearby sea and islands in the Taiwan Strait. To the east of its compound is Xiamen University, on the west is the upscale Overseas Chinese New Village (Huaqiao xin cun 華僑新村) residential area; restaurants and bookstores line the road outside its southern wall. Although Nanputuo attracts many worshipers and tourists, it has long been a tranquil Buddhist site.

The temple is distinguished by its colorful and ornamental southern-style architecture. The halls enshrining statues of the Buddha, Guanyin, and other deities are covered by red-tiled roofs topped by yellow, red, pink, blue, and green figures of phoenixes, flowers, dragons, waves, fairies, and heavenly palaces, ending in eaves resembling curled dragon tails. The stone pillars supporting the roofs are engraved with red and gold characters composing rhyming couplets (*duilian* 對聯) by famous persons. Paintings and texts of Buddhist stories on black lacquered-wood boards hang on the outside walls of the halls. More characters are carved into boulders behind the temple on Wulao Peak. The abundance of colorful characters and paintings on walls, pillars, and rocks visually produces the temple's semiotic space from its physical space to embody the teachings of the Buddha and the cosmology of Buddhism.[1]

In the first section of this chapter we discuss the physical space of Nanputuo Temple as it appeared in 1999, the year we did a comprehensive survey of the site. We describe how the layout and the buildings, including a hall dedicated to Guanyin, function within the semiotic space of the temple.[2] In the second section we portray the semiotic space of the temple by examining some of the engraved characters as they appear to visitors. We focus on those conveying poems, couplets, allusions, and stories chiseled or painted on pillars, walls, and stones. These profuse engravings, characteristic of a southern-style Buddhist temple, appealed to worshipers and tourists alike.

Physical Space: Layout of the Temple

When Nanputuo Temple was named and dedicated to Guanyin in the late seventeenth century, it acquired the typical layout of a Chan Buddhist temple. It grew over time with the addition of new buildings and courtyards. By the late 1990s, the temple had assumed its current scale, occupying twenty-six hectares, one-quarter of which is the built area.[3] The temple, sited on a north-south axis and facing south to the water, consisted of three compounds—central, east, and west. The central compound contained the main square, the most sacred space in the temple. It held the main halls for the Buddha, Guanyin, and significant deities and arhats, representing the Buddhist teachings and cosmology. All images and symbols of Buddhist teachings were located here, and many rituals, including chanting, were performed daily or on special occasions. The central compound also encompassed the front yard (containing a large pond) and back hills (covered with rocks and trees), which represented the heaven-like environment of Buddhism. The daily life and the activities of clerics, novices, and students that constituted the actual practice of the Buddha's teaching and its transmission through the BCM, charity foundation, and meditation hall took place in the west compound. Secular activities for believers and visitors that were related to Buddhism occurred in the east compound.

A wall encompassing the central compound's front yard, the main square, and the west and east compounds demarcated the temple from the secular world. It had been constructed in the early 1980s, along with two mountain gates (*shanmen* 山門) of white-gray granite placed at the east and west corners of the front yard. We describe below the temple's physical layout as visitors experienced it in 1999, the same year we observed worshipers at the October Guanyin festival (see chapter 9). By then, the physical space had been restored and further construction was expanding the temple within its compound. Our narration also touches on the history and functions of buildings we discuss later in the book.

Central Compound

FRONT YARD: Entering the temple through a mountain gate, visitors stepped into the temple's front yard. It occupied 3.1 hectares, one-eighth of the temple's total land area. The tranquil atmosphere of shade trees and the large Lotus Pond transported them from the noisy secular world to the sacred and pure land of perfect bliss. In pleasant weather, people strolled around, with the elderly, couples, and families with children chatting and enjoying time together. Walking along a gray flagstone path, visitors next encountered the Heavenly Kings Hall, the entrance to the main square of the central compound. Before going inside, they purchased tickets at the booth on the east side of the hall's entrance.[4]

With tickets in hand, most people paused at the entrance and turned to gaze southward at the magnificent sight of two eleven-story Longevity Pagodas and the Releasing Life and Lotus Ponds. Each pagoda was flanked by a flagpole, with the Buddhist flag flying on the west and the PRC flag on the east. A strip of land between the ponds held seven shorter white marble pagodas representing the Seven Past Buddhas.[5] The magnificent panorama contributed to the grandeur of the temple. Then, approaching the large incense box in front of the door to the Heavenly Kings Hall, people took out the incense sticks they had brought and pressed them between their palms. Turning south again, they bowed deeply to the Heavenly Emperor (*tiandi* 天帝), then faced back to the Heavenly Kings Hall and bowed again. After placing the incense sticks into the ashes of the incense box, they climbed four steps to enter the hall.

PHYSICAL AND SEMIOTIC SPACES

MAIN SQUARE: The main square, the temple's most sacred and significant part, was a rectangular-shaped space surrounded by a wall. Following Chan Buddhism, the main statues and halls for worship were concentrated here. The square contained several halls with cloisters extending up both sides, filled with images, statues, decorations, and symbols. All expressed the Buddha's teaching and represented the cosmology of Buddhism. The compound's entire structure, including halls and cloisters, and the images they housed, such as Buddha, Guanyin, bodhisattvas, deities, and arhats (*aluohan* 阿羅漢), represented the heavenly cosmology—mandala—of Buddhism. Here, in this structural space, the monks performed rituals during morning and evening service (*zaowan ke* 早晚課), and on special festive occasions, as the living practice of Buddhism. The monks' adherence to the precepts—the practice of the Buddha's teachings—showed people practically and visually what the Buddha taught. Visitors were able to walk freely around the central compound; enter each hall; worship the Buddha, Guanyin, and other statues; look at paintings; read the engraved calligraphy; and observe the monks walking through the compound and performing rituals.

The Heavenly Kings Hall was the door to the central compound, welcoming visitors and protecting the temple. The gray granite building was covered by a double-tiered roof of green tiles with upturned eaves ending in curled dragon tails. Above the entrance, a black lacquered sign proclaimed "Heavenly Kings Hall" in gold characters. Climbing the steps to the hall, visitors passed between two carved stone lions. Inside, a sizeable gold statue with a paunchy stomach, large bald head, and open laughing mouth greeted them. In Buddhist teachings, this was Mile 彌勒 (Skt. Maitreya), the Future Buddha. Many lay worshipers considered this jolly deity to be a symbol of wealth and good luck (sometimes called "Laughing Buddha" in English). In front of Mile was an incense urn and table for worship. The colorful and fearsome statues of the Four Heavenly Kings stood to protect Buddhism. They defended the temple from malevolent spirits attacking from the four directions—east, south, west, and north. Towering five meters high, they gazed down on all who came, checking for those harboring evil minds, bad character, or wrong behavior. Visitors frightened by these deities worshiped them by offering fragrant incense sticks. Behind Mile stood a statue of Weituo (韋馱, Skt. Skanda), a devoted guardian of Buddhism and the temple, who faced back toward the Great Buddha Hall.

As visitors stepped from the Heavenly Kings Hall into the main square, they gazed across the flagstones toward the Great Buddha Hall, the largest building on the square, and realized they had entered the most sacred space of the temple. Cloisters on the sides of the square ran along its entire length from south to north. The west cloister started from the Qielan Hall (Ch. Qielan dian 伽藍殿, Skt. Saṃghārāma)—dedicated to Guan Gong 關公, a general venerated in Buddhism and Daoism for dispelling calamities and evil—and was topped by the Drum Tower. The east cloister, which started at the Dizang Hall (Ch. Dizang dian 地藏殿, Skt. Kṣitigarbha prasāda), housed the bodhisattva who cared for dead souls and was topped by the Bell Tower. The striking of the drum and bell kept the daily schedule of the temple and reverberated throughout the neighborhood. People considered the sounds to be the voice of the dharma spreading Buddhist merit all over the world and indicating that the temple's practice of Buddhism was ongoing.

The Great Buddha Hall, the temple's cosmological center, represents the Buddha's supreme position. The magnificent gray stone structure was topped by a saffron-tiled roof with curling dragon-tail eaves, similar to the Heavenly Kings Hall but larger. Visitors climbed a half-dozen stone steps, passing between two carved stone lions, to reach the front veranda, and they could enter the hall when rituals were not being performed. Inside the large, dimly lit hall, which was a vast room, sat the three giant Buddha statues. In the center was Sakyamuni Buddha (Skt., Ch. Shijiamoni 釋迦牟尼), flanked by Medicine Buddha (Ch. Yaoshifo 藥師佛, Skt. Bhaiṣajyaguru) on the east and Eternal Life Buddha (Ch. Amituofo 阿彌陀佛, Skt. Amitābha) on the west. Directly in front of Sakyamuni Buddha was a smaller statue of a seated Thousand-Handed and Thousand-Eyed Guanyin. This statue was originally in the Great Compassion Hall, so its relocation to the Great Buddha Hall acknowledged the temple's dedication to Guanyin. People stuck burning incense sticks into urns at the hall entrance and bowed deeply. Visible in the dim light were the three statues in the hall reflecting the dull gold color of fluorescent lights high in the ceiling and the thin rays of daylight filtering through the lattice of small windows.

Twice a day, hundreds of monks, including BCM students, assembled inside the Great Buddha Hall to chant sutras for morning and evening services. The only laypersons allowed in the hall were Buddhist devotees participating in the rituals during these times, but people could request that special rituals be performed to send merit to their ancestors' souls (*chaodu* 超度). People standing at the door could witness the rituals being performed, while those walking around the temple could hear the chanting that taught Buddha's wisdom. The visual and audible effects of the hall evoked the long history of Buddhist practice in the temple and the teachings that remained alive among its devotees.

The sections of the east and west cloisters flanking the Great Buddha Hall housed the Eighteen Arhats (Shiba luohan 十八羅漢). Each side displayed nine gold statues of sitting figures depicting people who had attained the highest possible (human) level of Buddhism. Each statue had a highly distinctive posture and facial expression, some funny and others frightening, and bore a metal plate identifying each by name. Visitors enjoyed observing the faces, understanding that the arhats were people who chose to serve Buddha through self-cultivation.

The Great Compassion Hall, standing behind the Great Buddha Hall, was dedicated to Guanyin Bodhisattva offering mercy to save innumerable people. All lay visitors to the temple, even tourists who had rushed past the Great Buddha Hall, came to the Great Compassion Hall to worship the Guanyin statues housed inside. The Great Compassion Hall, a compact octagonal wood building, sat atop a five-meter-high concrete platform. It was covered by a triple layer of roofs, with colorful dragons poised and curled on the tip of each eave as if taking flight. The hall housed four statues of Guanyin, each facing one of the cardinal directions. The main one was a two-handed Guanyin, sitting serenely in a bed of lotus flowers facing southward toward the Great Buddha Hall. The other statues each had forty-eight arms radiating outward. Some hands had an eye engraved on their palms to let Guanyin see people in need anywhere in the world, while others held bows, swords, prayer beads, and other items representing powers to heal specific pains, misfortunes, and illnesses. For spreading Guanyin's mercy, the four doors were always open so that the bodhisattva could hear cries for help coming from any direction and extend compassionate hands.

To reach the hall, visitors had to climb thirty steps on the south side of its foundation as if they were actually ascending Mount Putuo, where Guanyin lived. Many worshipers offered food, fruit, and flowers, believing this imbued the offerings with Guanyin's power to assist people. They handed offerings to a monk standing by the main Guanyin statue, who presented them to Guanyin and then returned the offerings to the worshipers. They then took the offerings home to eat with family members, sharing Guanyin's blessing. After offering, people walked clockwise around the veranda, viewing Guanyin at each door and bowing deeply each time. During the day, elderly female devotees sitting on stools on the veranda chanted sutras in low voices, looking after Guanyin. They lived in Xiamen and had served Guanyin for a long time. Some were even said to have entered the temple secretly during the Cultural Revolution to care for Guanyin.

Although the center of the Buddhist cosmos is Sakyamuni Buddha in the Great Buddha Hall, the Great Compassion Hall is where people focus on expressing their core belief. We saw more people praying fervently for their wishes and healing than anywhere else in the temple. In the Great Compassion Hall, the Guanyin statues were almost close enough for people to touch, enabling them to pray directly to Guanyin without the intermediation of monks. During most days, a constant stream of worshipers would likely ascend the steps to this hall, but on Guanyin festival days they have to wait in line as their numbers are so large. The Great Compassion Hall is undoubtedly the semiotic center of Nanputuo Temple for the practice of Buddhism.

Lying behind the Great Compassion Hall was the Dharma Hall, the northernmost building in the main square. Its two-story construction and its location further up the slope just before Wulao Peak made it the tallest building in the main square. Only clerics and specially invited laypersons could enter, which made the atmosphere especially tranquil. Dharma lectures by clerics and special ceremonies and rituals took place on the first floor. The second floor housed the Sutra Library (Cangjing ge 藏經閣); it contained nine thousand sutras printed during various dynasties as well as valuable Buddhist treasures. The hall symbolized the supreme position of the temple as a place of knowledge, tradition, and the Buddha's teachings and thus reassured people that Nanputuo Temple strictly preserved the dharma as the guardian of Buddhism. But since the

Dharma Hall was closed to the public, most people turned to the right directly in front of it, and exited the main square at the northeast corner to walk to the back hills.

ANNEX: The annex was physically located in the east compound but was accessible from the main square. It contained facilities for the management and daily activities of a Chan Buddhist temple unrelated to the cosmology of Buddhist teachings. The main facilities were located in an administrative building constructed in 1995. They included the guest department (*ke tang* 客堂), an important headquarters for communicating with the outside world and monitoring the comings and goings of visitors (see chapter 4). Traditionally, a temple accepted traveling monks and let them stay for a period of time. The head guest prefect interviewed visiting clerics to judge their suitability for staying at the temple. At the same time, the conversation gave the visitor an impression of the temple as it was expressed in the guest prefect's dignity and the atmosphere of the office. Another administrative office was the management department (*ku fang* 庫房), which handled the economic aspects of the temple (see chapter 4). At Nanputuo Temple, this office was the window through which laypeople could commission rituals. Another facility was the dining hall, called the "purification hall" (*zhai tang* 齋堂). All monks, including BCM students, ate there three times a day. Eating is a significant part of Chan Buddhist practice. The monks sat for a short period chanting and then, guided by the sounds of a bell, picked up chopsticks and ate in silence.

BACK HILLS: The slopes of Wulao Peak rising steeply behind the Dharma Hall spread across more than half of the temple's land. The rock-covered ground with trees and bushes growing in crevices was quiet and misty in the morning. This was a relaxed spot where old souls rested, and people believed the location was magically efficacious.[6] In the early morning, when the power was deemed most potent, people walked on the hills after practicing tai chi in the front yard, appreciating the beauty of the sacred and natural environment as a paradise. To approach the hills, people walked along a gently rising path of stone steps that led from the main square to a small grassy clearing in front of the Buddha Rock (Fo shi 佛石) at the base of Wulao Peak.

The Buddha Rock was the second most significant focus of worship after the Guanyin statue in the Great Compassion Hall. This boulder had an engraved, red character for "Buddha" (*fo* 佛) that was four meters high and three meters wide. Popular belief held that the rock, specifically the "Buddha" character, had the magical power to heal people's suffering and realize their wishes. Carved in 1866 (*QGN*, 67), it reflected the belief that natural features, such as large boulders or caves, were magically efficacious. Unlike the worship of Guanyin, this popular belief in magic was not contextualized in Buddhist sutras. Thus, the Buddha Rock lay at an ambivalent position between the main square, which is the core representation of the structure of Buddhism, and the natural mountain with its rocks and trees. People from Minnan, in particular, believed that this engraved Buddha character was imbued with the extraordinary power to ensure a safe trip and return home when traveling in the world. Since the nineteenth century, people from Minnan embarking from the Xiamen port came to the temple to pray at the Buddha Rock for a safe voyage and success overseas. It was even said that young people sent to work in villages during the Cultural Revolution secretly came to pray for their safe return.

From the Buddha Rock, people could climb the steep stone steps that led to trails winding along Wulao Peak. They enjoyed this quiet area to meditate, exercise, and breathe the clean air. There were no statues here because the back hills symbolized nature. But people could visit stupas containing the relics of eminent monks who had played essential roles in the temple since its ecumenicization, including Zhuanfeng, Huiquan, Taixu, and Miaozhan, and relax in small pavilions. Those interested in the temple's history visited the small hut where Taixu had lived and meditated and the cave that housed Sizhou Temple, the earliest temple on the site. A grotto under a large overhanging rock was where people placed old statues of Buddha, Guanyin, and other bodhisattvas and local deities they no longer wished to keep. Candles along the grotto entrance gave it the appearance of a graveyard for statues.

West Compound

The west compound had two sections. One was the section that functioned as the monastery where the monks lived. Laypeople could not enter it, except for grounds staff, BAX officers, and lay instructors at the BCM. The other was the far west section, located outside the temple wall, which served as the focus of people's ancestor worship. It consisted of a piece of land stretching from the wall of the inner west compound to the Overseas Chinese New Village.

MONASTERY SECTION: This part of the west compound, with abundant greenery, was quiet and peaceful compared to the noisy central compound full of people. The portion of the inner section closest to the wall separating it from the main square contained buildings where clerics could live and pursue their education. At the northernmost point was the abbot's residence; its construction had been delayed until the other facilities were completed in the late 1980s. Next to the abbot's residence were dormitories for monks residing at the temple. Nearby were the BCM facilities, including a two-story classroom building and the Taixu Library, and a long two-story dormitory for students extending northward from the west gate that opened to the front yard. On the east side of this gate was the two-story headquarters of the BAX. From this perch, the BAX officers could observe the comings and goings of the monks and their visitors.

Located to the west of these residential and BCM facilities were two large buildings that housed new activities to express the teachings of Buddhism at Nanputuo Temple. One, was the Meditation Hall, a three-story octagonal building, with each story surrounded by red pillars supporting a roof with upward-curving eaves. It was consecrated in 1994 as the first facility for meditation at Nanputuo Temple. Its introduction to the temple reflected the view of abbot Miaozhan that student monks needed textbook education of the sutras along with cultivation through meditation practice. The Meditation Hall was intended for monks to practice meditation, but laypersons could attend special lectures and meditation sessions. The other building was the Nanputuo Temple Charity Foundation (Nanputuo si cishan hui 南普陀寺慈善會). It was the first religious charity in the PRC, and its free medicine expressed Buddhist teachings of compassion (see chapter 5). It was housed in a rectangular two-story building lying along the front of the inner section that people could enter directly from the front yard. This layout of the inner west compound brought together the key aspects of the teaching of Buddhism for clerics, namely academics and meditation, the charity foundation where clerics and laypersons interacted, and the BAX. The layout reflected the good management of the temple.

CONCEPT, SPACE, HISTORY

FAR WEST SECTION: The far west, a large piece of land lying outside the walled area of Nanputuo Temple, was bisected by a road that passed through a tunnel under Wulao Peak. A pedestrian bridge spanned the road. In front of the bridge was a furnace where people could burn spirit money, a practice banned inside the temple compound since the mid-1990s to conform more strictly with Buddhist teachings. Crossing the bridge, people came to a larger grassy area with graves filled with the ashes of monks who had once lived at Nanputuo Temple. People believed this was a special spot because the graves had not been destroyed during the Cultural Revolution, unlike the ancestor tablets in the Merit Hall. Therefore, many people performed rituals for their ancestors here. Beyond the graves were two guest hostels accessible from the adjacent Overseas Chinese New Village residential area.

East Compound

The east compound, directly accessible by the east gate from the front yard, contained activities for devotees and commerce. Unlike the main square or west compound, it neither represented the cosmology of a Chan Buddhist temple nor served the management needs of Nanputuo Temple. All could enter, including tourists, so it was not quiet and peaceful.

The east compound contained several buildings, each for a specific activity. Some were for devotees. The Sutra Chanting Hall (Nianfo tang 唸佛堂) was located in a two-story building along the southern wall separating the east compound from the front yard. The first floor was a dormitory for lay employees of the temple, while a large room on the second floor was used by a devotee group for morning and evening sutra chanting. It was conducted by elderly monks in the Minnan dialect and was popular among local devotees, especially older women, who only spoke the local dialect. Behind the Sutra Chanting Hall was the old Merit Hall, a two-story building originally built in the 1930s to house the ancestor tablets of the monks at the temple. People conducted rituals here to send merit to their dead ancestors. At the very rear of the east compound, built against the rock face at the base of Wulao Peak, was the four-story Zhengming Building 正命樓, constructed in the 1930s as a retirement home for elderly monks. Its resident clerics in the 1990s were primarily elderly Minnan-speaking clerics ordained before 1949. They were often visited by elderly Minnan-speaking female devotees who came to chat.

The east compound contained two vegetarian restaurants. One was the Haihuilou Restaurant 海會樓, opened in 1982 in a new three-story building built on the site of a hall where devotees had previously gathered to chant sutras. The menu featured modestly priced vegetarian dishes such as fried rice noodles and purple taro cake that appealed to local believers and tourists. Its name alluded to the Haihui Pagoda in western Fujian Province that, according to legend, was built by a monk who discovered gold and silver while digging in his vegetable garden. The other was the larger Puzhaolou Restaurant 普照樓 housed in a building constructed in 1985; it featured fancier dishes and private dining rooms for visiting dignitaries, high-ranking officials, and wealthier customers. Many visitors, disembarking in droves from tourist buses, came to the temple for the exceptional experience of tasting Nanputuo Temple's famous vegetarian fare.

Semiotic Space: Representation and Images

So far, we have explained the physical space of Nanputuo Temple by focusing on the layout and functions of its land and buildings as visitors experienced them in 1999. But the temple structure and the buildings also conveyed many semiotic meanings, revealing Nanputuo Temple as a place firmly following the teachings of the Buddha. Decorative paintings and poems adorning the walls and pillars have been a key attribute of the temple's semiotic space.

The profusion of Chinese characters expressing poems, couplets, and allusions—whether engraved on pillars, walls, and stones or painted on lacquered boards—are typical of southern-style Buddhist and Daoist temples in Minnan, as well as Taiwan, Hong Kong, and Singapore. Especially delightful to visitors, these expressions covered practically all vertical surfaces in the main square as if trying to leave nothing bare. These characters and paintings conveyed Buddhist teachings, legends, and the history of the temple, including stories of the life of Gautama Buddha, miracles, and the devotion of believers, saints, and deities. At the same time, the stories described good and bad deeds and their effects during the previous lives of the Buddha. Some praised the gloriousness of

Buddhism and Nanputuo Temple. They filled the temple with meanings and messages, making it a vibrant religious space of belief and teachings of the Buddha. Even when the temple was empty and silent, without clerics and visitors, these symbols kept the temple as a sacred space of Buddhism.

Characters also appeared engraved on the rocks and monuments dotting the slopes of Wulao Peak. Unlike the characters in the main square extolling Buddhism and the temple, those on the hill conveyed the words of famous monks, devotees, literati, generals, and entrepreneurs who commemorated their visits by praising the temple's beautiful natural environment. The engraved and painted poems, couplets, and phrases used metaphors, historical connotations, esoteric terms, literary references, and prosody that only cultured and educated persons could fluently read and comprehend. But even the people who recognized only a few characters retained vivid images that stimulated their imaginations. At the very least, by observing these characters and carvings, people realized that the temple and places in it were historically and intellectually significant, and they could synchronize their existence with them. Just glancing at engraved characters touched people's emotions as they read "beautiful heaven," "peace," "purity," "big ocean," "compassion," "selflessness," "stability," "limitless mercy of Buddha," "karma," and such local place names as "Nanputuo Temple" and "Wulao Peak." This abundance of carefully chosen characters was a powerful visual experience of the teaching and cosmos of Buddhism; just being surrounded by them generated the semiotic space of Buddhism and the power of Guanyin in Nanputuo Temple. This space created respect among visitors for the permanence of the Buddha's teaching and a sense that they were living in the heavenly pure land (Ch. *jingtu* 净土, Skt. *sukhāvatī*) that was visually represented (Belting 2011, 46–47).[7]

East and West Mountain Gates

Characters carved on the stone arches of the two mountain gates welcomed people with allusions that celebrated the history and location of the temple and its Buddhist character. On the top of both mountain gates, four characters were prominently engraved—Egret Island Majestic Mountain (Ludao mingshan 鷺島名山)—declaring that this was the spot.

Poetic couplets were engraved on the arches, with one line on each side.[8] The East Mountain Gate couplet read:

[right] The eyes delight to gaze upon a Buddhist temple beside university halls. 喜瞻佛刹連黌舍
[left]   The ears feast upon the sound of crashing waves carried by a heavenly wind. 飽聽天風拍海濤

The West Mountain Gate couplet read:

[right] The broad expanse of Xiamen Isle runs beside the vast and azure sea. 廣廈島連滄海 闊
[left]   The contemplations of the discerning mind are as lofty as Wulao Peak. 大心量比五峰高

As a pair, these couplets positioned Nanputuo Temple in the magnificent, open, and heavenly atmosphere—facing the ocean and incoming wind, with its back protected by Wulao Peak, and next to Xiamen University, a place of learning and knowledge. The references to nature in the West Mountain Gate couplet, which alluded that the glory emanating from the temple and Buddhism was as broad as the ocean and as high as mountains, highlighted the excellent feng shui of the temple, communicating to people that it was a most auspicious and sacred place for Buddhism. Other characters indicated the date of their engraving according to the Buddhist calendar (*fo li* 佛曆) as the year 2528 (1985). Some visitors could recognize the distinctive script of Zhao Puchu 趙樸初 (1907–2000), president of the Buddhist Association of China. His calligraphy engraved on the mountain gates indicated that Nanputuo Temple was blessed by the state.[9]

A couplet on the small gate in the wall next to the Heavenly Kings Hall read:

[right] The hills harbor auspicious energy. 山含瑞氣
[left]   The waters bear benevolent light. 水帶恩光

This couplet meant that the physical setting of the temple, with the ponds and sea in front and hills behind, showed the prosperity of Buddhism.

The gates demarcated the outside lay world from the sacred world within Nanputuo Temple, while the couplets differentiated the surrounding environment's auspicious air, mountains, and ocean from the temple, sanctifying it.

Heavenly Kings Hall

The Heavenly Kings Hall was the dignified and sedate entrance to the main square of the central compound. Above the hall's entrance was a large black lacquered board inscribed with the characters for "Nanputuo" in gold paint and "1926," the year the hall was built and when Taixu came to the temple. The thickness and grandeur of the characters told visitors that this was the rightful place of confidence and dignity for the prospering of Buddhism. On the hall's front veranda, visitors saw couplets carved on pillars that supported the overhanging roof. Twelve pillars flanked the large front door, six to the east and six to the west. Those on each side were subdivided into front and back rows, three to a row. A couplet's first line was carved on an east-side pillar and the second line on its west-side counterpart. They told of the temple and its attributes.

The first couplet a visitor saw while approaching the Heavenly Kings Hall was engraved on the two pillars of the front row immediately flanking the steps.

> [right] Stemming from sacred Luojia, this temple opened its doors to expound the dharma. 分派洛伽開法宇
>
> [left]   Parted by the strait from the towering Taiwu, the temple gate was raised. 隔江太武拱山門

The couplet underscored Nanputuo Temple's connection to Mount Putuo. The right line alluded to the temple's origin in Luojia Mountain.[10] This is the mythic mountain in India's southern ocean where Guanyin is believed to reside, as well as the most famous center of Guanyin worship in China. The allusion of the left line was that Mount Taiwu lay across the water from Nanputuo Temple, just as Luojia Mountain did from Mount Putuo (China's Putuoluojia consists of two adjacent islands, Putuo and Luojia). This could also mean that Mount Taiwu was the gate protecting Nanputuo Temple. In this latter allusion, Taiwu could refer to the three emperors infamous for suppressing Buddhism before the modern era.[11] But now Taiwu was protecting Nanputuo Temple, showing that Buddhism had recovered from its suppression by the previous cruel emperors and was flourishing. These multiple images conveying distinct meanings stimulated the imaginations of those pausing to read them.

Another couplet described the etymology and history of Nanputuo Temple.

[right]   A Buddha came south; thus, Heaven spread the Luojia teachings to another island. 一佛南來天為洛伽開別島
[left]   The great river flows east; I look out from this floating islet with hopes of merciful smooth sailing. 大江東去我從浮嶼望慈航

The right line indicated that Guanyin came to Xiamen from Mount Putuo to establish Nanputuo Temple for the spread of Buddhist teachings. In the left line, the characters for *cihang* 慈航, meaning "merciful sailing," contained multiple allusions. One was a prayer to Guanyin: it asked for safe ocean passage by merchants, fishermen, and overseas Chinese about to embark from Xiamen's harbor; and it expressed gratitude upon their safe return. Another allusion was to the lives of believers who sailed in the mercy of the Buddha, smoothly guiding them from the world of suffering in this life to nirvana. Additionally, the characters for *cihang* were the same as those for the name of a hermit who was another form of Guanyin, a further allusion to Mount Putuo.

Some couplets in the Heavenly Kings Hall welcomed people with their pronouncement of the Buddha's teaching, in which all those entering the temple were freed from the suffering of worldly attachments and pollution and could obtain the truth.

[right]   The profound sounds of a plucked lute shatter worldly suffering and reveal the emptiness of forms. 按琵琶玄彈破苦空色殻
[left]   The yawning cavern of the dragon's mouth swallows the pearl for abandoning earthly attachments. 張蛟龍口吞來離垢珍珠

The "plucked lute" referred to the sound of chanting, while "dragon mouth" alluded to the entrance of the temple, as well as the Buddha's teaching and the Buddhist cosmos. One of the hall's Four Heavenly Kings, named Realm Upholding King (Ch. Chiguo tianwang 持國天王, Skt. Dhṛtarāṣṭra), held the Chinese lute to convert others with the beauty of his music. Another guardian named All-Seeing King (Ch. Guangmu tianwang 廣目天王, Skt. Virūpākṣa) clasped a dragon snare. Thus, the couplet praised the virtue of the heavenly kings and explained their symbols and meanings in the context of the Buddha's teaching.

The following couplet expressed the truth of the Buddha's teachings in simple and evocative words.

[right] The essence of the four great universal substances [earth, water, fire, and wind] is to lack attachments, follow the endless cycle of the peach trees turning red and the willows turning green, produce variation, and continually renew the world. 四大本無情隨循環桃紅柳綠翻新世界

[left] The fundamental principle of the Way of the Heavenly Kings is to protect the land of the realm, expel evil, uphold justice, and bring peace to heaven and earth. 天王原有道護國土催邪扶正鎮定乾坤

The right line of the couplet described the essence of Buddhism in terms of cycles of renewal and ongoing change. The popular expression "peach trees turning red, the willows turning green" (*taohong liu lü* 桃紅柳綠) referred to the beauty that was both ephemeral and eternal because their existence as blooms recurred annually and they kept the same shape. The left line explained that Buddhism protected the country and kept it peaceful under the guardianship of the heavenly kings. Notably, the order of the characters conveyed a further aspect of meaning. The first character of the right-hand line was "four" (*si* 四), and the first one on the left-hand couplet was "heaven" (*tian* 天). Then, the right-hand second character was "great" (*da* 大), and the left second was "king" (*wang* 王). Together, these characters meant the "four heavenly great kings," referencing the Heavenly Kings Hall. Small characters engraved on this pillar attributed the couplet to Yinyue 印月, another name for Huiquan, the first abbot of Nanputuo Temple, and thus alluded to in the composition of this deeply effective couplet.[12]

Standing in the center of the Heavenly Kings Hall, the statue of Mile welcomed people with a couplet.

[right]   Cultivate the six virtues [Skt. *pāramitā*], and you shall expel all excess distress. 修六度波羅蜜多盡除有漏煩惱
[left]   A single cry to the merciful Buddha [Ch. Amituofo, Skt. Amitābha] hastens extinguishment in nirvana. 念一聲阿彌陀佛趣入無餘涅槃

This couplet stated that people passing through the Heavenly Kings Hall into the heart of the temple would all achieve nirvana, no matter their education or social status, if they followed the six virtues of good rules and chanted "Amituofo."

As people bowed to each of the four heavenly kings, they saw Weituo, the Heavenly King ordered by the Buddha to the significant role of protecting the temple and Buddhism. The couplet on the pillars flanking his statue read:

[right]   In olden times, the Buddha expounded on the dharma [to Weituo]. 昔日如来開教誨
[left]   In present times, he preserves the dharma, keeping the *sangha* at peace. 今朝護法鎮禅林

This couplet clarified his role and attributes, assuring people that Nanputuo Temple was forever well protected as a place to practice the dharma.

Great Buddha Hall

The Great Buddha Hall was the center of Buddhism in Nanputuo, and so the couplets told the history and attributes of the temple as a blessed place where Buddhism was flourishing. Key couplets were engraved on twelve large pillars arrayed along the front veranda of the hall, equally divided on the east and west sides. The couplets expressed carefully crafted poems showed the rightfulness, historical authenticity, and dignity of Buddhism at the temple.

The most eye-catching couplet, located on the front row pillars closest to the steps, said:

[right]   The wellspring of the sutras is as ancient as the reign of [Emperor] Kaiyuan in the Tang dynasty. 經始溯唐朝，與開元而並古

[left]   The light of the dharma blankets the island of Xiamen, more splendid yet opposite Taiwu. 普光被廈島，對太武以增輝

This couplet affirmed the long history of the site as a place of Buddhist teaching. The right line suggested the origins of a Buddhist temple on the site in the Tang dynasty during the reign of Emperor Kaiyuan (713–741), who protected Buddhism. In the left line, Taiwu had the double meaning that Buddhism had overcome suppression by Emperor Taiwu and was flourishing at Nanputuo Temple across the bay from Mount Taiwu.

Another couplet alluded to the ecumenicization of the temple.

[right]   How pleasing to point to this southern Chan school passing so near to Huxi. 禪派即南宗笑指虎溪通咫尺

[left]   How supreme the sound of the dharma, encircling Egret Islet [Xiamen] and resounding among its winding hills. 法音超上品環看鷺嶼繞迦陵

The right line suggested Nanputuo Temple's affiliation with the Linji sect of the southern Chan school. The characters for *huxi* 虎溪 referred to Huxiyan Temple, where Huiquan was tonsured and served as prior before becoming the abbot of Nanputuo Temple. The character linking southern Chan with *huxi* was *xiao* 笑 (translated as "pleasing"), which can mean "laugh": this could refer to the well-known parable "Three Laughing Persons at Tiger Creek" (Huxi san xiao 虎溪三笑). The parable recounts the visit of the Confucianist Tao Yuanming 陶淵明 (365–427) and the Daoist Lu Xiujing 陸修靜 (406–477) to the Buddhist monk Huiyuan 慧遠 (334–416), living in seclusion in the mountains during the Jin dynasty (266–420). While walking, the three men were so deeply engrossed in conversation that they inadvertently passed over Tiger Stream, which Huiyuan had vowed never to cross during seclusion. Upon realizing this, the three men burst out laughing, enlightened by the realization that true wisdom is attained by overcoming boundaries. This story conveyed the message that attachment to a single philosophy or religion was contrary to true wisdom. Similarly, the ecumenicization of Nanputuo Temple reached beyond the temple's Heyun religious lineage to select an abbot, Huiquan, from the Huangbo lineage of Huxiyan Temple. Thus, the couplet's reference to the parable suggested that ecumenicization had greatly enhanced Nanputuo Temple as a place of Buddhist teachings by creating a spectacular relationship with the older, more "authentic" and authoritative Huxi Temple. Additionally, it could refer to the fact that Huiyuan had founded the Pure Land school of Buddhism while Huiquan propounded the dual cultivation of Chan and Pure Land Buddhism (Chan jing shuangxiu 禪淨雙修) at Huxiyan Temple.

Another couplet recounted the origins of Nanputuo Temple.

[right]   What great changes face a Buddhist land; a new set of claws for the tiled mandarin drake. These vestiges of war, the work of Jing Hai hundreds of years before. 佛国幾滄桑鴛瓦重新爪 跡百年先靖海
[left]   Temple hermitage, surrounded by water and bamboo; I still my heart at the River of Lu. A petal of sweet fragrance for the ancient Gautama Buddha. 禪房饒水竹鷺 江永住心 香一瓣古瞿曇

The right line of this couplet recounted that after the troubled time between the Ming and Qing dynasties, Buddhism flourished again with the coming of Jing Hai, another name for the Qing admiral Shi Lang, who established Nanputuo Temple in the seventeenth century. The left line pointed to the continuity of Buddhism from the time of Gautama Buddha to Nanputuo Temple. Together, both lines emphasized the eternity of Buddhism and its validation through the temple's history.

Inside the Great Buddha Hall were four couplets engraved on pillars. These couplets were closest to the hall's central Buddha statue, therefore the most significant. Three were written by politicians and generals to show that secular powers patronized Nanputuo Temple and were disciples of the Buddha. The fourth was written by Huiquan. Their contents were similar to those on the outside pillars that praised Buddha and Guanyin, extolled the beauty of the temple, and recounted its history.

A remarkable attribute of the hall was the profusion of paintings and characters in gold on black lacquered wood decorating the outside walls that depicted scenes accompanied by narrative text about the Buddha. This was the only space in the temple where people could see and learn from these popular stories. Altogether, there were twenty-eight stories, four on the front wall and the rest on the rear wall (see table 2.1; the numbers correspond to our numbered descriptions of the stories below). Most came from *Stories of the Buddha's Deeds in Past Lives* (*Shijia rulai ying hua shiji* 釋迦如來應化事蹟), a collection of popular stories of the Buddha's previous and current life that conveyed his teachings.[13] The painting in the temple that accompanied each story highlighted its most dramatic moment. All images, including people, clothes, landscapes, buildings, and plants, were represented in Chinese style as if the activities of the historical Buddha occurred in China rather than in India, where the Buddha was born and lived.

The four large murals on the front of the Great Buddha Hall were especially significant because people saw them immediately, before anything else, as they approached. The text and murals for two stories appeared to the right of the entrance door. "White Dog Barks at the Buddha" (1) told of a dog yelping at the Buddha, prompting the Buddha to tell the dog's owner that his father had been reincarnated as this dog as a result of his miserliness. "Blind Boy Sees the Buddha" (2) told of a miser who died and was reincarnated as a poor and blind boy. One day the boy entered a rich man's house and was kicked out. Seeing this, the Buddha told the boy that he was born blind because he had been a rich miser in his previous life. This enlightened the boy, and he converted to the Buddha's teachings, after which his eyes opened. Both stories conveyed a clear message to people to be kind and share good fortune so as to be born with better karma. Otherwise, they would have bad karma and be reincarnated as a dog or blind person. But even so, the Buddha would help if they showed understanding.

To the left of the front door two significant tales from Gautama Buddha's life, "Born Under a Tree" (3) and "Raised by His Aunt" (4), recounted his birth and upbringing. These paintings of well-known scenes featuring beautifully clothed noblewomen, the Buddha's mother, stepmother, and the baby Buddha conveyed an understanding of the joy and appreciation of Gautama Buddha's birth in this world. These stories, along

TABLE 2.1 Stories of the Buddha's Life on Walls of the Great Buddha Hall

Parable	Title		
1	White Dog Barks at the Buddha	白狗吠佛	bai gou fei fo
2	Blind Boy Sees the Buddha	盲兒見佛	mang er jian fo
3	Born Under a Tree	樹下誕生	shuxia dansheng
4	Raised by His Aunt	姨母養育	yimu yangyu
5	Choosing the Birth Family	家选饭王	jia xuan fan wang
6	Riding an Elephant to Enter the Womb	乘象入胎	cheng xiang ru tai
7	Nine Dragons Bathing [Sakyamuni]	九龍灌浴	jiulong guan yu
8	Immortals Practicing Divination	仙人占相	xianren zhan xiang
9	The Buddha Leaving the Family	初啟出家	chu qi chujia
10	Buddha Cuts His Hair and Changes Clothes	落髮貿衣	luo fa mao yi
11	Chandaka Is Dismissed from the Palace	車匿辭還	che ni ci huan
12	Chandaka Returns to the Palace	車匿還宮	che ni huan gong
13	Buddha Turns into an Ugly Devil	佛化醜鬼	fo hua chou gui
14	Ugly Woman Changes Appearance	醜女改容	chounü gai rong
15	Salvation for Hunters	度捕豬人	du bu zhu ren
16	Offering to Heaven and Meeting the Buddha	祀天遇佛	si tian yu fo
17	Bringing Salvation to a Woman	度跂陀女	du ba tuo nü
18	Salvation for Thieves	救度賊人	jiu du zeiren
19	Origin of the Way to Attain the Pure Land	净土緣起	jingtu yuanqi
20	Origin of Food Offering Ritual	施食緣起	shishi yuanqi
21	Buddha Saves an Infant	佛救婴儿	fo jiu ying'er
22	Mulian Saves His Mother	目蓮救母	mu lian jiu mu
23	Tender Willow Twigs and Clean Water	杨枝净水	yang zhi jing shui
24	A Child Gives Earth as Alms	小儿施土	xiao'er shi tu
25	Making Pennants to Offer the Buddha	造幡供佛	zao fan gong fo
26	Four Kings Offering Begging Bowl	四王獻鉢	si wang xianbo
27	Plucking Flowers to Offer to the Buddha	採花獻佛	caihua xian fo
28	Infinite Life	無量壽会	wuliang shou hui

with similar ones on the rear wall, expressed the boundless mercy of motherhood through the Buddha's mother, Maya, who died seven days after he was born, and her sister Pajapati, who raised the baby Buddha.

All of the stories we list in table 2.1 fall under five story types. One type told the life events of Gautama Buddha from birth to death. Some especially well-known scenes were depicted on the back wall, including the bodhisattva choosing the family into which he would be born as the prince who became Gautama Buddha (5); his mother Maya realizing that she was bearing a sacred being when she dreamed that a white elephant entered her body (6); nine dragons bathing the Buddha when he was born (7); an enchanter divining that the baby would be the Buddha (8); the Buddha leaving his family (9); the Buddha cutting his hair and changing his clothes (10); the Buddha's servant leaving the palace (11); and the servant returning to the palace (12).

A second type described the conversion to Buddhism of various people, from kings to pariahs, to convey the compassion of the Buddha and equality of the devotion of all persons in Buddhism. Some stories of this type focused on individuals, such as an ugly man abandoned by his parents (13) and an ugly woman (14). Others told of entire groups converting to Buddhism, such as a tribe of hunters who had killed animals (15) and a pagan king who had sacrificed animals but then converted along with his subjects (16). The stories about groups showed that if a leader converted to Buddhism, the followers did likewise. Some even become clerics as a result of the Buddha's mercy, such as a pagan woman (17) and five hundred thieves (18).

A third kind of story concerned reincarnation by bad karma and salvation by the Buddha. This was conveyed in the especially well-known tale of the Buddha teaching his disciple Mulian how to save his mother, who was suffering in hell (22), which was the origin of the All Souls' Festival (Ch. Yulanpen 盂蘭盆, Skt. Ullambana). Yet another story told the origin of the belief that Guanyin's boundless mercy cured people's suffering (23).

A fourth type concerned the origins of specific rituals long practiced by people. One explained the way to attain the pure land (19) after death. Another showed the Buddha saving hungry and thirsty goblins and explained the origin of the release of burning mouths ritual (*fangyankou* 放焰口) to feed starving ghosts (20). The story of the Buddha saving a child kidnapped by a goblin and then promising to feed the hungry goblin (21) also explained this ritual.

The fifth kind of parable, about devotion and piety, taught that offerings made with a pure and pious mind were better than any treasure. One story told of a boy so filled with joy at seeing the Buddha that he offered the Buddha the earth on which he was praying (24). Other such stories told of the Buddha receiving offerings of banners (25), spurning bejeweled bowls for a stone begging bowl (26), and receiving flowers plucked by poor people obligated to give them to the king (27). Some stories (28) depicted glorious scenes of the world of the Buddha, his outstanding achievement of enlightenment, and other sacred existences.

The careful selection of the stories revealed the message that clerics at Nanputuo sought to communicate to visitors. All reinforced the message that the Buddha's life was the basis of his teachings, that a person's behavior in this life affected the next life, and that Buddha's mercy was for all, kings and pariahs alike. They encouraged people to behave well, and in so doing, they became good Buddhists, living their lives as the Buddha taught.

The Great Buddha Hall was the heart of a semiotic space of the temple, with Buddha statues in the center surrounded by statues of bodhisattvas and other deities. Couplets on pillars poetically expressed the Buddha's teachings, while murals on the outside walls visually represented the Buddha's teachings through popular stories. Together, these images made an awe-inspiring and full representation of Buddhism; indeed, in English, the hall is sometimes called the "image house." Ordinary people were often restricted from entering the hall and mostly viewed the statues through the front doors. Therefore, the vividly illustrated stories on the outside walls attracted people's attention and gave understanding of the everyday practice of Buddhism. Those who knew a story could tell it to their companions, such as a grandmother to her grandchild. Others were attracted by the pictures and paused to read stories aloud. Even those only glancing at the paintings received the message that the Buddha's teachings were glorious and embedded as stories and myths in their culture. This was the significance of the semiotic space.

Great Compassion Hall

During our observations of the Great Compassion Hall, dedicated to Guanyin and the focus of people's worship, no one left the temple without praying to the bodhisattva. Especially during the Guanyin festivals, the steps to the hall were covered by offerings of flowers, and people crowded its veranda to worship. Above the front door hung a tablet with characters that read "Great Compassion Hall" and the date 1928; the two characters for "great compassion" represented the virtue of Guanyin. The names of the donors who paid for the hall's construction were carved on a large incense urn and the lower wall. This conveyed the great devotion of believers to Guanyin and the deep ties of Guanyin to the people.

Couplets praising Buddha were engraved on the lower wall of the hall and the stone railings along the surrounding veranda. The couplet on the right and left sides of the central door housing the main Guanyin statue said:

> [right] Truth, behold; purity and tranquility too, behold; great wisdom and knowledge, behold them everywhere. 真觀清淨觀廣大智慧觀
> [left] Wonderful sound, the sound of lapping tides; the sound of victory over the mortal world. 妙音海潮音勝彼世間音

The couplet praised Guanyin and blessed the spreading sound of the dharma, likened to ocean waves. Its two lines were structurally symmetrical. In the right line, the character for *guan* 觀 was in the second, fifth, and tenth positions, while in the left line, the character for *yin* 音 was in the corresponding positions. In this way, the couplet repeated Guanyin's name six times to show reverence. The character for *miao* 妙 in the left line evoked the image and legend of Miaoshan 妙善, the human figure of Thousand-Handed and Thousand-Eyed Guanyin (Ashiwa and Wank 2019; Yü 2001). The character for *qing* 清 in the right line referred to the purity of Miaoshan as celibate and vegetarian.

A couplet in gold characters was inscribed on pillars by the hall's back door.

> [right] Nanputuo Temple takes its form from the Wulao Peak; its tranquility evokes the peace of Potalaka. 五老此留形清淨為心皆補坦
> [left] The universal gate has no fixed form; in great mercy and compassion, Guanyin rescues all creatures. 普門無定相慈悲濟物即觀音

The right line equated Wulao Peak with Potalaka to indicate that Guanyin was at the temple. The term "universal gate" (*pumen* 普門) in the left line alluded to the chapter in the *Lotus Sutra* (*Fahua jing* 法華経) that introduced Guanyin and her mercy. These couplets conveyed the message that Nanputuo Temple on Xiamen Island was equivalent to Potalaka where Guanyin resided, and the shape of the Great Compassion Hall was that of Potalaka.

Cloisters

The statues and inscriptions in the cloisters were concentrated alongside the Great Buddha Hall. For most people, the single most impressive characters in the temple compound were "no ego" (Ch. *wu wo* 無我, Skt. *anātman*) and "following karma" (*sui yuan* 隨緣) engraved on the east and west cloister walls, respectively, near the arhat statues. Their one-meter height and golden color, in contrast with the gray marble slabs, made them visible and dynamic. Unlike the esoteric characters in couplets, these were common characters, enabling anyone to understand these essential terms of Chan Buddhism. Educated devotees and monks could further appreciate them as the calligraphy of two influential priors of Nanputuo Temple in the nineteenth century, Shengji 省己 (n.d.) and Xican 喜參 (1848–1911) (see appendix 1). Worshipers walking from the front of the temple encountered these characters after passing the arhat statues.

Numerous carvings on stone slabs embedded in the walls separated the main square from the west and east compounds. Although few people stopped to read them carefully, their titles indicated their contents as the history and attributes of Nanputuo Temple. One, dated 1640, was a document of rent collection from the fields of Puzhao Temple, the predecessor of Nanputuo. It said, "During the time of Puzhao Temple, there was a natural disaster. The temple could not get rent from farmers, so many monks left. The Zhang family rented the field and paid the rent as prayers to have a baby son." The engraving showed that the temple was historically embedded in local society. The carving on another stone slab read, "During the Qing dynasty, there was a drought. So, the temples in Xiamen prayed for rain, and it fell. Believers' donations of gratitude were used to make a dragon shrine on the west side of the temple." This illustrated the mutually supportive ties between the temple and local society. Other slabs commemorating the rebuilding of Nanputuo Temple in 1792 and 1888 listed the names of donors. All these slabs served as public statements of the temple's great popular support throughout its history.

Some recent carvings conveyed additional information about the temple to visitors. One was an epigraph from the 1980s titled "Introduction to Nanputuo Temple." It summarized the history of the temple, listed its parts, described the scenery, noted the sophisticated southern-style architecture, and named the famous monks at the temple—Zhuanfeng, Taixu, Hongyi, Xingyuan—who trained clerics who subsequently spread throughout China and abroad. Another recent carving, titled "Introduction of Nanputuo Vegetarian Food," praised the fare offered at the temple's vegetarian restaurants by declaring that well-known people—including the intellectual Guo Moruo 郭沫若 (1892–1978) and the artist Feng Zikai 豐子愷 (1898–1975)—had dined at the temple in the 1960s, although no restaurant had existed at that time. The calligraphed appreciations from such patrons were used as symbols and advertisements for the Puzhaolou Restaurant, which opened in 1985. The characters describing the cuisine, as they were placed next to "no ego" and "following karma," conveyed the importance of Nanputuo Temple and its openness to visitors. Thus, the older slabs expressed the historical dignity of the temple, while the new ones conveyed its continuity by following traditional ways.

Dharma Hall

The Dharma Hall had two couplets on the outside pillars, engraved in the mid-1930s when the hall was renovated and enlarged. One said:

[right] The phenomenal world is nothing but an illusion, soon to vanish, transient as dew or a flash of lightning. 有為法如夢幻泡影露電

[left] In the final age, the time when Buddhism was weakened, we maintained our Buddhist faith, copying, reading, and chanting the sutras. 後末世能書寫讀誦受持

This couplet expressed how to transmit the dharma. Its right line reflected a phrase from the *Diamond Sutra* (*Jingang jing* 金剛経), while the left line instructed clerics to study and spread the dharma. The other couplet expressed the results of transmitting the dharma.

[right]   All who achieve the marvelous dharma will, in time, secure the peace of the pure land. 皆得妙法究竟清淨
[left]   The breadth of the dharma, spreading everywhere, is like a bridge to the Buddha world. 廣度一切猶如橋樑

By experiencing these carved and painted couplets in the main square, people obtained the image and sensation of Buddhism and the Buddha's teaching almost as if they were in heaven and were connected to the temple's past and spirit.

Wulao Peak

Leaving the symmetrical and built central compound, people entered the slopes of Wulao Peak. This was a space, as we introduced it earlier in the chapter, infused by nature—the rocks, trees, birds, and fresh air surrounding the temple created a tranquil atmosphere. To be considered "nature," the sloping hills and surrounding landscape did not have to remain untouched by human beings or preserved in a wild shape; instead, nature was the heavenly place in the imaginary cosmology of Buddhism, where everything was praised, named, and given meaning as symbolic nature in the context of Buddhism and its aesthetics. Informal comments as well as poetic and personal reflections left by famous visitors to Nanputuo Temple had been carved on the rocks and mountains of this natural environment. These inscriptions transformed untamed nature into symbols of Buddhism and at the same time extracted meanings from nature to enhance the symbolism. Ordinary people who read them could obtain a sense of nature's significance in the Buddha's teachings by learning how earlier visitors saw meanings of Buddhism in nature.

After leaving the main square for the backyard, visitors first encountered the Mind Purifying Pond (Xi xin chi 洗心池), which washed away all dirt from their thoughts. They saw characters engraved on the surrounding rocks. Several prominent engravings conveyed gratitude for Guanyin, such as, "We take refuge in the great Guanyin Bodhisattva" (*nanwu Guanshiyin pusa* 南無觀世音菩薩), carved in 1991. Characters engraved in 1701 read, "tucked into the sleeve of the East Sea" (*xiu zhong donghai* 袖中東海). These words of praise for the temple's environment imparted sensations of awe, acceptance, and release to the people. They prayed at the Buddha Rock, believing that the commanding strokes of the prominent "Buddha" character had the magical power to realize their wishes, especially for safe passage and prosperity when going abroad.

The narrow trails on Wulao Peak were bounded by rocks and monuments, including stupas of former abbots (Zhuanfeng, Huiquan, Taixu, Miaozhan), covered with engraved characters. The engravings were usually short passages by famous generals, poets, and others who were moved by their visit to the temple to write their feelings and impressions. People paid more attention to the engraved names and dates on Wulao Peak than they did to those in the temple's main square; the engravings in the back hills expressed the thoughts and emotions of visitors to the temple, whereas engravings in the main square conveyed the Buddha's teachings and the temple's historical character. People could link their sensations with the thoughts of earlier visitors and reinforce the continuity of the heavenly nature in which they existed. One engraving from 1606 read, "This islet, like a sleeping dragon, lies crouching amidst hillocks" (*long zhou wo gang* 龍洲臥岡) in characters three meters high and one and a half meters wide. An 1854 engraving read, "Leave all cares behind" (*dou fangxia* 都放下). One carved in 1904 read, "Extol the country, nourish the people" (*zhu guo you min* 祝國佑民). Another 1904 inscription announced the name of its rock as "Three Lives Rock" (*san sheng shi* 三生石), referring to previous, present, and future lives. In a 1928 engraving, "Forget the dust of the mortal world," the word "dust" referred to trivial secular matters. One epigraph from 1981 by an overseas Chinese read, "Always follow the path of Buddhist learning" (*chang sui foxue* 常隨佛學).

Many engravings evoked ships, the ocean, and travel. Gold and red characters carved in 1936 said, "Mindful of mercy, rough seas become tranquil" (*cibei wei nian niehai boping* 慈悲為念孽海波平). A 1948 engraving said, "Merciful voyage, pervasive grace" (*ci hang en pu* 慈航恩溥). The first two characters of each engraving alluded to Guanyin, indicating how engravings had multiple allusions. These inscriptions showed that Nanputuo Temple, located in a port city for travelers to Southeast Asia, was blessed by Guanyin. Many prayed at Guanyin and the Buddha Rock for safe passage before embarking, while returnees gave thanks for their good fortune overseas. From the pavilions on Wulao Peak, people could look out on the sea.

As the peak was said to resemble five old men gazing out to sea, it was as if the natural environment was sending off and greeting travelers.

Conclusion

We have seen how Nanputuo Temple developed over several centuries, first as a temple devoted to Guanyin and then as a center of the modern reform movement. It could develop in this fashion because its lesser significance relative to other temples in Minnan made it more receptive to popular expectations and new trends. Its position as a Chan Buddhist temple consecrated to Guanyin and open to the people revealed the overlap of its physical and semiotic spaces: it was a physical space of buildings and land, and a semiotic space of representing, practicing, and reproducing the Buddha's teachings and Buddhist cosmology in the routines and practices of the clerics. But, as we discuss in the following chapters, the temple was an institutional space of state regulations for controlling religious sites. The profusion of visual media appearing on vertical surfaces in the form of inscriptions and pictures conveyed stories, myths, poems, teachings, and impressions that inspired and channeled the imaginations, feelings, and thoughts of viewers. The symbols that conveyed meanings were strictly limited to the physical space to avoid semiotic behavior beyond the institutional space of religion. In this book's conclusion we show how symbols changed to conform with the shifting institutional space in the 2000s. Thus it is not completely accurate to say that the semiotic space was free from the restrictions of the physical and institutional spaces. Instead, political authorities made some effort to avoid direct criticism of the temple, and as long as the semiotic space did not touch on provocative issues in the institutional space, the freedom was almost boundless.

All visitors to Nanputuo Temple, be they worshipers or tourists, believers or atheists, were impressed by the magnificent atmosphere created by the buildings, statues, engravings, hills, and ponds. Witnessing the prospering of the dharma gave them a sense of being enveloped by the Buddha's teachings. In this way, the temple structure represented and produced a semiotic space of Buddhism integrated with people's experiences in the temple. Without semiotic space, religion has no existence; it would be something, but not religion.

3

Institutional Space and Nanputuo Temple's Historical Capital

THE INSTITUTIONAL SPACE OF RELIGION began again in the PRC with the opening-up policies launched in 1979; the process accelerated in 1982, when a new national constitution and comprehensive statement of CPC ideology repudiated the suppression of religion that occurred during the Cultural Revolution. In the first section of this chapter we discuss the state system of religion, including CPC ideology, bureaucratic organization, and local administration of religious activity sites. In the second section we describe how reactivated components of Nanputuo Temple's historical capital—the legacy of Taixu, transnational ties to overseas Chinese communities, and the leadership of an "old-generation" monk—positioned the temple in the opening institutional space. In the third section we offer a comparative view of the implementation of the religious policy in Fujian and the importance of Nanputuo Temple's historical capital for its recovery.

The years from 1979 to 1982 were a period of much uncertainty, as the previous institutional space from the Cultural Revolution that did not recognize religion intermingled with the new one that did. In 1979 Buddhist temples reopened, and some worshipers came. The following year in Beijing the Buddhist Academy of China reopened, and a ceremony to ordain clerics took place at Guangji Temple 廣濟寺 (Wen 2012, 71). But in Xiamen and other locales, people's thinking did not suddenly change. Local officials were unsure of what was permitted, and people still hesitated to worship in public. At Nanputuo new construction got underway, but the handful of elderly monks maintained their lay appearance, wearing clothing and hair styles imposed on them during the Cultural Revolution. Only in 1982, when the CPC clarified the institutional space of religion, did monks begin donning clerical robes; as Buddhist education revived, young clerics came, and the colorful Guanyin festivals restarted.

Dynamics of the State System of Religion After 1979

A 1979 article in the state media exhorting religious believers to work together with nonbelievers to realize the Four Modernizations was among the first signs of the reopening institutional space of religion. Another sign occurred in 1980, when an article quoting Marx's famous statement about religion as the "opium of the masses" asserted that Marx critiqued the use of religion by exploiting classes but did not call to eliminate religion (Yu 2015b, 281). Together with these ideological changes, the CPC restarted state religious administration, reopened religious associations and temples (and churches and mosques), and issued a new policy for returning temples occupied by local government and military units to religious communities (Guojia zongjiao shiwu ju 1980). But these new institutions acknowledging religion conflicted with the existing ones that denied religion. This was evident in the new 1978 PRC Constitution that replaced the "leftist" PRC Constitution drafted in 1975 during the Cultural Revolution. The 1978 PRC Constitution declared, "Citizens enjoy freedom to believe in religion and freedom not to believe in religion and to propagate atheism" (People's Republic of China 1978, art. 45).[1] Significantly, the right to propagate was extended to atheism but not to religion; this was a vestige of the 1975 PRC Constitution adopted during the Cultural Revolution that denied religion. Such ambivalence was also seen in efforts made by local state officials who encouraged religious communities to reclaim their religious property even while urging them to renounce their religious beliefs (Yu 2015b).

In 1982, the CPC reduced the ambiguity of its commitment to religion by issuing a new constitution and ideological statement on religion. The 1982 constitution declared:

Citizens of the People's Republic of China enjoy freedom of religious belief. No state organ, public organization, or individual may compel citizens to believe in, or not believe in, any religion; nor may they discriminate against citizens who believe in, or do not believe in, any religion. The state protects normal religious activities. No one may use religion to engage in activities that disrupt public order, impair the health of citizens or interfere with the state's educational system. Religious bodies and religious affairs are not subject to any foreign domination. (People's Republic of China 1982, art. 36)

Significantly, the PRC Constitution of 1982 no longer considered atheism to be covered by the right to religious belief, but it did introduce a new value under the label "normal religious activities." In other aspects, it adhered to all previous modern Chinese constitutions; freedom of religion only covered an individual's belief but not the propagation or founding of religions.[2]

The CPC's view toward religion was clarified in 1982 with an ideological statement titled "The Basic Viewpoint and Policy on the Religious Problem During Our Country's Socialist Period" (關於我國社會主義時期宗教問題的基本觀點和基本政策) and called by its issuing number as Document 19; it was distributed to guide local state officials confused by the sudden change in the CPC's approach toward religion. The three-thousand-character document synthesized earlier CPC ideas toward religion from the early 1950s into a tightly reasoned statement. Document 19, which is translated in full in MacInnis (1989), has been the subject of much scholarship (Chang 1983; Liu 1996; Morrison 2008; Potter 2003; Zhuo 2015), so we limit our discussion to discursive aspects that actors in Xiamen invoked in justifying intentions and actions, as we describe them in various episodes.

The State's Discursive Category of Religion

Notably, Document 19's title referred not to "religion" (*zongjiao* 宗教) but to the "religious problem" (*zongjiao wenti* 宗教問題). In CPC political discourse, a "problem" is typically a matter that does not conform to CPC ideology, necessitating "vigilance" and "guidance." According to the

CPC's materialist view in Document 19, religion in primitive society reflects people's awe of natural phenomena. In a class society, religion becomes a psychological salve for the immiserated working class and is used by the oppressing class to exploit the workers. In the PRC, where class oppression has been largely eliminated, religious belief persists because people's consciousness lags behind changes in productive forces. It follows that the "religious problem" is the persistence of religious belief even as the social conditions that generate it are largely eliminated in the socialist society. Although religion will eventually "disappear naturally" with rising economic development, educational levels, and scientific knowledge, Document 19 cautions that until it does, the CPC must keep "vigilance" over religion because of its "complex nature," including links to ethnic issues and foreign relations.

Document 19 identified three periods in the CPC's handling of the religious problem since the founding of the PRC. The first, from 1949 to 1965, was the "correct approach" that resulted in fashioning a religious policy and freeing religions from domestic and foreign domination. The second period, from 1956 to 1977, consisted of "leftist errors," such as "forbidding normal religious activities [and] . . . wrongly suspecting clerics and believers" (Document 19, quoted in MacInnis 1989, 12–13). In the third, from 1979, the CPC restored the correct approach of the first period by reopening temples, churches, and religious associations and using religion to support the international diplomacy of the state. The CPC was now handling the religious problem "properly as we work toward national stability and ethnic unity, as we develop our international relations while resisting the infiltration of hostile forces from abroad, and as we go on constructing a socialist civilization with both material and spiritual values" (Document 19, quoted in MacInnis 1989, 12).

The CPC's expectations for religions were conveyed in discursive values repeated throughout Document 19. The most frequent was "patriotic," appearing twenty-seven times, most crucially in the phrase "love country, love religion" (*aiguo aijiao* 愛國愛教) (hereafter "patriotic religion").[3] Notably, "country" came before "religion." No one ever said, "love religion, love country."[4] In practice, the phrase meant that religions must obey the CPC. This value also appeared in such terms as "patriotic religious organizations," "patriotic clergy," "patriotic believers," and "patriotic education."[5] Another value was "unity," appearing twenty-three times as in "united front," "unity of the people," "united masses," and "ethnic unity." It referred to overcoming ethnic and other divisions while signaling that religion was part of the united front strategy, as discussed below. A third value was "independence," appearing sixteen times as in "independence," "autonomy," and the prefix "self" (as in "self-managing"). It meant that religions in the PRC should be free from control by "hostile" and "counter-revolutionary" domestic and foreign actors. A fourth value was "normal," appearing eleven times. According to Document 19, the "clear delineation of the line dividing normal religious activities from criminal ones [enables] a crackdown on criminal activities . . . to protect normal religious activities" (quoted in MacInnis 1989, 23).

Document 19 distinguished between constitutionally protected belief in religion as an individual matter and such collective religious activities as teaching and ceremonies. Collective activities could only occur at "religious activity sites," which were temples, churches, and mosques authorized by the local state to hold them. "All normal religious activities held in places so designated [as religious activity sites] are all to be conducted by religious organizations and religious believers themselves, under the protection of the law and without interference from any quarter. . . . No religious organization, or believer, should propagate or preach religion outside places designated for religious services" (Document 19, quoted in MacInnis 1989, 18).[6] Document 19 justified this delimitation as necessary to protect the constitutional rights of nonbelievers to be free from proselytizing.

Organization and Operation

The state system of religious control reflected the broader restructuring of the state after 1979. The key was the dual authorities of party and government. The CPC was the dominant authority that formulated the ideology of state and society. The government was the administrative authority that drew on CPC ideology to create and enforce policies in functional areas (such as religion, economy, and environment). Each authority was a hierarchy with national, provincial, and local (city, county) offices. The party was headed by the CPC Central Committee, while the government was run by the PRC State Council. The CPC's dominance at each level was indicated by the appointment of party members as leaders of government offices to ensure the ideological correctness of governance.

Document 19 identified three actors responsible for religion. The most powerful was an organ of the party called the CPC Central United Front Work Department (Zhonggong zhongyang tongyi zhanxian gongzuo bu 中共中央統一戰線工作部). It was founded in 1939 to manage the party's relations with nonparty groups, such as religions, ethnic minorities, and overseas Chinese. Although not explicitly mentioned in Document 19, its involvement was clearly indicated by the term "united." The department ran "united front work" to develop the CPC's ideological position toward nonparty groups, create corporatist associations to represent them (including the Buddhist Association of China), and cultivate their leaders to support CPC projects (Groot 2004; Van Slyke 1967). Each state level (central, province, local city/county) established its own branch of this CPC organ.

The other two actors handled the routine governance of religion. The State Administration for Religious Affairs (Guojia shiwu zongjiao ju 國家事務宗教局) was a central government ministry established in 1954, abolished during the Cultural Revolution, and revived in 1979.[7] It translated the CPC's ideology into religious policies, managed religious associations by educating their leaders about CPC ideology and government policies, censored religious publications, and gave foreign religious visitors favorable impressions of religion in the PRC.[8] Local offices, called "religious affairs bureaus" (*zongjiao ju* 宗教局), belonged to the government within the local state administration. In Xiamen, the Xiamen Municipal Religious Affairs Bureau (XRAB; Xiamen shi zongjiao shiwu ju 廈門市宗教事務局) had a director and vice directors responsible for specific religions, including Buddhism, Protestantism, and Catholicism.

The Buddhist Association of China was founded in 1953 to educate Buddhist clerics and devotees about CPC ideology and ensure their compliance with religious policies.[9] When revived in 1979, its president was the pre–Cultural Revolution Buddhist leader, the devotee Zhao Puchu, who served until his death (see Ji 2017). Its officers were abbots of important temples, although some devotees served in the 1980s due to the lack of clerics at that time. In Xiamen, all three abbots of Nanputuo Temple since the Cultural Revolution have served as vice presidents of the

Buddhist Association of China, indicating the temple's importance. Its office was inside Nanputuo Temple and the president was the abbot, a tradition dating to the first Buddhist association established in Xiamen in the 1930s with Taixu as president (*XFZ*, 175–193). The BAX members consisted of the Nanputuo Temple abbot and priors of the city's local temples and lay nun halls.

The most local level of the state saw regular interplay among these three actors to administer Buddhism. The Buddhist Association of Xiamen Municipality (BAX; Xiamen shi fojiao xiehui 廈門市佛教協會) was under the administrative direction of the XRAB, and their interaction was guided behind the scenes by the local Xiamen United Front Work Department. This guidance—officially called "coordination" (*xietiao* 協調) in the CPC lexicon—worked to control discourses, approve personnel appointments, and generate conformity to CPC ideology and projects. The distance of local united front work departments from the routine administration of religion minimized direct confrontation between the party and Buddhism within temples. It also created a line, at least in principle, between religious authority and political authority (CPC) to conform with the Chinese view of modern secular state administration.[10] The interaction of the three actors in the national administrative system for religion is depicted in figure 3.1, with the coordination relation indicated by dashed lines.

Coordination proceeded in several ways. One involved overlapping personnel appointments between the united front work departments and the other two actors at all levels of the state. In regard to religious affairs bureaus, there were two kinds of overlaps. One was party discipline. Because religious affairs officials were CPC members, they were subject to party discipline, including the ban on members believing in religion. The other was the practice of concurrent office holding. In Xiamen, the director of the XRAB was seconded as a vice director of the Xiamen United Front Work Department, furthering the overall integration of religious affairs with the united front concerns in Xiamen, which centered on overseas Chinese. In religious communities the overlap came about with the selection of clerics to serve on two legislative bodies under the purview of the United Front Work Department: one was the Chinese People's Consultative Political Conference (Zhongguo remin zhengzhi xieshang huiyi 中國人民政治協商會議), which proposed legislation; and the

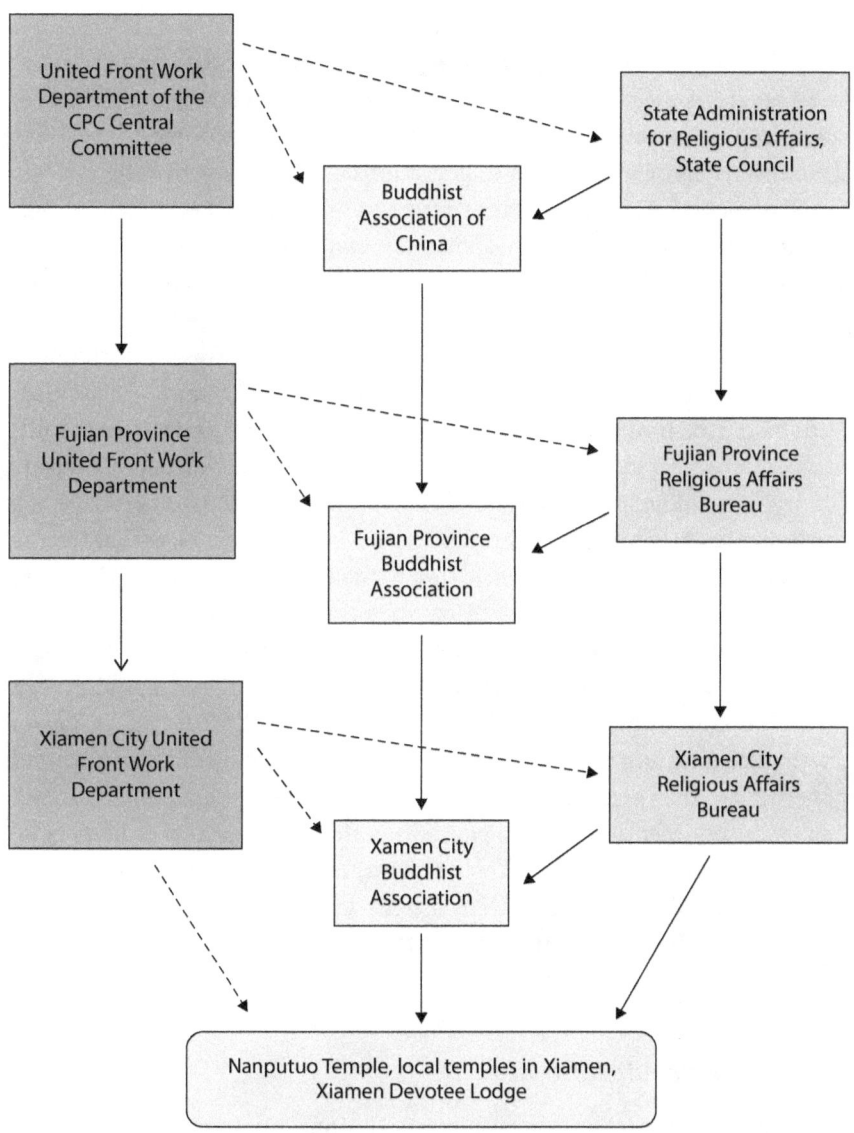

FIGURE 3.1 Hierarchy of state system of religious administration

other was the National People's Congress (Quanguo remin daibiao dahui 全國人民代表大會), which approved legislation. Both bodies had branches at all levels of the state. While representation gave clerics a modicum of voice in law-making processes regarding religion, it coopted them into the consensus regarding state expectations and projects for religion.

The participation of all three actors in regularly scheduled meetings also fostered coordination. Buddhist associations at the central and provincial levels held congresses to express goals and select leaders. Leading officials of the other two organizations also attended and gave keynote speeches reaffirming the CPC ideology. National congresses of the Buddhist Association of China, held every five or more years to articulate Buddhism's commitment to state projects, were especially important.[11] In 1980, at the Buddhist Association of China Ninth National Congress (Zhongguo fojiao hui quanguo daibiao huiyi 中國佛教會全國代表會議), the keynote speech was delivered by Xiao Xianfa 肖賢法, an official in the CPC Central United Front Work Department and director of the State Administration of Religious Affairs. Speaking to the clerics in the audience, he sought to dispel their concerns that the CPC's reacknowledgement of religion was "a temporary expedient" by reaffirming the party's historical commitment to religious freedom, as well as to the values of patriotism and unity (Xiao 1980). At the local level of city and county governance, the three actors met more frequently. For example, the BAX held monthly meetings of the Nanputuo abbot and priors of local temples. These meetings were often attended by officials of the XRAB and Xiamen United Front Work Department to discuss concrete problems faced by temples and Buddhists, and the policy and ideological issues at stake.

Local State Administration

The localization of the state system of religious administration occurred in several ways, one being the focus on religious activity sites. Document 19, as previously noted, delimits all aspects of religion, other than individual beliefs, to religious activity sites. Buddhist temples are where clerics reside and rituals and services are conducted, with larger ones housing Buddhist associations and academies. Thus, the Buddhist Association of China and Buddhist Academy of China were located at, respectively,

Guangji Temple and Fayuan Temple 法源寺 in Beijing, while the BAX and BCM were at Nanputuo Temple. There were national criteria for qualifying as a religious activity site, such as having clerics in residence and only holding "normal" religious activities. Local religious affairs bureaus could adapt them to local situations. In Xiamen, only a temple predating the founding of the PRC could be recognized as a religious activity site. This rule prevented new temple construction in order to limit the spread of religion and preserve land for commercial development.

Document 19 specified complementary roles for religious affairs bureaus and Buddhist associations in governing religious activity sites. A temple was under the "administrative control" of a local bureau, on the one hand, and, on the other, the "self-management" of "religious professionals," namely clerics at temples and local Buddhist associations. Officials and clerics were supposed to cooperate in maintaining religious activity sites for both "normal religion" and "tourism." But no practical guidelines distinguished "administrative control" from "self-management." This ambiguity engendered ongoing negotiations between clerics and local officials over their respective authorities.

As a religious activity site, a temple could not be privately owned. A large temple operating through the *shifang conglin* system was, in principle, legally owned by its resident clerics, who ran it according to the principle of "self-management." Implementing this principle was contentious at Nanputuo Temple, as we describe throughout this book. The numerous smaller local temples, historically the property of a master who passed it on to a disciple, were owned by the BAX in the case of Xiamen. Temples were run by a "democratic management committee" (*minzhu guanli weiyuanhui* 民主管理委員會) led by the prior. Depending on their size, they had five to seven Buddhist members and an accountant and cashier. In Xiamen, all committee members required the XRAB's approval, and the committees regularly reported the temple's activities and finances to the XRAB.[12] In this manner, committees enabled collective decision-making to prevent a temple from being used for private gain and facilitated the monitoring of the temple by the XRAB.

The second aspect of localization was decentralizing state governance at the start of the opening-up policies. This was intended to encourage initiative by local officials in governing according to local needs and situations.[13] Thus, the XRAB was part of the state hierarchy of religious affairs but also part of the local Xiamen Municipal People's Government 廈門市人民政府. The XRAB officials had to meet the expectations of the local state administration's concern to promote the development of the Xiamen SEZ and interacted with other local bureaus, such as public security and urban planning. Similarly, the BAX was enmeshed in local networks with other temples and government agencies while also connected to provincial and central state Buddhist associations. As a result, the politics in the institutional space proceeded in networks that wound their way through the local state administration and hierarchically in the state (Mertha 2009; Palmer 2009).

Decentralization enabled local states to selectively stress values in Document 19 in governing their jurisdictions. Thus, in Xiamen, with its extensive links to overseas Chinese communities, the local state administration emphasized the value of patriotism when seeking the compliance of religious actors. In jurisdictions with large ethnic minority populations, local states stressed the value of unity (Madsen 2000, 7–8). Additionally, in Minnan, local religious affairs bureaus allowed overseas Chinese donations to fund religious activities because they saw this as leading to investments in social services and business, as we explain later in this chapter. In contrast, in areas with few overseas Chinese ties, local officials viewed funds from overseas Chinese as security risks and restricted them (Madsen 2000, 7).

The Xiamen Municipal People's Government created organizations that merged its governance concerns regarding religions and overseas Chinese. One was the Religious Security Section (Zongjiao baowei ke 宗教保衛科), established in the early 1980s to handle such sensitive matters as requests by overseas Chinese clerics to reclaim temples and visiting religious dignitaries. It was led by the Xiamen vice mayor for public security, and members included the directors of the Xiamen United Front Work Department, the XRAB, the Xiamen Municipal Public Security Bureau (Xiamen shi gong'an ju 廈門市公安局), and the Xiamen National Security Bureau (Xiamen shi anquan ju 廈門市國家安全局) that dealt with foreign spies. It sought to ensure that the local state's deft handling of sensitive issues regarding overseas Chinese, such as reclaiming temples and staging large ceremonies. Another entity was the Religion and Overseas Chinese Group (Zongjiao huaqiao zu 宗教華僑組), established by the Xiamen United Front Work Department in the early 1990s. Its twenty members included clerics and representatives of other social groups in the Xiamen Municipal People's Congress. It annually inspected religious activity sites to ensure that the implementation of the religious policy would not "offend" overseas Chinese. This arrangement gave clerics some oversight of the XRAB, although the Religion and Overseas Chinese Group lacked enforcement power and could only try to persuade the XRAB to accept its recommendations.[14]

In sum, reopening the institutional space of religion created possibilities for actors. Local state officials sought to establish governance that met the expectations of the overlapping lines of authority in which they were embedded, while Buddhists sought to recover what they had lost in the first three decades of the PRC. Government officials and Buddhists alike invoked the discursive values of Document 19 to shape agendas, interactions, and negotiations.

Reactivating the Historical Capital of Nanputuo Temple

The relatively swift recovery of Nanputuo was facilitated by the value that the state placed on the temple including its legacy of Taixu and the networks with overseas Chinese. These legacies appealed to the CPC, not only for managing religion but also for reconnecting the country to the international market economy. The reactivation of these legacies was greatly furthered by the leadership of Nanputuo Temple's first abbot, the elderly Miaozhan. Aside from the buildings, his role as an "old generation" monk embodied the continuity of Nanputuo Temple.

Leadership of an Old-Generation Monk

The recovery of Nanputuo Temple was led by Miaozhan from 1979 until he died in 1995. His experience as a monk before the founding of the PRC gave him a clear vision to revive Buddhism as it had previously existed. His function as a living link to the influential clerics of the early twentieth century gave him the trust of overseas clerics of the same generation, as well as of Buddhists in Xiamen.

Miaozhan was born Chu Yongkang 褚永康 in 1910 to a farming family in Liaoning Province 遼寧省, northeast China. He was educated in a private school, attended a teacher training college, and became an elementary school principal. In 1937, Japanese occupation police imprisoned him on suspicion of anti-Japanese activities. During our observation at the temple, we heard stories that a fellow prisoner taught him Buddhist sutras, which Miaozhan chanted to calm himself. This supposedly convinced his captors of his innocence, and they released him. Miaozhan attributed his change of fortune to Buddhism and was ordained in 1939. He studied at the Zhanshan Buddhist Academy (Zhanshan foxue yuan 湛山佛學院) founded by Tanxu at Zhanshan Temple 湛山寺 in Qingdao City, Shandong Province 山東省青島市.[15] At that time, the Japanese, CPC, and the ROC armies were fighting in North China, so Miaozhan moved to the quieter south. In 1942, he went to Gaomin Temple 高旻寺 in Yangzhou, Jiangsu Province 江蘇省揚州市, to study under Chan master Laiguo 來果 (1881–1953). He remained at the temple for fifteen years, eventually serving as senior guest prefect.

In 1957, he came to Nanputuo Temple after a time of wandering (*yunyou* 雲遊), becoming prior (*jianyuan* 監院) the following year.[16] After being expelled from the temple compound during the Cultural Revolution, he grew his hair and wore lay clothing but remained by the temple, living in a lean-to along its outer wall. An overseas Chinese devotee visiting from Singapore recounted meeting him at Nanputuo Temple in 1973.

> When I saw Venerable Miaozhan, he was still relatively young. He lived in a small hut next to the temple and grew his own food. [He entered the temple] to sweep the courtyard. When I visited Nanputuo Temple, he came out and talked to me. . . . Then from 1979, more people came. When overseas Chinese came who were Buddhists, Venerable Miaozhan would go and greet them. . . . He encouraged us to worship at the temple and donate money. But he did not pressure us. He showed us around and told us what was needed. He did not ask directly.[17]

In 1976, the Xiamen Municipal People's Government opened Nanputuo Temple as a public park, and Miaozhan and a dozen other monks were hired to work at refreshment stands.

Then in 1979, Nanputuo reopened as a temple, and the Xiamen United Front Work Department designated Miaozhan as the temporary prior (*linshi zhuchi* 臨時住持). He was sixty-nine years old and one of the few monks educated in a Buddhist academy and possessing administrative experience.[18] Initially, he was a cautious leader and did not receive tonsure or wear clerical robes for fear of persecution. This became an issue when a Japanese Buddhist delegation of the Ōbaku sect (Jp. Ōbakushu 黃檗宗, Ch. Huangbo zong) visited Xiamen in 1980.[19] XRAB officials asked Miaozhan to shave his head and don clerical robes to give the visitors a good impression of Buddhism in Xiamen. But Miaozhan refused, so the officials found another monk willing to receive tonsure and wear robes. But this monk's weak textual knowledge of Buddhism disappointed the delegation and embarrassed the officials. The XRAB redoubled its pressure on Miaozhan, but he remained obstinate.

According to an XRAB official working at the temple at the time, Miaozhan refused for three reasons. First, the state attack on Buddhism during the Cultural Revolution had undermined his confidence in the staying power of the new policy. The official recounted to us the words that Miaozhan had told the XRAB director: "Today you tell me to put on robes, but tomorrow you will tell me to take them off. I don't like this."[20] Second, he objected to the XRAB's use of Nanputuo Temple for commercial purposes. In 1980, the XRAB had already constructed a restaurant inside the temple's east courtyard, and Miaozhan feared his cooperation would further the commercialization. Third, he felt he could help the temple recover without wearing robes and shaving his head. He said that being a Buddhist was based on the belief in one's heart rather than outward appearances (Wu 2014, vol. 7, book 1, 80–81).

Zhao Puchu, now president of the recently revived Buddhist Association of China, also worked to convince Miaozhan to receive tonsure and wear robes. During trips to Xiamen in 1980 and 1981, he unsuccessfully urged Miaozhan to assume a monk's figure. So, Zhao asked the XRAB to take Miaozhan to visit a few temples where monks wore robes again, to convince him (Wu 2014, vol. 7, book 1, 80–81). In October 1981, an XRAB official led Miaozhan and three other Nanputuo monks to visit Lingyanshan Temple 靈岩山寺 and Xiyuan Temple 西園寺 in Suzhou City 蘇州市 and Yufuo Temple 玉佛寺 in Shanghai. Soon after their return to Xiamen, the monks shaved their heads and donned robes (Wu 2014, vol. 7, book 1, 82–96). Miaozhan became an active and energetic leader of Nanputuo Temple, and Buddhism in Xiamen, provincially, and nationally for the next thirteen years until he died at age eighty-five.

Miaozhan's effectiveness as a leader stemmed from his background as an old-generation cleric. His memories of Buddhism fifty years earlier, before the founding of the PRC, gave him a clear view of the temple he sought to recover. Due to his long association with Nanputuo, he appreciated its character as a modern temple and the importance of the BCM. His approach reflected the views of Taixu, Tanxu, and other eminent clerics of the early twentieth century on the pressing need to educate the clergy. In his efforts to revive the temple, Miaozhan paid little heed to political considerations and simply did what he considered best for Buddhism. This attitude endeared him to Buddhists and inspired trust among the overseas Chinese clerics. At the same time, it heightened tensions with the local government in Xiamen, which worked to restrain and channel his aspirations for the temple. Miaozhan's ability to persevere reflected his prestige. Clerics and devotees alike respected him for his hardships during the Cultural Revolution to care for Nanputuo Temple and his sincere commitment to Buddhism.

His leadership was enhanced by ties with elderly Buddhist leaders in the PRC and overseas. He was close to Zhao Puchu. Both were the same age, disciples of Tanxu, and had experienced the troubled times in the 1930s and 1940s but chose to remain in China. Miaozhan could contact Zhao Puchu to discuss problems at Nanputuo Temple and ask for assistance. He established close ties with overseas clerics, most notably Hongchuan 宏船 (Hong Choon, 1907–1990) in Singapore. In 1984, Hongchuan gave Miaozhan a dharma transmission, making him the forty-eighth generation of Hongchuan's religious lineage (*Miaozhan heshang jinian ji* 1997, 99).[21] While the ostensible purpose was to give Miaozhan the authority to appoint the priors of local temples in Hongchuan's lineage (see chapter 7), the transmission boosted Miaozhan's prestige as the leader of Nanputuo Temple. It connected Miaozhan to Hongchuan, a former student of Taixu and the preeminent overseas Chinese monk in Southeast Asia in the late twentieth century, and to Hongchuan's master Huiquan, the first abbot of the ecumenicized Nanputuo Temple in the 1920s.

Miaozhan's rising stature after 1979 was reflected in his positions in the state's religious system. He held the three leading positions of Buddhism in Xiamen—abbot of Nanputuo Temple, rector of the BCM, and president of the BAX. Additionally, he became president of the Buddhist Association of Fujian, executive board member of the Buddhist

Association of China, abbot of Yongquan Temple 涌泉寺 in Fuzhou, and dean of the Fujian Buddhist Academy (Fujian foxue yuan 福建佛學院), among other appointments. In the last few years of his life, he played a leading role in the Buddhist diplomacy of the state, including the leader of the Buddha relic tour delegation to Thailand in 1994.

Xiamen's Buddhist communities held Miaozhan in exceptionally high regard because he respected local Minnan traditions of Buddhism. He let lay nuns study in the BCM alongside ordained nuns, continuing the respect for this community created by Hongyi and other clerics at Nanputuo Temple in the 1930s (Ashiwa and Wank 2019). He also enjoyed close ties with devotees. He worked with prominent elderly devotees to recover Buddhism in Xiamen and held ceremonies to confer the devotee precepts. He permitted popular local practices that were not part of more orthodox Buddhism, such as burning spirit money for dead souls and performing the release of burning mouths ritiual (see page 207).

Miaozhan even gained the sympathy and support of local state officials who appreciated the elderly northern monk's devotion to Nanputuo Temple. Some XRAB officials who worked closely with him were attracted to his straightforward demeanor; upon retiring from government service, they showed their dedication to him by working for the temple and the BAX. They drew on their in-depth knowledge of state administration and CPC ideology to advise Miaozhan. Their understanding of state officials' expectations as well as Buddhist clerics' desires made them invaluable mediators during the early phases of the recovery.[22] For all of these reasons, Miaozhan and the capital he embodied were critical for reactivating Nanputuo Temple's historical legacies.

The Legacy of Taixu

Taixu's association with Nanputuo from 1926 to 1933 gave the temple's recovery favorable attention from the CPC.[23] His image contributed to the view of Nanputuo as the desirable kind of modern Buddhist temple for the PRC's socialist society. This positive image may be traced to the 1950s when Taixu's disciple Juzan drew on Buddhism for the Human Realm to gain CPC recognition for Buddhism. Juzan's emphasis on the physical labor of clerics and this-worldly concerns helped gain CPC approval to found the Buddhist Association of China in 1953 (Welch 1967,

7–19). After 1979, Taixu's Buddhism for the Human Realm was the form of Buddhism that the CPC considered appropriate in the PRC (Ji 2013, 39–48), even though, given the sensitive nature of Taixu's cooperation with the ROC, the Buddhist Association of China did not (at first) openly acknowledge Taixu. Thus in 1983, when the association's president Zhao Puchu urged clerics to engage in physical labor, academic study, and international exchanges, he referred only to Chan Buddhist tradition without mentioning Taixu. Then, in 1987, the Buddhist Association of China began to acknowledge him by adopting a resolution to "advocate the active and progressive thought of Buddhism for the Human Realm" (Ji 2013, 51–52).

Under the leadership of Miaozhan, clerics actively promoted Taixu's legacy at Nanputuo Temple. The BCM's curriculum emphasized his mix of Buddhist and secular courses. The 1989 inaugural issue of the *Journal of the Buddhist College of Minnan* (*Minnan foxue yuan xuebao* 閩南佛學院學報) devoted articles to Taixu and his ideas on Buddhist education. Places in the temple were dedicated to him, such as the Taixu Library (Taixu tushu guan 太虛圖書館), completed in 1989. A hut on Wulao Peak where Taixu lived was restored and named the Taixu Pavilion. Monks viewed the administration innovations at the temple in the 1980s (see chapter 4) and a charity foundation that opened in 1994 (see chapter 5) as a way to extend Taixu's teachings of worldly engagement. Taixu could thus be considered the guardian of the recovery of Nanputuo Temple and a model for positioning religion in a "socialist society."

Nanputuo Temple benefitted from Taixu's massive influence on Buddhism outside of China. Many influential clerics in Southeast Asia were BCM graduates, including Hongchuan and Yanpei 演培 (Yen Pei, 1917–1996) in Singapore, and Zhumo 竺摩 (Chuk Mor, 1913–2002) in Malaysia. In Taiwan, two of the four leading Buddhist organizations were directly linked to Taixu and the BCM through Taixu's star disciple Yinshun 印順 (Yin Shun, 1906–2005). Yinshun became his spiritual successor and taught a generation of socially engaged clerics, most notably Zhengyan 證嚴 (Cheng Yen, 1937–), founder of the Compassion Relief Tzu Chi Foundation (Ci ji gongde hui 慈濟功德會). Other clerics were much influenced by Taixu's ideas, such as Xingyun 星雲 (Hsing Yun, 1927–2023), the founder of Fo Guang Shan 佛光山. These transnational links made Nanputuo

Temple a vital site for PRC engagement with overseas Chinese as well as with Taiwan and Hong Kong. During the 1980s, when Deng Xiaoping 鄧小平 viewed Singapore as a development model for China, the CPC Central United Front Work Department cultivated influential monks in Singapore with ties to Nanputuo Temple as opinion leaders among overseas Chinese.[24]

In the 1990s, Nanputuo Temple's links to overseas temples helped the Buddhist Association of China to make Buddhism more relevant in the PRC. They helped the association study new practices in Buddhist education, social welfare, and media that had begun in Taiwan, Singapore, and other overseas Chinese communities in the 1960s in response to expectations from their states and the growing middle classes (Kuah-Pearce 2003). Some of these practices, such as running a charity foundation and use of internet media, were then brought to China and first tried at Nanputuo Temple.

The state expressed its support for the temple by various means. One entailed the visits of national leaders to the temple from 1979, starting with Hua Guofeng 華國峰, Deng Xiaoping, and heads of foreign states (cf. *XFZ*, 28–45). A second involved conferring awards on the temple. In 1983, the central state designated Nanputuo as one of 142 key national temples (*hanzu diqu fojiao quanguo zhongdian siyuan* 漢族地區佛教全國重點寺院) with cultural and historical significance for Han Chinese. In Xiamen, the local state administration gave Nanputuo Temple sixty-nine awards in the two decades since 1981, starting with one for being an Advanced Unit for Maintaining Peace and Order ("Nanputuo si," n.d.). A third form of support occurred when the central state granted permission for Nanputuo Temple to pioneer new activities. In 1985, the state approved the reopening of the BCM, the first Buddhist academy in the PRC that was not linked to a Buddhist association.[25] In the 1990s, other examples include the innovations mentioned above in charity, social media, and Buddhist diplomacy of the state. The fourth manifestation of state support was the willingness of Zhao Puchu and the Buddhist Association of China to intervene in various matters on behalf of Nanputuo clerics in conflicts with the local state administration. Because Nanputuo was one of the first major temples to recover, the CPC Central United Front Work Department and the Buddhist

Association of China observed it closely to understand trends and problems in the state's religious administration. Additionally, the CPC saw the temple as important for cultivating relationships with influential overseas Chinese clerics.

Transnational Networks of Clerics

The transnational networks of Nanputuo Temple were formed by overlapping affiliations of religious kinship, loyalty, and regionalism among clerics (Ashiwa and Wank 2005). Throughout history, communication and resource exchanges among temples have proceeded through such affiliations, constituting the decentralized organization of Chinese Buddhism (Welch 1967, 403–408). Although Buddhism in the PRC had become more nationally integrated through the administrative structure of the Buddhist Association of China, the networks remained key to communication between temples in the PRC and Chinese temples overseas.

The strongest affiliation was religious kinship. It was a tie between clerics tonsured by the same master, who considered themselves dharma brothers. They had mutual obligations similar to blood siblings, even if their common master was several generations removed (Welch 1967, 403). Many elderly Chinese monks in Southeast Asia were dharma brothers, as evident in the prevalence of four *gatha* names among them—Guang 廣, Hong 宏, Hui 會, and Rui 瑞.[26] They had been tonsured or ordained at Nanputuo Temple or one of the other major temples in Minnan—Kaiyuan Temple 開元寺, Chengtian Temple 承天寺, Nanshan Temple 南山寺, and Xuefeng Temple 雪峰寺.[27] Many of these clerics shared weaker but significant religious kinship ties through experiences before 1949 while studying and teaching in the BCM and holding office at Nanputuo Temple. They then followed their masters overseas to found temples. When their masters passed away, they inherited the leadership of the temples as the second generation of overseas Chinese clerics (*XFZ*, 225–228).

Loyalty affiliations were created among clerics who held office or studied under Taixu and other master monks, such as Zhuanfeng and Xingyuan, at Nanputuo Temple and the BCM. Loyalty affiliations also linked Chinese clerics who propagated Taixu's teachings after 1949, even

INSTITUTIONAL SPACE AND HISTORICAL CAPITAL

if they had not lived or studied at the temple. Regional affiliations formed among cliques of Minnan-speaking clerics who invited other clerics from Minnan to their overseas domiciles. Minnan-speaking clerics headed many Chinese Buddhist temples in Southeast Asia, especially in Malaysia, the Philippines, and Singapore. Regionalism also linked devotees and worshipers to temples run by Minnan-speaking monks in overseas Chinese communities.

These affiliations facilitated resource sharing among the temples (Ashiwa and Wank 2005). For instance, carefully made abbatial appointments helped to resolve leadership issues among overseas temples, a growing problem for aging clerics who lacked successors. This is illustrated by Kong Meng San Phor Kark See Temple (Guangmingshan pujue si 光明山普覺禪寺) in Singapore and Seng Guan Temple (Xinyuan si 信願寺) in Manila, established, respectively, by Hongchuan and Xingyuan. When Xingyuan passed away in 1962, his disciple Ruijin 瑞今 (1905–2005) succeeded him as abbot of Seng Guan Temple. After Ruijin served twelve years as abbot, the maximum permitted in the temple (Dy 2013), Hongchuan, who was already abbot of Kong Meng San Phor Kark See Temple, was invited to succeed him. Then, in 1990, when Hongchuan passed away, Ruijin was invited to become abbot of Kong Meng San Phor Kark See Temple. We interviewed the ninety-six-year-old Ruijin at Seng Guan Temple in 2000. When we asked why he was selected as abbot of the temple in Singapore, his response invoked all three affiliations. "Hongchuan and I were classmates at the BCM [loyalty]. He is also from Jinjiang County. So we have known each other for a long time [regionalism]. Our master is Huiquan, so we are brothers [kinship]. Also, Hongchuan and I are disciples of Xingyuan [loyalty]."[28] His answer showed the power of the three affiliations in allocating resources, in this case, leadership, among Chinese Buddhist temples in Southeast Asia.

The reactivation of these transnational ties brought significant resources to Nanputuo Temple and, more generally, to Buddhism in Minnan. One was money. Many overseas clerics wanted to help Buddhism recover in the PRC. They funded the restoration of the temples and the creation of new facilities, such as the dormitories, classrooms, and library of the BCM. A second resource was the recovery of ritual knowledge that had been lost in the PRC over the past three decades. In the early 1980s, young monks from Nanputuo Temple went to temples in Singapore and Hong Kong to learn Buddhist rituals and bring their knowledge back to China.[29] A third resource was political support. Because the CPC considered overseas Chinese clerics to be important to party causes, state officials responded quickly to the clerics' requests. BAX officers said that lobbying by Hongchuan helped gain central state approval to revive the BCM. Furthermore, Buddhists in Xiamen learned how to use the solicitousness of local officials toward overseas monks. When the BAX sought to reclaim an occupied temple, it did so in the name of an overseas Chinese cleric. The local state administration would then fast-track the eviction of the government or military unit "to avoid harming the feelings of overseas Chinese."[30]

The transnational ties were also reciprocal, thereby ensuring their continuity. Funding the revival of the BCM served the needs of the elderly overseas clerics to find successors to lead their temples. In the 1990s, many graduates emigrated to serve in overseas temples that lacked successors. Additionally, overseas Chinese temples in Southeast Asia with insufficient clerics for large rituals invited delegations from Nanputuo Temple to participate. These visits provided ritual training to many BCM students.

Hongchuan was the most significant overseas monk for Nanputuo Temple in the 1980s. He was born in 1913 in Jinjiang County, next to Xiamen, and was tonsured at age twelve by Huiquan. In 1925, Hongchuan enrolled in the BCM, studied under Taixu, and moved to Southeast Asia in 1938 with his master Huiquan. His stature grew over the decades. He served as abbot of Beow Heong Lim Temple (Miaoxianglin si 妙香林寺) in Penang, built Kong Meng San Phor Kark See Temple in Singapore, and founded the Singapore Buddhist Federation, the Singapore Inter-Religious Organization, a free medical clinic, and a primary school. By the 1980s, he was the leader of Chinese Buddhism in Singapore and respected among Buddhists throughout Southeast Asia. In 1987, the King of Thailand bestowed him with the title "Supreme Chinese Monk" (Hongchuan fashi jinian tekan 1993). From 1982 to 1990, Hongchuan undertook eight well-publicized trips to the PRC that spurred the development of Buddhism in China and international relations between Singapore and the PRC. His meetings with high-ranking officials in the PRC furthered "friendly relations" between the two countries that lacked diplomatic relations until 1990 (Chia 2008). In 1988, Zhao Puchu made a reciprocal visit to Singapore, where he was impressed by the city-state's missionary schools and the technological savvy of Buddhists. He commented, "Buddhist organizations should learn from Singapore's successful experience" (cited in Chia 2008, 879), echoing Deng Xiaoping's view ten years earlier that the city-state was a model for China's economic development.

Devotees were also part of these transnational networks. Their donations, whether given through overseas clerics or directly, helped fund the recovery of Buddhism. They believed they accrued merit (*gongde* 功德) by donating funds to rebuild temples. Devotees also constituted pilgrimage networks between Southeast Asia and China. Many joined specialized worship tours organized by tour companies run by overseas Chinese.[31] These tours typically flew directly to Xiamen. The first temple that tourists visited was Nanputuo, where their ancestors had worshiped when departing to Southeast Asia. These tours also furthered transnational ties in other ways, as illustrated by the Singapore-based Jinta Tourism company. It was founded in 1980 by a woman, originally from Quanzhou, whose trip to the PRC in the late 1970s to visit her mother gave her the idea for a tour company. Initially, her tours visited scenic places rather than religious sites. Then, in 1985, she organized a tour of China's Four Sacred Buddhist Mountains (Si da fojiao mingshan 四大佛教名山) and was surprised that many Buddhist devotees from Singapore joined. She developed new tour itineraries focused on Buddhist temples because their religious, scenic, and religious aspects had broad appeal, to both elderly devotees wanting to worship and families with children exploring their cultural identity as "Chinese." In 1996, Jinta Tours was contracted by the Singapore Devotee Lodge, the Chinese devotee organization in Singapore, to organize a worship tour of devotees. Since then, the company has operated several worship tours annually.

The CPC valued good relations with overseas Chinese ties for manifold reasons, including furthering Buddhist diplomacy, tourism, and cultural awareness of China among overseas Chinese. For Nanputuo Temple, the ties provided such resources as funds and ritual knowledge and deepened relations with overseas devotees and believers. The resources accruing to Nanputuo Temple through these ties made it among the first temples to recover.

Comparative Perspective on a Precocious Revival

By the mid-1980s, Buddhists had reclaimed 85 percent of all temples in Fujian Province, a far higher rate than in other provinces at the time. By the end of the 1980s, the 3,000 registered Buddhist temples in Fujian constituted 80 percent of all registered temples in the PRC, while its 10,000 monks and nuns accounted for 25 percent of the national population of Buddhist clerics. During the 1990s, these numbers increased to 4,000 temples and 14,000 ordained clerics, although the national shares of temples and clerics they represented fell to 25 percent and 14 percent, respectively, as recovery picked up elsewhere.[32] In this section we examine the precociousness of the recovery in Fujian from the perspectives of local state implementation of the religious policy and the historical capitals of temples.

Proactivity of the Local State

When we asked people during our fieldwork why Nanputuo Temple recovered so rapidly, state officials and BAX officers talked about the quick and thorough implementation of the religious policy in Fujian Province and the Minnan region. Some emphasized the importance of state officials with the foresight and connections to get things done. They noted the commitment of Xiang Nan 項南, Fujian CPC party leader at the time, to the market reform policies, as well as his tie with Zhao Puchu, forged in 1954 when they served as representatives from Anhui Province at the first meeting of the National People's Congress.[33] In 1981, Xiang Nan arranged for Zhao Puchu to visit Nanshan Temple in Zhangzhou City near Xiamen. Zhao discovered that the temple grounds were being used as a zoo. He reported this shocking situation to Xiang Nan, who immediately ordered the local state administration to return the temple to Buddhists. Then, Xiang Nan launched an investigation of all Buddhist temples by a team that included members of the Fujian Province CPC Standing Committee, the Fujian Provincial People's Government, the Fujian People's Consultative Committee, and the Fujian Provincial People's Legislature. The team traveled throughout the province identifying the temples occupied by local states and military units. It reported the temples to the Fujian Religious Affairs Bureau, which ordered their return to Buddhists.

The high rank of the team members and their ties were crucial to the team's effectiveness, as explained to us nearly two decades later by a Fujian Religious Affairs Bureau official.

> At that time, even though there were only six or seven people in the Fujian Religious Affairs Bureau, our strength was actually quite big because we had the backing of Xiang Nan, who attached importance to religious work. Reclaiming temples could not have been accomplished without the support of powerful officials. Our religious affairs bureau is only an administrative department. But the investigative team was made up of leading organizations, so it was powerful. The rather quick implementation of the [religious] policy in Fujian was solely due to the recognition by the leading bureau [Fujian Province CPC leader] of the importance of religion.[34]

Personal ties were leveraged to get the People's Liberation Army to vacate local temples because the Fujian Religious Affairs Bureau could not compel the military. Many temples had been subject to military use as observation posts and storehouses because the coast of Fujian Province was on the front line of the hostilities with the ROC on Taiwan. But a member of the investigative team, who was the former chief of staff of the Fujian military region, persuaded military commanders to give up temples.[35] In Xiamen, a hardware factory and a primary school established at Nanputuo Temple in the Cultural Revolution were withdrawn, and lay nun halls and local temples, including those occupied by the military, were returned to Buddhists.

Our interviews with local officials from 1988 to 1990 suggested that the economic concerns of local state administrations in Minnan also spurred the implementation of the religious policy. They were keenly aware that, as an ancestral overseas Chinese homeland, the CPC expected the region to take the lead in attracting foreign investment, especially in the Xiamen Special Economic Zone. Whereas overseas Chinese were previously viewed as spies, local officials now saw them as key to gaining investment and international markets. To encourage their investment, officials sought to overcome the distrust of overseas Chinese toward the CPC that resulted from the party's socialist ideology and earlier poor treatment of returned overseas Chinese (*guiqiao* 歸僑).[36] Officials viewed the party's tolerant stance toward religion as an important trust-building gesture and expressed their attitudes in numerous interviews in the late 1980s.[37] For example, an official in the Fujian Religious Affairs Bureau said, "All overseas Chinese believe in religion. It is important to make them feel welcome by letting their temples and churches start. You can't ask them to invest their money here if you are suppressing their religion."[38]

Officials in economic and commercial bureaus offered various explanations of how tolerance toward religion and folk beliefs generated economic investment. An official in a commercial bureau said, "They [overseas Chinese] come back to visit their village and rebuild the ancestor hall. After they get here, they look around and see the favorable economic conditions, and so they invest in a business."[39] We heard apocryphal stories from officials of how religion had caused overseas Chinese businesspersons to invest. One such story involved a tile factory that was among the earliest overseas Chinese investments in the Xiamen SEZ. Its owner, an overseas Chinese devotee from Indonesia, accompanied Hongchuan on one of his first trips to Xiamen in the early 1980s. While in Xiamen, Hongchuan encouraged him to invest because economic growth would help the Chinese people and Buddhism. These stories also encompassed other religions. An official at the Nan'an Religious Affairs Bureau near Xiamen told us about an overseas Chinese Christian. Upon visiting China after many years, he was so moved to see people once again worshiping in churches in China that he invested 100 million yuan in a business.[40]

These interviews suggest the degree to which officials in local state administrations in Fujian linked economic development with religion. State officials at all levels of the provincial administration proactively implemented the religious policy as part of their efforts to fulfill central state expectations for Fujian to use its capital as an "overseas Chinese ancestral homeland" to be a national leader in creating an internationally integrated market economy.

The Importance of Historical Capital

Even within Fujian Province, the pace of recovery varied; temples with the historical capital equivalent to the kind Nanputuo Temple possessed—transnational networks and leadership of an "old generation" cleric—recovered earlier. The importance of such capital is highlighted by examining two other key temples in Fujian Province: Guanghua Temple 廣化寺 and Wanfu Temple 萬福寺.[41] Guanghua Temple had capital similar to Nanputuo Temple and recovered rapidly, though the characters of the temples were quite different.[42] In contrast, Wanfu Temple lacked equivalent networks and leadership—which, we argue, explains why its recovery did not get underway until a decade later.

Guanghua Temple was an old and famous site of Buddhist education. It was founded in 558, more than a thousand years before Nanputuo Temple, in Putian Prefecture adjacent to the Minnan region. By the eighth century it had become a center of Buddhist education and sutra printing and was patronized by emperors when Indian Buddhist monks came to teach and discuss Buddhism. In the early twentieth century, monks from Guanghua Temple established seven branch temples in Putianese-speaking Chinese communities in Malaya and Indonesia. During the Cultural Revolution, the several dozen monks at the temple were expelled, its statues smashed, and the compound turned into a factory. Its recovery from 1979 was led by Yuanzhuo 圓拙 (1909–1997) from Lianjiang County 連江縣, Fujian Province. He was tonsured in 1934, studied at the BCM and the Zhanshan Buddhist Academy, and was a disciple of Hongyi. In the 1950s, he returned to Guanghua Temple and then moved to nearby Kaiyuan Temple, where he worked printing sutras until he was forced to disrobe and become a farmer during the Cultural Revolution. In 1979, at the age of seventy, he became abbot of Guanghua Temple when it reopened.

Yuanzhuo mobilized the temple's transnational networks. A major overseas supporter was Yuanchan 圓禪, abbot of Yecheng Guanghua Temple 椰城廣化寺 in Jakarta, Indonesia. Overseas funds supported the founding of the Fujian Buddhist Academy (Fujian foxue yuan 福建佛學院) at Guanghua Temple in 1983. Yuanzhuo also achieved recognition within the Buddhist establishment, becoming president of the Buddhist Association of Fujian and vice president of the Buddhist Association of China. When we visited the temple in 1989 to attend an ordination ceremony, a hundred monks were in residence, including students of the academy. Its abbot was Yuanzhuo's disciple, Xuecheng 學誠 (1966–), who at age twenty-four was the youngest abbot in the PRC and would go on to be president of the Buddhist Association of China from 2015 to 2018.

The recoveries of Guanghua Temple and Nanputuo Temple underscored the importance of reactivating their historical capitals. Both temples relied on old-generation monks to mobilize their pre-1949 transnational networks and had Buddhist academies that provided personnel after 1979. But their characters were very different, with Guanghua Temple emphasizing traditional Buddhist teachings and its academy focused on educating Buddhist monks to be scholars. When we visited the temple in 1989, it was located in a quiet rural setting conducive to cultivation and study. In contrast, Nanputuo Temple was a center of modern Buddhist reform associated with Taixu and a school that trained monks to propagate Buddhism in the lay world. Its location in a cosmopolitan city next to a major national university also made it convenient as a tourist destination; its many daily visitors could easily access the activity of the city just outside the temple gates. Additionally, it had great popular appeal as a Guanyin temple. Worship focused on the Thousand-Handed and Thousand-Eyed Guanyin statue in the Great Compassion Hall, while its thrice-annual Guanyin festival was a major event.

Wanfu Temple recovered later. Founded in 789 during the Tang dynasty, it was located about 240 kilometers north of Xiamen in a rural area of Fuqing City 福清市. It was an authoritative temple in Chan Buddhism and the origin temple of Japan's Ōbaku sect.[43] The temple's reconstruction started in 1989, and it was consecrated in 1997. We visited in 1999, accompanied by officials from the religious affairs bureaus of Fujian Province and Fuqing City. Only ten clerics were living at the temple, which was empty and quiet. The abbot was a monk in his early thirties who had graduated from the Fujian Buddhist Academy. As we talked, an official from the Fuqing Religious Affairs Bureau listened carefully, a degree of monitoring we had not encountered elsewhere. At one point, the abbot took us aside to tell us that the officials were appropriating the donations for reconstruction provided by Japanese Buddhists for personal gain. He said that the halls had been built by construction companies owned by family members of religious affairs officials who had no experience with temples. To illustrate the shoddy construction, he thumped a pillar of the Great Buddha Hall, generating the hollow sound of a concrete pipe sheathed in marble tiles.

Wanfu Temple lacked an old-generation monk and the transnational ties that drove the earlier recoveries of Nanputuo Temple and Guanghua Temple. Although Japanese Buddhists of the Ōbaku sect supported its revival, none of the Japanese Buddhists who visited could speak Chinese. Therefore, all communication and funds for rebuilding went through officials of the Fuqing Religious Affairs Bureau. The abbot described another case of officials using the relationship with Japanese devotees as a chance for personal gain when he told us about his recent trip to Manpuku Temple (Jp. Manpuku-ji 萬福寺) in Kyoto, the main temple of the Ōbaku sect. A Japanese devotee had invited a six-person delegation from Wanfu Temple to attend a ceremony. The Fuqing Religious Affairs Bureau sent the abbot along with five officials. In Kyoto, the officials showed no interest in the ceremony but pestered the Japanese hosts to take them shopping for home appliances. Deeply embarrassed, the abbot asked us to translate and deliver a letter of apology to the Ōbaku devotee in Japan.

Juxtaposing these three temples highlights the importance of certain historical legacies. The Nanputuo and Guanghua abbots were connected to master monks of the early twentieth century and were renowned for their suffering during the Cultural Revolution. These experiences gave them the trust of overseas monks, who sent valuable resources to rebuild their temples and open Buddhist academies. As senior clerics, Miaozhan and Yuanzhuo held positions at all levels of the state's Buddhist establishment, including the Buddhist Association of China in Beijing. These ties gave the central state support for special projects, such as operating Buddhist academies, the graduates of which provided trained personnel for their temples. Through long association with their temples, the two monks understood their legacies and had clear visions for recovery, and the networks to support their efforts.

Conclusion

In 1979, the CPC reopened the institutional space of religion in the PRC by reacknowledging the existence of religion. In 1982, it issued Document

19 as a comprehensive ideological statement of how religions should exist in a socialist society. Over the next two decades, temples reopened, clerics and worshippers returned, and the state system of religious administration was restored in the new political context. Nanputuo Temple recovered rapidly due to its history as a center of the reform movement of Buddhism linked to Taixu, extensive transnational links to its location in a port city that was a special economic zone, and leadership by an old-generation cleric who was trusted by overseas Chinese.

The name tablet (*bian'e* 匾額) of Nanputuo Temple, made in 1926, hangs over the front gate of the Heavenly Kings Hall.

Front view of the central axis of Nanputuo Temple in 2017 showing the buildings in its main square. The Heavenly Kings Hall in the center is flanked by the Bell Tower (l.) and Drum Tower (r.). Behind the temple on Wulao Peak is Puzhao Temple. In front are two flags, the Buddhist flag (l.) and the national flag (r.).

Front view of Nanputuo Temple in 1999. The two tall Longevity Pagodas and seven shorter pagodas representing the Seven Past Buddhas lie between the Lotus Pond and the temple.

Nanputuo Temple in 1989, a decade after the temple reopened and the start of our research. The renovation of the entire compound had begun. The Lotus Pond was still a dry basin of grass and weeds, but the white stone fence along its edge was new. The Meditation Hall and Nanputuo Temple Charity Foundation were not yet built.

View of the Heavenly Kings Hall from the front yard in winter 1989. Most people came by bicycle, as private cars were still rare. The building on the right was built in Taixu's time, probably in the 1930s, as a sutra library and chanting hall in the modern style of the period. For a few years after 1979, Xiamen government officials on the temple's management committee lived there. It was demolished in the early 1990s.

This community center offering billiards and beer in downtown Xiamen was originally a temple confiscated during the Cultural Revolution. As of 1989, it had not been returned to Buddhists.

The East Mountain and West Mountain Gates demarcate the sacred from the world. The couplet on the East Mountain Gate was calligraphed by Zhao Puchu, the then-president of the Buddhist Association of China. Vendors were not allowed inside the gate. (photo 2017)

Murals depict stories of the lives of Gautama Buddha and other Past Buddhas. The murals at Nanputuo Temple have been renovated three times since 1979. First, simple lacquer panels were hung in the 1980s, reflecting the limited budget at that time. Second, in the 1990s, more permanent stone engravings were installed. Third, in the late 2000s, some murals were replaced by high-quality wooden ones of a more traditional architectural design. The increasing exquisiteness of the murals reflects the temple's growing wealth. For more on this mural, "Plucking a Flower to Offer to the Buddha," see page 343. (photo 2015)

The altar in the Great Buddha Hall. The three Buddha statues are Sakyamuni Buddha (c.), Medicine Buddha (r.), and Eternal Life Buddha (l.), the typical array in a Chinese Buddhist temple. In Nanputuo Temple, a Thousand-Handed and Thousand-Eyed Guanyin statue, originally in the Great Compassion Hall, is in front of Sakyamuni Buddha. This indicates the temple's devotion to Guanyin. Daily services and other rituals by the monks are performed here. (photo 2017)

The Great Compassion Hall is an octagonal building flanked by Bohdi trees and painted in magnificent colors. It is the focus of worship for people visiting the temple. (photo 2017)

Guanyin sits on a lotus flower in the Great Compassion Hall facing south toward the Great Buddha Hall. There are three other statues of Thousand-Handed and Thousand-Eyed Guanyin, each standing and facing one of the other cardinal directions. People typically worship by walking around the pavilion and bowing before each statue. (photo 1999)

The Buddha Rock at the foot of Wulao Peak. People believe it has magical power to fulfill their wishes, such as a safe voyage. The red color of the *fo* (Buddha) character was changed to gold in the early 1990s. There is always a stream of worshipers, particularly on special days like the Guanyin festival. (photo 1999)

Stones with engravings by prominent visitors throughout the temple's history abound on Wulao Peak. Some people stop to read the engravings, touch them, and throw coins for good luck. (photo 1990)

Puzhao Temple was built several centuries before Nanputuo Temple. It is a wooden structure attached to a cave on Wulao Peak and tended by a monk from Nanputuo Temple. It is a focus of local belief and worship, although tourists rarely visit. This scene from 1989 shows a group of elderly local women who came daily to sit and watch over it.

Hundreds of statues, including those of Guanyin, no longer used by people in their homes as well as newly donated ones, are collected in a cave on Wulao Peak. They are tended by a monk. (photo 2000)

PART II

Recovery and Development of Nanputuo Temple

4

Revival of Buddhist Practice and Education, 1982–1989

THE RECOVERY OF RELIGION ACCELERATED in 1982 with the CPC's issuance of Document 19. The ideological statement clarified the institutional space of religion, reducing uncertainties for local actors as to what they could do and to what extent. Religious followers could maintain their beliefs and practices as long as they supported the state's aims. This was expressed by Xi Zhongxun 習仲勳 (1913–2002), the national director of the CPC Central United Front Work Department and the lead drafter of Document 19.[1] In a 1986 speech to directors of local religious affairs bureaus, Xi said, "On the one hand ... the CPC and government thoroughly implement the freedom of religious belief policy. On the other hand, the mass believers and notable figures in the religious world maintain their religious beliefs and positively serve the establishment of the Four Modernizations, the unification of the motherland, and world peace. In this, we can completely coordinate" (quoted in Xue 2015a, 51). His words portrayed the relationship between the state and religions as mutually supportive coexistence. This remained the approach until the Tiananmen Square protest in 1989.

The period from 1982 until 1989 marked the first phase of Nanputuo Temple's recovery. It was a time of much energy in Xiamen, which was experiencing exceptionally rapid economic growth. As funds and support flowed in from overseas Chinese, the temple filled up with Buddhist teachings and clerics and worshipers, regaining its vibrancy as a popular Buddhist temple dedicated to Guanyin. In this chapter's first three sections we describe the recovery of the temple in terms of Buddhist education, clerical ordination, and monastic management. In the fourth section we explain how the temple's recovery led to a growing struggle between the clerics and local state officials. The former sought to rapidly rebuild the monastic order and temple, while the latter sought to use the temple for tourism to contribute to the economic development of the Xiamen SEZ (Special Economic Zone). In the fifth section we examine the temple during the Tiananmen Square protest, which confronted the monks with protecting Buddhism and the temple during a national political crisis.

Educating Clerics: Restarting the Buddhist College of Minnan

Restarting clerical education was key to replenishing the ranks of the monks in Nanputuo Temple. In 1982, a three-month remedial course in Chinese culture and reading skills was opened with a class of thirty-two monks. It was called the Buddhist Instruction School (Yang zheng yuan 養正院), the same name as the school created in 1934 by Hongyi. In 1983, the school started a two-year preparatory program (peixun ban 培訓班) in Buddhism. The first class enrolled fifty-eight male and female students. The BCM reopened in 1985 with a four-year undergraduate program (zhengke ban 正科班), that was considered equivalent to high school and the first two years of college. Its forty-four students consisted of twenty-nine nuns and lay nuns, and fifteen monks. The rector was Miaozhan, leader of Nanputuo Temple, and the first academic dean (jiaowu zhang 教務長) was Mengcan 夢參 (1915–2017), recruited from a teaching post at the Buddhist Academy of China.[2] The BCM had unparalleled resources due to the strong support from overseas Chinese. By 1989, these consisted of a new classroom building, library, and dormitories, salaried instructors, and scholarships for students covering their tuition, room, board, and a monthly stipend of 35 yuan.

The BCM adapted Taixu's curriculum to the needs of Buddhism after the Cultural Revolution by emphasizing both textual and ritual studies. Miaozhan expressed his thinking in his influential article, "New Ideas for Education" (Seng jiaoyu de xin gousi 僧教育的新構思), published in 1989.

Taixu was assuredly a great Buddhist educator. He left us more than forty years ago, and the motherland has since undergone earth-shaking changes. Now is a different time. The mission of history requires us to learn the master's spirit of continuous innovation. Therefore, how to develop a new way of education is a vital topic facing Buddhists. . . . Presently, Buddhist academies domestically and abroad follow the old path of the Buddhist institute established in the first four decades of the century that take their sole task as cultivating clerics proficient in the Buddhist canon. The knowledge of student clerics educated in this way is very narrow. Apart from knowing some famous names and scriptural ideas, they have absolutely no other specializations. As a result, their learning is not applied after graduation, leaving their futures problematic. . . . They cannot become the backbone of Buddhism and the pillars of the clerical community. . . . Therefore, Buddhist academies must transition from only teaching pedagogical knowledge to teach multilevel and multidisciplinary knowledge that meets the actual needs of Buddhism in China. (Miaozhan 1989a)

Miaozhan's point was that when Taixu developed his ideas in the early twentieth century, clerics already knew Buddhist chanting, meditation, and rituals but lacked theoretical and textual knowledge of Buddhist teaching. Following the Cultural Revolution, however, Chinese clerics lacked knowledge of both practice and theory. Therefore, it was now necessary to simultaneously emphasize the study of practice and texts. For textual study, Miaozhan revived Taixu's mixed curriculum of Buddhist canon and secular courses. But whereas Taixu had excused students from the ritual life of the temple to focus on textual study, Miaozhan required their attendance at morning and evening services, participation in rituals, and practice of meditation.

Miaozhan made other innovations at the BCM. One was the admission of nuns, reflecting his desire to replenish the clergy and give Minnan lay nuns the opportunity for education (Ashiwa and Wank 2019). When the BCM opened in 1985, the shortage of facilities meant that nuns and lay nuns had to study alongside monks in the same classrooms. This comingling was undesirable from the viewpoint of Buddhist teachings. Additionally, it was a hardship for the nuns who had to live scattered among three local temples and commute to classes held in Nanputuo Temple. In 1989, the BCM started holding separate classes for the nuns at Wanshilian Temple 萬石蓮寺 where the largest number of nuns lived. The BCM also started English courses, the first Buddhist academy to do so. The teaching of English reflected Taixu's idea to train clerics to spread Buddhism in the West among non-Buddhists as it did Miaozhan's openminded desire to replenish the clerical ranks both in China and abroad. Miaozhan encouraged BCM graduates to serve in overseas temples. The following account of the school is based on our fieldwork in 1989 and 1990.

Organization

At BCM the dean was responsible for overseeing admissions, curriculum, and faculty hiring. In 1989 a thirty-five-year-old monk was appointed to succeed Mengcan.[3] (The nearly four-decade difference in their ages reflected the gap in generational continuity among the clerics at that time; with no cohort of middle-aged clerics to serve, young monks in their twenties and early thirties filled management offices.) The new BCM dean was born in 1953 in Leqing City, Zhejiang Province 浙江溫州樂清市, to a Daoist family. His interest in Buddhism was piqued by reading books. He came to Nanputuo in 1981, among the first young clerics to do so. In 1982, he studied in the temple's newly revived remedial course of the Buddhist Instruction School. The following year he was ordained at Fuzhou's Yongquan Temple and entered the preparatory program of the BCM. Upon graduating in 1985, he enrolled in the first undergraduate class. He assumed administrative responsibilities in the BCM while still a student and was appointed dean upon graduating. The two vice deans were nuns who had graduated in the first BCM class. One oversaw the curriculum, student class monitors, and political thought, while the other managed book purchases and class attendance. Because of the personnel shortage, monks and nuns worked in the same office, with devotees handling the secretarial work. BCM's several dozen instructors at that time included clerics and laypersons.

The dean's primary concern was finding qualified instructors for the Buddhism courses; those teaching the undergraduate program were elderly monks and well-educated devotees from Xiamen and Shanghai.

Some devotees were monks who had disrobed during the Cultural Revolution. They taught at BCM in the 1980s to make up for the lack of qualified instructors who deeply understood Buddhist teachings. Some young instructors were 1985 graduates of the preparatory program who taught introductory courses in the three-month remedial program. In 1989, one-third of the forty-four graduates of the first undergraduate class were retained as instructors in the remedial and preparatory programs. Additionally, monks from other Buddhist academies and temples taught on a short-term basis; they mostly came from the Buddhist Academy of China, Fujian Buddhist Academy, Mount Putuo Temple, and Lingyanshan Temple.

Secular courses were taught by laypersons; they were teachers from Xiamen University and local schools of Chinese philosophy and history, and foreign languages. During the summer, professors from around China came to teach the classical philosophies of Confucius, Laozi, and Zhuangzi. They sought to teach at the BCM because the students were enthusiastic, and the pay supplemented the meager university salaries for humanities instructors. Instructors of secular courses were not required to be Buddhists but had to be favorably disposed toward Buddhism. We heard of a philosophy professor who was not hired because he had used Marxist-Leninist analysis to criticize Buddhism in his writings.

The teaching load was six hours per week. Instructors divided their time equally between teaching monks at Nanputuo Temple and nuns at Wanshilian Temple. Some instructors who were concurrently studying in the BCM had a reduced teaching load, allowing them to keep up with their studies. Depending on age and seniority, instructors were paid 140 to 180 yuan per month. Some positions were more highly paid, such as the BCM dean's 200-yuan salary and the 260-yuan salary for a prominent devotee from Shanghai. Bonuses were paid on Spring Festival and other holidays. The daily schedule for the BCM was the same as that of Nanputuo Temple (see table 4.1). Students awoke at 4:30 to join the temple's resident monks for the morning service and breakfast in the dining hall. During the day, they attended classes while resident monks worked at their jobs. In the evening when the monks in the temple practiced self-cultivation, BCM students attended a mandatory study hall in their homerooms. The summer curriculum was reduced to two hours of classes on Monday, Wednesday, and Friday mornings. Each class had two student monitors to keep

TABLE 4.1 BCM Daily Schedule

Time	Activity
4:30 a.m.	Wake up
5:00–5:55	Morning service
6:00–7:00	Breakfast and cleanup
7:00–8:00	Study or rest
8:00–10:50	Three 45-minute classes
11:00–11:30	Lunch
11:30–2:00 p.m.	Free time and rest
2:00–3:50	Two 45-minute classes
4:00–5:00	Evening service
5:00–5:30	Dinner
5:30–7:00	Free time
7:00–8:30	Study in mandatory study hall
8:30–9:30	Free time
9:30/	Lights out

attendance and clean the classroom. Students only left the school for family emergencies at home.

There were rules for daily life to help the young student monks observe the precepts. These included prohibitions on watching television and movies, reading novels, and eating in restaurants. Teachers randomly inspected movie theaters in Xiamen for students. We heard that some students evaded restrictions by eating in the private dining rooms of restaurants, and by watching television on display models in appliance stores. Teachers said it could be challenging to keep discipline in such a wealthy and cosmopolitan city as Xiamen. Most of the students were from rural areas and poorer northern cities and were curious about the urban life outside the gates of Nanputuo Temple.

Curriculum

The curriculum included Tripitaka scriptures, Buddhist-related topics, and secular subjects (see appendix 3).[4] Constituting about half the curriculum, the study of the Tripitaka focused on important scriptures in Buddhist Pure Land (Jingtu 淨土), Chan 禪, and Tiantai 天台 schools. They emphasized the middle way (*zhongguan* 中觀) and consciousness-only (*weishi* 唯識) views on the importance of the mind in shaping human experience, reflecting Taixu's philosophical approach toward Buddhism. The Buddhist-related courses were mostly taught in the preparatory program. They included introductory lectures about Buddhism (*foxue jiangyi* 佛學講義). Students read Taixu's *History of Scientific Thought* (*Kexue sixiang shi* 科學思想史) and Yinshun's *The Way to Buddhahood* (*Cheng fo zhi dao* 成佛之道), studied the biographies of eminent monks, and learned about rituals.

The secular subjects offered at BCM included humanities courses about China, such as religious history, Chinese history, philosophy and literature, and classical Chinese, as well as foreign languages. The inclusion of foreign languages expressed the aspirations of Taixu and Miaozhan to propagate Buddhism abroad. Additional courses were calligraphy, physical education, and political study. XRAB officials taught political study courses (*zhengzhi xuexi* 政治學習) covering Marxist-Leninist-Maoist ideology and religious policy. Even though monks were allowed to teach such courses, none did. Some political study instructors made the ideology courses relevant to Buddhism by lecturing on Marx's distinction between idealism and materialism and teaching modern Chinese history alongside communist theories of religion. Students studied religious policy by reading *Fujian Religion* (*Fujian zongjiao* 福建宗教) and *Chinese Buddhism* (*Zhongguo zongjiao* 中國宗教), journals published, respectively, by the Fujian Buddhist Association and the Buddhist Association of China containing news of Buddhist activities and policy-related matters. Pressing political events were also discussed in class, which greatly interested the students.

Admissions

Applicants to the BCM had to be eighteen to thirty years old, have taken their novice precepts, and graduated from junior high school. On the application form, they wrote their names, birthday, place of origin and family background, and information related to Buddhism, including the year and place of receiving the precepts and the names of two clerics as references. They submitted the form to their local Buddhist association, which could reject the application or pass it on to the BCM with a letter of endorsement. All applicants came to Nanputuo Temple for an interview with Miaozhan, as standard written entrance exams were not introduced until the late 1990s. Miaozhan assessed their motives for study and capacity for abstract thought, as seen in their eloquence. Practically all applicants were admitted, so the purpose of the evaluation was to determine their placement in either the three-month remedial program, the two-year preparatory program, or the four-year undergraduate program. Those from rural areas with little education entered the remedial program, where they studied language, history, and physical education. After three months, they could advance to the preparatory program and then to the undergraduate program.

The lack of fixed admissions criteria created disparities in academic performance. The largest occurred in the preparatory program, which included many academically weak students. Most of these students were recommended by elderly overseas Chinese monks who had returned to their ancestral villages in China to find successors to their temples in Southeast Asia and had little time to evaluate the motives, character, and intelligence of the young men who approached them with an interest in going overseas. After selecting and tonsuring their successors, the elderly clerics wrote to Miaozhan requesting the novices be admitted to the BCM. Miaozhan placed them in the preparatory program, but many begged to be allowed to skip the remedial program and directly enter the preparatory program, even prostrating at Miaozhan's feet. He typically acceded out of kindness and concern for quickly replenishing the ranks of the clergy. Unsurprisingly, the preparatory program had a high dropout rate of 20 percent. The first to leave were those who had become monks to escape rural life. They disrobed to take regular jobs in Xiamen. Next to go were those who could not cope with the rigors of study. They were sent to the remedial program, but some still foundered. Those with a strong will to be a monk became resident clerics at Nanputuo Temple and local temples, where they chanted and did other work.

The undergraduate program included graduates of the preparatory program, and its dropout rate was lower. The first undergraduate class, which entered in 1985, had forty-four students (see table 4.2). Two-thirds were nuns (66 percent, n=29) who tended to be academically stronger. More than half of the nuns (55 percent, n=16) were high school graduates compared to 13 percent (n=2) of the monks. Furthermore, nuns were

TABLE 4.2 Characteristics of 1985 Matriculating Class

Variable	Nuns	Monks	Total
Number	29 (66%)	15 (33%)	44
High school graduate	16 (55%)	2 (13%)	18
Urban background	18 (62%)	5 (33%)	23
Fujian origin	10 (34%)	7 (47%)	17
Age (mean/median)	23.7/23	21.8/21	

Source: Unpublished document (Buddhist College of Minnan 1989)

twice as likely to come from urban areas and wealthier rural areas with better schools. Among the seventeen students from Fujian, ten nuns came from the wealthier coast, while the seven monks were mainly from the poorer western regions. Only three students were from Minnan, including a monk from a wealthy business family and two lay nuns from Xiamen. This low representation from the wealthy Minnan region fit the contemporary view that those who became clerics were poor people seeking to secure their room and board and a chance to earn money by doing rituals.

Graduation

The BAX assigned jobs to graduates of the undergraduate program, paralleling the state job assignment practice for high school and university graduates. In principle, graduates were assigned to positions in the jurisdiction of the local Buddhist associations that had endorsed their admission to the BCM. This practice was rarely observed, however, because of the great demand for graduates to staff temples in Xiamen. Most graduates of the first few classes were assigned positions in Nanputuo Temple, the BAX, the BCM, or local temples in Xiamen. The job assignments of the 1989 graduates are seen in table 4.3. The two left-hand columns are the job assignments and the BAX assessment of their abilities. The two right-hand columns are the numbers of nuns and monks assigned to each job. A third of the 1989 graduates were assigned to the BCM, with fourteen as instructors in the preparatory program and one as an administrator. Most were nuns because of the urgent need for female instructors to teach the more numerous female students. Nineteen clerics received unspecified

TABLE 4.3 Job Assignments of 1989 Graduates of BCM Undergraduate Program

Job	Evaluation criteria	Nuns	Monks
Teacher at BCM	Excellent character and studies 品學兼優 Diligent and eager 勤奮好學 Good grasp of theory 有一定理論水平 Eloquent fluency 口語流利 Not very eloquent 口才較差 Capable 有一定工作能力	11	3
Academic monitor at BCM	Capable 有一定工作能力		1
Nanputuo Temple (unspecified job)		8	
Wanshilian Temple (unspecified job)		4	
Hongshan Temple (unspecified job)			7
BAX general affairs		1	
Assignment pending		1	2
Borderline cases	To be retained by temple or returned to place of origin 可留寺廟或回原籍	3	
Return to home area	Average 一般 Poor health 身體較差	3	

Source: Unpublished document (Buddhist College of Minnan 1989)

job assignments in temples, including Nanputuo Temple, Hongshan Temple 鴻山寺, and Wanshilian Temple. One lay nun was assigned to the BAX as a researcher for the *Gazetteer of Nanputuo Temple*. The remaining nine graduates included those whose assignments in Xiamen were pending, those awaiting a decision on whether they would be assigned in Xiamen or returned to their home regions, and those being returned to their places of origin due to poor health or abilities.

Ordaining Clerics

Twenty graduates from the 1989 graduating class of the BCM were among 552 novices ordained (*shoujie* 受戒) at a ceremony (*chuanjie fahui* 傳戒法會) organized by the Buddhist Association of Fujian. Novice monks took *bhikṣu* (Skt., Ch. *biqiu* 比丘) precepts at Guanghua Temple in Putian in October 1989, while novice nuns took the *bhikṣuṇī* (Skt., Ch. *biqiuni* 比丘尼) precepts at Chongfu Temple 崇福寺 in Quanzhou in January 1990. The novices had all applied to participate through their local Buddhist association, which certified that they were over twenty years old and had no handicaps that could hinder participation in the ceremony. Applications had to be approved by local and provincial religious affairs bureaus and finally by the Buddhist Association of China. Many ordinands were middle-aged and elderly former clerics who had laicized during the 1950s and 1960s. The ordination at Guanghua Temple was the first permitting elderly ordinands and could be seen as compensation for their suffering; the expenses of the poor ordinands to attend the ceremony were paid by overseas Chinese Buddhists. This purpose of the ordination helped account for the great number of ordinands; it was the largest since ordinations restarted after the Cultural Revolution.

The scale of the ordination at Guanghua Temple signified the growing recovery of Buddhism. At the first ceremony, held in 1980 at Guangji Temple in Beijing, thirty-nine ordinands who were nuns and monks in their twenties studying at the Buddhist Academy of China were ordained; the ordination master (*dejie heshang* 得戒和尚) was Zhengguo 正果 (1913–1987), a disciple of Taixu and the Guangji abbot. The much larger Guanghua ordination was the first to stage separate ceremonies for nuns and monks, indicating stricter adherence to Buddhist teachings. Additionally, the ordination lasted fifteen days, significantly longer than the three-day ceremony at Guangji Temple (Wen 2012). A longer ordination period enabled more thorough teaching of the precepts and rules for the proper behavior of a cleric before the actual ordination ceremony on the final day (see appendix 4 for the ordination schedule at Guanghua Temple). The increasing length of ordination periods over the decade reflected the Buddhist Association of China's growing confidence in the political situation for religion in the PRC.

Ceremony

The ordination at Guanghua Temple was presided over by three masters (*san shi* 三師): Miaozhan had been invited to be the ordination master; and the catechist (*jiaoshou shi* 教授師) and confessor (*jiemo shi* 羯磨師) were both senior monks from Guanghua Temple. Other monks served as the seven honored witnesses (*qizun* 七尊) and instructors (*yinli shi* 引禮師). Together, they ran the daily morning and afternoon sessions to teach ordinands the essential liturgies, the meaning of precepts, the proper way for a cleric to eat and dress, and answers to the questions on the final day of the ordination ceremony. Each day followed the same schedule. Ordinands arose at 3:30 and attended morning service in the Great Buddha Hall from 4:10 to 5:40. From 6:00 to 6:40, they ate breakfast followed by an hour's rest. From 8:00 to 10:30, they attended the morning session, followed by lunch from 10:40 to 11:20, and an hour of rest. From 2:00 p.m. to 3:30 p.m. they attended the afternoon session and evening services from 4:00 to 5:30. This was followed by thirty minutes for dinner and then study until lights out at 9:00 p.m.

The ordination instructor was Dingmiao 定妙, the ritual specialist at Guanghua Temple. He was born in 1912 in Xianyou County 仙游縣, Fujian. He had been a sickly child, so his mother sent him to live in a temple, vowing that he would become a monk if his health improved. At age thirteen, he renounced lay life, was ordained at Guishan Temple 龜山寺 in Putian, and learned rituals at Tiantong Temple. In 1948, he went to Guanghua Temple to serve concurrently as the precentor in charge of daily rituals, and the proctor (*jiucha* 糾察) who enforced disciplinary rules in the temple and its daily schedule. During the Cultural Revolution, he retreated to a local temple in his hometown and then, in 1979, returned to Guanghua Temple. As one of the few remaining monks who knew the elaborate, local Buddhist rituals in Minnan, he often visited other temples to perform them and teach young clerics. He had served as an instructor at ordination ceremonies in 1942 and 1945 at Tiantong Temple but told us that he had forgotten many of its rituals. He said, "When you begin, you will make some mistakes. So, you say you will not do it again. Or you start something and remember as you go."[5]

Ordinands

The 552 ordinands at the 1989 ceremony came from all over China, with 79 percent (n=434) from Fujian (see table 4.4). They were mostly under the age of thirty or over sixty (see table 4.5). The younger ordinands were students or graduates of Buddhist academies. Many older ordinands who had renounced lay life in the period between the 1920s and 1950s were forced to laicize during the Cultural Revolution, and then renounced lay life again after 1979. Some older ordinands had left their families in the

TABLE 4.4 Distribution of Ordinands by Region

Areas	Administrative Unit	Male	Female	Total
South	Fujian (434), Guangdong, Guangxi	218	227	445
Northeast	Heilongjiang, Jilin, Liaoning	6	33	39
North	Hebei, Inner Mongolia, Shandong	4	1	5
Central	Henan, Hubei, Hunan, Jiangxi	6	16	22
East	Jiangsu, Anhui, Zhejiang, Shanghai	8	19	27
Northwest	Shanxi, Gansu	1	7	8
Southwest	Sichuan	4	2	6
Total		247	305	552

Source: Unpublished document (Fujian Buddhist Association 1989)

TABLE 4.5 Ages of Ordinands

Age	Men	Women	Total
Over 80	1	0	1
70–79	11	16	27
60–69	75	81	156
50–59	48	49	97
40–49	23	29	52
30–39	32	31	63
20–29	54	96	150
Under 20	1	1	2
No answer	2	2	4
Total	247	305	552

Source: Unpublished document (Fujian Buddhist Association 1989)

1950s and 1960s but were not ordained because ordination ceremonies had ceased. A few were former government employees furloughed during the 1980s when their enterprises and bureaus downsized and were now leaving their families.

Gender disparities could be seen among the ordinands. Women were ordained in larger numbers than men: 55 percent versus 45 percent. Additionally, the national distribution of women was greater than for men, with 26 percent from outside the southern area as compared with 13 percent of the men. Finally, women were over-represented among the least-educated and most-educated ordinands. There were three times as many illiterate women as men (see table 4.6), but university-educated women outnumbered men three to two. The former were mostly elderly lay nuns, while the latter were young nuns who recently graduated from the BCM and Fujian Buddhist Academy. There were also gender differences in occupational status (see table 4.7): of the 552 ordinands, 279

TABLE 4.6 Distribution of Education of Ordinands

Level and years of school	Male	Female	Total
No schooling	26	76	102
Some primary school (1–5 years)	76	71	147
Primary school graduate (6 years)	56	48	104
Some junior middle school (7–8 years)	1	6	7
Junior middle school graduate (9 years)	47	39	86
Some senior high school (10–11 years)	6	7	13
Senior high school graduate (12 years)	15	14	29
Some university (13–15 years)	4	10	14
University graduate (16 years)	5	5	10
No answer	11	29	40
Total	247	305	552

Source: Unpublished document (Fujian Buddhist Association 1989)

TABLE 4.7 Distribution of Prior Occupation of Ordinands

Occupation	Male	Female	Total
Farmer	172	117	289
Homemaker	4	88	92
Student	22	49	71
Cadre	7	4	11
Worker in state enterprise	7	9	16
Worker in local government enterprise	8	5	13
Worker in service sector	10	11	21
Artisan	12	11	23
Teacher	1	4	5
Small businessperson	2	1	3
No answer	2	6	8
Total	247	305	552

Source: Unpublished document (Fujian Buddhist Association 1989)

were farmers (172 of whom were men). The second most common occupation was homemaker. These were mostly women, including many elderly lay nuns forced to marry during the Cultural Revolution. The third-largest occupation was student, mostly young novices from the BCM and Fujian Buddhist Academy.

The presiding ordination monks discussed some challenging aspects of the ceremony with us. One was that elderly female ordinands had difficulty participating because they lacked sufficient Mandarin ability to follow the ceremony. During the final stage of the ceremony, for instance, when the presiding monks questioned the ordinands, someone had to sit beside them to whisper the correct answers in their ears. Another challenging aspect of ordination was the politically sensitive practice of scarring the scalp with burning incense, a practice meant to show commitment to maintaining the precepts. At the first ordination ceremony in 1980, regulations did not forbid scarring of the scalp, although none of the forty ordinands in 1980 did so. But we were told that some burned their inner arms where the scars were less visible; such concealment may have reflected the political sensitivity of religion at that time.[6]

The large ordination ceremony at Guanghua Temple, which included many BCM graduates, was crucial for replenishing the clergy. The participation of so many elderly ordinands was compensation for their suffering at the hands of the state during the Cultural Revolution. Most were uneducated, and more than a few had forgotten how to wear robes and chant. The young faces of the BCM graduates stood out as signs of a new generation moving into leadership. They showed the youthful, energetic, and increasingly confident face of Buddhism in the PRC.

Establishing Temple Bureaucracy

The bureaucracy established at Nanputuo under Miaozhan combined the traditional offices of a large Buddhist temple with new ones reflecting contemporary concerns: it maintained the old spirit in the *Pure Rules of Baizhang* (*Baizhang qinggui* 百丈清規), the traditional rules for administration and daily life in a Chan Buddhist temple; and it addressed the need for an expanded temple bureaucracy to accommodate the activities of the rapidly recovering temple in a special economic zone. Monks at the temple described this bureaucracy as modern because of its innovations.

Altogether, there were seven departments. Four were traditional, including the management department (*kufang* 庫房) that handled the temple's economic matters and physical maintenance; the guest department (*ketang* 客堂) in charge of all comings and goings of visitors to the temple; the sacristy (*yibo* 衣缽), which functioned as the abbot's secretary; and the precentor (*weinuo* 維那) who managed the temple's routine rituals. The other three, reflecting contemporary needs and growth, included the ritual department (*fawu* 法務) to handle Buddhist rituals demanded by laypersons; the academic affairs department (*jiaowu* 教務) to run the BCM; and the enterprise department (*qiye* 企業) to manage the vegetarian restaurants and other commercial operations for tourists.

There were other innovations as well. One reduced the hierarchy of the offices, reflecting Miaozhan's view that all aspects of temple management were equally crucial at Nanputuo. To supervise the monastery's daily operation, he created a committee called the deacons meeting (*zhishi hui* 執事會) comprising the heads of the management, precentor, guest prefect, sacristy, ritual, education, and enterprise departments. It met at least once a month to discuss large cash expenditures, disciplinary problems, and long-range planning, and to give counsel to the abbot. Another innovation, reflecting the scarcity of administrative personnel in the 1980s, extended the traditional term of office from six months to one year, and clerics served multiple terms.[7] The temple administration was soon nourished by the talented young clerics who came to study at the BCM, as 1985 graduates of the two-year preparatory program were assigned to offices at Nanputuo Temple.

In the descriptions of the five departments that follow we draw on interviews with the monks who headed departments in 1989 and 1990 to explain their functions and organization at the time. Brief biographies of the monks illuminate the career paths of the first post–Cultural Revolution generation of monks and the personal characteristics considered desirable for those holding specific offices.

Management Department

The head of the management department was the prior (*jianyuan* 監院). He was in charge of the temple when the abbot was away or ill. His responsibilities included the financial accounts, buildings and grounds, and the kitchen. He could authorize small expenditures, although larger ones needed the approval of the deacon's meeting and the abbot. He was supported by three subpriors (*fusi* 副寺), each with their staff. A cashier authorized cash disbursements and supervised the lay accountants who recorded income from on-demand rituals, donations, and fees for storing ancestor ashes. A purchaser kept the temple stocked with daily supplies. A supervisor oversaw the cafeteria staff of fifteen laypersons—including a head cook, three assistant cooks, three rice cooks, a water boiler, and seven at-large assistants—plus five monks who served food. The management department included the provost (*dujian* 都監), who, according to Buddhist tradition, was a senior monk advising the abbot.

Several tasks were not traditionally part of the management department but reflected the needs of restoring the temple. One was supervising the Nanputuo Temple Construction Unit, established in 1982 to restore the halls. The unit had over a hundred artisans from rural villages with traditional specializations in temple-related arts and crafts. Carpenters and painters came from Xianyou County, and masons from Hui'an County. Both counties were near Xiamen, and the artisans came and went as needed for specific jobs. They took work back to their home villages, where they mobilized other artisans to help complete it, and then brought the finished products to the temple for installation. Another task was supervising the maintenance staff. Although the guest department had traditionally been in charge of maintenance, it was too busy handling the many visitors to the temple and applicants to the BCM. The management department thus supervised the temple's seventy electricians, janitors, gardeners, and watchmen.

The prior was from Wenzhou City, Zhejiang Province 浙江省溫州市. He had been a novice at Tiantong Temple 天童寺 in Ningbo, Zhejiang Province 浙江省寧波市, and was ordained in 1980. In 1983, he enrolled in the preparatory program of the Buddhist Instruction School. When he became prior in 1989, he was thirty years old. His youth emphasized the absence of a whole generation of middle-aged monks who would have typically occupied the high-ranking office of prior at a large temple. He was considered pious, modest, and honest, essential qualities for the cleric entrusted with the temple's money and property. He also taught in the BCM, underscoring the shortage of instructors. He subsequently held other offices including BAX secretary, director of the Nanputuo Temple

Charity Foundation, vice rector of the BCM, and Nanputuo Temple provost. (In 2004, he became the abbot of Tiantong Temple.)

Guest Department

The guest department was the filter between the temple and the outside world, responsible for all those in Nanputuo Temple. It was headed by the senior guest prefect (*da zhike* 大知客), assisted by a staff of ten monks.[8] Its office was easily accessible in the annex along the east side of the main compound. Its most important task was interviewing monks seeking to stay at the temple. A monk could request a short-term or long-term stay. No one was denied a request for short-term stay, which was limited to three nights and meant for wandering monks and those traveling to other temples. Monks seeking long-term stay desired to cultivate themselves at the temple. They could be refused if the temple was full or if their appearance, behavior, or answers to questions during the interview aroused the senior guest prefect's suspicion. At the same time, the conversation gave the visitor an impression of the temple as conveyed through the dignity of the head guest prefect.

Those seeking long-term stay who passed the interview filled out duplicate forms on their backgrounds, one for the temple and one for the XRAB. They went to a local hospital to check for infectious illnesses and hermaphrodism. Upon passing the health check, they agreed to abide by the *Nanputuo Temple Regulations for Permanent Residence* (*Nanputuo si changzhu guiyue* 南普陀寺常住規約), which regulated the temple's daily life.[9] They were given a temporary job based on their previous experience, education, and skills. After two months, they were assigned fixed jobs, which could consist of kitchen work, cleaning incense urns, Buddhist book sales, gathering alms, selling prayer beads, guarding artifacts in the sutra library, doing rituals, supervising buildings, or sanitation work. Monks received stipends ranging from 50 yuan for a tea pourer in the guest office to 140 yuan for the prior.

The guest department handled the burdensome administration of the state's residency permit (*hukou* 戶口) system. In the 1980s, visitors to a city were required to get a temporary permit at the nearby public security (police) station. The permit let them stay for six months. A longer stay required sponsorship by a local organization, such as a temple, to obtain a permanent residence permit. The guest department was busy handling the paperwork because monks constantly came and went. For example, in 1989, an average of 18 of the 170 monks in residence came or left each month. Additionally, the number of permanent residence permits was insufficient; the local state administration had allocated sixty permits in 1986, but only nine had been issued by 1989. The guest prefect had to reapply every six months to renew the temporary permits. He did acknowledge, however, that his good ties with the public security station reduced the burdensome paperwork; sometimes he only had to give oral reports to the police officers when they visited the temple. Significantly, the police did not require reporting of monks staying for a short term, which enabled the clerical practice of wandering.

The guest department was responsible for lay visitors to the temple, including overseas and domestic devotees and donors, tourists and tour groups, and families and relatives of monks in long-term residence. Special guests, such as donors and families of monks, could stay at the guesthouses, which were clean and cheaper than commercial hotels that were not well developed in the 1980s. Daily rates for room and board were 4 yuan for dormitory accommodations and 8 yuan for a private room. Families of monks could stay three nights for free, while charges for devotees were often waived. Tourists could visit the public places of the temple when they were open and eat in the vegetarian restaurants but could not stay overnight.

The guest department also worked to ensure that lay visitors did not violate the state religious policy while they were at the temple.[10] The guest prefect told us about a group of French Buddhists that included Taiwanese members. As soon as they entered the temple, the Taiwanese began handing out pamphlets titled "Immediate Enlightenment" (Ji ke kaiwu 即刻開悟). A Nanputuo monk saw the pamphlet was not Buddhist and reported this to the senior guest prefect who rushed to stop their distribution.[11] The guest prefect said that if he had not acted quickly, the local state could have investigated Nanputuo Temple for infiltration by Taiwan spies and abnormal religious practices. Another concern of the guest prefect was to prevent clerics from discussing politics with visiting laypersons. Such talk was not only unbefitting for a cleric, but could cause trouble if a monk's critical comments about the religious policy reached the ears of the authorities.

The guest department was the window for laypersons seeking services. When a ritual service was requested, the guest department notified the management department, which issued a notice of the type of ritual, date, and number of monks necessary for its performance. Another service was the storage of family ancestor ashes in the Merit Hall, which began in 1985. Demand was high because many ancestor halls in Minnan had been destroyed during the Cultural Revolution. Red Guards had dumped the ashes of family ancestors stored in Nanputuo's Merit Hall but did not touch those of deceased monks. Therefore, Xiamen residents saw Nanputuo Temple as a haven for ash storage and willingly paid the fee. Several monks chanted daily at the hall to send merit to the souls, with a larger assemblage chanting monthly.

The senior guest prefect was a twenty-nine-year-old monk from Xianyou County 仙游縣, Putian, born into a family that had been temple artisans for many generations. His five younger brothers all specialized in creating temple paintings that illustrated Buddhist stories and popular beliefs. When he was a child, a fortuneteller and a spirit medium predicted that he would become a Buddhist monk. At the time, he was training in Daoist meditation and had advanced far enough to see a bright light with his eyes shut. In 1981, while supervising repair work at Guanghua Temple, a Buddhist monk gave him some sutras. He read them and decided to study further. He took his novice vows at Nanputuo Temple, matriculated in 1983 in the preparatory program, and entered the BCM undergraduate program in 1985. Considering him to be a shrewd judge of people, Miaozhan appointed him class monitor and then guest prefect.

Sacristy

The sacristy department served as the abbot's secretary and assistant. It was run by the sacristan, who supervised housekeeping in the abbot's residence, scheduled his appointments, and drafted his correspondence.[12] Miaozhan received over a dozen letters a day from clerics, overseas Chinese, and state officials asking about the development of Buddhism at Nanputuo Temple and in China. He discussed each answer with the sacristan and dictated responses. Many letters appealed for funds for projects by Buddhists in poorer inland and northern regions of China. Miaozhan solicited the sacristan's advice on the use of temple income, the temple's development plans, and other matters. The most challenging part of the sacristan's job was maintaining the abbot's schedule because there were many last-minute tasks and meetings.

The sacristan's day was long. He rose at 4:30 every morning and ate breakfast at 6:00 in the dining hall with the other clerics. His office was in the Acolyte Building next door to the Abbot's Residence. He spent the day writing the abbot's letters, accompanying him to meetings, visiting other temples in Xiamen, and entertaining the abbot's many visitors. After dinner, he read and recited the *Lotus Sutra* until midnight. He selected four monks to assist him: two attended to the abbot's daily needs, such as cleaning his clothes, preparing snacks, and caring for him when sick; the other two monks accompanied the abbot in his ritual activities, such as carrying his ritual items and spreading his prayer cloth. The latter two monks were BCM students chosen by the sacristan for their interest in rituals and their physical attractiveness.

The sacristan was born in 1967 to a Buddhist family of traditional medicine doctors in a village in Chaozhou City, Guangdong Province 廣東省潮州市. His grandfather was a traditional Chinese medicine practitioner, his father a surgeon, and his mother a pediatrician. His grandfather, a pious Buddhist and a strict vegetarian, influenced his decision to leave his family, but his parents disapproved because he was the eldest of three sons. So he left home to become a novice, and eventually his parents approved. In 1984, he began studying in the BCM and was ordained the following year at Nanhua Temple 南華寺, Guangzhou. In 1985, he enrolled in the first undergraduate class of the BCM. An excellent student, he was appointed Nanputuo sacristan and a BCM instructor. When we met him in 1989, he was planning to emigrate to the United States to serve in the Young Men's Buddhist Association (Fojiao qingnian hui 佛教青年會) in New York City. But the rupture in diplomatic relations between China and the United States following the Tiananmen Square protest delayed his departure until 1992. (His story continues in chapter 5.)

Precentor and Ritual Department

All Buddhist rituals at Nanputuo Temple were managed by the precentor and ritual department. There were three kinds of rituals. One concerned the daily services performed by monks to praise the Buddha as part of the temple routine, which the precentor supervised. The second and third kinds involved calendrical rituals performed at fixed times and on-demand rituals commissioned by laypersons. They were the purview of the ritual department, created by Miaozhan in anticipation of the rising demand for commissioned rituals in the wealthy special economic zone.

The precentor was in charge of the morning and evening services (*zao wan gongke* 早晚功課) in the Great Buddha Hall presided over by the abbot and attended by all monks at the temple.[13] Supported by six assistants, he led the sutra chanting and offerings at the altar. The precentor also kept discipline in the meditation hall. There were many rules, and monks often made mistakes. But the state had banned the traditional practice of hitting a monk with the gong stick as punishment, so the precentor asked monks to self-report at a repentance meeting on the first and twenty-fifth of each month. A repenting monk bowed three times before the other monks and said, "Today, I repent to everyone" for failing to observe a rule. Yet the precentor noted that a repentance meeting was only for minor infractions; breaking a precept entailed greater disciplinary measures. He also said that the morning and evening services had been reduced from ninety minutes to sixty to give BCM students more time for study. He considered this lax because the Fujian Buddhist Academy at Guanghua Temple had not shortened the services for students.

The precentor was from Wenzhou City, Pinyang County 溫州市平陽縣. In 1981, he took his novice vows at Tiantong Temple, where he became engrossed in chanting. He taped the monks as they chanted and listened repeatedly to learn from them. That year he was ordained at Mount Wutai 五台山 in Shanxi Province 山西省 at the second ordination ceremony after the Cultural Revolution. In 1982, he enrolled in the three-month remedial class of Nanputuo's Buddhist Instruction School and then in the preparatory program. Upon graduating in 1985, he served as senior guest prefect and taught a class called "Basic Buddhist Knowledge" in the remedial class. In 1989, he was appointed precentor because of his excellent chanting in the Minnan dialect, although he was not from the region. He subsequently was appointed prior of Puguang Temple 普光寺 in Xiamen (see chapter 7).

The ritual department consisted only of the ritualist, who planned the ritual life of the temple in consultation with the abbot.[14] Calendric rituals were performed at fixed times, while on-demand rituals took place when

REVIVAL OF BUDDHIST PRACTICE, 1982-1989

commissioned. Rituals required several to dozens of monks, so the ritual specialist could ask any monk in the temple to participate. Each morning, he posted a notice of the rituals and their participants at the dining hall entrance so that all monks could see it on their way to breakfast.

Calendric rituals had multiple purposes, frequencies, and participants (see table 4.8).[15] The largest was the Guanyin festival, Nanputuo's signature event, held three times a year. Open to all, it was enormously popular, attracting tens of thousands of people. The most frequently performed service, usually called "first and fifteenth" (*chuyi shiwu* 初一十五), was held twice a month on the new moon and full moon days to show devotion to Buddhism. It combined the rituals of the auspicious mantra for eradicating misfortune (*xiaozai jixiang zhou* 消災吉祥咒) and the All

TABLE 4.8 Calendric Rituals at Nanputuo Temple in 1989 (per Lunar Calendar)

Month/Day (lunar)	Name	Description	Participants
1/1–15	初一十五 ch yi shiwu	Chanting for good fortune of the temple	Clerics and devotees
1/15	請職 qing zhi	Appointing temple administration personnel	Clerics only
1/15–25	拜萬佛 bai wan fo	Repenting before ten thousand buddhas	Clerics and devotees
2/16	拜千佛 bai qian fo	Chanting names of all buddhas and bodhisattvas	Clerics and devotees
2/19	觀音節 guanyin jie	Guanyin festival (birth)	Everyone
4/8	浴佛節 yu fo jie	Celebrating date of the Buddha's birth	Everyone
6/16	拜千佛 bai qian fo	Chanting names of all buddhas and bodhisattvas	Clerics and devotees
6/19	觀音節 guanyin jie	Guanyin festival (enlightenment)	Everyone
9/16	拜千佛 bai qian fo	Chanting names of all buddhas and bodhisattvas	Clerics and devotees
9/19	觀音節 guanyin jie	Guanyin festival (renunciation)	Everyone
10/15–21	水陸法會 shui lu fahui	Water and land assembly	Everyone
11th or 12th month	打七 da qi	Seven-day meditation (three times)	Clerics and devotees
12/27	請辭 qing ci	Resignation of temple's administrative personnel	Clerics only

Source: Data from interview with Nanputuo Temple ritualist, Yoshiko Ashiwa and David Wank, March 1990

Souls' Festival to thank the deceased monks of the temple. Sometimes, the day before the service, the monks gathered to refresh their memories of the precepts by chanting them (*busa song jie* 布薩誦戒).

There were two kinds of on-demand rituals. One was for living persons (*yansheng* 延生) and held in the Great Buddha Hall. These rituals consisted of blessings to eliminate disaster (*xiaozai* 消災), ensure security (*bao ping'an* 保平安), give thanks for a birthday (*guo shengri* 過生日), or ask for fortune (*yaoqiu facai* 要求發財). The other kind was for deceased persons (*wangsheng* 往生), usually commissioned by laypersons to worship their ancestors. The most common was sutra chanting (*nian jing* 念經), while the largest and most expensive was the release of burning mouths. During the 1980s, services for the deceased occurred in the Merit Hall in the east compound. While monks considered all commissioned rituals essentially the same, laypersons saw them as different because each had distinct words. They consulted their masters, friends, and family members to choose an appropriate ritual.

The rituals were relatively expensive, with the fee varying by kind of ritual and number of monks. For example, in 1989, a plenary recitation of Buddha's name (*pufuo* 普佛) with seven participating monks cost 500 yuan. More monks could be added at a higher cost.[16] Monks were paid according to their role: the hall master earned 22 yuan, the cymbal beaters received 18 yuan, and those who chanted received 14 yuan. Students from the BCM had the opportunity to learn on-demand rituals when asked on special occasions to participate. Some monks earned money by performing rituals at laypersons' homes, although the temple and the BAX discouraged this because it could be interpreted by the local authorities as propagating religion outside the temple in violation of the religious policy.

The ritualist was from Wenzhou. As a young child during the Cultural Revolution, his parents sent him to live at a local temple with a monk who had left Gushan Temple in Fuzhou when it was closed. In 1981, he became a novice at age twelve and was ordained at Gushan Temple. That year he came to Nanputuo Temple, one of the first young monks in residence after the Cultural Revolution. In 1983, he entered the preparatory program of the Buddhist Instruction School. He was fascinated with rituals and studied the intricate Minnan forms from elderly monks at the temple. He always carried a notebook to write down new ritual information and continually memorized ritual manuals. He frequently traveled to Chinese Buddhist temples in Southeast Asia to learn the rituals because knowledge of their performance in the PRC had been nearly destroyed by the Cultural Revolution. To perform elaborate rituals, such as releasing burning mouths, he invited the elderly ritual specialist, Dingmiao, from Guanghua Temple.

Relations Between Local State Administration and Nanputuo Temple

As the recovery of Nanputuo Temple proceeded, different views among the monks and local officials regarding its development took on greater significance. Tension over these views centered on the presence of local state officials in the internal management of the temple. Their presence had its origins in 1976 when Nanputuo opened as a public park under the jurisdiction of the Xiamen Parks and Forestry Bureau. To run the park, the bureau established the Nanputuo Management Office (Nanputuo guanli chu 南普陀管理處), located on the grounds, with six bureau officials assigned to it. In 1979, when the CPC reacknowledged religion, Nanputuo reopened as a temple under the jurisdiction of the newly revived XRAB. The management office and its officials were reassigned to the XRAB. The XRAB made some changes to the management office because Nanputuo was now recognized by the local state as a temple. First, the character for "temple" was added to the office's name; it was now called Nanputuo Temple Management Office (Nanputuo si guanli chu 南普陀寺管理處). Second, the XRAB appointed several elderly monks who had worked at the park's refreshment stands to serve in the management office with the XRAB officials. But the officials ran the committee, including supervising the temple's financial accounts.

The monks and officials sought to cooperate, but different expectations quickly became apparent. The monks, concerned with reviving Buddhist teachings, lacked knowledge about how to deal with the local state administration. They relied on the XRAB officials to obtain state funds for repairs, handle visiting dignitaries, run commercial activities, and organize public safety. The XRAB was concerned with furthering economic development in the Xiamen SEZ by promoting tourism at the temple. In 1980, the XRAB obtained investment funds from the Fujian

Province Tourism Bureau to build the Haihuilou Restaurant in the temple's east compound, which quickly became popular with local believers and tourists. While some monks considered it inappropriate to operate a restaurant inside the temple, they realized it encouraged visitors to visit the temple.

The issuance of Document 19 in 1982 compelled the XRAB to make changes within the Nanputuo Temple Management Office to conform to the document's principle of clerical self-management. The document stipulated that, "CPC and government cadres should . . . become adept in supporting and helping religious organizations to solve their own problems. They should not monopolize or do things these organizations should do themselves" (quoted in MacInnis 1989, 19). The XRAB made adjustments to the office that appeared to cede management authority to the clerics but still let the bureau keep control. One involved renaming the office "Nanputuo Temple Management Committee" (Nanputuo si guanli weiyuanhui 南普陀寺管理委員會). The term "committee" gave the appearance of a decision-making body of monks rather than a subordinate "office" of the XRAB. The number of Buddhists serving on it was increased to seven, with Miaozhan and another elderly cleric as director and codirector. Buddhists were now a majority on the thirteen-person committee and held the leadership positions. The second adjustment concerned the six XRAB officials. They remained on the committee but they took early retirement from the bureau; thus the committee appeared to have no state officials serving on it.

Despite these symbolic displays of clerical self-management, the XRAB continued to influence internal temple decision-making through its proxies—the six retired XRAB officials—on the Nanputuo Temple Management Committee. The proxies worked to control and allocate the temple's revenue and expand its tourism facilities. As their control became increasingly controversial, both sides drew on Document 19 and other state policies to justify their actions.

Growing Struggle to Control Temple Wealth, 1982–1989

The monks had self-management in regard to Buddhist rituals and teachings, but the XRAB controlled the temple's commercial businesses through its proxies on the Nanputuo Temple Management Committee.

Monks and a BAX officer identified the key proxy to us as someone whom we call Mr. Z. Previously a prison guard, he had joined the Xiamen Parks and Forestry Bureau in 1976 and began working in Nanputuo when it was a park. He managed the refreshment stands and was the accountant of the management office. When Nanputuo was recognized as a temple in 1979, he became an XRAB official and continued as manager and accountant. In 1982, he resigned from the XRAB to keep his position on the Nanputuo Temple Management Committee, still working as its accountant and to expand the tourism facilities at Nanputuo Temple.

To control allocation of the temple's revenue, Mr. Z classified it into two categories. "Service" (shiye 事業) income applied to revenue generated by the monks through fees for on-demand rituals, alms and donations, sales of Buddhist literature, and gate receipts. "Enterprise" (qiye 企業) applied to revenue from the tourist facilities, including the vegetarian restaurants, photo and refreshment stands, and souvenir shops.[17] Together, these tourism facilities were the Nanputuo Temple Enterprise (Nanputuo si qiye 南普陀寺企業). Mr. Z's job as accountant let him monitor both the service and enterprise income. He turned over service income to the clerics, but he kept control of the enterprise income and decided on its uses. The clerics saw his accounting procedures as violating Document 19's principle of religious self-management. They maintained that clerics ought to control all temple income, both service and enterprise. Nevertheless, the XRAB director declared that Mr. Z's accounting accorded with Document 19: he justified this on the grounds that the document permitted clerics to "sell a limited quantity of religious reading matter, religious articles, and works of religious art" (quoted in MacInnis 1989, 18) but did not mention other commercial activities. The XRAB also justified Mr. Z's accounting by asserting that Buddhist precepts forbade clerics from handling money; therefore a layperson had to manage the temple's tourist-related commerce, and this person was Mr. Z.

The XRAB also attempted to control donations to the temple, the only significant income for the monks that Mr. Z did not monitor. People donated by placing money in the alms boxes, giving it to the abbot, or donating money at the temple management department. This was permitted by Document 19, which said that people could give donations directly to clerics "as long as they are freely offered and small in quantity" (quoted in MacInnis 1989, 19). During the 1980s, donations from overseas Chinese to renovate the temple grew dramatically. By 1988, the monks' income was 1.4 million yuan, six times larger than the enterprise revenue of 240,000 yuan. The lion's share of the monks' income—1,280,000 yuan—came from donations.[18] These funds helped the monks build religious facilities, such as the classrooms and library of the BCM, and the abbot's residence. The XRAB tried to steer donations toward tourism facilities. It invoked Document 19's stipulation that large donations from persons outside China required local state approval. But overseas Chinese donated to increase their Buddhist merit and did not believe that building a hotel or expanding a parking lot did so. Facing the prospect of people withholding donations, the XRAB backed off.

With XRAB support, Mr. Z moved to maximize his income by shifting all expenses for running the temple to the income of the monks. For example, he refused to allocate enterprise income for upkeep of the temple's buildings and grounds, asserting that this was the self-management responsibility of the clerics. He also forced the monks to use their income to pay for resources that benefitted the Nanputuo Temple Enterprise. One day, having just mentioned to Miaozhan that the vegetarian restaurant needed a new stove, Mr. Z immediately bought one and sent the bill to the temple. The monks protested that such a large expenditure required the approval of the Nanputuo Temple Management Committee. Mr. Z claimed that Miaozhan, who led the committee, had verbally approved. But when Miaozhan insisted he had *not* given his approval, XRAB officials intervened on the side of Mr. Z. They characterized the situation as a misunderstanding caused by Miaozhan's poor memory, and they told the temple to pay the bill. A third example concerned Mr. Z's control of temple property intended for clerics, such as cars donated by overseas Chinese to the clerics. The XRAB declared that Buddhist clerics should not drive cars, permitting Mr. Z to hire their drivers and control their use.

These actions were deeply upsetting to the clerics. They felt that the cleanliness and beauty of the temple environment was a tourist draw that profited the Nanputuo Temple Enterprise. Therefore, it was unfair to expect the clerics to pay the entire temple upkeep through their services income. They saw Mr. Z's large purchases as a violation of the financial controls of the Nanputuo Temple Management Committee. Clerics also felt that Nanputuo Temple Enterprise personnel disrespected the clerics. Mr. Z let XRAB officials borrow temple cars for personal and bureau use, so cars were sometimes unavailable for the abbot and official temple business. Some enterprise employees were even said to have insulted monks to their faces, calling them lazy and unproductive.

At the same time, the clerics learned how to parry some tourist-related schemes of Mr. Z and the XRAB by using their own networks and lobbying in the local state administration. One very effective tie was Miaozhan's friendship with the Xiamen vice mayor in charge of the city's construction and land use. In the late 1980s, he enjoyed visiting Miaozhan to talk about the temple's restoration. He allowed Miaozhan to submit blueprints directly to the vice mayor's office for approval, bypassing the XRAB, which tended to oppose construction plans that did not fit its idea of tourism promotion. Another important relationship was with officials of the Xiamen United Front Work Department, who, as we noted in chapter 3, were very solicitous about overseas Chinese. For example, in the mid-1980s, the XRAB threatened to block the construction of a classroom building for the BCM unless the clerics also built tourism facilities. Miaozhan told the Xiamen United Front Work Department that the delay would "upset the feelings" of the overseas donors, and its intervention enabled the classroom building to be swiftly built. The clerics also appealed to the department to parry Mr. Z's proposal to convert a guesthouse for visiting overseas clerics into a luxury tourist hotel named the Nanputuo Villa (Nanputuo shanzhuang 南普陀山莊). The plan not only lacked any connection to Buddhism, but the new name suggested a rustic lodge where people enjoyed beautiful scenery while eating hearty food, including meat, and drinking alcoholic beverages. Miaozhan informed the Xiamen United Front Work Department that the hotel would offend overseas Chinese Buddhists and the idea was dropped.

These examples illustrate how clerics learned to use the different interests in the local state administration to their advantage. An officer of the BAX explained to us that the Xiamen United Front Work Department, as a local organ of the CPC, was primarily concerned with ideological issues, such as ensuring proper implementation of the principles in Document 19 and cultivating overseas Chinese. In contrast, the XRAB, as part of the local government, sought to meet the government's expectations for economic development by promoting tourism. Therefore, appeals by clerics to Xiamen United Front Work Department officials based on upholding the principles in Document 19, especially in matters involving overseas Chinese, could sometimes halt or limit XRAB projects.

Finally, another crucial network connected Nanputuo Temple to the central state via Miaozhan's position as vice president of the Buddhist Association of China and his friendship with Zhao Puchu. The importance of this connection can be seen regarding donations, as we mentioned above. Miaozhan had a practice of sharing donations to Nanputuo Temple with less prosperous temples and academies elsewhere in China, including the Buddhist Academy of China. The XRAB director opposed this practice as siphoning away local wealth, insisting that donations to Nanputuo Temple be spent in Xiamen to contribute to the special economic zone's economy. Of course, Miaozhan saw the purpose of the donations as furthering Buddhism regardless of geographic location. He overcame XRAB objections by obtaining a statement from the Buddhist Association of China supporting his donations to Buddhist schools. Miaozhan's ties to the central state became increasingly crucial in the context of the temple's growing conflict with the XRAB (see chapter 5).

Clerical Concerns of Secularization

The Nanputuo clerics and BAX officers increasingly viewed the Nanputuo Temple Management Committee as a Trojan horse for XRAB control and the secularization of the temple. In 1985, the XRAB built the upscale Puzhaolou Restaurant that featured private dining rooms with chandeliers. Only the strong objection of the monks prevented Mr. Z from serving meat and alcohol and operating a dance hall there. Additionally, Mr. Z began contracting out the shops of the Nanputuo Temple Enterprise to its employees, who began aggressively hawking their wares in the temple compound. Soon there was a photo shop by the Great Buddha Hall, a tea shop next to the Buddha Rock, and a booth selling calendars with pictures of scantily clad women near the temple's entrance.

The monks were also concerned that the Nanputuo Temple Enterprise had become an autonomous medium-sized business within the temple. By 1989, its 192 employees equaled the number of resident monks. It operated as a family firm with Mr. Z as the boss, his wife as cashier, and the spouses, relations, and friends of his XRAB colleagues serving in various capacities. The cooks and service personnel were said to be among the best compensated in the Xiamen catering industry, enjoying such benefits as holiday bonuses and free birthday parties for their children. XRAB officials could dine for free in Puzhaolou Restaurant, and entertained officials and visiting dignitaries there, also without paying the bill. Mr. Z covered these costs to keep a good relationship with the XRAB, his patron in the local government. But the monks saw this use of enterprise funds as serving secular purposes that had nothing to do with the temple as a site of Buddhist teachings.

The clerics' growing criticism of the XRAB reflected their increasing confidence and administrative experience. A turning point was the assignment of dozens of capable and talented 1985 graduates of the Buddhist Instruction School to positions in Nanputuo Temple. Unlike the elderly monks, they had no personal experience of religious persecution, were well versed in the religious policy, and more willing to challenge the XRAB's interpretations of Document 19. We even heard stories of monks publicly confronting XRAB officials, including one in the late 1980s described in the memoir of a BAX official.

> The monks had a distaste for the [XRAB] director. One cunning young monk from the BCM often spied on the Puzhaolou [restaurant] to see how often the director entertained guests.
>
> One night the young monk fearlessly approached the director's table in the banquet hall and called out, "Director, you come so many times to entertain guests. Don't you have to pay? Do you always have so much money for treating people?" The director ... was very embarrassed in front of the guests. Putting on a smile, he said, "Yes, I am paying." The monk shouted, "Let's see the receipt." Still smiling, the director said, "Isn't it usual to pay after eating?" The monk responded, "Director, you entertained here last night, too. Show me that receipt."
>
> Just then, Mr. Z, the boss, heard the voices and discerned the predicament of the director, his taskmaster. He smiled, patted the young monk on the shoulder, and said, "Don't shout! Don't shout! If the little master waits for the director to finish eating before paying the bill, I will show it to you. It is very embarrassing to speak this way in front of guests." But the young monk continued in a loud voice. "The officials of the people's government are the parents of the

people. How can they keep on entertaining guests so often? It is not worthy for an official. They are supposed to be our parents. This is awful! This is awful!" (Wu 2014, vol. 7, book 3, 70)

The growing anger of clerics towards the XRAB paralleled the bureau's declining importance as a conduit of state construction funds to the temple. This is suggested by viewing the total construction expenditures at the temple of 15.6 million yuan from 1986 to 1992. State funding constituted only 19 percent (3 million yuan) of the total, with the service income and donations controlled by clerics accounting for, respectively, 44 percent (6.9 million yuan) and 37 percent (5.7 million yuan) (*XFZ*, 10). Furthermore, the state funding tended to be invested in tourist rather than religious facilities, and it was of little interest to the clerics.[19] By the end of the 1980s, clerics viewed the Nanputuo Democratic Management Committee, the Nanputuo Temple Enterprise, and Mr. Z's presence as a conduit to siphon some of the temple's growing wealth for the well-being of XRAB officials and their relations.

Tiananmen Square Protest and Patriotic Religion

In 1989, as the renovation of Nanputuo Temple's main square neared completion, its monks faced the Tiananmen Square protest in Beijing. This event shook the state and created the biggest political challenge for Buddhism since 1979. As is well known, the protest began in spring 1989 in Beijing as university students mourned the death of Hu Yaobang 胡耀邦, a liberal member of the political elite.[20] It quickly encompassed demands for more political openness and an end to the corruption among state officials. The students attracted widespread sympathy and support from the general population. After two months of accelerating protests in Beijing and other cities around the country, the People's Liberation Army suppressed the movement on June 4, killing many people. The political crises tested Miaozhan's leadership of the temple. In the runup to June 4, he sought to prevent sympathetic BCM students from joining the student protestors. After June 4, he worked to limit the effects in the temple while acknowledging and reflecting people's sadness and fear at the violence and suffering.[21]

REVIVAL OF BUDDHIST PRACTICE, 1982-1989

When the protest began, students at Xiamen University boycotted classes. They sent representatives to Beijing who telephoned reports from Tiananmen Square that were broadcast by loudspeakers to crowds outside the student dormitories at Xiamen University. The students organized marches from the university to the city center. Passing Nanputuo Temple, marchers called to the monks. BCM teachers blocked the exits to prevent young monks studying at the BCM from joining the march. Miaozhan guarded the main temple gate, swatting at monks who tried to get around him. He knew that the local state would punish the temple if clerics, highly visible in their robes, were among the marchers. As a result of these efforts, no Buddhist clerics were visible in the student marches in Xiamen.

Buddhist monks were visible in demonstrations in Beijing, however, which prompted the State Administration of Religious Affairs to demand more political study in Buddhist academies. Shortly after June 4, the Fujian Religious Affairs Bureau summoned the heads of all local bureaus, Buddhist associations, and Buddhist academies in the province to an emergency meeting. It announced the increase in the political study courses. Clerics and association officers at the meeting were disturbed by the assumption that Buddhists were insufficiently patriotic. One participating BAX officer, a layperson, described the meeting to us along with his views.

> They [provincial religious affairs officials] requested that we strengthen our political study. We were told that just because one is a Buddhist monk does not mean they do not have to study politics. During the chaos in Beijing, monks participated in the demonstrations. The government said this was because the monks emphasized "love Buddhism" more than "love country." I beg to differ. We must ensure that our students have genuine faith in Buddhism. Otherwise, they cannot contribute to Buddhism. If their belief is false, they will waver at the first sign of disturbance.
>
> In 1952, China established the Buddhist Academy of China to cultivate successors in Buddhism. The standard then was Marxism-Leninism, and courses on Buddhism were taught as academic subjects. The political element was heavy. Some teachers who did not believe

in Buddhism taught philosophy courses on modern Marxist philosophy. So, during the Cultural Revolution, when the CPC destroyed all the temples, clerics who had received this education felt that Buddhism had no future, and they got married. You cannot blame them. But this shows their education failed to give them genuine belief. Otherwise, they would not have disrobed even when facing a mountain of swords and a sea of flames.

At the meeting, I said we cannot cultivate false monks—monks without belief. So how can it be said that "love religion" is overemphasized? In cultivating Buddhist talent, you must definitely "love religion." You cannot take "love religion and love country" as antagonistic. . . . The real issue is the righteousness of the actions of the CPC. If it is righteous, the CPC should not fear that Buddhists will not love it. I saw a World War II movie about Christian priests protecting underground patriots fighting against German fascism. The priests even sacrificed their lives to protect these patriots. So, the critical issue is whether or not the CPC is righteous. If the party is not righteous but keeps telling people to love it, who will? The document issued by the Fujian Religious Affairs Bureau calling for more political study did not get to the essence of the problem.[22]

The BCM replaced regular courses with intensive study of the religious policy. After several days, the students were upset at the disruption of their Buddhist studies. So, the BAX worked with sympathetic XRAB officials to make the political study more interesting by going beyond Marxist-Leninist theory and religious policy to include Chinese history and contemporary events. XRAB officials lectured on sensitive current topics, such as the fall of communist states in Eastern Europe, which the CPC labeled "the peaceful restoration of capitalism" to be prevented at all costs in China. They analyzed the popular uprisings, such as the Romanian revolution of December 1989, as an example of the chaos caused by popular challenges to the communist parties. Other courses were taught by BAX officers and Xiamen University professors. One course surveyed patriots in Chinese history, such as Yue Fei 岳飛 (1103–1142), a loyal general who fought the invading Jurchen armies, and the scholar-general Wen Tianxiang 文天祥 (1236–1283), who resisted Mongol invaders and refused to submit despite torture. In this way, the monks,

BAX, and XRAB officials cooperated to integrate the state demand for more political study into the curriculum without offending the sensibilities of the student monks.

Nanputuo Temple came under increased state surveillance to catch student activists fleeing from north China to sanctuary in Hong Kong. Immediately after June 4, the local government tightened the enforcement of residency permits at Nanputuo Temple. This was possibly due to the tradition of criminals disguising themselves as wandering monks to seek sanctuary in Buddhist temples. The senior guest prefect could no longer make oral reports on newly arrived monks but now had to submit written reports at the public security bureau substation. But the waiver for reporting short-term stays remained, in effect facilitating the possible movement of activists through Nanputuo Temple disguised as monks. Rumors circulated of clerical robes found on nearby beaches, left by activists who swam to Jinmen, the Taiwan-controlled island several kilometers off the coast. Such stories reflected widespread sympathy for the student activists and peoples' conviction that the clerics supported them. We heard first-hand from a foreign teacher at Xiamen University of a likely activist at Nanputuo Temple. While the teacher was visiting the temple, a young monk spoke to her in excellent English, unusual for a cleric at that time. He said that he had arrived in Xiamen two days earlier and was going south the next day. Expensive track shoes poked out under his robes, and a small tuft of hair stuck up from his shaved pate. He joked that his English name was "punk monk."

The senior monks we spoke with in the months after June 4 felt the temple was successfully navigating the political uncertainty. They supported Miaozhan's decision to block students from joining the protestors because it prevented the BCM from being shut down. One monk noted that classes had been halted at Buddhist academies in Nanjing, Shanghai, and Suzhou, where students had joined the protestors. One student monk at the BCM said that watching the demonstration pass by the temple gate had taught him to resist the temptation to get involved in secular politics.

The aftermath of the Tiananmen Square protest rippled through the ritual life of the temple. Several days after June 4, two tall flagpoles flying the Chinese and Buddhist flags were erected outside the Heavenly Kings Hall. This was done at the behest of the XRAB to show the temple's patriotism. A senior monk told us that the Chinese flag was higher, although this was not readily discernable. In August, the temple hosted a large Buddhist assembly to send merit to dead souls (*puli fahui* 普利法會). A banner across the temple entrance read "Praying for World Peace." A monk who helped organize the ceremony told us that a wealthy overseas Chinese devotee sponsored it. The ceremony "prayed for souls who died long ago and those who died recently."[23] We interpreted the ceremony as the clerics' acknowledgment of the deaths and sufferings in Beijing. While showing loyalty to the state, they could express the Buddhist character of the temple.[24]

Conclusion

By 1989, the semiotic space of Nanputuo Temple had recovered and was fully functioning as a site of Buddhist teachings. The four hundred monks at the temple were more than double the number during the earlier flourishing of the temple in the mid-1930s. While many visitors came daily to worship at the temple, tens of thousands came to the day-long Guanyin birthday festival three times a year. The physical space was nearing recovery, although piles of construction materials still dotted the side compounds, and the Lotus Pond was still a dry and dusty bowl in the front yard. But the institutional space of religion at the temple contained diverging interests, agendas, and interpretations of the religious policy. In the next chapter we explore the expansion of Nanputuo Temple and the deepening conflict with the local state administration in the changed politics after the Tiananmen Square protest.

5

Expansion and Conflict in the Space of Religion, 1989–1995

THE TIANANMEN SQUARE PROTEST, CULMINATING on June 4, 1989, in state violence against the student protestors, severely shook the CPC. It subsequently launched the massive campaign targeting student activists and other social groups, such as private businesspersons, that the party saw as supporting them. The political tension caused a downturn in the domestic economy, while international trade plunged as countries suspended diplomatic relations with the PRC to condemn the violence against unarmed citizens. In 1990, annual GDP growth fell by two-thirds to 3.9 percent. The CPC leadership was divided by infighting over China's direction, with some blaming the opening-up policies for the protests. The political repression and leadership split created deep uncertainty about the CPC's commitment to the opening-up policies. Then, in 1992, the situation shifted when Deng Xiaoping took a widely publicized tour of Guangdong Province, where the market reforms were most advanced. This signal of support for opening-up policies from the PRC's paramount leader helped restart rapid economic growth, with GDP tripling 14.2 percent that year (National Bureau of Statistics of China n.d.). This economic activity gave new resources to religions even as changes in the CPC's ideology profoundly affected the institutional space of religion.

The CPC now saw religion as a serious security threat, creating new demands toward it. This new view was expressed in a 1991 document called "Circular of the CPC Central Committee and the State Council on Several Issues in Regard to Further Improving Religious Work" (中共中央國務院關於進一步做好宗教工作若干問題的通知) (Zhonggong zhongyang 1991), hereafter referred to by its issuing number as Document 6.

> Hostile forces abroad have been using religion as a key means of pursuing the "peaceful evolution" strategy and continue to infiltrate and sabotage us. National separatists have also used religion to stir trouble, attack the party's leadership and the socialist system, and undermine the unity of the motherland and the unity of the ethnicities. In some places, a small number of hostile elements are rampant in establishing illegal organizations and competing with us for leadership of temples and churches; some illegally set up scripture schools and theological seminaries to compete with us for young people. Some temples have restored religious feudal privileges, oppression, and exploitation that had been abolished. At the grassroots level, religion is being used to intervene in state administration, the judiciary, and school education. (Zhonggong zhongyang 1991)

Document 6 demanded the "adaptation of religion to socialist society" (*zongjiao yu shehui zhuyi shehui xiang shiying* 宗教與社會主義社會相適應). Religions were expected to change their doctrines and activities to fit the needs of socialism as determined by the CPC. Party secretary Jiang Zemin explained this in a meeting with religious leaders on November 7, 1993:

> Adaptation does not require religious believers to abandon theistic ideology and religious beliefs, but rather to love the motherland [be patriotic] in politics, support the socialist system, and uphold the leadership of the CPC. At the same time, that which does not meet the socialist system of religion and religious doctrines must be reformed so that the positive elements of religious doctrines, religious codes, and religious morals may be used to serve socialism. (Jiang 1993)

Thus, the CPC's earlier encouragement in the 1980s for religions to revive as long as they supported the state's opening-up policies changed to demands that religions alter their internal characteristics and activities to better serve the state.

In the five sections of this chapter we present the events that occurred during the second phase of Nanputuo Temple's recovery, from the Tiananmen Square protest in 1989 to Miaozhan's death in 1995. During these six years, the central state became more directly involved in the temple. First, we cover the abbatial ascension ceremony (*sheng zuo* 升座) of Miaozhan in 1989, postponed for several months by the Tiananmen Square protest. Actors made accommodations to enable this crucial Buddhist ceremony to proceed during the extreme political tension. Second, we discuss the escalating battle between the monks and the XRAB officials, precipitated by Miaozhan's efforts to integrate the temple's semiotic space after becoming abbot. Third, we describe the expansion of the temple, revealing tensions, overlaps, and compromises in the physical, semiotic, and institutional spaces of religion. Fourth, we explain how the overseas migration of young clerics to Southeast Asia and North America reflected the historical legacies of Nanputuo Temple and political tensions after the Tiananmen Square protest. In the fifth and last section of the chapter we describe the funeral of Miaozhan in 1995. Unlike his ascension ceremony, the various actors could not sufficiently compromise, and a conflict broke out over the handling of his body.

Abbatial Ascension

A temple without an abbot is headless, lacking a complete structure. Therefore, the ascension ceremony is a crucial time in the semiotic, physical, and institutional spaces of a temple. The ascension ceremony of Miaozhan in 1989 showed the shape of the temple, which was approved by CPC ideology and recognized by the state administration. The three spaces came together in the ceremony as an idealized image that reflected compromises with the state. In this section, we describe the process of the ceremony and the auspicious sayings festooning the temple walls for the occasion.[1]

One compromise of the ceremony involved its timing. Many Buddhists already recognized Miaozhan as the de facto abbot of Nanputuo

Temple since 1957 and admired his long dedication to it. During the 1980s, as the temple rapidly revived under his leadership, Buddhists were increasingly upset by the lack of a ceremony to formally install him as abbot, especially since other senior monks, such as Yuanzhuo at Guanghua Temple, had been installed earlier in the 1980s. Some attributed the delay to the concern of the XRAB that Miaozhan's ascension as abbot would increase his authority, making him harder to control. In the end, pressure from Buddhists, including overseas clerics and the Buddhist Association of China, helped push the Xiamen Municipal People's Government to approve his ascension ceremony for July 1989. But the Tiananmen Square protest erupted the month before the ceremony, causing the XRAB to postpone it to October. According to a BAX officer, XRAB officials deemed it inappropriate to convene a large religious celebration so soon after June 4.[2]

A second compromise concerned the participants. Hundreds of invitations had been sent to overseas Chinese, and Buddhists in Singapore and Hong Kong had chartered airplanes to attend. In normal times, the state would have welcomed their presence as a sign of the patriotism of overseas Chinese. But in the political tension and insecurity after the Tiananmen Square protest, local state officials viewed their attendance in a different light. They worried that their attendance would highlight the large contribution that overseas Chinese had made to the temple's recovery, thereby diminishing the importance of the CPC's "correct" ideology toward religion and state funding for construction. Therefore, the number of attendees coming from outside of Xiamen was reduced to sixty. Despite Miaozhan's sadness that his staunch overseas supporters could not come, the ascension ceremony was held on October 9, 1989. The five hundred attendees were mostly from Xiamen.

The ceremony gave him religious recognition in Buddhism and institutional recognition in the state as the leader of Nanputuo Temple. Even XRAB officials attended to congratulate Miaozhan. The guest of honor was the Buddhist Association of China vice president Mingyang 明陽 (1916–2002), a disciple of Yuanying and the leader of several important temples. The critical role in the abbatial ascension ceremony of position-giving cleric (*song wei fashi* 送位法師) was typically filled by the retiring abbot. But Miaozhan was already acting abbot, and the previous abbot was long since deceased, so the position was filled by Yuanzhuo, abbot of

Guanghua Temple. Two dozen abbots and priors of other temples attended, resplendent in their bright red robes. The hundreds of clerics included many BCM students. Monks wore brown robes draped from one shoulder over yellow robes, while nuns donned light brown robes over darker brown ones, and many devotees wore brown robes. Scores of devotees in lay attire also attended.

The ceremony traversed the temple compound, starting with Miaozhan entering the temple at the mountain gate and ending inside the abbot's residence two hours later. Along the way, he worshiped at all parts of the temple in the following sequence: from East Mountain Gate 東大山門 to West Mountain Gate 西大山門, Heavenly Kings Hall 天王殿, Dizang Hall 地藏殿, Qielan Hall 伽藍殿, Temple Ancestral Hall 祖堂, Great Buddha Hall 大雄寶殿, Vegetarian Hall 齋堂, Great Compassion Hall 大悲殿, Dharma Hall 法堂, and finally to the Abbot's Residence 方丈樓. The climax occurred in Dharma Hall when Miaozhan expressed his authority as abbot by sitting in the abbot's dharma seat (*fa zuo* 法座) to preach to the attendees.

A ritualist team (*yizhang dui* 儀仗隊) of thirteen monks accompanied Miaozhan. One held aloft a jeweled canopy, a multihued cloth cylinder with tassels symbolizing the high position and character of the abbot. Its visibility signaled Miaozhan's presence as he moved through the temple, even when surrounded by the crowd. Two monks carried poles with vertical cloth banners with a couplet extolling Miaozhan's selfless assumption of the abbotship.

[right]	He acts not for his own tranquil happiness in the here and now. 不為自己茲安樂
[left]	But wishes that all sentient beings might cast away their hardships. 但願眾生得離難

Other ritualists carried the incense tray, lanterns, incense pot, dragon staff, white horsehair whisk, handbell, and begging bowl. Four monks stayed close to Miaozhan, handing him ritual items at appropriate moments and the microphone when he spoke. As he moved through the temple, the crowd followed. We next describe the ceremony and salient couplets with auspicious words hung on walls and pillars for the occasion.

Sequence of the Abbatial Ascension Ceremony

At 8:50 a.m. the bell rang three times, and the wooden clapper struck as Miaozhan rode in a car from the East Mountain Gate to the West Mountain Gate. These sounds marked his leaving the temple for the last time as an ordinary cleric. He held a gold-covered, S-shaped scepter symbolizing power and fortune as he alighted in front of the West Mountain Gate. At 9:00 a.m. the Nanputuo Temple prior presented Miaozhan with the red robe worn by previous temple abbots. Miaozhan draped it over his saffron robe and brown cassock. The monks bowed to Miaozhan. A ritualist handed him the monk staff. Miaozhan pointed it at the West Mountain Gate and spoke the following words: "The all-embracing gates of this Buddhist temple contain all the world's myriad forms. Everyone is filled with great delight, for this place is exceedingly auspicious (這個總持法門, 羅列森羅萬象, 出入皆大歡喜, 此處最為吉祥)." In a symbolic act meant to dispel ignorance and call out to all sentient beings, he pounded the bottom of the staff on the ground, and the metal rings at its tip jangled loudly. As the bell in Dizang Hall began to ring, he walked through the West Mountain Gate toward the Heavenly Kings Hall, where hundreds of attendees waited. Stopping in front of the hall, he pointed the staff at its door saying, "This Buddhist site is anointed by Guanyin; its capacity for mercy, compassion, joy, and surrender is immeasurable. Today, Miaozhan has come to enter the temple grounds; in great propriety and peace, this undertaking is exceedingly auspicious (此是觀音選佛場, 慈悲喜拾四無量, 妙湛今日來進院, 如意康寧最吉祥)." As he struck the monk staff on the ground, the jangling announced his presence. The door opened, and he entered the temple.

Inside the Heavenly Kings Hall, Miaozhan worshiped at the statue of Mile. Pressing his palms together, he bowed. A ritualist struck the handbell, and Miaozhan prostrated in front of Mile. He repeated this three times. Then he burned incense from the incense tray, which a ritualist had placed at the altar, and prostrated three times. He said:

> The Mile Buddha now inhabits Tushita Hall [one of the seven levels of Heaven]; yet dividing his body, he exists infinitely throughout the world. Those who respectfully worship him by providing

offerings will be first to receive the truth of his teachings under the dragon-flower tree (彌勒現住兜率院, 分身無量在世間, 恭敬禮拜供養者, 龍華三會授記先).[3]

Next, he worshiped at the statue of Weituo at the rear of the Heavenly Kings Hall. He said:

Gripping a *vajra* sword, he quells the demon armies; the three continents respond, revealing the might of this powerful deity. In those days, he received the Buddha's personal command at Ling Mountain; we, too, entrust this Heavenly General to protect the Buddhist way (手持寶杵鎮魔軍, 三洲感應顯威神, 當年親受靈山囑, 寄位天將護法門).

Miaozhan exited the Heavenly Kings Hall and walked east across the courtyard to the Dizang Hall 地藏殿. After worshiping, he said:

Only after all sentient beings cross over to the shore of enlightenment will Dizang ascend to enlightenment; so long as hell remains unemptied, he has vowed not to attain Buddhahood. His great will and power remain unmatched throughout all time. Bowing down to the ground, I gratefully receive the refuge of his compassionate mercy (眾生度盡方登菩提, 獄不空誓不成佛, 大願大力空前絕後, 稽首皈依慈悲攝受).

Exiting the Dizang Hall, he walked west across the main courtyard to the Qielan Hall. He worshiped and said, "Master of the temple, he adjudicates within its walls, undertaking the Buddha's command to partake in earnest surrender. May Qielan assist the Buddha in exercising his formidable power, and preserve the eternal peace of these temple grounds (闍寺權衡為主宰, 欽承佛敕共輸誠, 惟願輔佐施威力, 護持梵剎永安寧)." He left the Qielan Hall, walking north to the Ancestor Hall. After worshiping, he said:

How impressive are the multitude of monks who have served this temple! One generation after another, they have stirred up the influence of our Linji school. Miaozhan pledges to carry on the aspirations of the worthy men before him, and commits to training talented clerics of high character and intelligence at this Minnan academy (偉哉列祖龍象眾, 奕葉相承振宗風, 妙湛誓繼先德志, 定教閩院出賢聖).

He walked west across the front courtyard to the entrance of the Great Buddha Hall, where the abbots were waiting. He held a brown dragon cloth, an old-fashioned prayer cloth used before the creation of prayer cushions, which symbolized the position of abbot. The precentor struck a hand-chime, and the bell in the Dizang Hall, which had been ringing since Miaozhan entered the temple compound, stopped. Yuanzhuo came out from the hall to greet him. He took the dragon cloth from Miaozhan, and they entered the hall together. They faced each other across the prayer cushion, with Yuanzhuo on the west and Miaozhan on the east. Yuanzhuo raised the dragon cloth and placed it on the prayer cushion. This was the moment when Miaozhan was recognized in Buddhism as abbot. The two monks bowed toward the Buddha statue and turned to face each other with palms pressed together in prayer. Then, Yuanzhuo exited the hall. Miaozhan burned incense at the altar, pressed his palms in prayer, and said, "Within the heavenly realm and all that lies below, there is nothing like the Buddha; nor can anything in the ten worldly directions compare. I have seen all there is to see in the world; there is nothing in it like the Buddha (天上天下無如佛, 十方世界亦無比, 世間所有我盡見, 一切無有如佛者)." He prostrated three times.

Miaozhan exited the Great Buddha Hall. He turned west to walk to its front corner, north to its rear, and east across its back side to the dining hall. He said:

A rotation of food must be prepared before I preach the Buddha truth;
I look to you to shoulder the task of blending the hundred flavors.
This place will never lack for fragrant foods or excellent cooks. The multitudes of mortals are content, both men and deities are pleased (法輪來轉食輪先, 調和百味仰仔肩, 香積寶廚永不缺, 海眾安和人天歡).

He walked south and then west to the Great Compassion Hall and climbed the steps to the statue of Thousand-Handed and Thousand-Eyed Guanyin. He worshiped and said:

How sublime, the sound of Guanyin's holy name: the sound of Sanskrit and the sound of the tide, the sound that far surpasses all other earthly sounds. Thus, we must routinely chant it aloud, chanting and chanting without forming doubts, for Guanyin is a pure and holy saint. When facing suffering or distress, the name of Guanyin can be used for support (妙音觀世音, 梵音海潮音, 勝彼世間音, 是故須常念, 念念勿生疑, 觀世音淨聖, 於苦惱死厄, 能為作依怙).

He prostrated three times and walked down the rear steps of the Great Compassion Hall to the Dharma Hall.

The bell and drum began sounding in unison, and all attendees gathered in front of the Dharma Hall. A ritualist bearing the incense bowl entered, followed by Miaozhan holding the dragon cloth. Thereupon, everyone else entered. At the end of the large hall was a table-like altar covered by a yellow cloth. Behind it was the dharma seat, where the abbot sat when preaching the dharma. Yuanzhuo stood west of the seat, facing Miaozhan on the east. Miaozhan bowed to Yuanzhuo and raised the dragon cloth. Yuanzhuo took hold of it, and they lifted it together. Yuanzhuo placed the dragon cloth on the dharma seat, saying, "I offer humble wishes to the eminent monk Miaozhan that his good fortune and wisdom may grow, that his Buddha-body may remain healthy, and that this place of learning where he resides may become more prosperous with each passing day (敬祝妙湛大和尚福慧增長, 法體康泰, 常住學院蒸蒸日上)." Miaozhan responded, "Miaozhan pursues his course in accordance with the Buddha's teachings, leads the multitudes in self-cultivation, trains clerical talent, and ensures the long-standing existence of the rightful dharma (妙湛依教奉行, 領眾熏修, 培育僧才, 令正法久住)." Yuanzhuo stepped back from the dharma seat and stood to the side. Miaozhan walked to the front of the altar and faced the dharma seat. He said, "This lion's seat [the seat of the abbot] has been passed down to us from the founder of our school. Today, this old monk will ascend to this revered place, for he is destined to preach the dharma to all the beings assembled here (這個獅子座, 佛祖所流傳, 老衲今登臨, 廣度諸有緣)." The precentor began singing the "Fragrant Furnace Incantation" (Lu xiang zan 爐香贊). Miaozhan lit an incense stick, bowed three times, and sat in the abbot's seat. Four monks stood by him, two to a side. Miaozhan held the white whisk that symbolized ridding the world of suffering. It is a symbol of the abbot because its bearers are responsible for the spiritual and physical well-being of all communities in Buddhism. Holding its handle, Miaozhan waved it back and forth and then laid it on the table before him. He stood up and bowed. The proctor unfolded the dragon cloth and chanted three times, "May the canopy of incense clouds covering the world serve as an offering to all bodhisattvas (香雲蓋菩薩)." Following each time, he struck a handbell, and Miaozhan bowed.

Miaozhan stood before the altar, facing the assemblage for his first dharma talk as abbot. The precentor announced the talk by chanting, "Monks and people gathered in the Dharma Hall, behold this first righteous deed (法筵龍象眾, 當觀第一義)." A ritualist handed Miaozhan an incense stick. He lit it and said:

> This stick of incense existed prior to the heaven and earth, and is brighter than the light of the sun and moon. I place it into the urn to burn. I declare to worship the eternal Three Precious Treasures of Buddhism in all ten directions, and our ancestral clerics in the Western Heavens [Buddhas] and in the Eastern Land [China], who magnify our school and extend its teachings by propagating its munificent knowledge all across the world. I abide by the hope that Buddhism will become more glorious by the day, and that the dharma wheel will keep on turning (此一瓣香, 先天地而有, 超日月之光, 爇向爐中, 專申供養十方常住三寶, 西天東土歷代祖師、天下弘宗演教諸大善知識, 伏願佛日增輝, 法輪常轉).

The ritualist gave him a second incense stick. Miaozhan lit it and said:

> This stick of incense is embedded in the past, present, and future; its luxuriant fragrance blankets the ten directions. I place it into the urn to burn. I offer my wishes that the country may prosper, society may progress, the people may find contentment and happiness, households may be merry, the world may be at peace, and the weapons of war may forever cease (此一瓣香、根盤三際, 葉茂十方, 爇向爐中、端為祝愿: 國家昌盛、社會進步、人民幸福、家庭快樂、世界和平、干戈永息).

The ritualist passed him the third stick of incense. He lit it, saying:

> This stick of incense is to honor the cultivation of Buddhist precepts, with their powerful utility; I place it into the urn to burn. I declare my reverence for the master who taught me the dharma, the exalted old monk Huiquan; and the old monk Zhuanfeng, who ecumenicized this temple. This is meant to repay their kindness in bestowing the nourishment of the dharma (此一瓣香, 戒定熏修, 力用具足, 爇向爐中, 專申供養得法本師、本寺堂上上會下全老和尚、本寺改子孫為十方的開創者上轉下逢老和尚、用酬法乳之恩).

The ritualist gave him a fourth incense stick. Miaozhan lit it and said:

> I place this stick of incense into the urn to burn, declaring to worship the old monk Quanlang, the master who ordained me; the old monk Jinxiu, the respected teacher who tonsured me; the old monk Tanxu, who imparted to me the Buddhist teachings; the old monk Laiguo, who taught me to meditate; all of the many teachers who instructed me in acquiring the great knowledge of Buddhism; and all of the eminent masters who are elder monks of this temple. This is meant as recompense for their kindness, which led to my accomplishments (此一瓣香、爇向爐中、專申供養得戒本師上全下朗老和尚、剃度恩師上進下修老和尚、學教法師上俠下虛老和尚、學禪禪師上來下果老和尚、諸方參學受教諸大善知識、本寺前輩耆德長老、用報成就之德).

The four ritualists stood aside, and a monk wearing black robes handed Miaozhan the dragon staff. Topped by the golden head of a dragon, it symbolized the authority of dharma and, therefore, that of the abbot. Taking the staff, Miaozhan sat in the abbot's seat and said, "These Buddhist monks, gathered before the Wulao Peak, are here to strive diligently in studying the dharma. We have a soaring ambition: to stop at nothing to achieve enlightenment and become Buddhas (五老峰前龍象儔, 爭向法苑學無為, 丈夫自有沖天志, 不證菩提不罷休)."

Remaining seated, Miaozhan spoke directly to the gathering about his experiences and wishes for Nanputuo Temple.

I, Miaozhan, have frittered away my eighty years. It has already been fifty years since I left home to become a Buddhist monk; and yet my learning remains insufficient, and I have still not achieved results from my meditation practice. I have passed this time fruitlessly, for I remain unchanged. When I came to Nanputuo Temple in 1957, it was originally my plan to examine the sutras and, in so doing, enrich my life. After laboring in my studies for one year, I became the head of the temple, and continued in this position for the next thirty-one years. Yet I have done so little for this temple where I have lived so long. Today, members of both temple orders [clerics and devotees] have nominated me to become the abbot of this temple. I cannot refuse, and must strive to take on this difficult job. This thriving monastery is, in my view, the foremost ecumenical temple in Minnan [Southern Fujian]. At the same time, the task of restoring the BCM is arduous, and I am ashamed that my humble talents and shallow learning will make it difficult for me to successfully carry out this heavy responsibility. I strongly hope that those who hold administrative positions, regardless of their duties, will work together diligently, and will bravely shoulder the burden of carrying out this vital responsibility (妙湛虛度八十歲, 出家已有五十年, 學教未成. 參禪為就, 光陰空過, 依然故我. 五七年到南普陀本來打算看看佛經, 充實自己, 來後參加勞動一年, 當家三十一年, 對常住並無甚麼建樹, 今承兩序大眾推舉住持法席, 辭不獲已, 只得勉為其難, 第念這個(此)十方叢林道場, 乃我閩南首剎, 並恢復閩南佛學院, 任務非常艱鉅, 妙湛自慚才疏學淺, 難能勝此重任, 深望首領上座, 諸位執事, 大家齊努力, 勇挑此重擔).

Miaozhan stood up, holding the dragon staff, and said:

For many years, Buddhism has been in the autumn of decline; and it is a great pity that "the green and yellow do not meet."[4] It is my profound wish that the young monks studying the dharma become good successors and reinforce the work of their senior peers (佛教垂秋已有年, 青黃不接實堪憐, 深望青年學法者, 煉成龍象好接班).

He prostrated three times as the precentor chanted, "Examine the dharma of the Sakyamuni Buddha; the dharma of the Sakyamuni Buddha is just so (諦觀法王法, 法王法如是)."

Miaozhan exited the Dharma Hall accompanied by the ritualists and by the crowd. Heading south, he walked down the steps into the second courtyard. He turned east, walked to the vegetarian hall, and then south to the Great Buddha Hall. In the front of the hall, he turned west, crossing to the west corridor. Exiting through a door on the wall of the west corridor, he entered the west compound, which contained the academy and the abbot's residence. Turning north, he went to the abbot's residence. The two dozen abbots and priors lined the sides of its entrance to greet him. He entered from the main door. Inside, he bowed, burned three incense sticks, bowed again, and handed the dragon cloth to Yuanzhuo. They approached the abbot's seat together. Yuanzhuo then departed. Grasping the jeweled canopy, Miaozhan said, "I have entered the hall of the former worthies, and have ascended to the seat of the ancestral teachers. I will proclaim the teachings of the Buddha, and will walk on the rightful path (入先德之堂，登祖師之座. 宣佛祖之教，登入正之道)." When he finished speaking, devotees approached to give him flowers. This was the first time he received offerings as abbot of the Nanputuo Temple. The assembled clerics bowed three times.

Now, the mood lightened. People congratulated Miaozhan and took pictures with him in a festive tone. Then, everyone went to eat lunch in the temple. Most attendees went to the temple dining hall, while special guests dined in Puzhaolou Restaurant.

Engraved Couplets on Walls and Pillars

Couplets with joyful and hopeful words celebrating Miaozhan's ascension festooned the temple compound. The two strips for each couplet were placed next to or opposite each other on the doorways, pillars, and walls of the temple along the path he traversed. The largest numbers were at the Dharma Hall, where Miaozhan preached the dharma for the first time as abbot of Nanputuo Temple.

Couplets written by the students of the BCM were located at the most meaningful and visible places, such as the pillars in the center of the Dharma Hall. Many referred to the power of the teachings of the Buddha.

[right] Perfect integration of the phenomenal and profound, both form and intention, manifest at once across the universe. 妙相圓融即色即心遍十方而示現

[left] Essential Buddhahood ever-residing, neither coming nor going, forever endures the trials of ten thousand *kalpas*. 法身常住無去無來歷萬劫以長存

We interpret the right line to say that Buddhism naturally flourishes because it is compatible with reality. The left line said that problems in the world can be overcome because there are always people who preserve the teachings of the Buddha. This couplet meant that the abbot led in preserving Buddhist teachings.

Another couplet on the round pillars in the center of the Dharma Hall read:

[right] Dharma is the master of all Buddhas; may all beings on earth or in heaven submit to it. 法為諸佛所師一切人天皆供養

[left] The sutras are chanted across the five embodied forms; may all sages across the universe abide by them. 經通五人共說 十方聖賢盡皈依

The right line proclaimed the great need for the teachings of the Buddha to solve problems in the world. The left line said that the Buddha, disciples, deities, bodhisattvas, and reincarnations followed the Buddha's teachings and propagated them all over the world.

Many couplets hanging on the walls of the Dharma Hall were from eminent monks and devotees. The guest of honor, Mingyang, who represented the Buddhist Association of China, gave three couplets. One said:

[right] With virtuous wisdom and dignity, one achieves the Buddha path. 福慧莊嚴成無上道

[left] With compassionate mercy and joyful charity, one becomes a person of the Buddha. 慈悲喜拾度有緣人

In the right line, "fortune" signified the flourishing of Buddhist teachings, and "wisdom" referred to those who followed them. In the left line, "this predestined man" meant Miaozhan, who was becoming an abbot.

EXPANSION AND CONFLICT, 1989–1995

Zhao Puchu, who was not in attendance, wrote the most beautiful couplet. Befitting his status as president of the Buddhist Association of China, the couplet was on the wall directly behind the dharma seat where Miaozhan gave his first dharma talk.

[right] Ascendant to the lion's seat, [Miaozhan] proclaims the teachings of our school; under this heavenly rain, precious flowers bloom, their scent sublime and pure. 升獅子座宣揚宗風天雨寶花妙香潔

[left] Dwellers far and wide in the Purple Bamboo Woods aspire alike to ride the raft of mercy to the far shore; their minds clear and pure, like the moon reflected on placid water. 住紫竹林廣開慈筏心同水月湛清華

In the right line, "lion's seat" indicated the abbotship, and therefore Miaozhan, while the "teachings of the school" referred to the Linji sect of Chan Buddhism. This line congratulated Miaozhan for becoming abbot and expressed the hope that he would propagate the teachings. In the left line, "Purple Bamboo Woods" was the mythological place where Guanyin lived; in the context of the ceremony, it referred to Nanputuo Temple, underscoring the temple's importance for propagating the teachings of the Buddha. Additionally, the two lines contained the characters for Miaozhan's name, further honoring him; the thirteenth character of the right line was 妙 (*miao*), and its equivalent on the left was 湛 (*zhan*).

Some couplets in the Dharma Hall came from associations and temples. Two couplets were jointly presented by the Chaozhou Buddhist Association and Kaiyuan Zhenguo Chan Temple 開元鎮國禪寺 in Chaozhou, Guangdong Province. They were arrayed such that each couplet's first and second lines were hung on opposite walls.

[right] A flowery rain permeates the quiet Chan mind. 華雨禪心寂

[left] A fragrant cloud floats above the dharma seat. 香雲法座高

The right line refers to the teachings of the *Garland Sutra* (Ch. Huayan jing 華嚴經, Skt. Avataṃsaka sūtra), the most significant sutra in Chan

Buddhism. The sutra's name was indicated by the first character, which was 華 (hua). The left line indicated the beneficial effects of the abbot.

[right] Nominated by rulers of heaven and earth. 龍天推出
[left]   [Miaozhan] proclaims the dharma like a roaring lion. 作獅子吼

Other couplets hung in other locations in the temple. In the abbot's residence, another couplet from Mingyang read:

[right] So lofty his virtue, stern and sublime, as high as the mountain peaks. 妙嚴德望名山領
[left]   So placid is his mind, clear and pure, extending across Egret Islet. 湛淡襟懷鷺島揚

The "mountain peaks" in the right line referred to Wulao Peak behind Nanputuo Temple, while "Egret Islet" in the left line was the old name for Xiamen Island. By highlighting the beauty and completeness of the temple's physical setting, the couplet conveyed that an abbot in residence made the temple whole. Additionally, when combined, the first character of each line formed Miaozhan's name, increasing the beauty and significance of the couplet.

A couplet from the Heilongjiang Buddhist Association in northeast China, Miaozhan's home region, hung outside the guest office. It was the only one to mention patriotic religion.

[right] Love for country, love for religion, shining ever-brighter in partnership. 愛國愛教肝膽相照
[left]   Bathing the world in merciful light, the dharma wheel forever turns. 慈光普照法輪常轉

"Love country, love religion," as we explained in chapter 3, was a political slogan used to broadcast the fundamental precondition for the CPC's tolerance of religion in the PRC. It was necessary for the clerics to post a couplet with such a message at least once to show that they had not forgotten the party, even on such a momentous Buddhist occasion as the ascension of the abbot of a major temple. It is possible to interpret this couplet on the whole as an expression of conformity to state policy and ideology, and to construe the characters meaning "love country, love religion" to indicate the CPC's supremacy over religion. But from the perspective of Buddhism, the couplet could express an entirely different, even opposite, meaning. Although it started with the four characters "love country, love religion," it ended with the "dharma wheel eternally revolves." This could mean that states and political parties are ephemeral, whereas the teachings of the Buddha are eternal. Additionally, it is noteworthy that the couplet was posted outside the guest office rather than in the more religiously significant Dharma Hall where the abbot preached.

The rich and complex couplets and the dignity of the ceremony attended by both Buddhists and officials, including representatives from the Buddhist Association of China and other important temples in China, communicated the increased authority of Miaozhan as abbot. For the next six years, he exerted full authority as abbot to expand the temple as a center of Buddhist teachings in new directions while navigating local and national politics.

Battling Over Temple Wealth

On the eve of his ascension as abbot, Miaozhan notified the local state administration of his intention to reaffirm the *shifang conglin* system at Nanputuo Temple, or, in other words, clerical control over all its facilities. He proposed eliminating the Nanputuo Temple Management Committee established by the XRAB in 1982 to control the vegetarian restaurant and shops of the Nanputuo Temple Enterprise. Instead, the enterprise would be under clerical management. Not surprisingly, the local state administration opposed this move. Miaozhan's exertion of the full power of the abbot brought the growing tension between monks and officers into open conflict. This escalation drew the central state directly into the temple's affairs.

In describing the conflict from Miaozhan's ascension as abbot in 1989 to his death in 1995, we draw on two data sources: oral accounts of the conflict related to us by BAX officers and clerics, and unpublished documents—letters, reports, and meeting transcripts—circulated between the temple, the Xiamen Municipal People's Government, and the Buddhist

Association of China in Beijing. This section's four parts are in chronological order.

Central State Intervention

On October 1, 1989, Miaozhan sent a three-page report to Zhao Puchu detailing the local state's opposition to his new administrative plan for Nanputuo Temple and asking the Buddhist Association of China for help. The report was titled "Opinion on Restoring the *Shifang Conglin* Temple System at Nanputuo Temple, Xiamen" (關於廈門南普陀寺恢復十方叢林制度的意見). It began by describing local officials' reaction to his intention to eliminate the Nanputuo Temple Management Committee.

> Everyone [XRAB and Xiamen United Front Work Department officials] appeared very surprised [by my administrative plan]. They connoted their reasons for opposing it by saying, "After changing to the *shifang conglin* system, what to do with the large collective enterprise [the legal status of the temple]?" "What to do with the Nanputuo Temple Management Committee accounts?" "Are monks able to manage?" They even said, "The flourishing of Nanputuo Temple every year since 1979 is because of the correct direction of the Nanputuo Temple Management Committee. It cannot be removed. Doing so would deny the success of the XRAB." (Miaozhan 1989b)

The report characterized the Nanputuo Temple Management Committee as competing with the abbot's authority. It was especially critical of the committee's long-serving accountant, Mr. Z, a former official of the XRAB (see chapter 4).

> The Nanputuo Temple Management Committee is only concerned about financial income and does not consider things from the perspective of religious persons. When they [retired XRAB officials on the committee] see a piece of land or a building, they only think of constructing a hotel or a non-vegetarian restaurant or store. Because . . . [Mr. Z] is backed by the XRAB, he controls the personnel and the economic power . . . [of the Nanputuo Temple Enterprise]. He puts the

> needs of the temple and BCM . . . on the back burner. . . . and spends no energy on the work of religious education. Moreover, he arbitrarily sees clerics as only suitable for chanting sutras and performing services, and incapable of managing finances and business or even being taught to do so. (Miaozhan 1989b)

Miaozhan blamed the officials in the local party and government for hindering the development of the temple.

> We have spent years training clerics to assume responsibility for all kinds of temple work. If we do not open up opportunities and a future for them, we are putting the cart before the horse. If this situation is not corrected, how will it be possible for Chinese Buddhist talent to emerge? How will it be possible to promote Chinese Buddhism? We will never be able to control our fate with our own hands to develop the future of Buddhism in China. . . . We must reclaim all of our management authority. This is a most urgent matter. . . . To sum up, it is entirely a matter of the Xiamen United Front Work Department and XRAB using their authority to interfere. (Miaozhan 1989b)

Zhao Puchu arranged a meeting on July 18, 1990, in Beijing for Miaozhan to discuss the matter with officials in the State Administration of Religious Affairs. Zhao's proactivism showed the importance that the central state attached to Nanputuo Temple. Accompanied by Buddhist Association of China officers, Miaozhan met with the State Administration of Religious Affairs deputy director.[5] He presented his case for dissolving the Nanputuo Temple Management Committee. First, Miaozhan said, it created the unfortunate perception that the temple was a "government-run temple" (*guanban de simiao* 官辦的寺廟). For example, the temple's official seal read "Nanputuo Temple Management Committee" rather than "Nanputuo Temple." Miaozhan claimed this challenged the temple's religious legitimacy as a Buddhist temple. Second, the actions of a layperson (Mr. Z) on the committee violated state religious policy by "interfering in the economy and personnel of the Nanputuo Temple Enterprise" and "blindly developing the enterprise" without considering the temple's religious character (Zhongguo fojiao xiehui 1990). His point was that the

Nanputuo Temple Enterprise was increasingly operating as an independent enterprise without concern for the religious character of the temple. After listening to Miaozhan, the deputy director affirmed that the Nanputuo Temple Enterprise was an inalienable part of the temple. But rather than eliminating the Nanputuo Temple Management Committee, he determined that the special status of the Nanputuo Temple Enterprise should be formalized by legally leasing it to Mr. Z.[6]

Five months later, on November 21, 1990, Zhao Puchu visited Nanputuo Temple to discuss implementing the solution proposed at the July meeting by the deputy director of the State Administration of Religious Affairs.[7] A heated exchange of views occurred at a meeting attended by Zhao, monks, BAX officers, and officials from the XRAB and Fujian Religious Affairs Bureau. Miaozhan and XRAB officials justified their opposing views by referencing state religious policies. Miaozhan pointed to a "contradiction" between, on the one hand, the self-management of the temple and, on the other, the presence of the Nanputuo Temple Management Committee. He claimed the committee's existence violated the principle of religious self-management in Document 19 and demanded its elimination. In response, the XRAB deputy director denied that there was any contradiction. He claimed that the Nanputuo Temple Management Committee was necessary for communication between the temple and local government. He said that many international tourists and dignitaries visited the temple, requiring coordination with police and other agencies to ensure their safety. Additionally, the XRAB deputy director said that clerics could not handle money, so the lay members on the Nanputuo Temple Management Committee were necessary to manage the Nanputuo Temple Enterprise. In his view, the committee fully accorded with state religious policy and the Buddhist Association of China guidelines for temple management.[8]

Finally, an agreement was reached for implementing the solution that had been proposed earlier in Beijing.[9] It called for replacing the Nanputuo Temple Management Committee with a new entity composed entirely of clerics to manage the temple. The new organization was called the Nanputuo Temple Affairs Committee (Nanputuo si siwu weiyuanhui 南普陀寺寺務委員會), its director was the abbot, and other members were the clerics serving as department heads in the temple. As for the Nanputuo Temple Enterprise, it would become a financially independent unit inside the temple with its own seal and bank account and renamed the Nanputuo Temple Business Agency (Nanputuo si shiye she 南普陀寺事業社) (we continue to refer to it as "Nanputuo Temple Enterprise" to avoid the confusion of multiple names). It was leased to its manager, Mr. Z, for three years at an annual fee of 140,000 yuan. This solution gave both parties a partial victory. The clerics obtained the dissolution of the Nanputuo Temple Management Committee while the XRAB, working through its proxy Mr. Z, retained control of the Nanputuo Temple Enterprise.

But the solution effectively split the institutional space of the temple. The leasing of the Nanputuo Temple Enterprise turned a commercial entity intended for the self-sufficiency of the temple (as stipulated in Document 19) into a privately managed firm operating by collective enterprise regulations and run for the profit of laypersons. This split was reflected in the opening of separate bank accounts and seals for the temple and the enterprise. Mr. Z no longer needed the abbot's approval for expenditures, and thus had a freer hand.

Detaching the Enterprise

Upon leasing the Nanputuo Temple Enterprise, Mr. Z deepened his control over it by detaching it from the temple.[10] First, he renamed the Nanputuo Temple Enterprise as Nanputuo Business (Nanputuo shiye she 南普陀事業社). This name, printed on all enterprise shopping bags, did not indicate that the enterprise was part of a Buddhist temple. Then in 1991 Mr. Z secretly changed the name of the enterprise's legal representative (*fa ren daibiao* 法人代表) from the abbot to himself. The clerics only learned of this a year later when they happened to see a list of new legal representatives of Xiamen business firms published in the local newspaper. Miaozhan protested to the XRAB that this move was illegitimate because the temple owned the enterprise, so the legal representative had to be a cleric. The XRAB dismissed his protest, claiming that there was no rule specifying that a cleric had to fill this position.

Mr. Z used his new authority as the legal representative of the Nanputuo Temple Enterprise to expand its business scope. He obtained a license to open a department store that sold toys, clothes, home appliances, and other commodities that had nothing to do with Buddhism. He ignored Miaozhan in matters relating to the enterprise and stopped sending monthly financial reports to the clerics on the Nanputuo Temple Affairs Committee. When Mr. Z needed approval for a matter, he got it from the XRAB. These moves greatly angered the clerics. They saw dropping the character for "temple" in the new name of the enterprise as severing it from the temple. They likened this to the Cultural Revolution ideology that had denied religion. Furthermore, they saw Mr. Z's legal representation of the enterprise as violating the principle of clerical ownership that the State Religious Affair Bureau had reaffirmed in July 1990. Finally, they saw Mr. Z's actions as an affront to the abbot's authority and a further challenge to the temple's integrity as a site of Buddhist teachings.

Mr. Z continued to corner the monks to acquire temple resources as described in chapter 4. For example, in 1992, a building in the east compound containing a shop of the Nanputuo Temple Enterprise needed repairs. So, the clerics asked Mr. Z to temporarily move the shop to another building. Mr. Z refused by counterdemanding that Miaozhan allocate land in the temple's front yard for a new building to house the Nanputuo Temple Enterprise headquarters and a department store. Miaozhan offered a strip of land by the East Mountain Gate along the wall separating the temple from Xiamen University. Mr. Z promised that the enterprise would pay all construction costs, and he obtained a 240,000-yuan loan to erect the new building by the East Mountain Gate and repair the old building in the east compound. But he inserted a clause into the loan contract that these buildings were for the exclusive use of the Nanputuo Temple Enterprise. Miaozhan saw this as a transfer of property rights and insisted that Mr. Z cancel the loan—which he did only after extracting a guarantee from Miaozhan that the temple would pay for the new building by the East Mountain Gate.

The XRAB continued to back Mr. Z in various ways. One was to raise his status. In 1993, it nominated him as a member of the Xiamen People's Political Consultative Conference and, the following year, arranged his selection as a province-level model worker. These positions increased Mr. Z's networks and status. Miaozhan objected that these actions were illegitimate because the enterprise was part of the temple, so Mr. Z's nominations and awards required the abbot's approval. But XRAB countered that there was no such requirement and also moved to undermine the BAX by targeting several former XRAB former officials who worked there. They had served on the Nanputuo Temple Management Committee in the early 1980s, become sympathetic to Miaozhan, and were hired to work in the BAX. They used their insider knowledge of local state administration to give Miaozhan and the clerics very effective counsel in handling the XRAB and Mr. Z. In 1993, during the quadrennial election for BAX officers, the XRAB engineered their removal by declaring that CPC members could not work in the BAX. But the XRAB strategy seemed to backfire. The newly elected BAX officers were all young monks who were very critical of the XRAB and were not afraid to accuse its officials of violating the constitutional rights of clerics and the religious policy.

Resistance of the Monks

In 1994, as Mr. Z's lease for the Nanputuo Temple Enterprise was about to expire, the monks began making plans for assuming its management.[11] The Nanputuo Temple Affairs Committee approved a resolution in July titled "Strengthening the Construction of Nanputuo Temple and Maintaining Clerics' Autonomous Management of the Temple and Sovereignty" (加強南普陀寺自身建設, 維護僧人自主管理寺廟和主權) (referred to as the July Resolution). It declared that the Nanputuo Temple Affairs Committee had authority over all matters inside the temple and that the enterprise was an inalienable part of the temple. It specified rules for managing the enterprise, including clerical selection of the lessee and legal representative. To support these rules, the July Resolution cited state religious policies that reaffirmed the principle of religious self-management. One was "Methods for the Management of National Han Buddhist Temples" (全國漢傳佛教寺院管理辦法), adopted by the Buddhist Association of China on October 21, 1993. The other was "Rules for Managing Religious Activity Sites" (宗教活動場所管理條例), issued by the State Administration of Religious Affairs on January 31, 1994.

The July Resolution shocked local officials. Realizing that the resolution challenged XRAB control over the Nanputuo Temple Enterprise, they sprang into action to get the monks to retract it. On July 11, they ordered monks to study a speech by Jiang Zemin that called upon social groups to support the state in order to ensure social stability. The monks saw this as ideological intimidation and refused to retract the resolution.

On July 15, the XRAB convened another meeting, attended by an official from the Xiamen Municipal Industry and Commerce Bureau, which issued business licenses. He announced that monks could not serve as the legal representatives of business firms. The clerics countered that they only wanted to decide who the representative should be. Again they refused to retract the July Resolution. So, the XRAB officials stepped up the intimidation by meeting individually with each monk on the Nanputuo Temple Affairs Committee. They warned that the monks would be accused of disobeying the state if they did not retract the July Resolution. Still, the monks stood their ground.

Suddenly, on July 22, the XRAB sent a car to bring Miaozhan to the XRAB headquarters, insisting he come alone. There, officials rebuked him for causing problems between the XRAB and Nanputuo clerics. Then they made him sign a summary of the meeting that blamed him for the problems. The summary read:

> The XRAB met with Miaozhan on the afternoon of July 22 to further discuss the actions taken by the Nanputuo Temple Affairs Committee since the beginning of July to handle the problem of the Nanputuo Temple Business [Nanputuo Temple Enterprise]. These actions violate the principles of the minutes presided over by the State Administration of Religious Affairs when it came to Xiamen in 1990 [the December meeting]. The Nanputuo Temple Affairs Committee has adopted irregular organizational activities, disregard for the government, and persistence in sticking to its old ways. This wrong behavior has obstructed the coordinating work of the government bureau responsible for administration. Venerable Miao has indicated his acceptance of this well-intentioned criticism and will make corrections. To ensure smooth progress in this coordinating work, he has again agreed to the following four principles about handling the enterprise problem and, moreover, takes responsibility for good work regarding the monks at the temple.[12]

The four principles stated that (1) the initiative in solving all matters concerning the Nanputuo Temple Enterprise lay with the XRAB; (2) the principles agreed on in the 1990 meeting at Nanputuo Temple were correct; (3) emphasis should be on unity and harmony and avoiding destabilizing actions; and (4) the two sides (XRAB and Nanputuo Temple) should work together as one. Taken together, these principles negated the July Resolution. XRAB officials sent Miaozhan back to the temple with instructions to return the next day. He returned to XRAB headquarters as directed, this time accompanied by six monks. They insisted that the document Miaozhan had signed was full of Cultural Revolution hyperbole. They objected to the characterization of the monks' actions as violating state religious policy. So, the officials deleted the third and fourth sentences of the meeting summary while retaining the four principles that negated the July Resolution. Miaozhan signed this revised document. Thereupon, the XRAB renewed Mr. Z's lease of the Nanputuo Temple Enterprise for another three years.

On September 10, 1994, the BAX sent a report to Zhao Puchu describing the conflict between the clerics and the local government. It linked the conflict to the vagueness of the religious policy by describing how differently the clerics and officials interpreted the rules for managing religious activity sites.

> The temple deacon says, "To thoroughly implement Document 145 issued by Premier Li Peng 李鹏 on October 11, 1994, we [BAX] think that the bureau responsible for administering religion [XRAB] did not obtain the agreement of the Nanputuo Temple Affairs Committee and the abbot. The unauthorized signing of the application for the legal representative of the Nanputuo Temple Enterprise is wrong and violates the spirit of the central state's religious policy." [But] the XRAB director says, "Premier Li Peng's Document 145 only contains principles and is abstract. It is not as concrete as a public security ordinance. It can be interpreted this way or that way. It does not mention that the abbot must be the legal representative of the temple."[13]

The BAX report concluded in an exasperated tone, stating that "if it is possible to have somewhat more detailed regulations, this would significantly reduce trouble in the future."[14] It requested that the Buddhist Association of China and the State Administration of Religious Affairs come to the temple to resolve the problem.

Uprising of the Monks

In May 1995, the conflict turned violent.[15] The spark was a plan drafted by the monks to manage the Nanputuo Temple Enterprise after regaining control. When the XRAB learned of the plan, it moved to block its implementation by invoking security concerns.[16] On May 17, it called a snap meeting in Puzhaolou Restaurant to discuss the enterprise. Participants included XRAB officials, Xiamen Public Security Bureau officials accompanied by twelve policemen, Mr. Z, the monks on the Nanputuo Temple Affairs Committee, BCM teachers, and BAX officers. The monks were suspicious because the meeting had been called when Miaozhan was away in Beijing. When a monk began to film the proceedings, the XRAB director ordered him to stop. So the monk hid the camera under his robes and continued filming.

The XRAB director began the meeting by announcing a new system to manage the Nanputuo Temple Enterprise.[17] It called for its employees to elect its manager, who would then be its legal representative. The director justified this arrangement by referring to the "Village and Township Collectively Owned Enterprise Regulations" (城鎮集體所有制企業條例) issued by the State Council in 1990. He announced a new "three-party management" system for the enterprise that consisted of personnel from the XRAB, Xiamen Public Security Bureau, and the monks. He explained that this was necessary to ensure the safety of the tourists and dignitaries who dined at the restaurant. As the director spoke, he waved a piece of paper, saying that it was the approval for the new management system issued by the Xiamen Municipal People's Government. When monks demanded to see the document, he refused to show it and abruptly ended the meeting.

The monks were incensed: the new management system deemed the purpose of the Nanputuo Temple Enterprise to be for entertaining tourists rather than furthering the economic self-sufficiency of the temple, and thus had denied the monks' claim to control the enterprise. The monks streamed out of Puzhaolou Restaurant and locked the gate of the east compound to prevent officials from leaving. A standoff ensued between the officials inside the building and the monks outside who surrounded it. The officials demanded that the monks on the Nanputuo Temple Affairs Committee enter the building one by one for questioning. A table was set up in a second-floor room for this purpose. The prior went first. As soon as he entered the building, police locked the door to prevent other monks from following. Immediately, the monks rang the temple gong in a prearranged signal of alarm. Hundreds of young BCM students rushed over and swarmed the courtyard. Smashing windows, they entered the building and ran up the stairs to rescue the prior. Police officers were guarding the doors to the room, so the monks went back outside. They made large wall posters demanding that the local officials observe their constitutional rights and self-management, and they hung the posters outside the temple walls within public view.[18] Later that afternoon, a police force swept down from Wulao Peak behind the temple to free the trapped officials.

The XRAB labeled the incident a "political affair" (*zhengzhi shijian* 政治事件) because the clerics had disobeyed local state officials and used force against them. This was a serious matter. The police took the prior and several other monks away for questioning. Miaozhan rushed back from Beijing, and Zhao Puchu promptly dispatched a team from the Buddhist Association of China to investigate the matter. The team interviewed monks and viewed the wall posters. It concluded that the incident was not a political affair because the monks had not criticized the CPC or the government but only asked the XRAB to respect the constitution and religious policy. It recommended that no monks be punished.

A few days later, the monks wrote a strong letter of protest to the Xiamen Municipal People's Government blaming the "nondemocratic dictatorial style" of the XRAB officials for fomenting the violence at the meeting. "Some clerics raised difficult questions . . . which were quite reasonable. But [XRAB officials] used such threats as 'causing trouble' and '6/4' [Tiananmen Square protest] to cover up their illegal goals. This incited the fierce dissatisfaction and criticism by all deacons and clerics of Nanputuo Temple."[19] The letter accused XRAB officials of violating the constitution and religious policy, and of being personally corrupt.

> The XRAB wants to . . . strengthen its leadership of the Nanputuo Temple Enterprise. There is a reason for this. To put it directly, there is a widespread saying, "Nanputuo Temple is a piece of choice fatty meat. Everybody wants to find some excuse to take a bite." This is precisely the desire of the XRAB in regard to strengthening its

leadership of the Nanputuo Temple Enterprise. Do you now see how the real power is held in the hands of . . . [Mr. Z] and his group of friends and relatives? This is corrupt politics; those who submit will prosper, and those who resist will perish. When the child of a leading cadre has a birthday, the enterprise pays for their birthday party at a restaurant. The enterprise gives gifts of wine and cigarettes to cadres and pays their expenses to go abroad and travel to scenic spots in China under the innocuous label of "study tour." So, it is not surprising that the bureau in charge of religious matters in Xiamen is clinging to the enterprise to the very end regardless of CPC and national policies. . . . The central state is now trying to root out corruption by looking into its underlying causes and symptoms. In our view, if the government authorities that manage religion are allowed to continue to stick their hands into the choice piece of fatty meat that is the Nanputuo Temple Enterprise, this will corrupt the party and government cadres. The soiled reputation of the party and government will be a big disaster that harbingers the decadence of our party and country. The Nanputuo Temple Enterprise should be returned to the monks to manage. We will do better and cleaner management that will bring honor to Xiamen.[20]

The letter concluded by making six demands of local officials: (1) recognize the Nanputuo Temple Enterprise as part of the temple and under the authority of clerics; (2) protect the temple from outside interference and respect the feelings and legal rights of clerics; (3) make the abbot the legal representative of the Nanputuo Temple Enterprise; (4) recognize that the enterprise manager should be first chosen by the Nanputuo Temple Affairs Committee and then reported to the XRAB; (5) recognize that all people working in the temple [including employees of the Nanputuo Temple Enterprise] were under the management authority of the clerics; and (6) revoke the government notice authorizing the XRAB's new three-party management system.

On June 16, a month after the affair, Zhao Puchu sent a letter to the Fujian Religious Affairs Bureau supporting the clerics. He wrote: "I feel that the contradiction between the temple and the management system of its business firm is a disastrous and long-standing problem. It is mainly due to the excessive interference of the city authorities responsible for religious work and their attempts to do things that others should do" (Zhao 1995). This letter drew on phrases in Document 19 to accuse the XRAB officials of violating the principle of religious self-management stipulated in the document. In his letter he called the new management plan a self-serving scheme that fanned conflict by violating the monks' property rights. But the letter had little effect. The matter of the Nanputuo Temple Enterprise remained unresolved and was soon overshadowed by Miaozhan's death and administrative turmoil, as we describe in chapter 6.

The conflict split Nanputuo into two institutional spaces: the space of religion and the space of collective enterprise. In this section, we have described how the local state administration used the collective enterprise policies to avoid claims of clerical self-management that existed in the institutional space of religion. But in other matters, it encouraged the clerics to move outside of the space of religion, especially in the case of the new charity foundation we describe next.

Expansion of the Temple

Miaozhan expanded the physical and semiotic space through multiple projects at Nanputuo Temple. He waited almost two years after his ascension to begin this work because political tension lingered after the Tiananmen Square protest. We describe four of the most significant projects in this section; the Nanputuo Temple Charity Foundation, the BCM nuns campus, the Meditation Hall, and the temple's twin eleven-story Longevity Pagodas. The completion of these projects created new possibilities for Nanputuo Temple to express Buddhist teachings, including outside the physical space of its compound in the case of the charity foundation. As they worked on the projects, the clerics navigated the local state administration's efforts to expand tourist facilities at the temple, and lingering security concerns after the Tiananmen Square protest.

Nanputuo Temple Charity Foundation

The Nanputuo Temple Charity Foundation opened on December 14, 1994, as the first religious charity in the PRC.[21] It gave the clerics new uses for alms to the temple, which were growing larger in the prospering society, by converting them into grants to other nonprofit charity providers. The opening of the foundation met the CPC's demand for the "adaptation of religion to socialist society" by using Buddhism to provide social services. At the same time, Buddhists saw it as propagating the Buddhist teachings of compassion, in keeping with Taixu's call for Buddhism to address people's needs. The foundation's mission statement borrowed Miaozhan's saying: "Do not forget the many among us who suffer hardship" (wu wang shishang ku ren duo 勿忘世上苦人多). Additionally, the foundation was helpful to clerics by establishing a link with the Xiamen Civil Affairs Bureau, which administered charity foundations. This reduced the dependency of clerics on the XRAB and likely forestalled its attempts to steer alms toward tourism projects.

The foundation was located at the front of the temple's west compound, making it easily accessed by people from the front yard. It had a staff of thirty-five persons, mostly devotees and believers, who administered the foundation's donations and grants, medical activities, and Buddhist gift shop under the leadership of clerics (NSZ, vol. 2, 278–279). In its first year, five thousand domestic and overseas members paid its nominal membership fee and donated to fund disaster relief, orphanages, nursing homes, schools in poor areas, and an onsite clinic. Many people came to obtain the foundation's medical services at its clinic, which had the status of a city-level hospital. When entering the clinic, people stepped into a Buddhist temple, experiencing Buddhist compassion as if it were free medical care and at-cost medicine provided by trained clerics and retired doctors. It had Eastern and Western medicine departments specializing in orthopedics, acupuncture, massage, gynecology, and pediatrics, as well as an electrocardiography room and pharmacy. Additionally, the clinic offered outreach treatment in nursing homes, orphanages, handicapped centers, and in poor regions.

In 1999 we gained insight into the clerics working at the clinic by interviewing a nun who was a provider of Chinese traditional health care. She was born in 1961 in Liaoning Province.[22] When her parents were diagnosed with cancer, she became a nurse to care for them. In search of a cure, she visited Pushou Temple 普壽寺, a nunnery on Mount Wutai. Her audience there with the abbess convinced her to become a Buddhist nun. She visited many temples before deciding to enroll in 1985 in the BCM's four-year program. After graduating, she taught in the school and supervised the female students. But she found the position stressful and jumped at the opportunity offered by the famous devotee Nan Huaijin 南懷瑾 (1918–2012) to sponsor six nuns from BCM to study in the five-year traditional medicine course at Xiamen University. After completing her medical studies, she worked in the foundation clinic. She aspired to get a doctorate in religious studies at the Buddhist-affiliated University of the West (formerly Hsi Lai University) in Los Angeles and dedicate herself to using acupuncture as a low-cost medical treatment for poor communities. Personal stories like hers exemplify the foundation's reach within Buddhism and beyond.

Significantly, the foundation was positioned outside the institutional space of religion. It was legally registered with the Xiamen Civil Affairs Bureau as a "social organization" (*shehui tuanti* 社會團體) for the purpose of charity work, despite being located inside the temple and based on Buddhist teachings. This institutional positioning as "charity" created new possibilities to express Buddhist teachings beyond the religious policy's confinement of Buddhism as "religion" to the temple's physical space. This potential can be seen in a ceremony held in May 1995 at an elementary school in Xiamen where Miaozhan presented a gift from the foundation of twenty thousand books (*Cishan* 1995a, 27). Resplendent in the brilliant red and gold robes of a Buddhist abbot, he gave a speech to students on the importance of study. It was clear to all present that the charity was Buddhist because the foundation's name included the characters of Nanputuo Temple, and Miaozhan was a Buddhist monk. Moreover, his speech was like a dharma talk, even though he delivered it in a public school.

Another possibility was disseminating Buddhism through media formats that covered charity news. The foundation's news journal, *Cishan* (*Charity*), was not classified as a religious publication, therefore it could be distributed outside the temple even though its content was devoted to the activities and pictures of the temple and abbot. For example, the journal published news of a ceremony at Nanputuo Temple held on September 2, 1995, to acknowledge the foundation's donation of 65,000 yuan and 6,000 pieces of clothing to flood-stricken Jiangxi Province. The article included a photo of Buddhist clerics and state officials in front of the Great Buddha Hall under a large banner proclaiming, "Ceremony to warmly hand over donations from the Xiamen SEZ to an old revolutionary base area" (*Cishan* 1995b, 19).[23] Word of this remarkable image—a Buddhist temple representing the Xiamen SEZ as it offered charity to a revered CPC historical site—circulated outside the temple through *Cishan* and the journal's regular coverage of charity news likely brought more attention to the event. Furthermore a television camera crew was visible in the photo filming the ceremony; this suggests that it may even have been a news broadcast on the state media.

Notably, one of the largest grant recipients was the CPC-affiliated Project Hope (Xiwang gongcheng 希望工程), initiated by the Communist Youth League in 1989 to support schools in poor rural areas. Project Hope quickly became the largest nongovernmental welfare provider in the PRC. It was portrayed in the state-controlled media as an expression of the CPC's concern for poor people and received positive international media coverage; this helped repair the image of the CPC after the violent suppression of the Tiananmen Square protest. Because of the project's mission, Nanputuo monks felt that granting money to Project Hope expressed Buddhist compassion. There was some gap, however, between donors' intentions and the foundation's grants. In table 5.1, showing the second-quarter statement from April to June 2000, "donor earmarks"

TABLE 5.1 Donation Flow at Nanputuo Temple Charity Foundation, April–June 2000

DONOR			FOUNDATION		
Earmark	Number	Yuan	Grant	Number	Yuan
Charity	811	115,000	Facility construction*	10	246,000
Sutra printing	100	30,000	Project Hope	47	88,000
Releasing life	124	20,000	Medical care	41	41,000
Project Hope	3	2,000	Poverty alleviation**	28	12,000
Total	1,038	167,000	Misc.	1	8,000
			Total	127	395,000

Figures calculated from data in *Cishan* (2000, no. 2: 3). The currency amounts in yuan are approximate.
 *Facility construction involved schools and orphanages, including one elementary school in a Buddhist temple.
 **Poverty alleviation included several allocations for the travel expenses of poor clerics.

are the four projects that individual and corporate donors chose to fund, and "foundation grants" are the projects that received grants from the foundation.

Remarkably, while less than 1 percent of donors chose to send funds to Project Hope, it received a third of the foundation's grants and 25 percent of its funds.[24] We asked monks and devotees why so few people earmarked their donations to Project Hope. They mentioned several reasons, including that people believed they could not receive Buddhist merit by donating to the CPC and feared CPC officials might use the money for their personal benefit. The grants by the Nanputuo Temple Charity Foundation to Project Hope were a particular "adaptation of religion to socialist society" whereby people's donations to accrue Buddhist merit could help burnish the image of the CPC.

Buddhist College of Minnan Campus for Nuns

The 1996 opening of a special campus for nuns at the BCM was another of Miaozhan's outstanding achievements and a reflection of the support from overseas Chinese donors. The new campus solved housing and other logistical problems for nuns who had previously needed to live and study in several local temples. Its founding also indicated a surge in the number of female applicants, who generally had better educational backgrounds than male applicants (see table 5.2). The dean when we visited in 2000 was a nun from Heilongjiang Province 黑龍江省 in north China who graduated in 1991 from the BCM; most of the other teachers were also BCM graduates. Of the one hundred students in each class, most had graduated from high school; some who had graduated from college and even from other academies, such as the Sichuan Buddhist Institute for Nuns (Sichuan nizhong foxue yuan 四川尼眾佛學院) at Tiexiang Temple 鐵像寺

TABLE 5.2 Student Matriculation in BCM

Entering Students	1985	1987	1989	1991	1993	1995
Monks	16	18	14	20	12	29
Nuns	23	28	29	30	45	85
Total	39	46	43	50	57	114

Source: Nanputuo Temple website (accessed 2011, no longer available)

and the Fujian Buddhist Academy, had come to BCM to further their Buddhist education. Their presence reflected the excellent resources and high quality of the modern Buddhist education at the BCM. In contrast to other academies devoted to educating nuns, the dean said that the BCM "offered a broader range of classes and is not that separated from contemporary society. . . . Students have to deal with external matters after graduating, so we encourage them to have contact with many things."[25] The nuns section continued to closely coordinate with the monks' section at Nanputuo Temple by using a common curriculum, sharing lay teachers for secular subjects, and holding joint entrance exams.

Miaozhan named the campus Zizhulin 紫竹林 after a convent on Mount Putuo. It occupied a 1.8-hectare site in a beautiful natural setting next to a public park about six kilometers from Nanputuo Temple. We heard that the site previously had a small temple named Dongneiyan 董内岩 that the People's Liberation Army had used as a military storehouse. The campus, constructed over two years from 1993, had the facilities of a Buddhist temple, including a mountain gate, Great Buddha Hall, Merit Hall, guest prefect office, dining hall, and housing for resident clerics, as well as a library, student dormitories, and classroom building.

During the construction process some disputes arose involving land use and tourism. The Xiamen Parks and Forestry Bureau, which managed the adjacent park, had included some Zizhulin land in its plan to upgrade the surrounding park. Heated negotiations ensued over several plots: on the one intended for the school's library, the bureau planned a teahouse, knowing that the Buddhist buildings on campus would provide an attractive backdrop. On another plot in front of the campus, originally intended for a lotus pond, the bureau planned a parking lot. Additionally, the bureau wanted to build a public restroom by the outside wall of the temple's kitchen. Miaozhan fought these plans by repeatedly visiting government bureaus, not only to explain the need for the new school campus but also to remind them that the land had historically "housed" a temple. The XRAB supported the clerics because its officials understood the importance of the new campus.

Further complications arose from requests by major donors for private apartments on the campus. Miaozhan approved a request by the main donor, a Singapore family in the construction business. The family set up an ancestral altar in the apartment, although they rarely stayed there. When we interviewed them, the donors explained that the ancestral hall in their village in Minnan had been ransacked during the Cultural Revolution and the bones went missing. Years later, a person claiming to have the bones approached the family seeking payment for their return. The family saw the campus as a safe haven for the recovered bones and expected the nuns to perform daily ancestral rites.[26] The nuns objected to worshiping ancestors in a temple intended for a Buddhist academy and to allocating space for a private residence for laypersons. Some nuns asserted that the apartment was their dormitory by sleeping in it at night, at which point the family relinquished the apartment. Another case involved the rector of a nuns academy in Taiwan who asked for the return of her donation after Miaozhan denied her request for an apartment.

Meditation Hall

Miaozhan's vision for Nanputuo Temple included a meditation hall to educate young monks in the BCM. This reflected his experience of practicing Chan meditation from 1942 to 1945 under Laiguo at Gaoming Temple, a center of Chan Buddhism. For Miaozhan, building such a hall would make it possible to carry on the tradition and repay Laiguo's benevolence. Planning for a hall in the west compound behind the charity foundation began in the late 1980s. The XRAB opposed the project, claiming that the hall's large size would spoil photo shots of the temple for tourists. But the Xiamen vice mayor in charge of construction had already approved the plan, so the XRAB officials invoked national security claims to derail it. These claims, made in the political tension immediately after the Tiananmen Square protest, gained traction because the funding for the Longevity Pagodas—the Nanputuo project we discuss next—was linked to the devotee Nan Huaijin. The CPC viewed Nan, a prominent scholar who had helped popularize Buddhism, with suspicion because he had been a member of the Nationalist Party and ROC military officer who went to Taiwan in 1949.

Nan Huaijin's involvement in the pagoda project began in 1986 as he attempted to forge ties with Buddhists in the PRC. He started with Nanputuo, since the temple was one of the first to recover and thus approachable because of its overseas connections. (As we explained earlier in the section about the Nanputuo Temple Charity Foundation, he contributed funds for six nuns studying at the BCM to study traditional medicine at Xiamen University.) Then, in spring 1989, just before the Tiananmen Square protest, a wealthy Taiwanese disciple of Nan visited Nanputuo Temple. Miaozhan described his vision for a meditation hall to the disciple, who offered to pay for its construction. The disciple told Miaozhan about modern temples in Taiwan and Japan with meditation halls and other facilities used by clerics and laypersons. He explained that Japanese politicians who visited temples in Japan to relax in their meditation halls went on to become patrons of the temples. Intrigued by these ideas, Miaozhan expanded his vision to a complex that included the hall, dormitories, a large auditorium, and a cafeteria. Nan's disciple hired a well-known Taiwan architect, whose tour of temples in Japan provided the appropriate inspiration, to design the Nanputuo complex.

In late 1989, Miaozhan unveiled the blueprints in the abbot's residence at a showing attended by the Taiwan donor and architect. The XRAB deputy director came and derisively commented that the design looked like a Japanese temple and that the meditation hall was just a place for lazy monks to sleep. He took photos of the blueprints and left without acknowledging the Taiwan guests. A few days later, agents from the Ministry of State Security, which tracked foreign spies, visited the temple to inquire about the businessman and the architect. Then, the XRAB prohibited Miaozhan from accepting funds from the businessman, concerned not only by his Taiwan connection but also about Nan Huaijin's background. Miaozhan could not object, considering the heightened concerns of the state that had surfaced just after the Tiananmen Square protest about hostile foreign actors using religion to destabilize China. The project came to a halt.

Then, in 1991, Nan Huaijin contacted Miaozhan, offering to pay for the meditation hall. The timing was propitious. The state's security concerns had lessened, and Nan Huaijin's standing in the eyes of the CPC had risen. He was now an investor in a large railway project in Guangdong Province and the host of secret talks in his Hong Kong residence, between PRC officials and Taiwan politicians, to further rapprochement. The XRAB deputy director said he would approve the meditation hall only if its height was lower than the Great Buddha Hall. To deflect the deputy director's concern, Miaozhan hired a famous specialist in ancient Chinese architecture as a project consultant. The consultant favored the taller building, and the project went forward with the planned height of the meditation hall. But to forestall further XRAB demands, Miaozhan dropped the idea of a dormitory, auditorium, and cafeteria and hired the city government architecture office to design a meditation hall in traditional Chinese style. The hall was consecrated in February 1994 at a ceremony attended by Nan Huaijin and hundreds of Buddhists from Taiwan and overseas. Nan Huaijin gave a talk attended by many students from Xiamen University, much to the consternation of university authorities.[27]

Longevity Pagodas

In the early 1990s, the front yard of Nanputuo Temple was still an eyesore of dusty earth and weeds. As part of his restoration design, Miaozhan had the Lotus Pond refilled and built two new Buddhist pagodas in front of the temple. Common among temples in north China, pagodas symbolically house the Buddha's remains. Although Nanputuo had never before included pagodas, Miaozhan, being a northern monk, thought of them as necessary structures to complete the temple's overall plan. In 1993, construction started on two eleven-story white Longevity Pagodas (Wanshou ta 萬壽塔). Funding came from a Hong Kong devotee who ran a Chinese medicine firm and considered himself Miaozhan's disciple.

Opposition from the XRAB, however, threatened the project. Just as the construction crew broke ground, the XRAB's deputy director issued a statement calling the pagodas harmful for tourism. The concrete plaza to anchor the pagodas would block tour buses, he charged, and the pagodas' height would disrupt photo shots of the temple. He asked the Xiamen City Planning Commission to suspend the project's construction license, demanding the plan be changed to a single, shorter pagoda with a smaller base. An officer in the BAX explained to us the gap in the perspectives of the officials and clerics.

> Those officials in the XRAB do not understand temple construction and design but still want to give their opinion. So, this always becomes an obstacle. They are happy if you ask their opinion; if you don't, they are angry.... Officials make judgments based on common perceptions of attractive and unattractive. But Elder Miao uses the perspective of religion. If there is a temple, there should be a

pagoda. So, building the pagoda reveals the difference in perceptions of the government officials in religious work and people who believe in religion. It also shows that government personnel in charge of religion greatly lack knowledge of Buddhism.[28]

The deputy director's attempt to thwart the project may have also been a move to regain XRAB oversight of new temple construction. As we described in chapter 4, in the late 1980s Miaozhan had developed a tie with the Xiamen vice mayor in charge of construction, who let the abbot submit plans for religious buildings to him for direct approval, bypassing the XRAB. In 1993, shortly after the vice mayor approved the pagodas, he was arrested on sweeping corruption charges (Lam 1994, 2–12), creating an opening for the XRAB to reassert authority over temple construction.

Miaozhan moved to surmount XRAB opposition. He visited the Xiamen City Planning Commission director, who appeared flattered by the abbot's attention. The director admitted that he had halted construction only at the XRAB's request but knew little of the actual situation. So, he agreed to Miaozhan's request to evaluate the pagoda construction plans. In October 1993, Miaozhan convened a group of engineers; officials from the XRAB, culture and tourism bureaus of the Xiamen City People's Government; and architects (including the Xiamen University architecture department chairperson) to visit the site of the planned pagodas. The group concurred that Miaozhan's plan accorded with traditional Buddhist architecture, and a large base was necessary to prevent the pagodas from sinking. Construction resumed, and the Longevity Pagodas were consecrated in 1994. This episode shows how the XRAB's persistence in promoting tourism extended to demanding changes in the semiotic and physical space of the temple. It also showed the clerics' growing skill to parry these demands by lobbying the local state administration and using outside experts.

These multiple projects expanding the physical and semiotic space of Nanputuo Temple overlapped with the institutional space. The positioning of the Nanputuo Temple Charity Foundation outside the institutional space of religion opened new possibilities to propagate Buddhist teachings while the other three projects expanded Buddhist teachings in the temple. The temple expansion was satisfying to clerics, but the conflicts with the local state administration disillusioned some of the young BCM graduates staffing the temple offices.

Transnational Movements of Clerics

In the early 1990s, young graduates of the BCM began emigrating to serve at overseas temples. This transnational movement reflected the legacy of Taixu, as the academy was the only one in the PRC at the time encouraging its graduates to propagate the dharma overseas and providing foreign language training to support them. Here we recount the experiences of six clerics from Nanputuo Temple who went to Southeast Asia and North America. We met them in 1989 and have continued to visit them at their temples abroad and see them in China.

Southeast Asia

Two monks emigrated to Southeast Asia through the deep ties Nanputuo Temple established in the region. Both monks had enrolled in 1983 in the two-year preparatory program at the Buddhist Instruction School. By the late 1990s, they were priors of temples in Singapore and Manila. (We refer to them by the pseudonyms Monk A and Monk B.)

Monk A was born in Xiamen in 1961 to a family whose grandmother was a prominent devotee. After graduating from high school in the late 1970s, he became a high school teacher. In this period, just after the Cultural Revolution, he was critical of Marxism because he felt that materialism could not solve societal problems. He started accompanying his grandmother to Nanputuo Temple and then went on his own. There he met Miaozhan, who encouraged him to renounce lay life. Miaozhan, who did not take disciples because he led an ecumenical temple, introduced him to the elderly monk Guangjing 廣淨 (1910–1997). Guangjing had been prior of Nanputuo Temple before emigrating to Singapore in 1952, where he became prior of Longshan Temple 龍山寺. After 1979, Guangjing strongly supported the recovery of Buddhism in the Minnan region, funding the restoration of thirty temples (*NSZ*, vol. 1, 170–171). Monk A graduated from the Buddhist Instruction School in 1985 and went on to become an administrator in Nanputuo Temple and then prior of Nanshan Temple in Zhangzhou. There he founded a youth group to discuss literature. During the Tiananmen Square protest, its members joined demonstrations, which led police to investigate him. Disillusioned, he emigrated to Singapore to join Guangjing, becoming prior of Longshan Temple in 1995. But despite continued police suspicion in China, he often returned because he felt his work lay there. He eventually became the abbot of Nanshan Temple.[29]

Monk B was born in the 1960s in Minnan, taking his novice precepts in 1983 at Xichan Temple 西禅寺, Fuzhou. After graduating from the Buddhist Instruction School in 1985, he entered the undergraduate program at the Nanjing Buddhist Academy. In 1989, he returned to Xichan Temple and held administrative positions. In the mid-1990s, Buddhist devotees in the Philippines invited him to be prior of Manila Buddha Temple 普陀寺. The temple's founder was Ruman 如滿 (1910–1983), a disciple of Xingyuan. Ruman gave dharma talks to lay devotees, eventually founding the temple in 1978 as a cultivation hall in Manila's Chinatown (*NSZ*, vol. 1, 158–160). After Ruman died in 1983, devotees managed the temple for a decade before asking the Fujian Religious Affairs Bureau to send a Minnan-speaking cleric to be prior. The bureau asked Monk B, and he went in 1996. When we interviewed him in 2000, he said that Buddhist activity in Manila's old Chinatown had declined as the overseas Chinese population moved to the wealthier suburbs. But donations from the Chinese community were steady, enabling Putuo Temple to fund disaster relief work and run a free clinic. Additionally, he cooperated with the Tzu Chi Buddhist Compassionate Mercy Foundation, a Taiwan-based Buddhist charity. The charity had money and organization but few clerics. So he gave dharma talks to its followers, who then donated to Putuo Temple.[30]

North America

Young clerics emigrated to North America along channels previously forged at midcentury by two Chinese Buddhist clerics, Ledu 樂渡 (1923–2011) and Miaofeng 妙峰 (1928–2019). Both Ledu and Miaofeng had been ordained in China in the mid-1940s, and they traveled to the United States in the 1960s to establish Buddhist temples. In the mid-1980s, they asked Miaozhan to send young clerics to support their work. Miaozhan selected seven of the top graduates of the BCM's 1989 class for Ledu and

Miaofeng to sponsor. But their departure was delayed by the diplomatic freeze between the PRC and the United States after the 1989 Tiananmen Square protest. They left in the early 1990s on U.S. visas for religious professionals to serve their ethnic communities.[31] We focus on the stories of three young clerics to illustrate the migration patterns of all seven.[32]

The first of these stories concerns Miaozhan's sacristan (see chapter 4), a young cleric whose emigration to New York City was sponsored by Ledu. Like Miaozhan himself, Ledu was a disciple of Tanxu, who propagated Buddhism before 1949 by founding temples, as well as academies to educate clerics. Ledu had studied in the 1940s at the Zhanshan Buddhist Seminary 湛山佛學院 founded by Tanxu at Zhanshan Temple 湛山寺, Shandong Province. In 1964, Ledu went to New York City at the invitation of well-educated devotees from Shanghai to establish a Buddhist temple. He founded Dajue Temple 大覺寺[33] and the Young Men's Buddhist Association of America in the Bronx; afterward he devoted himself to translating Buddhist sutras into English (Yu 1997, 375–385).[34] In the 1980s, an elderly devotee, also a Tanxu disciple, began teaching at the BCM and told Ledu of the academy's revival. Ledu then contacted Miaozhan and asked him to send a promising young monk. Notably, the information and personnel circulated within the strong religious kinship among Miaozhan, Ledu, and the devotee as Tanxu's disciples.

The young monk, who was the top student in the 1989 graduating class of the BCM, left for New York in 1992. There Ledu encouraged him to study English and attend college. He majored in psychology at City College of New York and obtained a master's degree in history, writing a thesis on different versions of the *Lotus Sutra*. In 2003, he received a dharma transmission in the Tiantai school, eventually becoming prior of the Cham Sham Temple (Zhanshan jingshe 湛山精舍) in Toronto, founded by Ledu's dharma brothers.[35]

The other two clerics, a nun and monk, were sponsored by Miaofeng, a disciple of Xuyun 虛雲 (1840–1959). Miaofeng was born in Guangdong Province and went to Taiwan in 1949, where he studied under Yinshun. In 1962, Yinshun answered an appeal from Chinese Americans in San Francisco for a Cantonese-speaking cleric by sending Miaofeng. The following year, Miaofeng went to New York to found Fawang Temple 法王寺 in Manhattan's Chinatown and several other temples (Yu 1997, 394–402). In the late 1980s, he asked Miaozhan to send young clerics to help serve the influx of new Chinese immigrants from Fujian and Zhejiang provinces coming to New York. Altogether, Miaofeng sponsored a dozen BCM graduates to the United States.

The nun was born in 1965 in Liaoning Province to parents who were factory workers. Being talented, hardworking, and ambitious to propagate Buddhism abroad, she was appointed as a BCM teacher and BAX officer while still a student. When she arrived in New York in 1991, Miaofeng sent her to his Cihang Prayer Hall 慈航精舍 in Queens. She kept busy doing rituals for immigrants from the PRC and had no time or opportunity to learn English. Furthermore, she felt disrespected because the hall's devotee managers never consulted her about its operation despite her higher religious status as an ordained cleric. She left the shrine, going first to Dajue Temple, and then to a prayer hall in San Francisco, both established by Ledu. There she was joined by her dharma sister from Nanputuo Temple. When we saw her in San Francisco in 2000, she said she had plenty of time for cultivation because few people visited the hall.

The monk Miaofeng sponsored was born in 1967 in Chaozhou, Guangdong Province. In 1989, he graduated from the BCM and taught there for several years. He then emigrated to New York to serve in Cihang Prayer Hall. While there he felt that his role as an ordained cleric was being used solely to raise the status of the prayer hall. So he moved to a private prayer hall in Queens owned by a devotee. A few years later, his master in Chaozhou appointed him prior of Kwan Ying Buddhist Temple (Guanyin si 觀音寺) in Los Angeles because he spoke the Cantonese dialect of the elderly worshipers. Later, he became prior of his master's temple in Chaozhou and traveled back and forth between the PRC and the United States.

The career tracks of these clerics reflected the expectations of their masters and their gender. Most served Chinese communities overseas, including Minnan speakers in Southeast Asia, Cantonese speakers in North America, and new PRC immigrants. Only one was encouraged by his master to learn English and propagate Buddhism beyond the overseas Chinese community, which opened many doors for him. As for the nun, her self-cultivation in Los Angeles was quite removed from her ambition to propagate Buddhism. It reflected the lack of opportunities for nuns to head temples.

Funeral of the Abbot

In 1995 Miaozhan weakened, worn down not only by age but also by his efforts to restore the temple amid conflict with local state officials. He fell ill in November while attending a meeting in Guangzhou. He was diagnosed with stomach cancer and, after brief stays in hospitals in Beijing and Xiamen, returned to Nanputuo Temple to die. On December 14, he wrote his final words, "Do not forget the many among us who suffer hardship," and died four days later. Immediately the Master Miaozhan Funeral Committee (Miaozhan heshang zhisang weiyuanhui 妙湛和尚治喪委員會) formed to give notice of his death and arrange the funeral. It was led by Zhao Puchu and consisted of thirty nationally and locally prominent Buddhists and state officials. The highest-ranking cleric was Yuanzhuo, abbot of Guanghua Temple, who had been the "sending seat cleric" at Miaozhan's abbatial ascension ceremony six years earlier. The highest-ranking state official was Ye Xiaowen 葉小文, the director of the State Administration of Religious Affairs.

Like the ascension ceremony, the funeral was an occasion for the physical, semiotic, and institutional spaces to come together in harmony. But divergent views of how to handle Miaozhan's body reflected the long conflict with the local state; clerics revered it as the vessel of a great teacher, while the XRAB treated it as a corpse to be disposed of. Therefore, the three spaces did not align as the struggle over his body ensued. In this section, we first describe the mourning period, organized by the monks, and the condolences from the central state. Then we describe the final conflict between monks and XRAB officials about Miaozhan's cremation.[36]

Mourning

According to Buddhist tradition, the body of an abbot lies in repose in his temple for seven days and is then cremated on the grounds of his temple. As soon as Miaozhan died, the young monks of the BCM turned the Dharma Hall into a mourning hall (*ling tang* 靈堂). They covered the outside with banners praising Miaozhan. A horizontal banner from the second-floor balcony had fifteen gold characters saying, "Master Miaozhan of Nanputuo Temple Passed away Peacefully (南普陀寺方丈妙湛大和尚安祥示寂)." Seven gold-colored banners praising Miaozhan hung from the stairs leading to the hall. The stairs to the entrance were lined with green wreaths intertwined with white and gold flowers and a gold swastika representing the dharma. The walls of the mourning room on the first floor were covered in gold cloth. Here is a selection of the phrases that appeared on the banners and cloths:

Master Miaozhan's mercy is like rain, cool and sweet as dew. 妙湛大和尚慈悲雲雨甘露

Master Miaozhan's power of prayer is boundless. 妙湛大和尚願力無邊

The master's words are like a string of pearls, filled with great insight; they will continue to instruct the next generation. 妙語連珠妙趣橫生誨後生

Master Miaozhan achieved complete enlightenment and went to heaven. 妙湛大和尚圓滿菩提

Master Miaozhan's compassionate heart is broad. 妙湛大和尚慈心廣大

Master Miaozhan: we offer prayers that he will come again. 妙湛大和尚乘願再來

Master Miaozhan's merciful heart will ferry all living beings [to salvation]. 妙湛大和尚悲心渡群生

Master Miaozhan's benevolence and grace are universally bestowed. 妙湛大和尚惠澤普施

Master Miaozhan gives medicine and care to the elderly. 妙湛大和尚扶藥濟老

His disciples will wholeheartedly carry on their master's legacy. 湛心切切潮師源

Miaozhan's body lay in repose in a glass case against the far wall. He was lying on his side in the Buddha's death position, wearing a red robe, his head and one hand resting on a gold pillow. The case was on a dais surrounded by yellow and white lotus flowers. A large black and white photo of Miaozhan hung above it. A yellow banner above the photo had four black characters that read, "Wishing that he [Miaozhan] come again" (乘願再來). Yellow banners hung on each side, each containing twelve characters to form a couplet, the first character of each line combined to form Miaozhan's name, augmenting respect.

[right] With insight, he penetrates the sublime dharma; noble of character, with sterling integrity, admired by men and deities alike. 妙道凝玄亮節高風人天共仰
[left] With profound kindness, immeasurably vast, he restored the academy and rebuilt the temple, complete in both fortune and wisdom. 湛恩汪濊興學建寺福慧雙全

In front of the dais was an incense table covered with a gold cloth upon which rested four plates holding apples, pears, oranges, grapes, and two large red candles. A low stool in front of the table was covered in gold cloth for people to kneel in reverence. Dozens of academy students wearing saffron-colored robes sat against the walls in silent vigil. Behind them stood devotees in black robes who continuously chanted.

Condolences poured into the BAX via fax and telegraph from central and local state agencies, other temples, academies, associations, and clerics, both domestically and overseas. Those from state agencies expressed the ideal image of a cleric in the eyes of the CPC. A message from the State Administration of Religious Affairs sent on December 22 said, "For his advocacy of the leadership of the CPC and the socialist system, advancing Buddhist attainments, and lifelong efforts to cultivate patriotic Buddhist talent, he can be considered a model of loving country, loving religion" (*Miaozhan heshang jinian ji* 1997, 91). A telegram from Zhao Puchu on December 19 expressed the view of the Buddhist Association of China.

> Master Miaozhan joined the sangha in his early life, learned from Buddhists across the country, and intensively studied the teachings of the Buddha, concentrating on both learning and practice. He devoted many years promoting the Buddha's teachings, benefitting

the masses with his effort. In recent years, he shouldered responsibility for the Fujian and Xiamen Buddhist associations, served the country and Buddhism, helped the government to implement religious policies, restored Buddhist temples, educated Buddhist clerics, established Buddhist charity, and assisted the work of foreign relations for the Buddhist community and the country. In all of this, he made extraordinary contributions. In his lifetime, Master Miaozhan was a dedicated and highly responsible person and monk. He possessed great compassion and desire for the salvation of the masses, exerting all his strength for this to the end. The demise of Master Miaozhan is an immense loss for the Buddhist community. We hope that the Nanputuo Temple community and BCM faculty and students will carry on the great virtue of Master Miaozhan to love and serve the nation and Buddhism with a strong spirit of selflessness, persistence, and striving. We hope you maintain unity in focusing on the big picture, dedicating to Buddhist practice and study of the Five Precepts, and properly managing the temple and the BCM. (*Miaozhan heshang jinian ji* 1997, 94)

In contrast to these idealized views of Miaozhan by the CPC and in Buddhism, the local XRAB viewed him physically as a corpse in need of disposal. Next, we describe the events that stemmed from this view of the local state administration.

Final Conflict

Behind the scenes, conflicts erupted between the monks and XRAB officials over Miaozhan's funeral. The monks wanted the funeral to proceed with all the dignity befitting an eminent abbot, including cremation on the Nanputuo Temple grounds, a tradition existing before 1949 for previous Nanputuo abbots. But immediately after Miaozhan's death, the XRAB director, citing health and fire concerns, announced the mourning period would be limited to three days and that cremation would occur at the municipal crematorium. The monks, who considered the funeral of the abbot to be an internal matter of Buddhism with no opening for the state to control the semiotic space, were aghast. Three days of mourning was highly disrespectful, and it was unimaginable for an abbot to be cremated alongside laypersons. But the Xiamen Municipal People's Government refused to permit the construction of a temporary crematorium. The XRAB director ordered the monks to deliver Miaozhan's corpse to the municipal one in three days, or the police would come to fetch it. This further infuriated the clerics, especially the young BCM students. The officials' treatment of Miaozhan's body as a corpse, just like any other, ignored his high religious status.

Monks saw the disrespect of the local state administration as revenge for Miaozhan's recalcitrance over the years. The BCM students, ignoring the three-day mourning period decreed by the XRAB, declared seven days of mourning. They kept a round-the-clock vigil to prevent the police from taking Miaozhan to the crematorium. The local state administration moved carefully because it was under the scrutiny of high-ranking Buddhists and officials on Miaozhan's funeral committee. The matter was settled by the Religious Security Section of the Xiamen Municipal People's Government, which handled politically sensitive matters regarding religion. It approved the seven-day mourning period and negotiated a compromise for the cremation of Miaozhan. The Nanputuo clerics could take his body on December 25 in a funeral procession to Guanghua Temple, which had a facility to cremate clerics.

A final conflict occurred on the day of the procession to Guanghua Temple, 170 kilometers away. The local state ordered the procession to leave early in the morning to avoid disrupting daytime traffic. The clerics viewed such timing as further disrespect for Miaozhan because the darkness would prevent mourners along the route from seeing the procession. The power of a Buddhist abbot would be cloaked. The clerics delayed the departure on various pretexts until dawn. Police cars led the way, followed by Miaozhan's hearse, dozens of buses filled with clerics and academy students, and carloads of devotees, Buddhist association officers, local state officials, and Miaozhan's family members from Manchuria. Mourners had waited for hours along the route, some with bloody foreheads from repeated prostration.

The procession arrived at Guanghua Temple in the late morning. The path from the mountain gate to the crematorium was lined with monks in saffron robes standing to one side and devotees in black robes on the other. Miaozhan's body was carried in its glass case by BCM students and then placed in the crematory on a bed of pine and cypress wood.

Cremation began shortly before noon, and the ashes were removed several hours later. They were divided into five bowls and carried back to Nanputuo Temple.

That evening, a large fire broke out on the ridge between Xiamen's old and new downtowns. It blazed so fiercely that army troops were called to help extinguish it. At dawn people realized an entire section of the ridge, from its base to the peak, had been reduced to smoking earth. Buddhists believed the cause of this devastation to be heaven's anger at the local state for sending Miaozhan away from his temple to be cremated. Later that day, Yuanzhuo eulogized Miaozhan at a memorial service at Nanputuo Temple. By tradition, such a service should occur on the same day as the cremation, but it had been postponed to transport Miaozhan's body to and from Guanghua Temple. His death symbolized the rapidly disappearing continuities of Buddhism with the earlier turmoil of war and revolution. The experience of the sufferings of such elderly monks as Miaozhan had been resources for the revival of temples after the Cultural Revolution. These legacies at Nanputuo Temple ended with his death.

Conclusion

During his final six years, Miaozhan served as abbot with the full formal acknowledgment of the religious authority of Buddhism and the institutional recognition of the state. Significantly, his ascension ceremony positioned him at the top of the semiotic space in Buddhism. The exertion of authority occurred amid the heightened security concerns of the state that placed new demands on religion. Nevertheless, Miaozhan significantly enlarged the semiotic and physical space of Buddhism at the temple by creating a charity foundation, a BCM campus for nuns, a Meditation Hall, and pagodas, and encouraged graduates of the BCM to go overseas.

But the expansion of Nanputuo Temple aggravated contradictions in the institutional space of religion as the clerics challenged XRAB control of the temple. Miaozhan used his position as president of both the BAX and Buddhist Association of Fujian, as well as his friendship with Zhao Puchu, to obtain help from the central state to manage the local conflict. Central intervention blunted local state actions but led to the deeper implanting of central state authority in the temple. While a completely free semiotic space in a temple could not be said to exist in the institutional space of religion defined by the CPC, it did in the imaginations of those who believed in Buddhism, such as Miaozhan. The local state officials failed to understand this. They could only conceive of handling Miaozhan by applying continuous pressure to thwart his growing authority.

The death of Miaozhan in 1995 left these conflicts unresolved. It created a gaping hole in the leadership and structure of Nanputuo Temple through which individuals and factions emerged who held different expectations for the next abbot, the future of the temple, and its relationship with the state. Although his death ended a pivotal connection to the historical legacies of the temple, it enabled new approaches for moving beyond the conflicts in the institutional space of religion. It opened possibilities for a new leader who could promote greater cooperation and even a symbiosis of religion and state in the PRC's market economy and socialist society.

6

Aligning with the Central State, 1996–2004

RESURGENT ECONOMIC GROWTH IN THE 1990s created new wealth and independent social organizations that challenged the administrative control of the state.¹ In religion, new trends occurred outside of its institutional space, such as unregistered temples and qigong practice groups. The state sought to standardize (*guifanhua* 規範化) its administration of society and economy by defining national standards and laws for businesses and social organizations, including religions. The movement toward standardization was also driven by the international aims of the CPC, such as shielding the domestic economy from the 1997 Asian financial crisis and being admitted to the World Trade Organization, which occurred in 2001. As part of this broad trend, the State Administration of Religious Affairs issued national policies for religious activity sites and foreign religious personnel, overriding numerous administrative practices developed locally in the 1980s.²

The third phase of Nanputuo Temple's recovery took place between 1996 and 2004. The new abbot Shenghui fostered structure in the temple's semiotic space, cooperation within the institutional space, and selective reorganization for the physical space. We explain the process of his selection as abbot, which brought central authority directly into the temple, in the first section of this chapter. In the second section we describe Shenghui's key accomplishments during his first term as abbot

ALIGNING WITH THE CENTRAL STATE, 1996-2004

from 1996 to 1999. He disciplined Buddhist teachings at Nanputuo Temple and standardized its procedures according to national guidelines as an ideal temple for the CPC in the state administrative system. We cover his accomplishments during his second term, from 2000 to 2004, in the third and fourth sections. He used Nanputuo Temple and his abbotship as a platform to represent state-approved Buddhism nationally and internationally when engaging the Buddhist diplomacy of the state and the campaign against Falun Gong. These initiatives made Nanputuo Temple a model of state control of Buddhism, although quite removed from how a temple was viewed and existed in Taixu's time.

Selecting a New Abbot

After Miaozhan died in 1995, the monks moved to choose a new abbot for Nanputuo Temple. They wanted to follow the *shifang conglin* system of abbot selection—based on merit, not lineage—that had been established when the temple ecumenicized in 1924. But it had been decades since the last abbot was selected, so there was uncertainty about the process. The monks' desire to discuss candidates until a consensus emerged was further complicated because the XRAB had to approve the nominee.

The sacristan, a monk in his late twenties, initiated the deliberations to elect a new abbot. He claimed that Miaozhan had confided a successor's name to him, an elderly monk in Sichuan Province who was Taixu's disciple. When the elderly monk declined the nomination, citing poor health, the sacristan nominated himself as the next abbot.[3] Some monks, however, suspected that Miaozhan had not named a successor, and as a result they saw the elderly monk's nomination as part of the sacristan's calculated plan for his own ascension. Unable to gain support, the sacristan withdrew his name from consideration. The second nominee was a native of Putian in his mid-thirties who held a high administrative office in the temple. Although XRAB officials who saw him as a pragmatist willing to bargain favored him as someone who could communicate with them in the Minnan dialect, other monks deemed his character as unsuitable for the abbotship. The third nominee was the prior and interim BAX secretary, widely seen as pious and a skilled administrator. But the XRAB opposed him because he had led the temple during the 1994 uprising described in chapter 5. So the prior withdrew from consideration, citing health reasons as well. This disappointed his supporters, who expected he would stand firm against the XRAB, as Miaozhan had. Some said that the prior had a good heart but was too timid.

The process stalled. The prior led a delegation to Beijing to consult with Zhao Puchu, who was deeply concerned about the leadership of such a prominent temple. He wanted to ensure that the next abbot would build on Miaozhan's work to make the temple a center of Buddhist teachings. So he proposed Shenghui, an ambitious and promising "new-generation" monk in his mid-forties born just after the founding of the PRC and among the first graduates of the Buddhist Academy of China after the Cultural Revolution. In fall 1996, Shenghui came to Xiamen and met all the stakeholders in the selection process over the course of several months, including clerics, BAX officers, and local state officials. A consensus emerged to make him abbot, and his ascension ceremony occurred in December 1996.

Each of these local actors could see advantages in Shenghui's selection. Zhao Puchu got recognition for installing a Nanputuo abbot with excellent ties to the Buddhist Association of China and a firm grasp of the religious policy. Shenghui's ascension offered hope to the local state administration in Xiamen for resolving conflict and implementing centrally standardized policies at the temple. The XRAB was able to reduce the power of the Nanputuo abbot by extracting an agreement from Shenghui to not serve concurrently as BAX president, unlike Miaozhan. For the clerics in Xiamen, Shenghui's ascension resolved the year-long leadership crises. They had high hopes for this rising star in the Buddhist establishment, although some noted his lack of ties to the temple.

A New-Generation Abbot

Shenghui was born Sheng Qinghui 盛清輝 in 1951 in Mao Zedong's home region of Xiangtan County, Hunan Province 湖南省湘潭縣. In 1981, he was tonsured at Mount Jiuhua 九華山, Anhui Province, and enrolled in the Buddhist Academy of China. His class, the first after the Cultural Revolution, was part of a new elite generation expected to succeed elderly abbots of significant temples. He wrote his master's thesis on the history of the administrative system of Buddhist temples and graduated in 1987. His education in the national capital made him politically astute, while his master's thesis grounded him in temple management. The Buddhist Association of China identified him as a leader, elevating him to important positions in Buddhism and the state.[4] He was rumored to be a leading candidate to succeed Zhao Puchu as president of the Buddhist Association of China.

Among Buddhists in Xiamen, we heard two views about Shenghui's potential as abbot of Nanputuo Temple. Some thought he possessed the political adroitness and management skills that "old-school" Miaozhan had lacked, and they expected him to be adept at handling local officials. Others viewed him as an opportunist sent by Beijing who had no ties to the temple or Minnan people. Some even called him a "political monk" (*zhengzhi heshang* 政治和尚). This derisive term had been applied to Taixu in the 1930s and 1940s by those critical of him for cultivating ties to politicians, accepting their money, and holding political views. In discussing Shenghui with us, clerics and devotees drew comparisons with Miaozhan. These comments also gave insight into generational change in Buddhist leadership.[5]

One comment concerned the two abbots' stances towards the CPC. Some saw Shenghui as too ready to accommodate the CPC's ideology and projects in contrast to Miaozhan's determination to consider only what was best for Buddhism. Such a view was expressed to us by a nun who worked as a doctor at the Nanputuo Temple Charity Foundation.[6] She said that Shenghui had not supported her plan for a preventive healthcare project in poor villages and suspected that he considered her Taiwan donor to be politically problematic. In contrast, she imagined that Miaozhan would have supported her project because it expressed Buddhist compassion, noting his perseverance in building the meditation hall despite the XRAB's objections to its Taiwan funding. Her comments suggested the view that Shenghui's attention to the political concerns of the state was not always in the best interests of Buddhism.

Other members of the Buddhist community saw Shenghui's political sensitivity as an asset. One monk, who had graduated from the BCM and was prior of a temple in Singapore at the time of our interview, told us:

> Some Sangha members do not understand Master Shenghui. He is very tenacious. Buddhism needs this kind of strength—neither too weak nor too strong—to form a connecting link between the top

and the bottom. Shenghui is able to not only handle government matters but also guide the monks in the temple while adjusting relations between the CPC and the monks. The Buddhist world in China needs talent like Shenghui, yet some people do not understand the difficulties that he faces in his position. He has to occasionally accept officials' opinions to be a connecting link. This is a good thing. People in the Buddhist world are either too politically left and always listen to the government or too right and oppose the government. Both ways are unhelpful to China and Buddhism.[7]

This monk saw Shenghui's ability to factor CPC ideology into his decision-making as best for Buddhism in the PRC. He implied that Miaozhan's view, in which political concerns had no place in Buddhism, had created confusion among local officials and exacerbated tensions.

Another insight concerned Shenghui's attachment to Nanputuo Temple. Some Buddhists we spoke with saw him as a careerist who used his ascension as abbot of Nanputuo Temple to further qualify him for becoming president of the Buddhist Association of China. They felt his commitment to the temple was weak: he spent much time away from Xiamen, they noted, and had declined the presidency of the BAX, which broke the local tradition of the Nanputuo abbot becoming the leader of all Buddhists in Xiamen.[8] Yet others saw these actions in a favorable light. Shenghui's absences from Xiamen befitted a monk of his stature, and his many national and international commitments raised Nanputuo Temple's profile. His decline of the BAX presidency was a shrewd move to minimize getting entangled in local politics, enabling him to focus on improving the temple rather than battling the XRAB.

The two abbots also projected very different images. Shenghui was large and fleshy, with a pale and reserved demeanor evoking a high-ranking official. He was aloof and did not often stop to chat with younger monks. In contrast, Miaozhan had a stocky, muscular frame conditioned by tai chi practice and hands hardened by manual labor. One BCM instructor wrote that "Venerable Miao had the demeanor of a Chan person, a straightforward personality, a simple life, and is kind and approachable," and he enjoyed being with BCM students (Jiqun 2000). These differences were reflected in their rhetoric and speaking styles. When we asked Miaozhan in 1990 to name overseas temples with close ties to

Nanputuo Temple, he answered simply, "All temples are connected through Buddhism."[9] When we asked Shenghui the same question in 1999, he gave an eloquent answer that touched on multiple themes—international Buddhist exchanges, the modernization of Buddhism, adaptation of Buddhism to socialist society—all of which echoed the state religious policy. In his public talks, Shenghui could sound like a CPC cadre exhorting the masses, his voice rising to punctuate key points.

Some devotees observed that criticism of Shenghui reflected nostalgia for the "old-style Buddhism" that existed in China before 1949. Miaozhan had spent his formative years during the vitality of the modern Buddhist reform movement and had survived a half-century of political turmoil under multiple regimes—ROC, Japanese military government, and PRC. These experiences gave him a clear idea of how to recover Buddhism as well as a skepticism that state power had any role to play in this. In contrast, Shenghui was born in the PRC and took CPC control of religion as a given. He was educated in the Buddhist Academy of China, the state-approved seminary in Beijing, where he learned how Buddhism should get along with CPC ideology and state administration of the religious policy. Now that Nanputuo Temple under Miaozhan's leadership had recovered and expanded, it needed a new leader better able to cooperate with the state power in the PRC.

Realigning Local Politics

Shenghui's decline of the BAX presidency scrambled local politics, creating openings for the XRAB to exert control. It moved to coopt the new BAX leadership through the 1997 quadrennial election of BAX officers. Invoking its authority to approve the nominees for officers, the XRAB sought to ensure the election of officials it favored. It played on distinctions between two influential regional groups whose young monks had been the first to arrive at Nanputuo in the early 1980s and subsequently assume leading positions in the temple. One group was from the Putian region adjacent to Minnan, and the other from Wenzhou Prefecture, lying just north of Fujian Province in Zhejiang Province. Some local Xiamen residents informally called these groups, respectively, the "Putian gang" (莆田幫) and "northerners" (北子).[10] While local devotees generally viewed the Wenzhou monks as more pious and grounded in Buddhist teachings, XRAB officials considered them troublemakers for their loyalty to Miaozhan. The officials favored the Putian monks, who seemed more open to bargaining, and some were conversant in Minnan dialect. During the 1997 election, XRAB officials approved the nomination of Putian monks for president and secretary. Their subsequent election weakened the close ties between the BAX and the Nanputuo abbot.

The XRAB sought to cooperate with the new BAX leadership in several ways. One was encouraging the BAX to reduce its financial dependence on Nanputuo Temple. With a funding source created under the previous abbot Miaozhan, the BAX budget came from selling the ashes of spirit money, which had been burnt at the temple by worshipers for dead souls, to farmers for use as fertilizer. But now, the XRAB officials encouraged the new BAX leadership to become independent of Nanputuo Temple. In doing so, XRAB officials played on the desire of the new BAX leaders to make their mark. The XRAB director encouraged the new BAX president and secretary to exert more authority over all Buddhist temples in Xiamen and thus overcome the appearance of BAX subservience to Nanputuo Temple. The BAX leader turned their attention to the local temples that had recovered during the 1990s and became wealthy by performing on-demand rituals. In 1997, the BAX ordered the temples to give it 15 percent of their annual revenue and required the purchase of a license to perform rituals. The XRAB enforced these demands by threatening to withhold approval for new construction at local temples that did not comply, although some temples refused.

Another form of cooperation was a real estate scheme of the XRAB to develop Miaoshi Temple 妙釋寺, a three-hundred-year-old temple in downtown Xiamen. The BAX would approve the site's development, and the XRAB would obtain a bank loan to finance the construction of a commercial complex with stores, offices, and a hotel. The scheme would give the XRAB steady rental income while the BAX would acquire rent-free office space, enabling it to leave Nanputuo Temple. But the plan encountered opposition from various quarters. Other city agencies objected because the site was in a park in the city's urban development plan. Buddhists objected because the temple had historical significance as a site designated by Taixu for devotees' activities. Some BAX officers and clerics feared the new physical separation would undermine the BAX's ability to work with Nanputuo Temple. The project did not get off the ground. The

BAX office was nevertheless moved, but only within Nanputuo Temple. The new abbot Shenghui considered its location next to the Heavenly Kings Hall in the main square to be inappropriate and relocated it to the west compound by its gate. Although the BAX office was no longer among the first things visitors saw when entering the temple, the new location let officers keep a closer eye on the comings and goings of the abbot and BCM students.

Cooperation between the BAX and XRAB created new political tensions. One was a rift between the BAX and local temples. Some priors, who refused to pay the fee for the ritual license or turn over temple revenue, began boycotting BAX meetings. Tension also grew among the BAX leaders. Its president was too busy with his work as the temple prior to pay much attention to the association and had delegated its management to the secretary. The secretary arranged the cooperation with the XRAB without consulting the president. As a result, the president tightened oversight by appointing a monk to attend all association meetings and report directly to him. The secretary viewed this monk as a spy and stopped holding meetings, thus halting many association activities. The situation was resolved in 2001 with the election of new BAX officers, including Shenghui as president. These events underscored the need for the BAX leadership and the Nanputuo abbot to cooperate in the institutional and semiotic spaces of Buddhism in Xiamen.

Standardizing the Temple

As soon as he became the abbot, Shenghui tightened discipline in the temple through multiple projects of "standardization" according to central state guidelines, which also transformed the semiotic space. He was determined to make the temple a more disciplined Buddhist temple, raise its status to a more national-level temple, and clear up the messy local situation left by Miaozhan and his supporters.

Furthering Discipline in Temple Life

Shenghui reversed the growing laxity in management and daily practice that had occurred as the temple expanded in the final years of Miaozhan's time. The measures that Shenghui adopted also showed his astuteness regarding CPC ideology and religious policy. His first step was issuing the *Nanputuo Temple Rules and Regulations* (*Nanputuo si guizhang zhidu* 南普陀寺規章制度) in the same month as his abbatial ascension. This thirty-one-page booklet contained 113 rules governing the personal conduct of monks and management of the temple, such as selection of the abbot, etiquette in dormitories, rules for drivers, and the financial accounts. Significantly, the first rule defined the ideal image of a monk in the PRC. "Monks in temples must be patriotic, uphold CPC leadership and the people's government, adapt to socialist society, respect the constitution and laws, implement relevant policies, care for residents of temples, assiduously cultivate the precepts, meditation, and wisdom, and overcome greed, anger, and delusions" (*Nanputuo si guizhang zhidu* 1996).

Next, Shenghui set out to create a more disciplined observance of Buddhist teachings at the temple by focusing on the behavior of clerics. He launched the Six Priorities Activities (Liu jiang huodong 六講活動) initiative, a name that evoked a state campaign. In fact, his initiative was coterminous with a CPC national campaign called Three Priorities Education (San jiang jiaoyu 三講教育), which targeted the behavior of corrupt officials.[11] In the CPC's political lexicon, "priority" meant the proper values and discipline that people must observe in thinking and behavior. The Six Priorities pertained to the proper behavior for clerics: they had to study ideas, ethics, and practices that mixed Buddhist teachings, temple management, and state imperatives. Priority 1 was the "awakening of Buddhist mind" (*faxin* 發心), which referred to the spirit of compassion expressed in the Nanputuo Temple Charity Foundation. Priority 2 was "training" (*xiuchi* 修持); it called for stricter observance of temple rules for meditation, participation in daily rituals, and meal attendance. Priority 3 was "upholding the precepts" (*chijie* 持戒) in interactions with temple visitors and handling donations. Priority 4 was "karmic cause and effect" (*yinguo* 因果), which applied to transparency in the decision-making of temple administration. Priority 5 was "study" (*xuefeng* 學風); it emphasized patriotism and legal compliance by clerics to promote social stability, environmentalism, and contributions to society. Priority 6 was "special character" (*daofeng* 道風). It stressed adhering to the rules in the administrative charters of Nanputuo Temple, the BCM, and the Nanputuo Temple Charity Foundation (Nanputuo si 1999).

ALIGNING WITH THE CENTRAL STATE, 1996–2004

The Six Priorities Activities showed not only that Shenghui recognized Nanputuo Temple's place in the national spotlight but also that he was determined to upgrade the temple as a model for linking Buddhist terms and concepts with CPC ideology. There was a consensus among monks we spoke to that the campaign had positive effects. They noted the decline of monks loitering in the courtyard, greater transparency in the Nanputuo Temple Management Committee, and fewer lay visitors to the monks' dormitories. At the same time, some criticized the mixing of Buddhist teachings with the CPC's political sloganeering techniques.

Upgrading Education

In 1997, Shenghui reformed the BCM to align with the Buddhist Association of China's new national standards to raise the academic quality of Buddhist education and scholarship.[12] He changed the start of the academic year from spring to fall to conform to other academies and shifted from the interview-based admissions process to a written exam covering Buddhist teachings and secular subjects, including classical and modern literature, English, contemporary affairs and politics, history, and geography. Four hundred applicants took the first exam in 1997, with ninety accepted and almost all enrolling. The selectivity and retention rate reflected the high reputation of the academy for its excellent facilities and pleasant surroundings. Underscoring its national scope, the accepted students were mainly from the northeast provinces of Heilongjiang, Jilin, and Liaoning, and the southern provinces of Guangdong, Zhejiang, and Hunan. The few from Fujian came from the coastal Putian and Mindong 閩東 regions, with none from Minnan.

Shenghui upgraded the educational quality of the BCM. In 1997, he eliminated the three-month remedial program established for those deprived of education during the Cultural Revolution. The same year, he started a three-year graduate program. The inaugural class had five nuns and two monks. The teaching staff included instructors from the other BCM programs, such as the rising-star monk Jiqun 濟群 (1962–), and such nationally prominent Buddhist scholars as Fang Litian 方立天 (1943–2014). But it was still too politically sensitive to invite instructors from Taiwan to teach. Shenghui instituted competitive faculty appointments to encourage scholarship, digitized the 45,000 volumes of the Taixu

Library, and turned the biennial *Journal of Minnan Buddhism* into an annual publication. Other initiatives included pioneering new practices for Buddhist academies in the PRC. In 1999, the BCM became the first Buddhist academy to offer courses in digital media and the internet and give personal computers to all instructors. Its students made a website for Nanputuo Temple, among the first for a temple. In 2001, the BCM became the first academy to accept international degree students (four nuns from Vietnam), and academy graduates began going abroad for advanced study of Buddhism, mainly in Sri Lanka and Japan.

These efforts furthered the national reputation of the BCM. In 1999, the State Administration of Religious Affairs praised it for excellence following a national inspection of academies. The BCM had seventy instructors, including nineteen monks, twenty-seven nuns, and twenty-four university professors. According to an official from the Fujian Religious Affairs Bureau, a total of three hundred students were enrolled in the BCM's programs, constituting one-third of all students in China's approximately fifteen Buddhist academies at the time.[13] The four-year program had graduated 415 clerics since the first class in 1989. They were much demanded by temples and Buddhist academies in China and overseas owing to their training in Buddhist and secular subjects, grounding in practice, and abilities in handling the secular world gained by living in an urban temple that was a major tourist attraction in the cosmopolitan Xiamen city.

Disengaging from Local Buddhist Communities

As standardization aligned Nanputuo Temple more closely to the central state, the temple became disengaged from Buddhists in Xiamen. This occurred in various ways. One began with a change in the BCM's admissions policy for nuns. Under Miaozhan, lay nuns could study in the school alongside ordained nuns. His policy respected the local Minnan culture of these women, who lived celibate, communitarian, and vegetarian lifestyles similar to that of Buddhist nuns, yet wore lay clothing, did not shave their heads, and held regular jobs. But Shenghui required all female applicants to have taken their novice vows, including shaving their heads and wearing clerical robes. So, beginning in 1997, a lay nun had to be ordained as a nun to continue her study of Buddhism. This change profoundly affected the lay nun community (see chapter 8).

Nanputuo Temple became further disengaged from local Buddhism when Shenghui halted the practice of popular Buddhist rituals. For example, he discontinued the release of burning mouths, which freed the spirits of wandering ghosts—persons who had died by accident, murder, or natural disasters. The dramatic elements of this elaborate and vivid ritual made it very popular. The lead monk performing it represented Dizang, the bodhisattva in charge of dead souls. At the high point of the ritual he symbolically spread sutras and drops of water (signifying sacred dewdrops) into the burning mouths of the ghosts who sought release from purgatory. In the "modern" view of religion, the ritual facilitated ancestor worship, with audience members serving as ancestor/ghosts. Such rituals could be considered superstition and had nothing to do with the Buddhist practice that Shenghui emphasized.

After 1997, the plenary mass (*shuilu fahui* 水陸法會) was the only large mortuary rite performed in Nanputuo Temple. While structurally similar to the release of burning mouths, it had a far longer history in Buddhism. Attendees prayed for peace and healing from the violence of wars and disasters that had killed people. The plenary mass was permitted at the temple because it spread the Buddha's merit to the dead and living, and it was performed at the behest of the temple and even state rulers. Another practice Shenghui banned was the burning of spirit money offerings to ancestors so they could bribe the king of hell to get out of purgatory and purchase items for their comfort in the afterlife. In 1989, we had seen many participants at the Guanyin festival bring bags of paper money to burn inside the temple. People now had to go to the furnace outside the west compound to burn the money themselves.

The decline of Nanputuo Temple as a center for devotee activities represented another detachment from ritual life, one that we observed in a sutra-chanting group that had begun back in the early 1980s. For two decades, devotees met every Sunday to chant inside a building in the east compound. The group included middle-aged and elderly women with local roots, as well as fortune-tellers and palm readers trying to show that they were Buddhists. Devotees were very close to the elderly Minnan-speaking monk, who supported their chanting and even advised them on personal matters. Every Sunday after chanting, devotees visited the elderly monk in the retirement home in the east compound. When Shenghui became abbot, the building where they met was demolished, and they had no place in the temple. Unlike Miaozhan, who enjoyed talking with devotees and administering the devotee precepts (*wujie* 五戒) to people when they asked, the devotees felt that Shenghui ignored them. Feeling unwelcome at Nanputuo Temple, the devotees arranged to have a temple built in the suburbs to conduct their activities.

The detachment of Nanputuo Temple occurred in tandem with the recovery of local temples in Xiamen during the 1990s. People found it more convenient to visit the temple closest to them or find a temple with a character more suitable to their tastes. Shenghui's restrictions on rituals and his cooler attitude toward devotees and believers hastened this movement of worshipers to local temples. These local temples catered to popular demands by holding chanting sessions, dharma talks, and other activities that were in decline at Nanputuo Temple. Furthermore, newly banned rituals at Nanputuo, such as the release of burning mouths, could still be commissioned at local temples. In these ways, upgrading Nanputuo Temple to fit central state requirements as a standardized Buddhist temple affected developments among local Buddhists in Xiamen.

Persisting Problems

Despite his efforts, Shenghui was unsuccessful in stopping the commercialization of the temple and XRAB control of the Nanputuo Temple Enterprise. His frustration was expressed in a large-character poster, titled "An Important Village in Chinese Buddhism: Nanputuo Temple" (Zhongguo fojiao zhongzhen—Nanputuo si 中國佛教重鎮—南普陀寺). It was hung inside the temple on June 4, 1999, the tenth anniversary of the Tiananmen Square protest. The date had become a day for airing public grievances against state officials. The poster, displayed on the wall of the left temple corridor where monks regularly posted news of the temple and Buddhist teachings, displayed the official seal of Nanputuo Temple and thus signified the poster's approval by the abbot. It described the temple's history, the results of the Six Priorities Activities, and unresolved issues at the temple. Such a public statement on divisive temple matters

ALIGNING WITH THE CENTRAL STATE, 1996–2004

was highly unusual and expressed the will of Shenghui, as an abbot sent by Beijing, to enforce discipline in the temple.

The poster called attention to three problems. First was the commercialization of the temple.

> As a sacred place in Chinese Buddhism, the atmosphere of Nanputuo Temple should be quiet and peaceful. However, the commercial atmosphere is too thick and has won out. As soon as visitors enter the gate, there is a retail store, while the path is lined with small stalls, photographers, cold drinks and snacks, and even places selling cigarettes and tea (there are three tea houses—one inside the East Mountain Gate, and two on the mountain behind the temple). One of the teahouses is on the spot where Master Hongyi made a retreat. The clerics in our temple wish to build a commemorative pavilion for Master Hongyi, but a tea vendor occupies the place. All of this has an enormous influence on the temple's religious atmosphere and the maintenance of its environment. We oppose the superstitious burning of spirit money, yet there are some who sell it (and they are not clerics). (Nanputuo si 1999).

The second problem was the constant stream of tour buses discharging passengers in front of the Heavenly Kings Hall, causing congestion in front of the temple. The poster called for constructing a parking lot near the temple to divert the buses. The third problem was the extremely sensitive issue of Miaozhan's funeral four years earlier, still a festering sore for Buddhists in Xiamen. According to Buddhist tradition, an abbot should be cremated at the temple where he had served, and the poster bemoaned the lack of such a facility at Nanputuo Temple. It said that the cremation of Miaozhan outside of Xiamen "greatly hurt the hearts of the mass of believers" (Nanputuo si 1999).

The poster obliquely attributed these problems to the local state. The commercialization was blamed on laypersons who disrespected Buddhism. This may have referred to Mr. Z (see chapter 5), who did the bidding of the XRAB inside the temple. Of course, most visitors to the temple knew nothing of the conflict between the monks and the XRAB. But those reading the poster's final plea for "all officials to please help in solving these problems" could realize that the monks blamed state officials. Shenghui's brave decision to publicly post this document showed his willingness to push back at what he considered unjust actions by local state officials. And it underscored his commitment to transparency in administration. No doubt, he was confident that his status as an elite monk sent by Beijing made him immune to local repercussions.

Repositioning Charity

In the late 1900s, as part of efforts to reorganize government administration of increasingly diverse and wealthy social organizations, the central state imposed a series of nuanced standardization procedures affecting the Nanputuo Temple Charity Foundation. New national regulations in 1998, for instance, required a social organization to be supervised by two administrative government agencies: one was the Civil Affairs Bureau, in charge of licensing, and the other was the bureau charged with supervising the activities of a social organization (Guowuyuan 1998). The 1998 charter of the Nanputuo Temple Charity Foundation thus acknowledged both the Xiamen Civil Affairs Bureau and the XRAB as administering it. But most significantly, this new charter recognized the foundation's Buddhist character by defining it as "a department for the clerics of Nanputuo Temple to put into practice the ideas of saving the world through Buddhist compassion" (*Cishan* 1998, 7). When the foundation was established in 1994, its charter did not mention its Buddhist character and listed only the Xiamen Civil Affairs Bureau as its administrative supervisor.

This new institutional description of the foundation as both "religion" and "charity" reflected a more integrated state system to administer religion in the complexities of the market economy. To emphasize its importance, we recall from chapter 5 the conflict over the Nanputuo Temple Enterprise in the first half of the 1990s. At that time the XRAB justified its control of the enterprise by insisting it was only an "economic" entity for generating revenue rather than a "religious" entity for propagating Buddhist teachings. Placing the enterprise outside of the space of religion had enabled the XRAB to act with impunity toward the enterprise, even installing a layperson as its director despite its being part of Nanputuo Temple. The 1998 Nanputuo Temple Charity Foundation charter precluded the possibility of the civil ministry taking control of the foundation as a "charity" entity by recognizing that the foundation head and administrators had to be clerics because it was also a "religious" entity.

The 1998 charter enhanced the clerics' confidence in their control of the Nanputuo Temple Charity Foundation. This confidence was expressed by the foundation's director.[14] We asked him if the 1998 charter's recognition of the XRAB's administrative authority over the foundation gave an opening for the XRAB to control donations. He said this was impossible because the charter clearly defined the discrete administrative functions of the XRAB and the Xiamen Civil Affairs Bureau, with financial oversight by the latter. Thus, standardization of state administration enhanced clerical self-governance, as stipulated in Document 19. It achieved this by recognizing the various functions of a temple and its more flexible positioning in multiple institutional spaces.

Buddhist Diplomacy of the State

Nanputuo monks played a prominent role in the Buddhist diplomacy of the state. A tour by Taixu in 1939, sponsored by the ROC to garner support from Buddhist countries in the war with Japan, became the modern Chinese state's diplomacy prototype (Welch 1968, 63). After 1949, the CPC expanded its diplomatic efforts to improve bilateral relations with other Buddhist countries by lending them the Buddha tooth relic that was housed in China.[15] Buddhist clerics were encouraged to participate in international Buddhist conferences and organizations to influence their agendas in support of CPC positions (Welch 1968, 211–214). Finally, the Buddhist Association of China organized "friendly" visits of overseas Buddhist delegations to the PRC, hoping to impress them with how Buddhism was active under the CPC.[16] These three avenues of Buddhist diplomacy stopped in the early 1960s and then reappeared after 1979. In the 1980s, it was largely oriented toward gaining overseas Chinese support for China's economic reforms. Then, in the 1990s, as the PRC integrated into the international market economy, Buddhist diplomacy practices were revived, with Nanputuo Temple playing an outsized role. The temple's involvement fit its cosmopolitan character and transnational ties. Its clerics were confident and adept at interacting with clerics, laypersons, and politicians of different nationalities. Its abbots were trusted by the CPC, as evidenced by their leading roles in the diplomacy; Miaozhan headed the first relic tour after the Cultural Revolution, and Shenghui led a politically sensitive tour to Taiwan. The temple's location in Minnan also provided cultural closeness to Buddhists in overseas Chinese communities, Hong Kong, and Taiwan.

Relic diplomacy revived in 1994 through tours to Burma and Thailand, with Miaozhan heading the delegation to the latter. The trip to Thailand marked the first international tour of the Buddha finger relic discovered in 1987 in Famen Temple 法門寺, Shanxi Province 陝西省. The official purpose of the tour, which lasted from November 1994 to February 1995, was to celebrate the Thai monarch's seventy-fifth birthday. A PRC communique declared that the tour "further strengthened the traditional friendship between the two peoples and promoted bilateral cooperation in cultural, religious and friendly exchanges" (Zhonghua renmin gongheguo 1994).

With all the pomp of a state visit, the relic tour began on November 3, when it was brought from Famen Temple to Beijing for a veneration ceremony attended by diplomats from Myanmar, Sri Lanka, Japan, and Laos. On November 28, the Thai foreign minister Thaksin Shinawatra flew to Beijing on a Thai air force jet to receive the relic. He was greeted by Premier Li Peng and met with Vice Premier and Foreign Minister Qian Qichen. The plane carrying the finger relic then proceeded to Thailand, where the Thai prime minister and Chinese ambassador were waiting at the airport. The prime minister received the relic on his head, following the traditional practice of the secular leader of Buddhism, such as the king or prime minister of a Buddhist country. The practice gave the highest honor to the person receiving the relic for symbolic legitimacy as head of the secular world. Then the Thai navy personnel escorted the relic to Bangkok in a grand procession of monks, Chinese lion-mask dancers, floats, and a brass band. The event was broadcast nationally, and huge crowds worshiped the relic during the three-month tour (Li 1995; Qiming 1995). For Thailand, the tour reaffirmed the Buddhist character of the Thai state, where Buddhism was practically the state religion. For the PRC, the tour conveyed cultural and religious affinities between the two countries to assuage the Thai populace uneasy with China's rising power and economic interests in the region. At the same time, the tour emphasized the cultural superiority of Chinese Buddhism, and therefore China, for possessing such a sacred and precious relic symbolizing the Buddha's words and deeds.

Shenghui's participation in Buddhist diplomacy began in 1999 during the finger relic tour to Hong Kong, held from May 20 to 29. The CPC wanted to celebrate China's reunification with Hong Kong, which had taken place two years earlier, while looking ahead to Macao's return from Portugal in December 1999 and beyond to reunification with Taiwan. Zhao Puchu led the tour delegation with Shenghui, who served as the senior monk. The tour was intended to celebrate three events: the fiftieth anniversary of the PRC, Macao's return to China, and the Hong Kong government's designation of the first day of the lunar new year— the Buddha's birthday—as a public holiday (Lingguang si, n.d.). Hundreds of thousands of people, including Hong Kong politicians, viewed the relic on display in a sports stadium. The Chinese monks met with leaders of other religions in Hong Kong to display unity and harmony.

In 2002, Shenghui led a tooth relic tour to Taiwan from February 23 to March 31. The tour occurred amid political tension from the recent election of a president in Taiwan who advocated independent statehood. The reunification of China and Taiwan was of utmost importance to the CPC, and it used Buddhism to emphasize cultural affinities. Hsing Yun, leader of the powerful Fo Guang Shan Buddhist organization in Taiwan and a supporter of unification, initiated the tour. Shenghui's participation was crucial in this sensitive diplomacy. The CPC trusted him because of his strong links to the central state. His position as abbot of Nanputuo Temple embodied cultural affinities with Taiwan, such as the fact that Yinshun, the most eminent monk in Taiwan, had studied at the BCM under Taixu. Shenghui selected twenty BCM students to participate in this important tour, including Zewu, who would soon succeed him as abbot of Nanputuo Temple (*NSZ* 2011, 318).

Shenghui adroitly handled the tour's religious and political implications even as Taiwan media reports suggested ambivalence towards it. Enthusiastic crowds, including politicians, worshiped the relic, while political groups denounced the tour, charging that the CPC's use of Buddhism amounted to propaganda (*China Post* 2002). In media, Shenghui delivered nuanced messages conveying Buddhist teachings as well as the CPC's message of unification. His eloquence in this diplomacy was evident in an interview in the *Taiwan Strait News* 台灣海峽時報, published by the PRC state-owned *Fujian Daily News* 福建日報, to promote closer ties between the PRC and Taiwan.

> The worship of the Buddha's finger bone relic in Taiwan is a significant event for Buddhist communities on both sides of the strait. It is a civilian Buddhist exchange that meets the years-long aspirations of the Buddhist community in Taiwan. This exchange activity among Buddhists lets many Taiwan compatriots pay homage directly to the Buddha finger relic. It will strengthen the close relations of Buddhists on both sides of the strait who have the same roots and origins and are nourished by the same Buddhism. Many high-ranking persons from the Nationalist Party, the People's Progress Party, and other political parties participated in the worship. (*Taiwan haixia shibao* 2002)

By commenting that politicians from opposing parties in Taiwan venerated the relic, Shenghui suggested that cultural unity could surmount political divisions. By noting that people in China and Taiwan were "nourished by the same Buddhism," he implied that the authenticity of Buddhism lay in the PRC and that the cultural unity of China and Taiwan was integrated through the PRC. In these ways, Buddhist relic diplomacy advanced the geopolitical ambitions of the CPC.

Since the mid-1990s, Nanputuo abbots have played a prominent role in the efforts of the Buddhist Association of China to create international Buddhist organizations led by Chinese clerics. In 1995, the establishment of the China-Korea-Japan Buddhist Goodwill Congress (Zhong han ri sanguo fojiao youhao jiaoliu huiyi 中韓日三國佛教友好交流會議) demonstrated that Buddhism was once again active in China. Zhao Puchu proposed it as a "golden sash," reflecting the historical interaction of China, Japan, and Korea via Buddhism. The initiative of clerics in the PRC to establish the congress and host the first meeting implied that the authenticity of Mahayana Buddhism in East Asia came from China. In his speech at the inaugural meeting of the congress, Miaozhan had called for cooperation among Buddhists of the three countries to establish Buddhist colleges and libraries (Miaozhan 1995).

ALIGNING WITH THE CENTRAL STATE, 1996-2004

In 1997, Shenghui served as the deputy leader of the Chinese delegation to the second goodwill congress, held in Kyoto. His youthful visage displayed the vitality of Chinese Buddhism, contrasting with Zhao Puchu and other delegation leaders who were twice his age. At the 2001 meeting held in Beijing, Shenghui led the Chinese delegation. He used the meeting's theme, "Buddhism and Environmental Protection," to attack Falun Gong, a key CPC concern at the time, calling it "environmental pollution" (Shenghui 2001a). We devote the next section of this chapter to the challenges Buddhism faced as it attempted to align itself with the Chinese state and oppose this popular religious movement.

Delegations of monks organized by the Buddhist Association of China and local Buddhist associations extended friendly exchanges to countries with growing populations of new overseas Chinese and large Taiwanese communities in Australia, North America, and elsewhere. They created goodwill and ties with overseas Chinese Buddhists and expanded China's cultural presence in countries of economic and political importance to the PRC. These tours visited multiple temples, coordinating their movements with Chinese embassies and consulates. We learned of one tour organized in 1999 by the Buddhist Association of China from a participant who was the prior of a local temple in Xiamen.[17] An influential and wealthy overseas Chinese businesswoman from Taiwan, who lived in Australia and was a disciple of Hsing Yun, initiated the tour by inviting the Buddhist Association of China to attend a temple consecration ceremony in Australia. The association sent a six-person delegation of four monks from Guangji Temple, the association's headquarters, and two young BCM graduates who were rising leaders in Xiamen's Buddhism. The tour visited Fo Guang Shan temples including Nan Tien Temple (Nantian si 南天寺) near Sydney, the largest Buddhist temple in the southern hemisphere; Chung Tian Temple (Zhongtian si 中天寺) near Brisbane; and smaller Fo Guang Shan meditation halls and Guanyin temples. At each temple, the monks joined discussions on the development of Buddhism in the contemporary world.

The tour served the needs of various actors. It gave the Buddhist Association of China a chance to observe innovative aspects of modern Buddhist temple management in the global operations of Fo Guang Shan, such as digitized sutras, multifunctional conference halls, religious and secular courses offered by Buddhist academies to laypersons, and adaptations of Taixu's modern reform Buddhism to the contexts of non-Buddhist societies. These observations gave the Buddhist Association of China and leading clerics new ideas, whether for scholarship or for adapting Buddhism to the needs of society and the Buddhist diplomacy of the state. Chinese diplomats could use the tour to develop ties with Australia's large and influential Taiwan community; expand the PRC's cultural influence in Australia, a growing source of raw materials and foodstuffs for China and a destination for overseas investment; and deepen ties with Fo Guang Shan and its influential leader Hsing Yun. As for the Nanputuo monks, they welcomed the chance to develop new ties between their temples in Xiamen and overseas Buddhist temples, while their presence also helped build goodwill with Taiwanese Buddhists in Australia through their shared Minnan culture. In these ways, Buddhist diplomacy, with Nanputuo Temple's participation, cultivated relations with overseas Chinese, furthered bilateral relations, and helped project the PRC's cultural influence as a growing global power.

Distinguishing Buddhism by Opposing Falun Gong

In July 1999, the state crackdown on Falun Gong created a challenge for Buddhism because Falun Gong claimed to be Buddhist. Shenghui's leadership of Buddhism locally and nationally in the crackdown positioned Buddhism more securely in the institutional space of religion while aligning Nanputuo Temple and himself more tightly with the state. As is well known, Falun Gong 法輪功, also called Falun Dafa 法輪大法 or Great Dharma Wheel Practice, was a new cultivation practice founded in the early 1990s by the qigong practitioner Li Hongzhi 李洪志. Combining qigong, meditation, and moral teachings, such practices have existed for over a thousand years in various styles and lineages that combine Buddhism, Daoism, martial arts, and folk beliefs. Falun Gong, the most popular of the many new schools, grew rapidly in the 1990s to have tens of millions of followers. The activities of these groups generated much income, enabling them to pay state-recognized associations for sponsorship to gain recognition in the state administrative system. In 1993 Falun Gong established the Falun Dafa Research Society (Falun dafa yanjiu hui 法輪大法研究會) as a branch of the state-run China Qigong Science Society (Zhongguo qigong kexue yanjiu hui 中國氣功科學研究會).[18] Because Falun Gong was centered in northeast Chinese cities hit hard by state-industry layoffs, its members came from all walks of life, including officials and unemployed workers, who met regularly in public parks to practice.

Although the CPC initially tolerated such practices, it soon saw Falun Gong as a threat because its strong ideas and decentralized national organizations could mobilize many people in multiple locales. The spark that led to the crackdown was the enforcement of new national state regulations in the mid-1990s to standardize the regulation of social organizations. In 1997, the Falun Dafa Research Society was dissolved, threatening its existence. Falun Gong sought recognition from the Buddhist Association of China as a Buddhist organization but the association refused because Falun Gong did not meet its criteria for Buddhism. On April 25, 1999, thousands of Falun Gong followers protested their treatment by the state in a silent vigil that surrounded the residential compound of CPC leaders in Beijing. The action shocked the party into launching a massive state campaign on July 20 to suppress and eliminate Falun Gong (Otehode 2009; Ownby 2008; Penny 2003).

The campaign was the first to target a religious community in China with some links to Buddhism since the Cultural Revolution. Falun Gong leaders were arrested and gatherings banned. The state media broadcast attacks on Falun Gong, calling it an evil cult and its founder Li Hongzhi a charlatan. The crackdown began just days before we arrived for two months of fieldwork in Xiamen, so it was very much on people's minds. Buddhists were confused and frightened because of overlaps in beliefs and practices between Falun Gong and Buddhism: such vital concepts in Falun Gong as dharma and karma came from Buddhism; its founder claimed to be a bodhisattva; and the practice of qigong was also widespread among Buddhists. For these reasons, Buddhists were anxious that the crackdown on Falun Gong would envelop Buddhism. Rumors circulated about arrests of Buddhist qigong practitioners and investigations of monks and devotees.

But the relentless state media attack on Falun Gong did not mention Buddhism. After a week, Buddhists relaxed. A senior monk at Nanputuo

Temple expressed his confidence to us that the crackdown on Falun Gong had nothing to do with Buddhism.

> [The crackdown] will not affect the big five religions [Buddhism, Daoism, Catholicism, Islam, Protestantism]. But Falun Gong is like the White Lotus Society.[19] It has an organization and political goals.... Why does Falun Gong have so many followers? It is because the masses lack a sufficient understanding of religion. They cannot distinguish true religions [zhengjiao 正教] from cults [xiejiao 邪教] and are easily deceived. From now on, the government will pay more attention to distinguishing rightful religion from evil cults to eliminate them.[20]

To ensure that people and state officials did not confuse Buddhism and Falun Gong, the monk said Buddhists had to teach people how to distinguish between them. One source of confusion was their shared conceptual terminology. Another source of confusion was Buddhism's growing popularity among laypersons in groups and networks outside temples. This trend began after the Tiananmen Square protest as students, intellectuals, and professionals turned from politics to safer religious activities, such as organizing sutra study and meditation groups. After the start of the crackdown on Falun Gong, the monks were concerned that these independent activities might be seen as part of it. We explain below the efforts in Xiamen by monks, devotees, and BAX officers to distinguish Buddhism from Falun Gong, especially those made by Shenghui during his national leadership in the anti–Falun Gong campaign.

Buddhist Responses in Xiamen

Shenghui moved swiftly to coordinate activities in Nanputuo Temple with the state crackdown on Falun Gong. He was familiar with the movement because he was the vice president of the Buddhist Association of China in 1997 when it first denied Falun Gong recognition as a Buddhist organization. Several days after the crackdown began, copies of articles in the state media attacking Falun Gong were posted in the temple's central compound on a public announcement board used to disseminate teachings of Buddhism. Some articles charged Falun Gong with being an illegal organization. One headline announced, "Decision of the Civil Affairs Ministry of the People's Republic of China Regarding the Ban on Falun Gong Dafa Research Society" (*Xiamen ribao* 1999). Other articles attacked the character of Li Hongzhi, such as one headlined "The Life of Li Hongzhi" (*Xiamen wanbao* 1999). Another statement drew a line between Buddhism and Falun Gong by explaining Buddhist teachings and terms used by Falun Gong. Noticeably, no responses or comments were issued in the name of the abbot and monks of Nanputuo Temple.

An intellectual devotee serving on the BAX executive board explained the monks' lack of response to us. He said that most Buddhist monks did not know how to criticize Falun Gong as superstition without criticizing Buddhism. "The issue of superstition puts monks in a difficult position. There are superstitious aspects to Buddhism. Even monks can be unable to distinguish Falun Gong from Buddhism clearly. So, if you criticize Falun Gong poorly, it will backfire on you."[21] He illustrated this point with the Buddhist concept of karma, which Falun Gong interpreted as the reason an individual's sickness and poor health in this life could be attributed to behaving badly in a previous life. "How can a Buddhist criticize this concept [karma]? It is part of Buddhism, so if you criticize it, you are criticizing yourself."[22] To challenge Falun Gong, a cleric needed an excellent understanding of its teachings and practices. But younger monks knew nothing about Falun Gong because their text-based education in state-approved Buddhist academies did not expose them to the popular Buddhist practices of laypersons. Furthermore, the state religious policy discouraged young clerics from venturing outside temples into society to experience the popular practices of Buddhism widespread among the people. According to our devotee observer, the young clerics could not understand the needs of the mass of Buddhist believers, even though they could see the sufferings of laid-off workers, poor farmers, and others.

The only clerics who understood the state-recognized Buddhism practiced in temples and the popular Buddhism practiced by people in society were elderly monks ordained before 1949. They knew the psychology of the people, the cultural background of popular beliefs, and the level of people's understanding of everyday Buddhism. Many had recently passed away, such as Miaozhan. Those still alive wanted nothing to do with Falun Gong; they would not even write articles distinguishing

Buddhism from Falun Gong as part of the state campaign to suppress it. We asked the devotee what these monks feared because the Buddhist Association of China had publicly criticized Falun Gong since 1997. He replied, "Now [in 1999], the situation is different. Falun Gong has been labeled an illegal organization, so the criticism has become political. . . . People are afraid that if they make a mistake in how they criticize Falun Gong, it will be a political mistake that will hurt them."[23]

This devotee, an expert in local Minnan religious customs and traditions, used the example of karma to explain how he distinguished Buddhism from Falun Gong.

> Falun Gong says sickness is caused by wrongdoing in your previous life. So, you cannot be cured by a doctor but only by practicing Falun Gong. If you do not get well, this is because you did something terrible in your previous life. This idea in Falun Gong comes from the Buddhist idea of karma. But I distinguish it as follows. Karma in Buddhism emphasizes the present life. For example, goodness and evil are repaid. This encourages people to do good deeds and be kind. . . . But in Falun Gong, karma emphasizes the previous life. It says to endure if you are sick because you did evil in the previous life.[24]

Because the devotee understood Buddhist concepts so well, the BAX had asked him to write an article on Falun Gong's appropriation and misuse of them. The article was to be titled "Raising the Banner of Buddhism to Oppose Buddhism: Denouncing the Fallacies of 'Falundafa'" (打着佛教旗號反佛教的魔鬼邪教—斥"法輪大法"的歪理邪教). But even though he was writing the article, he told us, it would be published with a prominent younger monk listed as coauthor to give more authority.

BAX officers and government officials offered yet another explanation for why the monks at Nanputuo Temple did not write articles critical of Falun Gong: with almost no local Falun Gong followers, monks had no need to do so. According to a BAX officer, Xiamen had only one hundred Falun Gong followers, and an official of the Fujian Religious Affairs Bureau said that were only seven thousand Falun Gong followers in the entire province. In a somewhat self-congratulatory tone, they attributed these low numbers to the successful implementation of the religious policy in Fujian, which had taught people the difference between "orthodox religions" such as Buddhism and "cults" such as Falun Gong.²⁵

National and International Platforms

Shenghui became the national voice of Buddhism to condemn Falun Gong. From 2000, he served as vice president of the newly created National Anti-Cult Association (Quanguo fan xiejiao xiehui 全國反邪教協會), along with representatives of the other four state-recognized religions. The association aimed to discredit Falun Gong through exhibitions, conferences, and media events. Shenghui made speeches condemning Falun Gong, such as one in 2001 titled "Rid Evil, Oppose Cults, Eliminate Falsities, and Correct Rightfully" (除惡反邪去偽匡正) at a meeting of the Chinese People's Political Consultative Committee (Shenghui 2001c).

Shenghui used Nanputuo Temple as a hub for his efforts. For example, a spring 2002 National Anti-Cult Association meeting held at the temple attracted 140 national representatives of the five recognized religions who presented sixty-five papers criticizing Falun Gong. BCM students staged cultural events, such as reciting a poem titled "To the Souls of Those Harmed by Cults" (致被邪教殘害的靈魂) and performing a chant "that vividly reflected the widespread Buddhist prayer for positive prosperity, societal peace, and the good wish to actively save the souls of those hurt by cults" (Chen 2002). Shenghui gave a speech, saying:

> In religion, cults are the opposite of orthodoxy. All traditional religions regard as cults those forces that violate, distort, and falsify their teachings and deviate from moral traditions. Li Hongzhi and his cult organization "Falun Gong" stole religious concepts, especially Buddhist ones, fabricated the so-called Falun Dafa, confused people, defrauded them of money, and destroyed lives. This seriously endangers society and people, grievously damages our rightful Buddhism, and harms the religious feelings of all Buddhist believers. Therefore, cults are not religions, but religion is the natural nemesis of cults. Precisely because of this, the earliest resistance

to the "Falun Gong" cult was our religion. In particular, our Buddhism. As early as 1996, our beloved deceased president, Mr. Zhao Puchu, pointed out the cult nature of "Falun Gong." (Shenghui 2001c)

Shenghui stressed the need for Buddhists to lead in exposing the cult character of Falun Gong. His mention of the date "1996" showed that the Buddhist Association of China had denounced Falun Gong three years before the CPC's national crackdown.

Shenghui's condemnation of Falun Gong on international platforms articulated an emerging CPC view of religion tailored for a global audience. In 2001 he went to Geneva to speak about the situation of religion in the PRC to the United Nations Human Rights Commission. His immediate aim was to tamp down criticisms of the suppression of Falun Gong in the PRC as a violation of human rights, but his speech also reflected how the CPC discourse was shifting from its position two decades earlier in Document 19. We quote this remarkable speech in full:

> At the close of the historical processes of the twentieth century, there is an even greater need for peace by humanity in the new century and millennium. Peace is not just a theme of the times but a problem necessitating ongoing efforts to solve.
>
> The distinctive characteristic of Chinese culture that "harmony is most valued" deeply permeates the beliefs and practices of all religions in our country. We deeply understand that the success of these activities requires a peaceful environment. Without peace, there can be no human rights and development, so first, it is necessary to have peace in order to have human rights and development! Peace-loving is a fine tradition of religion in China. Although the five major Chinese religions—Buddhism, Daoism, Islam, Protestantism, and Catholicism—have different origins and doctrines, there has never been large-scale conflict and nothing resembling the brutal religious wars in Western history.
>
> In today's China, the harmonious coexistence of religions is entering a new phase. Freedom of religion stems from its enshrinement in the constitution, and under its protection, we enjoy complete and total religious freedom. Regardless of their size, the five

major religions have equal status, mutually respect each other, and independently conduct religious activities. They make positive contributions by smiting evil to promote good, purifying people's minds, and working for national construction and benefits. Those of us in religious circles consider now to be a golden era.

However, we also note that not every place is illuminated by peaceful sunlight in today's world, as war and poverty remain rampant, and humanity is still suffering unbearable pain. Some violence and evil in the world are even carried out in the name of "religion." There are people who use religious differences to incite racial hatred and the "clash of civilizations." They use the excuse of protecting religious human rights to trample the sovereignty of other countries. They use the banner of religion to deceive the public, gain trust and split the motherland. Moreover, heretical cults plagiarize religious terminology and uphold the banner of religion to oppose religions, deceive the masses, and kill for profit. For example, the rampant spread of Falun Gong in China was due to its theft of religious doctrine. Its use of Buddhist terms, such as "dharma wheel" and "completeness," transmitted for two thousand years to make the Great Law of Dharma Wheel Practice, has confused people, swindled money, and destroyed lives. The Falun Gong heterodox cult is similar to the United States' Branch Davidians, Japan's Aum Shinrikyo, and Uganda's Restoring the Ten Commandments of God Movement. In China, Falun Gong killed a thousand people. Moreover, in its schemes to get money by whatever means, it distorts and misrepresents other religions by saying such things as, "All religions are false." "God does not recognize religions." "All religions nowadays—Buddhism, Christianity, Catholicism, and even Judaism—cannot save people and are lowly." Therefore, the heterodox cult Falun Gong is a dark force that destroys religious freedom and human rights. In particular, Buddhism, along with knowledgeable people in science and technology, law, journalism, and other walks of life, have struggled to expose the plot for five years. Finally, in 1999, our government outlawed the Falun Gong cult.

Unfortunately, the Falun Gong cult leader Li Hongzhi went to a powerful country where he tells lies and complains loudly about alleged injustices, confusing his adherents in China. Nurtured by its money and support, he even incites self-immolations in Tiananmen Square. The merging of this power and evil has become today's biggest obstacle to human rights and religious freedom.

As a representative of China's religious circles, both as director of the United Nations Association of China and vice president of the Buddhist Association of China, along with over one hundred million adherents, I am bitter about this. In this regarding, Chinese religious circles, based on the United Nations' principles and charter, advocate as follows:

First, hold the peace banner high, and safeguard the purity of religions. Oppose the use of religion to pursue power politics. Oppose the use of religious resources to split the motherland. Oppose the endangerment of world peace by religious extremism. Oppose heterodox cults' misappropriation of religious terminology, trampling on religions, and breaching the peace.

Second, promote the spirit of religious tolerance and peace, and create an environment of peaceful coexistence. Directly face differences between civilizations and religious beliefs by mutual respect, seeking common ground, strengthening dialogue among civilizations and religions, treating them equally, and avoiding confrontation. Expand the advantages of different civilizations and religious beliefs, promote national unity, ethnic unity, dispute-free relations among religions and big and small countries, the equality of peoples, and maintain peace and common progress.

In the new millennium, let us seize the bond of peace that is religion, in keeping with the spirit of saving the world, to create the comprehensive, lasting, and just worldly paradise that humanity is seeking. (Shenghui, 2001b)

We consider Shenghui's speech to be an early expression of the CPC's new ideological approach toward religion in the wake of Falun Gong. It employed Document 19's discursive style of positively and negatively valued dichotomies in a tightly reasoned and self-referential argument. One dichotomy was between the West, with its history of religious conflict and war, and China, where religions coexist because they have absorbed the value of harmony from Chinese civilization. (Of course, Shenghui did not mention the CPC's suppression of religion during the Cultural

Revolution.) The other dichotomy was religion and cult: the former purifies people's minds, benefits society, and promotes national unity, whereas the latter confuses people, causes social chaos, and undermines the nation and state. Crucially, these dichotomies were not rooted in the Marxian historical materialism seen in Document 19, but they appeared to draw on the growing field of religious studies in the PRC that saw religions as embodying traditional values and creating social capital (see Lü and Gong 2014). This ideological shift suggested that in the quest for a less divisive approach in the wake of Falun Gong, the CPC would incorporate folk beliefs and practices as cultural expressions of national identity and as policies to promote social stability.

The selection of Shenghui, as a Buddhist monk, to deliver this important speech to an international audience also had multiple significances. Its alternative discursive framing of religion deemphasized the issue of human rights in ways favorable not only to China but also to the CPC's growing aspiration for the PRC to be recognized as a world power. The selection of a leading Buddhist monk to make this statement reflected the growing role of Buddhism, and important temples such as Nanputuo, as sites for new forms of Buddhism as religion and culture.[26]

Conclusion

The third phase of Nanputuo Temple's recovery occurred within the CPC's attempts to create a more administratively standardized and centralized state system to govern the rapid economic growth and new social forces in the wealthier society. Using the opening created by Miaozhan's death, the Buddhist Association of China installed a new abbot, Shenghui. As a monk educated in the Buddhist Academy of China in Beijing, the country's political center, Shenghui had excellent knowledge of Buddhist teachings and a grasp of CPC ideology toward religion and its expectations for Buddhism. He furthered the integration of Buddhism's semiotic and physical spaces in Nanputuo Temple with the institutional space of religion to develop its image as an ideal Buddhist temple for the CPC. While some criticized Shenghui as a political monk, his understanding of the CPC's ideology had dual significance for Buddhism in the space of religion. On the one hand, he sought to serve the CPC by speaking in ways the party expected. On the other hand, he strove to maintain the relevance and status of Buddhism under the CPC. His efforts as abbot for eight years from 1997 enhanced the temple's alignment with central state expectations while disengaging it from local Buddhist communities in Xiamen. By the early twenty-first century, with its recovery complete, Nanputuo Temple was ready to meet the needs of Buddhists in the expanding middle class and the CPC's expectations for Buddhism as both religion and culture.

The ceremony for the release of burning mouths lasts an entire night, ending at dawn. It invites wandering ghosts that died in unusual circumstances, such as natural disasters, wars, and accidents. At the top center is the ritual master acting on behalf of the Dizang bodhisattva to save wandering ghosts by feeding them sacred water and bread. This photograph, taken in 1990, shows the ritual specialist Dingmiao presiding over one of the first performances of the ceremony since Nanputuo Temple's reopening. He was one of the few elderly clerics after the Cultural Revolution who remembered the ritual practice (see page 122). This performance of the ceremony at Nanputuo Temple transmitted knowledge of its practice to young monks.

The start of Miaozhan's abbatial ascension ceremony on October 9, 1989. He entered Nanputuo Temple through the West Mountain Gate in the early morning. He was led by the monk Dingmiao, serving as master of ceremonies. A young monk carried an incense tray to purify the path.

Miaozhan offered flowers to the Buddha after becoming abbot at his ascension ceremony.

Senior clerics attending the abbatial ascension ceremony as guests. Miaozhan (c.) was flanked by Mingyang (l.), a vice president of the Buddhist Association of China, and Yuanzhuo (r.), abbot of Guanghua Temple. They were in front of the abbot's residence.

(*left*) Ordinands learn how to put on their robes as part of the two-week ordination training at Guanghua Temple in October 1989.

(*right*) An instructor teaches an elderly novice to make a formal bow as part of the ordination training.

Ordinands eat at the dining hall during the ordination training. They are learning dining manners for monastic life, such as eating in silence and waiting for the gong sound to pick up the bowl.

Three elderly novices with tense expressions wait to receive the precepts for reordainment. They hold the robes they will wear after being reordained. The monk on the right is an instructor (*yinli shi* 引禮師), also recently ordained.

After fifteen days, the newly ordained monks are happy and relaxed as they wait for buses to go home.

Newly ordained nuns filed into the Great Buddha Hall at Chongfu Temple in January 1990. The ordination ceremony was the first only for nuns since the Cultural Revolution.

PART III

Nanputuo Temple and Local Buddhist Communities

7

Dynamism of Local Temples

WE NOW SHIFT OUR GAZE from Nanputuo Temple to look at the space of religion in Xiamen's other Buddhist temples. Some had been occupied by the military and local government units in the 1950s and razed to make space for military buildings and factories; others had been destroyed by Red Guards during the Cultural Revolution. The few original buildings still standing were in great disrepair. Some temples were reclaimed by the BAX as early as 1979 and rebuilt with funds from overseas Chinese clerics. Compounds were rebuilt as multistoried structures on a much larger scale to maximize available floor space on limited land. In 1997, according to our survey, about half of the forty-one temples on Xiamen Island had recovered and were registered as religious activity sites, actively creating niches within neighborhoods, business communities, and overseas Buddhist networks. Their appeal increased in 1997 when the abbot Shenghui banned popular on-demand practices and rituals at Nanputuo Temple to focus on educating monks (see chapter 6). Although tourists still went to Nanputuo Temple for the experience, Xiamen residents increasingly turned to local temples for worship. These temples welcomed their support, responding to their needs as a semiotic space to connect with history, ancestors, and local culture through Buddhism.

In this chapter we consider the recovery of local temples as a process of positioning in the physical, semiotic, and institutional spaces of religion. In the first section we provide an overview of the types of temples recognized by the BAX in Xiamen's Buddhism. Hongshan Temple, the only temple directly administered by Nanputuo, is our subject in the second section. Third, we describe three dharma transmission temples. And in the fourth section we examine how flexibilities in the space of religion contributed to the positioning of three local temples. The recovery process of a temple was shaped by its links to Nanputuo Temple, ties to overseas Chinese and other historical capitals, and the prior's character and abilities.

Types of Local Temples in Xiamen

The *Gazetteer of Xiamen Buddhism* classified temples in Xiamen's Buddhism into three types (see table 7.1).

The twenty-three extant "Buddhist temples" (*fojiao si* 佛教寺) in the table were founded in the sixteenth and seventeenth centuries by Buddhist monks from the Linji, Caodong 曹洞, and Yunmen 云門 schools of Pure Land Buddhism. Over half included the character for "temple" (*si* 寺) in their names. One was called a "yard" (*yuan* 院), a term typically referring to a temple's residence for elderly clerics. Eight were called "cave" (*dong* 洞) and "crag" (*yan* 岩), indicating quiet and scenic locations for cultivation. Their physical space conformed closely to the ideal of a

TABLE 7.1 BAX Classification of Buddhist Temples in Xiamen City

Type	Temple Form	Description	Extant	Forsaken
Buddhist temple	Temple	"Three halls, five courts" on north-south axis, founded in Ming and Qing dynasties.	14	5
	Crag, cave	Located in beautiful, secluded places. Founded in Ming dynasty.	8	6
	Small temple	For elderly clerics. Founded in Song, Yuan, Ming dynasties.	1	2
Lay nun hall	Hall, grove, hermitage	In residential areas. Founded in late Qing dynasty and ROC.	10	16
Daoist, folk belief temples	Temple, shrine	Sites where Buddhist monks once lived, founded in Ming and Qing dynasties.	8	24
Total			41	53

Source: XFZ, 105–113.

Buddhist temple layout, with halls and courts oriented to the worship of the Buddha (*XFZ*, 49). As for the caves and crags, noted the *Gazetteer*, "although they are small, their construction takes the main shrine hall as the center surrounded by appropriate courts. Therefore, they have not lost the special characteristics of a Buddhist temple" (*XFZ*, 67–68). In the 1990s, caves and crags began to include the character for "temple" in their names as they expanded in size.

Ten extant sites were called "temples where lay nuns reside" (*zhu caigu de si* 住菜姑的寺), hereafter referred to as lay nun halls. The lay nuns were celibate and pious women who lived communally. In the eighteenth and nineteenth centuries they were affiliated with folk religious movements, but in the early twentieth century Hongyi and other Nanputuo monks recognized them as a special category of Buddhist. The names given to their places of residence contained the characters for "hall" (*tang* 堂, *yuan* 苑), "lodge" (*lin* 林, also translated as "grove" or "forest"), and hermitage (*jingshe* 精舍, *an* 庵). These multistoried residence sites did not conform to the single-plane layout of a Buddhist temple, but the BAX considered them Buddhist because the lifestyle of the lay nuns was similar to that of ordained nuns and centered on the worship of the Buddha and Guanyin. In the early 2000s, many halls were transformed into Buddhist temples for ordained nuns and adopted the character for "temple" into their names, a trend we discuss in the next chapter.

The *Gazetteer of Xiamen Buddhism* included eight sites in a category called "temple where [Buddhist clerics] have resided" (*XFZ*, 109).[1] Their names contained the characters for *gong* 宮 or *miao* 庙, indicating they were Daoist and folk belief temples, of which there were two hundred in Xiamen City. The eight mentioned by the *Gazetteer* were founded in the eighteenth and nineteenth centuries to worship powerful deities including Mazu 馬祖, the Sea Goddess and protector of seafarers; Baosheng Dadi 保生大帝 (Great Life Preserving Emperor), the medicine deity with extraordinary curative power; and Guandi 關帝, who controlled evil spirits. Their location in the city center and perceptions of their magical efficacy made them very popular with Xiamen residents.

We focus in this chapter on temples with ordained clerics in residence. Most of them were classified in the *Gazetteer* as "Buddhist temples," although the categories were flexible, and some reclassification occurred. Table 7.2 highlights some of their characteristics.

TABLE 7.2 Characteristics of Selected Local Buddhist Temples in 1999

Temple	Leadership	Residents	Niche
Hongshan Temple 鴻山寺	Prior appointed by Nanputuo abbot	10 monks, some devotees	Downtown location, salon for artists and intellectuals
Puguang Temple 普光寺	Prior selected in consultation with Nanputuo abbot	16 monks	Performed locally popular rituals commissioned by overseas Chinese
Huxiyan Temple 虎溪岩寺	Prior selected in consultation with Nanputuo abbot	8 monks, some devotees	Scenic location and center for devotees
Bailudong Temple 白鹿洞寺	Prior selected in consultation with Nanputuo abbot	15 monks, some lay nuns and devotees	Scenic location, emphasized Minnan culture
Wanshilian Temple 萬石蓮寺	Succession resolved by Nanputuo abbot becoming prior	10 nuns and lay nuns, some devotees	Previously served as nunnery for BCM nuns
Guanyin Temple 觀音寺	Founded by monk with Nanputuo and XRAB connections	4 monks	New temple located on a prominent ridge
Tianzhuyan Temple 天竺岩寺	Managed by BAX through Xiamen Devotee Lodge		Earth God temple converting to Buddhist temple

Source: Data from 1999 survey, Yoshiko Ashiwa and David Wank

Hongshan Temple: A Branch of Nanputuo

Hongshan Temple's location close to Xiamen's old downtown helped make it a meeting place for intellectuals, artists, and youth. The temple was founded in the sixteenth century and rebuilt in 1889 by Xican 喜參 (1848–1911), a former prior of Nanshan Temple. Xican led Hongshan for two years and then became prior of Nanputuo Temple (Nanputuo and Nanshan Temples had Heyun religious lineage). When Nanputuo Temple was ecumenicized in 1924, Hongshan became its branch temple (*xia yuan* 下院), with its prior appointed by the Nanputuo abbot.

Hongshan Temple was closely associated with the modern reform movement of Buddhism. In the 1920s, young activist devotees propagating Buddhism made it their headquarters, and many eminent monks gave dharma talks there. After the Japanese invasion in 1937, clerics abandoned the temple, and lay nuns moved in. In 1958, the army made Hongshan an observation post and storeroom; then, in the last year of the Cultural Revolution, it became a public park (*XFZ*, 52–53). The temple's recovery from 1987 was aided by Guangjing, prior of Longshan Temple in Singapore, and Miaohua 妙華 (1922–2009), who had founded and restored temples in the PRC, the United States, and Vietnam. Although Miaohua had no ties to Hongshan Temple, the Nanputuo abbot Miaozhan appointed Miaohua's disciple Fayun as prior.[2]

Temple Prior and Local Capital

Fayun 法雲 was an energetic monk in his early thirties when we first met him at Hongshan. He was born in 1966 in Xiapu County 霞浦縣, north of Fuzhou City. His mother was Buddhist, and from a young age Fayun enjoyed reading sutras. He decided to become a monk even though his father opposed the idea. He first went to a local temple in nearby Fuding City 福鼎市 and then to the larger Ziguo Temple 資國寺 for further study of Buddhism. Fayun's teacher was Ti'an 題安, a Buddhist monk in Fuding who had studied at a Buddhist academy and kept the precepts during the Cultural Revolution. Ti'an had many disciples, so he asked Miaohua, his younger dharma brother, to be Fayun's master. Fayun was ordained at Jiuhua Temple, Anhui Province, in 1986 and enrolled in the BCM. He was twenty-four years old when he became prior of Hongshan in 1989, even before he graduated. He became a locally elite cleric, assuming official positions in the Xiamen and Fujian Buddhist associations and the Siming District People's Consultative Committee in Xiamen. Additionally, he received state awards, such as XRAB recognition as an "advanced individual in religious circles serving the construction of socialist society and the two civilizations" (宗教界為社會主義兩個文明建設服務先進個人). Deng Xiaoping had promoted the concept of "two civilizations" in the 1980s to foster economic and spiritual development; the award thus conveyed that Fayun fit the CPC's image of an ideal Buddhist monk. In 1997, the Nanputuo abbot, Shenghui, gave Fayun a dharma transmission for the Linji and Caodong sects of Shenghui's religious lineages. This reflected Shenghui's high esteem for Fayun as a young, rising cleric.

Fayun reconnected the temple to its history by revitalizing it as a center of devotee education and an intellectual and artistic salon. To encourage conversation and contemplation, he built a scenic teahouse displaying artwork by Xiamen artists. He gave dharma talks on humanistic

Buddhism and sutras, believing that they were more effective in propagating Buddhism than chanting because they spread Buddhist reasoning. His acts of charity included providing the tuition of poor children and BCM students, paying medical expenses of poor devotees, and repairing infrastructure and temples in disaster areas. When we visited the temple in 1999, the residents included ten monks, two lay nuns, and a devotee who was the prior's uncle and accountant. There were few fixed positions among the monks; each was assigned by the prior as needed. A dharma talk every Tuesday, a great compassion dharma assembly (*dabei fa hui* 大悲法會), and a ten-thousand-buddhas worship assembly (*wanfo fa hui* 萬佛法會) in September were among the temple's regularly scheduled activities.[3]

Fayun's successful leadership of Hongshan Temple exemplifies how connections to local capital in Xiamen's Buddhism contributed to the temple's recovery. First, the Nanputuo temple abbots appointed him as prior and actively supported him. Second, as a BCM graduate grounded in Buddhist teachings and secular subjects, Fayun was capable of giving dharma talks relevant to laypersons' lives. Third, his appointments in the BAX and district legislature gave him status and networks to manage the temples and interact with officials. Fourth, he had a clear understanding of the temple's history and how to build on its legacy to appeal to worshipers. Fifth, he was outgoing in his way, which helped him connect with people.

Narrative of Rebuilding and Patriotism

In 1996, a large stele was erected in Hongshan Temple's courtyard to commemorate its rebuilding. Generally, a narrative of a temple's history and rebuilding is engraved in characters on the stone surface. This information is meant to bolster the prestige of the temple by referring to highly valued resources in its contemporary context, which in imperial times were land and patrons (Walsh 2010). At Hongshan the new stele, an imposing rectangular slab of black stone atop a pedestal, narrated the temple's history in a way that expressed values of patriotism, modernity, state patronage, self-sufficiency, and overseas Chinese and popular support. The red engraved characters conveying the history appeared under the title "Inscription of Rebuilding of Xiamen's Hongshan Temple"

(Chongjian Xiamen Hongshan si beiji 重建廈門鴻山寺碑記). Even if people did not stop to read, the imposing stele's presence signified the grandeur and significance of the site.

The narrative began by establishing the temple's position in Buddhism. "It is for worshiping Guanyin Pusa. All who worship here will have their prayers realized" (*chongfeng guanyin renshi fan you qiqiu* 崇奉觀音人士凡有祈求). The message also indicated the temple's popular appeal because Guanyin was widely worshiped in Minnan. Because the temple was a branch of Nanputuo Temple, no mention was made of Hongshan's lineage or denomination. An allusion to the temple's ancient age, however, was meant as a reminder that the Buddha's teachings are timeless: "There is no way to know the origins of the temple" (*mi bu li ying kaishan shiji yi wu ke kao* 靡不立應開山事蹟已無可考).

The account of Hongshan's history on the stele began with an event meant to express the temple's patriotism in resisting foreign power: on November 26, 1622, a Ming dynasty official executed several Dutch sailors who were raiding Xiamen. This execution had been recorded on a rock at the temple titled "Engraved rock of Xu Yiming [Ming official] attacking and suppressing the red barbarians [Westerners]" (*xuyiming gong jiao hong yi ke shi* 徐一鳴攻剿紅夷刻石). According to Fayun, the rock was the reason the provincial state recognized the temple in 1985 as a "Fujian Province Cultural Protection Unit" (Fujian sheng wenwu baohu danwei 福建省文物保護單位).

The stele narrative went on to explain how the temple's rebuilding over centuries had depended on believers and military governors, thus conveying deep historical support for the temple and Buddhism. Moving into the modern era, the narrative told of the temple's rebuilding by Xican after it had been destroyed during the Taiping Rebellion (1850–1864), a detail alluding to Hongshan's link to Nanputuo Temple. It listed prominent devotees who studied at the temple in the 1920s and organized the New Buddhist Youth Association (Fojiao xin qingnian hui 佛教新青年會), highlighting its importance in the movement for the modern reform of Buddhism.

The narrative then recounted the temple's recovery.

> In 1987, Venerable Miaohua from Singapore visited and saw how decrepit Hongshan Temple had become. He felt that the old temple

was a famous site in such a wealthy place as Xiamen. He felt that it would be a good place to propagate Buddhism. It was also a branch of Nanputuo Temple. There was a monk from Longshan Temple in Singapore named Guangjing. Guangjing was also invited by Venerable Guangchu to help rebuild Puguang Temple. Ven. Guangjing communicated a lot about Hongshan Temple and got the permission of the government. Thereupon, he took all his savings and raised more money. He asked Nanputuo Temple's Ven. Miaozhan to take charge of restoring Hongshan Temple.

This passage established the support of Buddhists for the temple's recovery, including overseas Chinese and its close cooperation with Nanputuo Temple. A list of the buildings in the compound in order of restoration was engraved on the stele, indicating that Hongshan Temple was complete as a Buddhist temple.

The narrative concluded with a paean to the temple's successful recovery. "It is now eight years since Hongshan Temple was restored. Now is a good era. The country is strong, and Buddhism is strong [*guo qiang fo qiang* 國強佛強]. There are more and more believers. Hongshan Temple is once again open. Venerable Miaohua asked that the reasons for restoring the temple and the restoration process be recorded. I have therefore recorded what I know so that those who come later will know." The author's name was listed at the bottom, Lin Ziqing 林子青 (1910–2002), a devotee from Xiamen with a national reputation who worked in the Buddhist Association of China and taught in the BCM (see chapter 8). His authorship heightened the grandeur of the stele and Hongshan Temple.

Dharma Transmission Temples and Their Niches

The leadership of the dharma transmission temples was complicated by history and religious policy, so here we provide some useful context. Clerics considered each temple as belonging to a dharma transmission lineage of masters and disciples from one of the Buddhist schools who would pass the priorship among themselves. An elderly overseas Chinese cleric who funded the rebuilding of a temple, for instance, expected the new prior to be from his lineage. But lineage inheritance was complicated because the religious policy forbade a monk who was not a PRC citizen from leading a temple. The problem arose because the overseas clerics were neither PRC citizens nor did they have disciples who were. The Nanputuo monks, BAX, and XRAB cooperated to overcome these problems in a manner that respected the authority of both dharma lineage and religious policy. Typically, Miaozhan introduced a young monk studying at the BCM to the elderly overseas monk funding the restoration of a temple. The elderly monk would then give a dharma transmission—an understanding of the teaching of Buddhism passed down through the generational lineage—to the young cleric.[4] The transmission was a private ceremony to inscribe the name of the young cleric into the lineage scroll of their new master as the youngest generation of dharma receivers. Then the BAX, which legally owned the temple, appointed the disciple as the prior.

Puguang Temple: Upcoming Wealthy Temple with Great Popular Support

Puguang Temple was founded as a Pure Land temple in the Ming dynasty. The military had used it as a storehouse from 1958 to 1977, and then villagers farmed its land for the next decade (XFZ, 55–56). Its recovery from 1986 was led by Guangyu 廣餘 (1920–2006), prior of Miaoxianglin Temple in Penang and a disciple of Zhuandao. He was the dharma brother of Guangshu 廣樹 (1914–1979), the previous prior of Puguang Temple from 1937 to 1946 (XFZ, 176–177). To find a prior, Guangyu consulted with Miaozhan, who recommended Anjing 安景, a BCM graduate and the Nanputuo precentor (see chapter 4). Guangyu then gave Anjing a dharma transmission to include him in his lineage, making him prior in 1993 (XFZ, 55–56). Under Anjing's entrepreneurial leadership, Puguang rapidly became the wealthiest local temple.

The temple's largest revenue source came from the fees and donations generated by performing locally popular rituals. The largest ritual was the plenary mass for wandering souls (*shuilu fahui* 水陸法會) held from September 13 to 19 every year, starting in 1994. It was so large that over a hundred clerics were invited from Nanputuo Temple and Mount Tiantai 天台山 in Zhejiang Province to help perform it. It attracted thousands of worshipers, earning the temple several million yuan. The temple then began holding an annual water and land assembly as well as a monthly Medicine Buddha dharma assembly attended by a thousand worshipers. The temple's location on the new highway to the international airport made it convenient for overseas Chinese to commission rituals, while the growing number of area residents in the urbanizing neighborhood became temple supporters. Additionally, Anjing refused to pay the new BAX licensing fee for ritual performances imposed in 1997 and retained all income for the temple.

Anjing also noted that his temple's appeal shot up from 1997 when Nanputuo Temple stopped performing locally popular rituals. He said that the assembly that year was the largest performed in Xiamen after the Cultural Revolution and earned his temple over 3 million yuan. The BAX warned him to stop holding the ritual, citing the temple's failure to obtain a license to perform it (a new requirement by the BAX described in chapter 6) and that the transportation to the temple was inadequate. But Anjing went ahead and held it. He reasoned that the religious policy did not require approval for conducting rituals from the XRAB or BAX but only required reporting the plans to conduct them. He kept good relations with believers by letting them burn paper spirit money and follow other folk belief practices that were now banned at Nanputuo and discouraged by the BAX. He explained, "The masses want to avoid disaster and have a long life. Buddhism must adapt to these desires. Paper spirit money takes the Buddha as a spirit. It is superstition, but there is no way to explain this to people. So, burning money can increase temple income for repairing temple buildings. Isn't this a good thing?"[5]

Storage fees for family ancestor tablets (*shenzu paiwei* 神祖牌位) also provided much income for the temple. Anjing claimed that Puguang Temple stored the most tablets of any temple in Xiamen because it had the lowest fees. In 1999, housing a tablet at his temple cost 4,500 yuan compared with 6,000 yuan at Huxiyan Temple and over 7,000 yuan at Nanputuo Temple. According to Anjing, there were two reasons for the Xiamen tradition of keeping ancestor tablets in Buddhist temples. One stemmed from the lack of ancestral halls in urban districts. The second began when people started to store ancestor tablets and ash urns in Buddhist temples during the Cultural Revolution to protect them from destruction by Red Guards. So Anjing believed that storing ancestor tablets "accorded with the desire of the masses."[6]

The temple's closeness to the people was also reflected in characters engraved on the memorial stele for Ruizhi 瑞枝 (1891–1937), a former temple prior. Lin Ziqing, who wrote the narrative for the Hongshan Temple stele described above, composed this account of Ruizhi's life.

> In 1917 Ruizhi became prior of the temple. He managed it for ten years and started to rebuild the . . . halls. The appearance of the temple was renewed. Venerable Ruizhi was very frank and open toward people and always loyal. He [knew Chinese medicine and] was especially good at curing lung disease and setting broken bones. Those he cured were very thankful. When I was young, I knew him well. He was very knowledgeable about Buddhism in Minnan and often told stories about its history. He worked hard to propagate Buddhism and was especially helpful to young people who wanted to study Buddhism. In 1936, Xiamen's economy was very depressed. At that time, Nanputuo Temple had financial problems. The monks at Nanputuo Temple felt that Venerable Ruizhi knew many people and asked him to be the prior of Nanputuo Temple to solve its problem. So in the time that he could spare from giving medical treatment, he often went to Nanputuo Temple. He performed countless good deeds for the temple, and many people admired him. At that time, Nanputuo Temple ran the BCM and the Buddhist Instruction School, and over one hundred people lived there. They depended for daily necessities on Venerable Ruizhi. The following year the Marco Polo Bridge Incident [Lugou qiao shijian 盧溝橋事件] occurred, and the situation in Xiamen became very tense.⁷ Many monks fled Nanputuo Temple. A Nationalist Party army from Guangdong came to Xiamen and occupied all the temples, causing the most trouble for Nanputuo Temple. Venerable Ruizhi was suspected of a crime and imprisoned. He then died and no one defended him. Already half a century has passed. There is still no pagoda to commemorate his contribution. Is this not a tragic matter?

In stressing Ruizhi's qualities as a monk through his selflessness and knowledge of Buddhism, the temple also conveyed values expressed in Document 19, including patriotism, unity, and loyalty. The stele inscription notes that, unlike the other monks who "fled" China during the Japanese occupation, he remained in Nanputuo Temple to administer it. This suggests his loyalty and concern for the local people. While the nature of his "suspected crime" is not specified, it implies patriotism because he died at the hands of soldiers of the Nationalist Party, the enemy of the CPC.[8] To laypersons, the inscription also conveyed the values of loyalty to lineage and gratitude to a master. This was especially evident in the final words. "Venerable Ruizhi's disciple Venerable Guangyu, who has long lived in Southeast Asia, felt that he had left Venerable Ruizhi too early and could not look after him. Until now, he has been unable to repay his kindness. So he rebuilt Puguang Temple and created this memorial pagoda as an eternal memorial. Because I knew of Venerable Ruizhi's circumstances, Venerable Guangyu asked me to write this tablet to tell those who will come later. So I have written this history of him."

When we visited in 1999, Puguang Temple was one of the largest local temples. It had reclaimed half of its original 8,000 square meters of land, and its new buildings had 10,000 square meters of floor space. About twenty monks resided there, all in their teens and twenties, except for one in his sixties. Those under the legal age of eighteen had taken novice vows in secret. Anjing was the only BCM graduate at the temple, although several monks were studying there. The temple's business office managed finances and served as guest prefect. A general affairs office supervised the kitchen and grounds maintenance. The accountant and cashier were laypersons retired from a local community college. In 1998, Puguang Temple became the first temple in Xiamen to hold a Buddhist summer school (*xialingying* 夏令營). Twenty-five elementary students studied traditional Chinese culture and the *Diamond Sutra* and *Lotus Sutra* for two months. This did not violate the religious policy prohibition of religious education for minors as it was considered a "cultural activity." Anjing dreamed of starting a primary school. He said, "This would enable me to spread Buddhism into society. If everybody is kind, then there would be peace with no need for police."[9]

Anjing (1958–2004) was born to a farming family in Wenzhou, Zhejiang Province. His parents practiced folk religion. He said that he decided to become a monk when, at age thirteen, during the Cultural Revolution, some neighbors brought a Buddhist statue rescued from destruction to their home for worship. The sound of sutra chanting intrigued Anjing.

But his parents did not want him to become a monk because he was the oldest child. He felt that his parents looked down on Buddhist monks, which he said was a common view among people in Wenzhou, in contrast to Xiamen residents who respected clerics. In 1981 he was tonsured at Tiantong Temple, Ningbo City, Zhejiang Province, and was ordained at Mount Wutai (*wutaishan* 五台山) in Shanxi Province. The next year he enrolled in the Buddhist Instruction Academy and then the BCM, graduating in 1989. Anjing was part of the trio of young Wenzhou-born clerics who had studied together in the academy from 1982 and went on to assume high administrative positions in Nanputuo Temple. After graduation, he taught at the BCM and was senior guest prefect and precentor at Nanputuo. This experience in administrative matters, organizing rituals, and teaching made him an effective prior of Puguang Temple. Anjing described himself as a strong leader who decided everything without consulting others. People called him "boss" (*laoban* 老闆) because of his forceful management and fundraising style. His efforts to meet people's expectations were evident in the many announcements of rituals and events at the temple.

Huxiyan Temple: Center for Devotees

Huxiyan Temple was significant in Buddhism as a gathering place for devotees. It was founded in 1615, destroyed in fighting between the forces of the Ming and Qing dynasties, and rebuilt in 1701 by a navy admiral who invited the monk Yuanfei 元飛 to be prior. Yuanfei, the fourth-generation disciple of Yinyuan 隱元 (whose travels to Japan in the seventeenth century started the Ōbaku sect there), gave Huxiyan Temple its name. It acquired considerable status and held many large rituals and assemblies.

In 1909, Huiquan, the twelfth-generation disciple of Yuanfei and a leader of the modern Buddhist reform movement in Xiamen, became prior. Together with Hongyi, Huiquan made Huxiyan Temple a center of clerical education. He was succeeded as the temple prior by his disciple and then by his dharma brother Honghui 宏輝. In 1958, the temple was occupied by the military and destroyed in the Cultural Revolution (*XFZ*, 78–79). In 1982, it was reclaimed by the BAX and rebuilt with funds sent by Huiquan's disciple in Singapore, Hongchuan, abbot of Kong Meng San

Phor Kark See Temple. In 1986 Honghui's disciple Kaizheng 開正 became prior and the XRAB recognized the temple as a religious activity site open for public worship.

When we visited the temple in 1990, only half a dozen monks and several devotees lived there, but large numbers of devotees attended its Guanyin, Medicine Buddha, and other dharma assemblies. To help perform them, the temple invited monks from Nanputuo Temple, including BCM students whose participation was part of their Buddhist education. The temple was also a gathering place for the Xiamen Devotee Lodge (see chapter 8). Every month, a hundred devotees came to conduct chanting and share a meal they cooked in the kitchen. These local ties gave the temple solid financial support from businesspersons who worshiped regularly. Some who were wealthy gave large donations, but most donors gave modestly, such as a fisherman who donated 50 yuan after every fishing trip and a construction firm owner who gave cement for temple construction. The temple had enough revenue to provide resident clerics with a monthly stipend, and it was the first local temple to do so. To raise large sums for special projects like repairs, appeals for donations and descriptions of the project were hung in the temple. Those giving 1,500 yuan (in 1990) had their names engraved on the rocks surrounding the temple. Although the majority of donors were local businesspersons, overseas Chinese also gave to the temple, sometimes contributing enough to have their names engraved on multiple stones.

The beautiful setting of the temple near the city center made it an object of struggle as Buddhists and the XRAB attempted to control its development. In the early 1990s, Kaizheng planned a vegetarian restaurant to earn money. The XRAB opposed it, possibly because it would have competed with the restaurant at Nanputuo Temple, from which the XRAB benefitted. The bureau pressured the BAX to withhold approval, but the BAX recognized the revenue needs of the temple and refused to block the restaurant. The restaurant opened, but business lagged as a result of insufficient parking facilities and the temple's seclusion. So Kaizheng sought local state designation for the temple as an official tourist site, hoping to cater to organized tour groups. But the XRAB opposed this too, possibly because the venture would have interfered with its own plans: by the late 1990s, the XRAB had lined up investment from a Singapore businessperson to develop the temple as a tourist site.[10]

When Kaizheng opposed the Singapore-backed project, the XRAB sought to remove him from office. The officials obtained the account books from the accountant on the temple democratic management committee and charged Kaizheng with financial misdeeds. But the account books revealed no wrongdoing, and the charges were dropped. Then, XRAB officials tried to oust Kaizheng for incompetency. They mobilized other local clerics who were resentful that Kaizheng, who had little Buddhist education, was the leader of a prominent temple. These clerics wrote to the provincial and national Buddhist associations accusing Kaizheng of mismanagement, but eventually, as we explain below, the strong support of the BAX and Nanputuo abbot Miaozhan allowed Kaizheng to prevail.

Kaizheng's leadership style exacerbated the problems at Huxiyan Temple. A BAX officer noted that he was headstrong, unwilling to admit mistakes, and treated subordinates imperiously. His inability to grasp basic administrative protocols posed another challenge for the XRAB. The officer said, "Kaizheng thinks he does not have to pay attention to the democratic management committee because it consists of old monks and devotees. But the XRAB controls the committee because it approves all members."[11] As shown by the scrutiny of the account books and the accusations of resentful colleagues, Kaizheng had detractors within local Buddhist communities whom the XRAB used to try to remove him from office. But the Nanputuo abbot Miaozhan appreciated Kaizheng's doggedness and assigned a BAX officer to help him interact with local officials. Miaozhan's successor, Shenghui, boosted Kaizheng's status by giving him a dharma transmission to make him the forty-second-generation descendant of Shenghui's dharma line and promoted him within the BAX. Of course, this transmission also helped Shenghui, an outsider sent by Beijing, to create allies among clerics in Xiamen.

We learned about Kaizheng's background from people who worked with him at the temple.[12] He was born in Xiamen in the late 1940s, the eldest of six brothers, and had four older sisters. His father was an accountant in a Chinese medicine store. After graduating from primary school, he supported his family by scavenging coal cinders and wood chips that fell from freight trains to sell as cooking fuel. Malnourishment in childhood stunted his growth: being only 150 centimeters tall, he was too short to be a worker and too light to be a soldier, so he worked as a furnace stoker in a medical equipment factory. He was repeatedly selected as a model worker but his appearance prevented him from finding a wife. When he decided to become a monk, he got a job as a gate watchman at Nanputuo Temple. Miaozhan noticed him and introduced him to Honghui, who became his tonsure master in 1982 and selected him as prior of Huxiyan Temple.

The story of Kaizheng and his priorship at Huxiyan underscored the importance of a temple leader's role in securing its fate. Kaizheng's weakness placed Huxiyan Temple on contested ground during the 1990s. The XRAB sought to control the temple by placing pliable devotees on the democratic management committee, but Miaozhan's dispatch of a BAX officer to work with Kaizheng helped thwart its strategy. In some ways, this situation resembled that between the XRAB and the Nanputuo Temple clerics described in previous chapters. The conflicts centered on resources with commercial value, involved XRAB manipulation of internal temple management, and invoked a higher authority for support, in this case, Nanputuo abbots.

Bailudong Temple: Emphasizing Minnan Speakers

Bailudong Temple was the only significant local temple in Xiamen where all monks were from Minnan and its dialect was their daily language. The temple was built in the Ming dynasty and belonged to the Caodong school 曹洞宗. Its hilltop location offered a panoramic view of the city and port. The Fujian provincial government had designated the temple as a Fujian Province Cultural Treasure in the 1950s, but it was occupied in 1958 by the military during the Taiwan Strait crisis as an observation post and destroyed in the Cultural Revolution. In 1988, the BAX paid half a million yuan to the People's Liberation Army to reclaim it (*XFZ*, 79–80). The funds were raised by Yuanguo 元果 (1929–1998), president of the Hong Kong Buddhist Association.[13] Although he had no tie with Bailudong Temple, Miaozhan gave him responsibility for the temple because he was of the Caodong school. Subsequently, Yuanguo appointed his brother Changqin 常欽 to be prior of the temple. In 1989, the temple's rebuilding got underway.

Changqin made Bailudong Temple a center for Minnan culture.[14] He did not like to speak in Mandarin and conversed with us in Minnan dialect (through an interpreter). This embrace of Minnan culture gave Bailudong strong local support. It facilitated relations with local officials as Changqin could converse with them in dialect. He was especially friendly with the directors of city government agencies who were compatriots from Hui'an County, including the XRAB director. Some officials were regular worshipers at Bailudong. Changqin explained to us that excellent ties with the XRAB made it possible for him to hold dharma assemblies at the temple before its official designation as a religious activity site, and his embrace of Minnan culture attracted wealthy local businessmen to become patrons. In his view, the other local temples in Xiamen were controlled by Nanputuo Temple, which was run by "northern monks," a term Changqin applied to any cleric not from Minnan. He proudly told us about his brilliant female disciple from Minnan, who had studied in the Chinese literature department at Xiamen University and then enrolled in the BCM. After graduating, she spurned a teaching post in the school because she could not get along with the northern nuns. She accepted a post at the Quanzhou Buddhist Academy (Quanzhou foxue yuan 泉州佛學苑), revived in 1987 to educate Minnan lay nuns.

When we visited in 1999, fourteen monks and thirteen workers were in residence, all in their twenties, all from the Minnan region. Only three monks were ordained, the rest were tonsured, and five were studying at the BCM. For temple management, Changqin was advised by a ninety-year-old devotee; he had been a cleric and Nanputuo guest prefect before 1949 and then politically labeled a "rotten egg" and imprisoned for thirty years. The temple was still expanding, with the Merit and Dizang Halls serving as columbaria. The temple held a plenary mass every October from the fifteenth to the twenty-first to commemorate the reopening of the temple. It held a ten-thousand-buddhas service from the first to the fifteenth day of the first month of the year and performed rites for the dead. Several hundred persons gathered on the eighth day of each month to burn incense, worship the Buddha, and afterward partake in a meal. The temple was very lively on holidays as a retreat for city residents. It also ran a free clinic staffed on weekends by doctors and members of a charity founded in 2000.

But temple finances had declined since Yuanguo passed away in 1998, Changqin told us, and fewer worshipers than expected came to the temple. We corroborated this latter point in interviews with devotees and others in Xiamen; they told us they had never gone to the temple because they had forgotten it existed, or because other local temples were more active and also attracting local worshipers. Changqin shared some of his ideas for generating income with us. In the new ancestor hall, he would charge 3,050 yuan for a tablet, undercutting Puguang Temple. He also talked about making a tablet for living persons for long life and a "cleansing" that would cost 100 yuan.

Changqin was born in 1931 in Hui'an County to a Buddhist farming family. His elder brother was the monk Yuanguo, as noted above. Changqin had four sons, all businesspersons, and a daughter who was a lay nun, of whom he was especially proud. He had worked for decades as an official in the county government bureau that managed the local artisanal industry and then, in 1984, was reassigned to the religious affairs bureau. The new position was problematic because he was a Buddhist, but he had hidden this part of his identity because he was also a CPC member. His brother encouraged him to resign from his job and renounce his party membership to become a monk. When Yuanguo was abbot of Chongfu Temple in the 1980s, Changqin served under him as prior.[15] In 1989, at age fifty-nine, he was ordained at the ceremony for elderly ordinands at Guanghua Temple (see chapter 4). Changqin was skilled in calligraphy, the abacus, feng shui, and Shaolin martial arts. He conducted divinations for large buildings, including for the local state and the military. Yet he felt that monks should not profit from their powers of divination and did not accept payments for divining gravesites. Due to his government experience, the religious affairs bureaus in Hui'an and Xiamen tried to appoint him to various positions, including on the Superstition Management Committee after the crackdown on Falun Gong. But he refused all requests because he did not want to suffer through long meetings. He had already built a small temple in his home village for retirement.

Changqin regaled us with a saga intended to show his fearlessness, but it also illuminated political tensions stemming from the state's administration of local temples within Xiamen's Buddhism. The story concerned his conflict with the neighboring Huxiyan Temple on the other side of the hill. The two temples shared a well for water and constantly faced water shortages. During Bailudong's opening ceremony in 1996 a tanker truck was brought in to supply drinking water for attendees. But the water was tainted, and everyone got diarrhea. After the ceremony, the XRAB suggested that Changqin build a reservoir to ensure his temple's water supply. However, this new reservoir reduced the available water for Huxiyan Temple. Its prior, Kaizheng, confronted Changqin and called him a water thief, provoking Kaizheng's disciple to try to punch Changqin. The situation escalated when Changqin hit Kaizheng, knocking him down. After this, Kaizheng avoided him.

Kaizheng and a BAX official told us the other side of this story.[16] As they explained it, the XRAB had pressured Kaizheng to widen the access road to his temple for tour buses. Kaizheng refused because this would have destroyed the natural environment of the temple. So the XRAB began to harass him by encouraging Changqin to poach Huxiyan's water. The accounts of the two priors show how patterns of interaction between the local officials and clerics at Nanputuo Temple also existed among local temples.

Flexibilities in the Space of Religion

The situation of several local Buddhist temples in Xiamen illustrates considerable flexibility in the space of religion. The case of Wanshilian Temple shows the multiple uses of a formerly Daoist temple and the resolution of competing claims to leadership during its recovery. Guanyin Temple is an unusual case of establishing a new temple despite the state's prohibition to do so. Finally, Tianzhuyan, a site of Earth God worship, illustrates how a folk belief temple converted to a Buddhist temple. In all three temples, connections to Nanputuo Temple for personnel, status, and legitimacy helped position them in the space of religion in Xiamen.

Wanshilian Temple: Leadership Competition in a Nunnery

Wanshilian Temple, a site of natural beauty on the opposite side of Wulao Peak from Nanputuo Temple, was founded in the sixteenth century as a Daoist temple with the name Wanshiyan 萬石岩, meaning "Ten Thousand Rocks Crag." In the seventeenth century, it was rebuilt as a Buddhist temple by the Qing admiral Shi Lang when he built Nanputuo Temple. The multiple traditions venerating the site were evident on the rocks surrounding the temple, where Daoists, Buddhists, and literati left engravings to extoll its beauty. The temple had an illustrious modern history. In 1933, Huiquan, after serving as Nanputuo abbot, became Wanshiyan's prior. He rebuilt Wanshiyan and made it into a center of clerical education by founding the Wanshi Buddhist Research Society (Wanshi foxue yanjiu she 萬石佛學研究社), which enrolled over sixty monks from Fujian and Guangdong Provinces, and Taiwan. He planned to set up a Buddhist college and received a large donation from the family of Chen Jiageng 陳嘉庚, the famous Xiamen native and overseas Chinese businessperson in Malaya who had founded Xiamen University a decade earlier. But the Japanese occupation of Xiamen in 1938 halted this venture. After World War II, the monk Xingyuan sought to revive Buddhist education at the temple by starting the Dajue Buddhist Studies Society (Dajue foxue she 大覺佛學社). It opened in early 1949, presided over by the monk Yinshun, with two dozen students. But classes soon stopped when Yinshun left Xiamen for Taiwan. In 1958, the temple was used as a military storehouse, and in 1962 the local state redesignated the site and its environs as a public park named the Wanshiyan Botanical Garden (XFZ, 80–81).

In 1979, the BAX reclaimed the temple from the military, and a lay nun named Kaiyin 開因 (1923–2016), a disciple of Hongyi, became its head.[17] Her service reflected the critical role of lay nuns during the early recovery when there were few ordained clerics. In 1984, Huiquan's disciple, Singapore-based Hongchuan, donated money to repair the temple. He also renamed the temple "Wanshilian" (Ten Thousand Rocks and Lotuses Temple 萬石蓮), to distinguish it from the surrounding botanical garden. Miaozhan asked Kaiyin to supervise the temple's rebuilding. But Hongchuan and Kaiyin disagreed on the new prior. Hongchuan gave a dharma transmission to a young monk from the BCM to make him prior, while Kaiyin favored an elderly monk who was a disciple of Huiquan. Both Hongchuan and Kaiyin had justifications for claiming authority to designate the prior: Hongchuan was the disciple of Huiquan and funded the recovery of the temple; Kaiyin had suffered in China for decades to preserve Buddhism and managed the recovery of the temple after 1979. Miaozhan solved the impasse by receiving a dharma transmission from Hongchuan to become the prior of Wanshilian Temple. The day before the temple's reconsecration ceremony, however, the XRAB objected to the transmission as illegal foreign interference in religion. Miaozhan immediately telephoned Zhao Puchu in Beijing, who approved the ceremony to proceed.

Under Miaozhan, the temple was used as a dormitory for female students of the BCM. In addition to rebuilding its halls, a new dorm was constructed for the students. By the late 1980s, about a hundred female BCM students lived in the temple. But the number of female students coming to the BCM continued to grow, and two more temples managed by lay nuns were pressed into service as dormitories. The scattering of the nuns among several temples caused problems in scheduling classes, adding to tensions between young nuns and elderly lay nuns living together (see chapter 8). Therefore, when the nuns' campus at Zizhulin Temple opened in 1996, many students moved out of Wanshilian Temple. Its remaining residents consisted of a small number of young nuns, elderly lay nuns, and devotees. Its financial situation deteriorated as the subsidies from the BCM dried up. Furthermore, its alms income was meager because the temple was inside a public park, and people were loath to pay the park admission fee to enter the temple.

Guanyin Temple: Making a New Temple

Guanyin Temple was the first new Buddhist temple in Xiamen built on land where a temple had not existed historically. Its construction appeared to contradict the XRAB policy of only permitting temples to be built on the site of a preexisting one. This policy was intended to preserve more land for commercial development, prevent the "waste" of money on building new temples, and limit the number of Buddhist temples. Guanyin Temple sat on the side of the ridge separating Xiamen's old and new downtowns. The site's elevation and the temple's thirteen-story pagoda made it highly visible. While the land was a compact 400 square meters, the multistoried buildings had several thousand square meters of floor space. Although it lacked a stele when we visited in 2000, it was the first local temple with a website. The website described the temple compound and halls in detail, noting that Guanyin Temple was the third largest temple in Xiamen (after Nanputuo and Puguang Temples).[18] This attention to the temple's physical space was understandable given the temple's brief history.

We heard two overlapping explanations from BAX officers about how the Guanyin Temple came to be despite that ban on new temples.[19] According to one explanation, the Guanyin Temple was built on land given to the BAX as restitution for another temple the local state had requisitioned in the 1950s, but that it could not return to Buddhists because a hospital had subsequently been constructed on it. Therefore, the Guanyin Temple was not considered a "new" temple but rather a relocated one. Another reason was that Guanyin Temple was built on a site that once had a temple; the BAX classified such sites as "forsaken" (*fei* 廢). Thus, Guanyin Temple was a renewal of the earlier temple. For these reasons, the Guanyin Temple did not violate the ban on building new temples. Furthermore, the BAX officers noted that the status and networks of the temple's prior enabled him to get the local state approval for the temple. Although the prior was from the Butian region, he established local connections as a BCM graduate, a former senior guest prefect at Nanputuo Temple, and from serving on the BAX. His excellent ties to the Xiamen Municipal People's Government were seen in his appointments to the standing committee of the Xiamen All-China Youth Federation and the city district People's Consultative Committee, both under the Xiamen United Front Work Department.

The temple's construction was financed by the prior's overseas master and his prodigious fundraising. In 1999, the prior told us he simultaneously "preaches and constructs."[20] His choice of words referred to his use of Buddhist teachings and rituals to fund the temple's expansion to further more teaching and rituals. A large plaque in the temple compound not only solicited donations for rituals and construction, but also specified the amount and kinds of construction materials that donations could buy (see table 7.3). It proclaimed: "Contributions for constructing Guanyin Temple and eliminating disaster, and praying for longevity, wealth, and family security."

Before construction was finished, the temple was designated a religious activity site, enabling it to earn money through rituals. It convened a great compassion prayer ceremony on the nineteenth of each month and a buddha prayer assembly (*nian fo fahui* 念佛法会) every Saturday. In January and June, the temple convened a ten-thousand-buddhas service (*wan fo fahui* 萬佛法会). In addition, the Putian atmosphere of the temple was quite strong, reflecting the prior's Putian origins. All four resident monks were from his home region when we visited in 1999.

TABLE 7.3 Costs to Donate Construction Materials

Construction materials	Cost
One bag of cement	20 yuan
Buddha statues in the Thousand Buddhas Pagoda	2,000 yuan
Pillar in the Great Compassion Hall	10,000 yuan

Rituals	Cost
Praying for security and safety (effective for one year)	120 yuan
Disaster elimination and longevity (effective for one year)	120 yuan

Patronage	Donation
Have name carved on a tablet on temple wall	5,000 yuan

Source: Poster on temple wall, observed by Yoshiko Ashiwa and David Wank, September 1999

Tianzhuyan Temple: Transitioning from Folk Belief to Buddhism

Tianzhu Crag was transitioning from a folk belief site to a Buddhist temple when we visited in 1999. According to historical records, a crag dwelling (*yan yu* 岩宇) has existed at this isolated hillside in the city since the early eighteenth century. In the 1930s, a Buddhist monk built a 300-square-meter compound that burned down several years later. But villagers continued to venerate the abandoned temple as the Mountainside Earth God (Banshan tudi gong 半山土地公) and built a shrine in 1998 (XFZ, 83). It held the official status of "folk religion" (*minjian xinyang* 民間信仰) temple under the urban district government administration, as indicated by a prominent notice in the shrine titled "Huli District Folk Belief Temple Temporary Administrative Method" (湖里區民間信仰公廟暫時管理辦法). When we visited, the site had already been recognized by the BAX as a Buddhist temple, as revealed in its new stele calling it South Mountain Tianzhuyan Temple 南山天竺岩寺. The reason for choosing this particular site to convert, instead of one among hundreds of other local sites, was probably linked to the belief that the Earth God's magical efficacy was especially potent. The local state could not prevent people from worshiping, and local officials may have shared this belief, so the local authorities converted it to bring it under the control of the XRAB and BAX.

The local state's concerns regarding the site were suggested in a district government notice's ban on parading the deity (*you shen* 遊神) and greeting the deity (*ying shen* 迎神). These popular folk practices consisted of parading deity statues housed in temples through the streets during festivals. Parades generated much tumult and excitement as they crossed government administrative boundaries of neighborhoods, districts, and villages. They were sizeable networks of prestige, commitment, and resources among the people (Dean 1998) and therefore viewed as disruptive by the local authorities. The first step in converting the shrine was establishing a management committee for it whose members were Buddhist devotees. This task was assigned to the Xiamen Devotee Lodge, the state-recognized devotee association in Xiamen (see chapter 8).[21] The devotees saw no contradiction in managing a folk belief temple because they, too, worshiped these deities. But devotees understood the distinction between Buddhism and folk beliefs and were trusted to manage the temples. This solution gave all parties some benefit. The local state could better control the sites, the Xiamen Devotee Lodge demonstrated its usefulness, and the BAX gained new temples for the growing number of BCM graduates.

To be considered a Buddhist temple, a Daoist or folk belief site had to meet the criteria of the BAX. One was conformity to a Buddhist temple's traditional layout. A Buddhist temple compound is aligned on a north-south axis, but few folk belief sites met this criterion. But as long as the temple was centered on Buddhist worship, it could be considered a Buddhist temple.[22] Tianzhuyan conformed to this criterion because the central hall had a Guanyin statue, with the Earth God statue relegated to a left-side hall. To convert some other sites, however, a deity statue had to be moved from the main shrine to a side court to make way for a statue of the Buddha or a bodhisattva. The other criterion was the organization of daily routine according to Buddhist rules and teachings. This required a prior who was an ordained cleric, a collective lifestyle centered on the daily performance of morning and evening services, and the maintenance of celibacy and vegetarianism. This criterion was just being implemented when we visited the temple. The temple's management committee, led by a devotee, organized Buddhist rituals, including worshiping Guanyin on the first and fifteenth of each month, thousand-buddhas services on January 4 and December 16, and a ten-day-long ten-thousand-buddhas assembly from August 15. A dozen monks, including BCM graduates, lived in a building across the street, preparing to move into the temple.

The conversion to a Buddhist temple was a sensitive issue, as we realized when we tried to talk to the monks. No one answered our knocks on their doors, although someone watched us from a window. The devotee leader of the Tianzhuyan management committee told us that he, too, had been ignored by the clerics who were BCM graduates. He said that, in general, Buddhist clerics did not like being in converted temples because many visitors came to worship deities other than the Buddha. However, the devotee observed that monks might feel more comfortable at Tianzhuyan Temple because of its relative isolation.

Conclusion

During the 1980s and 1990s, the recovery of local temples in Xiamen's Buddhism depended on the connections to Nanputuo Temple created earlier in the twentieth century. The temples that recovered rapidly and smoothly were led by clerics who had ties to Nanputuo and held positions in the BAX. These networks activated the physical, semiotic, and institutional legitimacy of the space of religion. Dharma transmissions brokered by the Nanputuo abbot Miaozhan in the 1980s and early 1990s semiotically reconnected lineage to rebuild the physical space. And physical spaces could be altered to fit the semiotic space in Buddhism and the state's institutional concerns regarding administration and control.

The development of the local temples was furthered by the increasing detachment of Nanputuo Temple from local devotees and believers starting in 1997. They had more room to fully activate their capital, whether in the form of commitment, prestigious connections, or other local resources, to meet the expectations of Xiamen residents. But the detachment of Nanputuo Temple also weakened its ties to other local communities of Buddhism, as we explain in the next chapter.

8

Devotees and Lay Nuns

MANY PEOPLE ACTIVE IN BUDDHISM are not ordained, and their activities take place outside temples where clerics live. In this chapter we examine such people and their positions within the space of religion. A survey of all unordained people would be unwieldy, so we limit the focus to those who express serious commitment to Buddhism by taking the five precepts (*wujie* 五戒) to forswear killing, stealing, adultery, lying, and drinking alcohol. In chapter 9 we discuss the majority of mass worshipers who do not take the precepts, and who for the most part limit their participation in Buddhism to attending festivals and occasional worship at temples.

Two groups of laypersons in Xiamen took the five precepts. Buddhist religious doctrine recognized one group as devotees, with males called *youpuosai* 優婆塞 (Skt. *upāsaka*) and females called *youpuoyi* 優婆夷 (Skt. *upāsikā*). Their status in Buddhism was lower than ordained monks and nuns, who are called, respectively, *biqiu* 比丘 (Skt. *bhikṣu*) and *biqiuni* 比丘尼 (Skt. *bhikṣuṇī*).[1] Devotees (*jushi* 居士) lived with their families, and their lifestyles were indistinguishable from laypersons except for vegetarianism. The second group, known as pious women, were colloquially called "vegetarian women" 菜姑 (*caigu*), a unique Minnan tradition.[2] Like ordained nuns they were celibate, vegetarian, and lived communally, adhering to the worship of the Buddha and Guanyin. Yet similar to devotees, they were assimilated into Xiamen society because they kept their hair, wore regular clothes, and held jobs. To express this ambiguous position between an ordained nun and a devotee, we call these women by the contradictory term "lay nun."[3]

The devotees and lay nuns in Xiamen were greatly affected by their ties to clerics from Nanputuo Temple. The growth of both communities in the early twentieth century occurred with the resounding support of the Nanputuo clerics. From 1979, both groups became active again, working closely with the Nanputuo monks to recover Buddhism. But by the 1990s, both communities faced issues of continuity linked to trends in the semiotic and institutional spaces of religion, the recovery process within each community, and generational challenges to their existence.

Devotees: Practicing Buddhism in Local Communities

Devotees have conducted their activities with much independence from clerics by maintaining places apart from Buddhist temples for worship, services, sutra chanting, and study groups. This separation gives devotees a closeness to local cultures and concerns that clerics living in temples do not have. Such closeness has been a source of creativity and innovation throughout history in devotee Buddhism. It was manifested in new religious sects, some of which embraced political aims, such as the Zhaist groups from the Song dynasty and the White Lotus movement in the late seventeenth century, inciting state suppression. At the same time, the independence of devotees from clerics let them avoid the persecution of Buddhism at times in history. In particular, educated devotees have contributed to the continuity of Buddhism, such as Yang Wenhui and Zhao Puchu. In this section we describe several noted devotees who connected Buddhist communities to Nanputuo Temple, to the state-recognized devotee association, and to trends among young devotees emerging in the 1990s.

Devotee Leaders

The devotee leaders we describe here were sons of well-to-do business families active in Buddhism in the Minnan region before 1949 and who helped lead its recovery in Xiamen after 1979. Lin Ziqing 林子青 (1910–2002),

born in Zhangzhou City in Minnan, was a devotee with a national reputation. He was ordained as a monk at age eighteen with the Buddhist name Huiyun 慧雲 and enrolled in the BCM in 1927, where he studied under Taixu and other eminent clerics. He then taught in the BCM, and the Nanshan Buddhist School 南山佛化學校 at Nanshan Temple, Zhangzhou. In the 1930s, he served on the executive board of the newly founded Xiamen branch of the China Buddhist Association 中國佛教會廈門分會, the first national Buddhist association, and edited its journal *Buddhism Forum* 佛教公論. In 1938 he also participated in a field ambulance crew of Buddhist monks dispatched from Shanghai to Wuhan 武漢 in the battle against the Japanese army. Next, he spent several years wandering, visiting many temples in China and Taiwan. On a trip to Taiwan to transmit the precepts at Kaiyuan Temple 開元寺, Tainan City 台南市, Lin was arrested by the Japanese colonial government and spent a year in prison (*Fojiao shuji wang* n.d.). During the 1940s he also studied at a Buddhist university in Japan.[4] In 1948 he worked in the Shanghai Buddhist Association and taught the history of Indian Buddhism at the Jing'an Buddhist Academy (Jing'an foxue yuan 静安佛学院), where Taixu's disciple Yinshun was one of his students. Through his wide-ranging experiences and travels in China, he met many eminent clerics as well as younger ones who became prominent after 1949 in Taiwan, Hong Kong, and overseas Chinese communities.

In the PRC, Lin began working in 1957 at the newly formed Buddhist Association of China in Beijing, editing the association's English and Japanese publications and teaching in the Buddhist Academy of China. During the Cultural Revolution, he was sent to the countryside to do agricultural labor in a May Seventh Cadre School (Zheng 2002). In 1978 he returned to his position in the Buddhist Academy of China, becoming an executive director of the Buddhist Association of China; a member of the Buddhist Culture Research Institute (Zhongguo fojiao wenhua yanjiu suo 中國佛教文化研究所), established in 1987; and a member of the editorial board of *Fayin* 法音 (*Voice of Dharma*), the association's national journal. His scholarship focused on a yearbook commemorating Hongyi's life, culminating in the publication of the ten-volume *The Complete Works of Master Hongyi* (*Hongyi dashi quanji* 弘一大師全集).[5] His high standing in Chinese Buddhist circles was evident in the 2001 publication of a collection of his lectures and essays on Buddhism and Chinese literature by Dharma Drum Mountain 法鼓山 in Taiwan, established by Shengyan (Sheng Yen 聖嚴) (1931–2009).

Lin Ziqing also contributed much to the recovery of Nanputuo Temple and Buddhism in Xiamen. At the BCM, he taught courses and helped rebuild its curriculum. He aided the recovery of local temples by contributing narratives for their stelae, as described in chapter 7. His persecution during the Cultural Revolution for his Buddhism may have shaped the themes of patriotism and loyalty in those narratives. All visitors to his apartment in Beijing in the 1990s sat on a couch over which hung a scroll with a calligraphed inscription cautioning about fair-weather friends.

The second person, Cai Jitang 菜吉堂 (1904–1996), was a devotee leader in Xiamen. Born in Taiwan, his family moved to Xiamen, where his father owned a steel products firm. His parents often took him to Nanputuo Temple, and the visits fostered his interest in Buddhism. He took the devotee precepts from Yinguang 印光 (1862–1940) and studied under Taixu and Hongyi. In 1924, Cai helped organize the World New Youth Buddhist Propagation Troupe (Fo hua xin qingnian shijie xuanchuan dui 佛化新青年世界宣傳隊) to promote the "rightful belief of Buddhism and oppose superstition" (*XFZ*, 120). That same year he published articles distinguishing Buddhism from superstition and also founded Buddhist study groups. During the Japanese occupation, he chaired the Xiamen Mahayana Buddhist Society (Xiamen dasheng fojiao hui 廈門大乘佛教會), a Japanese organization to promote ties between Japan and China through Buddhism. According to the *Nanputuo Temple Gazetteer* (*NSZ*, vol. 2, 221–222), he assumed the position to help the well-being of the local people; he never called for "Sino-Japanese friendship" but instead used his position to request shelters for refugees.[6] These actions may have prevented him from being executed after the war as a collaborator.

In the PRC, Cai continued as a leader of Buddhism and the business community. In the 1950s, he became BAX vice president, BCM vice rector, vice president of the Buddhist Association of Fujian, and executive board member of the Buddhist Association of China. At the same time, his private company was among the first to institute socialized ownership in Xiamen, and he became president of the state-run Xiamen Chamber of Commerce. During the Cultural Revolution, he was persecuted politically for being a Buddhist and a capitalist. In 1966, he was paraded through the city streets in a tall dunce cap and draped with prayer beads, a wooden fish, and other Buddhist ritual objects. Hanging from his neck were two signs of self-denunciation: "Unearth Xiamen's biggest charlatan Cai Jitang, the corrupt capitalist Cai Jitang who slipped through the net," and "The reactionary charlatan Cai Jitang must be beaten to the ground, never to turn over again" (Wu 2014, vol. 7, book 1, 147–148). In 1979, the state restored his reputation, and he helped revive Buddhism. He served on the preparatory committee to restart the BAX, becoming its vice president in 1989, served as an instructor and vice rector of the BCM, and made fundraising trips to Singapore to restore Nanputuo Temple. Additionally, he became vice president of the Buddhist Association of Fujian and served on the executive board of the Buddhist Association of China. His status was such that the Xiamen United Front Work Department appointed him as a delegate to the Xiamen City People's Consultative Committee and vice president of the Taiwan Compatriots Friendship Association.

When we interviewed Cai in 1989 and 1990, his criticism of contemporary Buddhism reflected themes of the Buddhist reform movement half a century earlier. He said monks were absorbed with their salvation and did not serve the people. "Just worshiping Buddha, burning incense, and chanting sutras cannot help the country and society. . . . Buddhism is useless if it cannot help people's thinking and frame of mind."[7] In his view, mass worshipers lacked knowledge of Buddhism. "Ordinary people do not understand the true teachings of Buddhism. They only go to temples to worship wooden statues. . . . This is superstition. Worshiping . . . to get money and benefits in life is not in line with Buddhist principles."[8] He saw Christianity as a model for revitalizing Buddhism. "Just beating the wooden fish and banging the gong is not enough. We should take a cue from the West and use the piano. If we play the piano while we chant, people will like it. We have to modernize. We need art and music, and to appeal to young people."[9] He advocated a "devotee Buddhism" (*jushi fojiao* 居士佛教) in China modeled on Buddhism in Japan. "Japanese monks can leave temples and wear Western clothes just like lay persons. They think scientifically, write scholarly articles, and give lectures."[10] He advocated establishing Buddhist schools, for teaching not clerics but laypersons.

The third devotee, Zheng Mengxing 鄭夢星 (1933–?), had a deep knowledge of both the Buddhism practiced by clerics and the popular

Buddhism practiced by people, making him an effective link between the Buddhist lay communities and the BAX. He was born in 1933 in Yongchun County 永春縣, Minnan, to a family in the tea export trade. When he and his school classmates heard that the famous monk Hongyi was at Nanputuo Temple, they dared each other to visit him. Dropping in unannounced, they asked Hongyi why he became a monk. He answered that they would understand when they become older. Visiting Hongyi sparked Zheng Mengxing's interest in Buddhism, and he began to study on his own. In the late 1940s, Zheng joined the Nationalist Army as a clerk and then became the principal of a school for orphans at Kaiyuan Temple, Quanzhou. He received the devotee precepts from the temple's prior Guangyi 廣義 (1914–1995), a disciple of Hongyi. In 1948, Guangyi sent Zheng to a remote temple in western Fujian to avoid arrest for joining a protest against the Nationalist Party. Disguised as a monk, he lived there for over a year learning the routines and rituals of a Buddhist temple. He painted pictures of Buddhist deities for villagers, who invited him to their folk belief practices. Returning to Quanzhou, he opened a primary school for poor children in a Daoist temple and then worked in the Quanzhou culture and propaganda bureau painting propaganda posters. In the 1980s, he was assigned by the Quanzhou Municipal People's Government to compile gazetteers on the history, education, religion, and transportation of Jinjiang County. In 1989, the BAX invited him to Xiamen to compile the *Gazetteer of Xiamen Buddhism*.[11]

Zheng's broad knowledge of Buddhism and folk beliefs made him an effective link between the BAX, devotees, and lay nuns. He was on the executive board of the Xiamen Devotee Lodge, which reopened in 1989, designing its new headquarters in a former Daoist temple to conform to the semiotic space of Buddhism. His research for the gazetteer brought him into much contact with lay nuns. He effectively communicated the religious policy in ways the lay nuns found acceptable. We noticed this capability when we accompanied him in 2000 during his survey of lay nun halls in Xiamen. While interviewing the head lay nun of one hall, he realized that a three-year-old orphan girl was living there. In an officious-sounding voice, he warned the head lay nun that indoctrinating minors with Buddhism violated the religious policy. Then, in a softer tone, he opined that caring for an orphan was a charitable act. In this way, he told her that she was potentially violating the religious policy but would probably not get in trouble as long as she did not adopt more orphans.¹²

Xiamen University scholars and local officials respected Zheng as a "local intellectual" (*difang wenren* 地方文人) for his detailed knowledge of Minnan beliefs and religious practices. He was often invited to speak at academic events and contribute to scholarly publications. In these venues, he argued forcefully for a clear boundary between Buddhism and folk religion. During the campaign against Falun Gong in 1999, he wrote an article distinguishing it from Buddhism (see chapter 6).

The Xiamen Devotee Lodge

The Xiamen Devotee Lodge embodied the long tradition of Buddhist devotees conducting activities independent of temples and clerics. It was founded in 1952 as a state-recognized association for devotees. The lodge amalgamated Xiamen's many sutra chanting groups into a single organization with two thousand devotees. The lodge organized Buddhist teaching and welfare activities for devotees and promoted patriotic religion and Taixu's Buddhism for the Human Realm. Its members foreswore such superstitious practices as hungry ghost feeding (*pudu* 普渡), spirit worship, fortune telling, and divination (*XFZ*, 196). Lodge members were divided into ten neighborhood groups, each holding activities. To show patriotism during the 1950s, the lodge mobilized its members' participation in political activities, such as donating funds to support China's war efforts against the United States in Korea and marching in labor day parades. In 1958 the lodge was shut down, and during the Cultural Revolution, Red Guards ransacked members' homes to confiscate Buddhist texts.

In 1989, the Xiamen Devotee Lodge was among the first of the devotee associations in Fujian to restart. Its bylaws pledged loyalty to the CPC, obedience to the state, acceptance of the CPC definition of religion, and contributions to society. Additional aims mentioned in our interviews with the society's officers included preaching orthodox (*zhengxin* 正信) Buddhism, preventing superstition, and simplifying rituals. It had 1,400 registered members and several hundred other regular participants. To join, a person needed a certificate indicating they had taken the devotee precepts and to pay a 1-yuan monthly membership fee. Its first leaders in 1989 were Cai Jitang and Liu Zhengsong 柳正松 (1917–2001), who had founded the lodge in the 1950s. They soon retired, becoming honorary presidents until their deaths. The next secretary was a retired bureau director in the city government, and the vice secretary was a retired truck driver for the military.[13] The lodge was registered with the XRAB and supervised by the BAX, who appointed its officers for four-year terms. It had departments for rituals, general affairs, accounts, and maintenance. Its budget came from overseas donations, membership fees, on-demand rituals, alms, and funds from Nanputuo Temple and local temples. The Singapore Devotee Lodge provided funds to renovate the lodge building.[14]

The lodge operated independently of clerics. Regular dharma talks were given by elderly devotees, including Cai Jitang, who had excellent knowledge of Buddhism. BAX and lodge officers gave us several reasons why monks from Nanputuo Temple were not invited to talk. First, most monks could not speak the Minnan dialect, and most elderly devotees had difficulty understanding Mandarin. Second, the dharma talks of the monks were often not relevant to the daily lives of the devotees, unlike those given by Cai Jitang and other devotees. Monks were welcome to attend the dharma talks, but few did because of concerns about their status: for instance, according to rules in Buddhism, monks could not be seated at the same level as laypersons. So clerics attending a dharma talk at the lodge could not sit in the audience facing the speaker. Instead, they had to sit on a platform facing the audience, which was awkward because they had no part in speaking at the talks. Devotees only really needed the monks to administer the devotee precepts.

The lodge held sutra chanting and dharma talks several times a week and monthly services on the eighteenth and thirtieth. Annual rituals included Mile's birthday, worshiping Sakyamuni Buddha, and a thousand-buddhas assembly, and the hungry ghost service, as well as rituals not in Buddhism, such as the pure brightness festival (*qingming jie* 清明節), worshiping Guandi 關帝, and the dragon boat festival. These activities attracted hundreds of participants. There was a ritual for Guanyin's birthday a few days before the much larger Guanyin festival at Nanputuo Temple. Additionally, the lodge organized trips to Mount Putuo, to other Buddhist temples, as well as to folk belief sites, including shrines for Mazu (Sea Goddess) and Zushi Gong (Clear Stream Patriarch).

The local state used the devotees of the Xiamen Devotee Lodge to manage popular Daoist temples, as described in chapter 7. During the 1950s, the lodge headquarters was Danxia Temple 丹霞宮, devoted to Mazu and Baosheng Dadi (Life Protection Emperor). In 1989, the headquarters was Yangzhen Temple 養真宮, dedicated to Baosheng Dadi. Then in 1996, the BAX redesignated Yangzhen Temple as a Buddhist site named Nengren Temple 能仁寺, and eight Buddhist monks moved in.[15] The lodge was reassigned to Neiwu Temple 內武廟, dedicated to Guandi. Lodge officers saw no contradiction in Buddhist devotees using temples to house non-Buddhist deities because many devotees also worshiped them. But lodge officers noted that devotees understood the difference between popular belief and Buddhism, unlike other worshipers who may have seen the deities as part of Buddhism. The officers said that the devotees did not try to dissuade people from worshiping the deities or explain their differences from Buddhism because doing so violated their freedom of belief.

Despite these activities, the Xiamen Devotee Lodge faced problems related to its generational relevancy and appeal. By 2000, two-thirds of its members were over age sixty, with very few under thirty. The elderly members were the original ones from the 1950s, while the younger ones were their sons and daughters. The lodge sought to expand membership by offering classes on introductory Buddhism to prospective devotees and dharma talks for younger people. But the lodge secretary said that few young people came. They preferred going to Nanputuo Temple because it better fit their image of Buddhism.[16] Additionally, the growing number of young, well-educated clerics at Nanputuo Temple and local temples were now capable of giving dharma talks that interested young people. So the lodge's leadership shifted to support its aging and poor members. Every spring festival, the lodge distributed blankets and food to the members and other poor people. In the late 1990s, the lodge began planning a nursing home for elderly devotees. Various fundraising programs were discussed, including a vegetarian restaurant and religious tourist agency. The lodge secretary distinguished these businesses from those run by temples. "Temples have a business to raise money to support the monks, but we can use all our income for charitable purposes."[17] He saw the tourism business as especially promising because Minnan contained sites for seven religions—Hinduism, Manichaeism, and the five state-recognized ones.

DEVOTEES AND LAY NUNS

The devotee Liu Zhengsong played a significant role in enabling devotees to worship and cultivate independently from clerics. He was born in Xiamen to a family that ran businesses in the Philippines. After graduating from primary school, he worked in a relative's traditional medicine store in Hong Kong. The experience sparked his interest in Buddhism, and he began reading sutras. In the 1930s, he returned to Xiamen and took the devotee precepts. While organizing sutra chanting groups, he got the idea to gather the Buddhist texts needed by devotees in one book, just like the Christian Bible. The result was the *Buddhist Cultivation Handbook* (*Fojiao xiuxue yaodian*) 佛教修學要典, published piecemeal from 1948 to the early 1950s. In the 1950s, Liu helped form the Xiamen Devotee Lodge and served as vice president. He was violently attacked during the Cultural Revolution, and Red Guards seized his extensive collection of books. Miraculously, he found them in a storehouse in the 1980s.[18]

Liu's *Buddhist Cultivation Handbook* became very popular among devotees. Its 730 pages had six sections, including morning and evening services (*ke song* 課誦), sutras (*jingzhang* 經章), ritual prayers (*li chan* 禮懺), ritual procedures (*yi gui* 儀規), praising-Buddha chants (*zan yi gui* 讚儀規), and Liu's essays on how to live as a Buddhist devotee. Shortly after 1949, a devotee brought a copy of the *Buddhist Cultivation Handbook* to Hong Kong, where a complete edition was published in 1959 with a foreword by Xingyuan.[19] It became widely used in Hong Kong and was reprinted in Taiwan, the Philippines, and Singapore. By the 1980s, no copies remained in Xiamen. So devotees obtained one from Hong Kong, and the Nanputuo abbot Miaozhan asked the Buddhist Association of Fujian to print copies at Guanghua Temple. We saw many devotees in 1989 and 1990 at sutra chanting groups in Nanputuo Temple holding new copies.

During the 1990s, Liu revised the book to simplify rituals to reduce their time and cost, and eliminate elements that he considered superstitious, such as offerings to the celestial beings (*gongtian* 供天) and the food offering ceremony for all sentient beings (*mengshan* 蒙山). He explained that these rituals were inappropriate because they respected ghosts and deities (*jing guishen* 敬鬼神).[20] The revised edition was titled *The Buddhist Cultivation Handbook for Believers* (*Fojiao xinzhong xiuxue shouce* 佛教信眾修學手冊). Some aspects were controversial, such as a new essay on the Buddhist family that could be interpreted as encouraging the propagation of Buddhism to minors. Unable to find a publisher in the PRC, Liu printed five hundred copies at his own expense for personal distribution.

We asked him why a lay person rather than a monk compiled the book. He answered, "Few monks can write well, while those who can have different ideals from us. They preach how to leave the lay world (*chushi fa* 出世法), but we need to know how to engage the lay world (*rushi fa* 入世法)."[21] He advocated flexibility in following Buddhist teachings to avoid discouraging devotees from observing the precepts. "Buddhist devotees need not be strict vegetarians, as it is very difficult to do so. The Buddhist 'three pure laws' precept (*san jing lü* 三淨律) says meat can be eaten as long as it is 'not seen being killed, not heard being killed, and eaten inadvertently.'"[22] He also tolerated popular practices that were not in Buddhism but met people's needs. For example, he said that using divination blocks was not superstition but "just tradition.... Sometimes a person with a problem needs to find out yes or no. Divination blocks do this."[23]

Young Devotees Outside the Institutional Space of Religion

The early 1990s saw growing interest among educated youth in Buddhism. This trend reflected their turn to religion and philosophy after the Tiananmen Square protest as a safer way to seek answers to fundamental questions than through political involvement. Organizing groups around nonpolitical activities, such as literature, philosophy, and religion, was less controversial. In this section we trace the development of several interlinked organizations and networks that were neither part of the Xiamen Devotee Lodge nor recognized by the state.

The Buddhist Culture Seminar (Fojiao wenhua yantao ban 佛教文化研討班) was founded in 1993 through the cooperation of Nanputuo monks and professors at Xiamen University. The key monk was Jiqun 濟群, born in 1962 in Fu'an City 福安市, on Fujian's northeast coast. He was tonsured in 1979 and graduated in the first class of the revived Buddhist Academy of China. In 1989, he began teaching at the BCM, where he met monks from Taiwan who had graduate degrees and were skilled in lecturing to laypersons. These meetings motivated him to attend graduate courses at the history department of Xiamen University, where his fellow student was Zhanru 湛如 (1964–), who also taught at the BCM (1989–1991) before moving to Beijing University (*NSZ*, vol. 2, 262), the first Buddhist monk to teach there. An encounter with Taiwanese monks also gave Jiqun and Zhanru ideas for propagating Buddhism to youth. In 1991, they gave their first public lecture at Nanputuo on the *Healing Sutra* (*Yaoshi jing* 藥師經) and the *Vimalakīrti Sutra* (*Weimo jiejing* 維摩詰經), the latter centering on the experiences of a layperson. In 1992, they held lecture series at Nanputuo Temple on "Authentic Buddhism Course" (Zhengyan fojiao xilie 正言佛教系列) and "Buddhism for Human Life" (Rensheng fojiao 人生佛教).

In 1993, Nanputuo monks and young Xiamen University instructors held a two-week Buddhist Culture Seminar. They obtained permission from the history department and planned events inside the temple, observing the religious policy ban against propagating Buddhism outside temples. To publicize the event, the university's art department designed a poster with the banner "explore the true meaning of life, open the door of the dharma" (*tantao rensheng zhendi, koukai fofa damen* 探討人生真諦, 叩開佛法大門). These posters were hung throughout the university. The seminar attracted almost a hundred students who were interested in visiting temples, meditation, and discussion (Jiqun 2000).

We interviewed members of Xiamen University who had participated. One was a philosophy professor who had helped recruit students. His interest in Buddhism started through qigong practice, and he began attending Jiqun's dharma talks at Nanputuo Temple. He was greatly impressed by Jiqun's encouragement to go beyond studying Buddhist concepts and history to meditate on the fundamental questions of human existence. The instructor began using Buddhist concepts to teach qigong to his students and took the devotee precepts from Miaozhan. When he attended the Buddhist Culture Seminar, his qigong students went with him. Building on the seminar's success, the instructor helped found the Youth Chan Society (Qingnian chanxue she 青年禪學社), which held weekly lectures by Jiqun for the university students and ran a circulating library at Nanputuo Temple.[24] At the end of 1993, the Youth Chan Society organized a Buddhist Culture Week (Fojiao wenhua zhou 佛教文化周), a series of lectures by Jiqun and other monks on the *Lotus Sutra* and Consciousness Only school. This event attracted over a hundred students, including many of the most talented in the humanities departments, as well as young faculty members. Many participants subsequently took the devotee precepts at Nanputuo Temple. But the strong interest in Buddhism among students at the elite Xiamen University alarmed university authorities, who ordered the Youth Chan Society to disband. We asked the instructor how the university authorities could stop the society if its activities complied with state religious policies. He responded, "Although the activities were inside the temple, some students, after listening, felt confused in their beliefs and reported this to the authorities."[25] Thus, authorities could claim to be protecting students by halting the society.

After the disbanding of the Youth Chan Society, two movements surfaced among youth in Xiamen. One was linked to the revival in 1997 of a new version of the Buddhist Culture Seminar by Shenghui, who was newly selected as Nanputuo abbot. He oriented it to members of the broader society, especially the elderly, since it was less controversial than involving university students. This orientation could also be seen as fitting the new CPC expectation for religions to "adapt" to China's socialist society by providing leisure activities for the growing population of senior citizens. Soon Jiqun stopped giving dharma talks at the society's meetings, ostensibly because of his busy schedule. Some younger participants asked Nanputuo abbot Shenghui for permission to establish a small circulating library at the temple for self-study. The result was the Xiamen Youth Buddhist Book Club (Xiamen qingnian foxue shushe 廈門青年佛學書社), which opened every Sunday in the basement of the Meditation Hall. The main organizer was a woman in her late thirties who was an accountant in the city government. The club had over one hundred members, mostly in their twenties and thirties, including private businesspersons, company employees, government workers, and unemployed persons. We met one young man from a rural village who was self-studying with the idea of renouncing lay life. The organizer told us that none of the members were Xiamen University students. She became a Buddhist in 1981 when, at a difficult time in her life, she felt better after a friend took her to a Buddhist temple. We asked if a government employee could organize a Buddhist group. She replied, "I am doing nothing wrong by being a Buddhist and am willing to openly say that I am Buddhist." Our interview with her took place in August 1999 at the height of the state's anti–Falun Gong campaign. Nevertheless, she spoke freely, secure in being Buddhist because the crackdown distinguished Buddhism from Falun Gong.[26]

The other movement arose from interest in Tibetan Buddhism among young urban professionals and intellectuals, including former members of the Youth Chan Society, pursuing personal spirituality. Their activities centered on circuits of traveling Tibetan monks outside of Buddhist temples. We met one such person, Wang Haoxue (pseudonym), a former core member of the Youth Chan Society.[27] He was born just after the Cultural Revolution to a poor farming family in Anhui Province. Despite excelling in the village school, he failed the university entrance exam. Then, his parents pressured him to marry, so he left home. After wandering for some time, he came to Xiamen in 1992 to visit a friend. He obtained a job in the Xiamen University library and self-studied for an associate degree in Chinese literature at Fujian Teachers College. This study sparked his interest in Buddhism, as the texts answered questions about the meaning of life. He joined the Youth Chan Society and took the devotee precepts from Miaozhan. Soon, he quit the university job to manage the society's library in Nanputuo Temple. When the society was disbanded, Wang thought of becoming a monk but first wanted to deepen his understanding of Buddhism. In 1995, a devotee introduced him to a job in a bookstore (across the street from Nanputuo Temple) stocking many books on religion. This exposed him to books on Tibetan Buddhism. Then he met a Tibetan monk visiting Xiamen who invited him on a twenty-day retreat in Sichuan Province. He traveled with a group of young urban professionals—predominantly women in their mid-twenties to forties, including doctors and foreign firm employees, but no one from government bureaus or state enterprises—who came from Xiamen, Fuzhou, Quanzhou, and Guangzhou cities. In Sichuan, they lived for a week in a mountaintop temple. Ten people, again mostly women, stayed an extra month for secluded meditation (*biguan* 壁観).

Tibetan Buddhism appealed to Wang because he viewed its monks as less materialistic than Chinese monks who, he felt, were too concerned with building and running temples.

> I have faith in Tibetan Buddhism not because I think Han Buddhism cannot solve problems but because the situation of Han Buddhism is not very good. From the outside, all the [Han] temples seem to be flourishing. But many who enter the gate of Buddhism [i.e., become clerics] are motivated by a desire for money or to escape reality. So,

they lack commitment to cultivation and they are no different than laypersons. . . . This is quite common. Many temples do rituals to earn money. Few monks devote themselves to Buddhism for propagating and teaching the dharma.[28]

His criticism of Chinese clerics echoed that of such elderly devotees as Cai Jitang. But while Cai stressed the need for better-educated clerics to improve Buddhism, Wang rejected Han Buddhism in favor of Tibetan Buddhism. Wang and other devotees in the growing urban middle class could pursue their interest in Tibetan Buddhism because it was recognized by the state as part of Buddhism and was inside the PRC, making it easily accessible.

Repositioning Devotees in the Space of Religion

By 2000, devotees were increasingly marginalized in the institutional space of religion. During the 1980s, devotees were needed to do administrative work at Nanputuo Temple and the BAX and teach in the BCM, reprising their cooperation with Nanputuo monks in the early twentieth century. By the 1990s, however, there were many educated clerics who could perform these tasks, and devotees were no longer necessary. The relationship was further weakened by the growing detachment of the temple from local Buddhist communities. When Miaozhan was abbot of Nanputuo Temple, he visited the Xiamen Devotee Lodge to administer the precepts and let devotees hold their chanting group meetings in Nanputuo Temple. But from 1997 the new abbot Shenghui halted these practices, undermining the closeness of the devotee community to Nanputuo clerics.

Marginalization was also seen in the XRAB practice of using the Xiamen Devotee Lodge to manage Daoist and folk religion temples. Lodge officers put a positive face on this. They said that those coming to worship popular deities would be exposed to Buddhism by the presence of the devotees, while their alms propagated Buddhism. But it was undeniable that these temples were given to devotees to manage because they were not Buddhist temples and, therefore, unsuitable for clerics. This situation underscored how the XRAB and BAX saw the Xiamen Devotee Lodge as useful for controlling folk religion rather than propagating

Buddhism. At the same time, the authorities opposed attempts by educated youth to cooperate with monks, as in the Youth Chan Society. The educational authorities saw religion competing with the CPC for the minds and loyalty of educated youth. Unable to establish their activities, some youth joined networks of Tibetan Buddhism outside the institutional space of religion. These trends reflected the waning of the state-approved devotee community.

Lay Nuns: Legacies of Minnan Culture

Lay nuns were greatly respected in Minnan, but their status in Buddhism was ambiguous, as there was no doctrinal category for an unordained laywoman who has renounced lay life.[29] Their existence reflected the historical lack of ordained nuns in Minnan and was also deeply embedded in local culture through traditions and customs of celibate female communities, popular beliefs regarding vegetarianism, and Guanyin worship.[30] Their worship of Guanyin as the central figure in their halls linked the lay nun tradition to Nanputuo Temple, which was devoted to Guanyin. In the sections below we first describe the deep ties between the lay nuns and Nanputuo clerics that emerged in the early twentieth century, bringing the lay nuns into Pure Land Buddhism. We then examine continuity issues in the lay nun community stemming from how the BCM introduced the tradition of ordained nuns to Minnan in the 1980s. Next we present case studies of five lay nun halls affected by the introduction of the nuns' tradition to Minnan: two halls were converted into temples for ordained nuns graduating from the BCM; two halls adapted by transforming into sites of state-approved forms of culture; and a new lay nun hall was founded by lay nuns determined to preserve the tradition.

Acknowledging Ascetic and Pious Women, 1920s–2000s

In the early twentieth century, the lay nun culture that had long existed in Quanzhou and other parts of Minnan came to Xiamen. Growing international trade and the influx of rural residents seeking work provided financial support and recruits for their halls. By around 1930, twenty-one lay nuns lived in eight halls in the city, a number that, by 1939, swelled to eighty women in nineteen halls (*XFZ*, 124). Lay nuns who lived in a hall considered themselves a family, pooling income from handicraft production, ritual fees, and alms. Their care of orphans and the elderly made them close to the people who greatly esteemed them for their compassion. Lay nuns adopted female orphans who would become their disciples, care for them in old age, and inherit their halls.

Since the 1920s, lay nuns have had close ties with Nanputuo Temple. Monks outside Minnan who came to Nanputuo were greatly impressed by these devout women who worshiped Guanyin and led a communal lifestyle similar to ordained nuns. Hongyi called them "ascetic and pious women" (*fanxing qingxin nü* 梵行清信女) (Hongyi 2010, 626). His appreciation reflected the monks' interest in educating women in the model of Christian nuns who served as nurses and teachers. Monks saw a similar role for lay nuns in Minnan, although no nuns lived there when Hongyi did, in the 1930s. Monks did not advocate lay nuns, becoming ordained but accepted them as a special kind of Buddhist. Hongyi saw their potential to propagate Buddhism because they could work alongside laypeople to provide nursing and teaching, unlike ordained nuns, who were prohibited by Buddhist precepts from working in society. Monks incorporated lay nuns into Buddhism by giving them the devotee precepts. In 1948, Xingyuan and Guang'an established a school called the Jüehua Women's Buddhist Academy (Jue hua nüzi foxue yuan 覺華女子佛學苑) to teach them to read and acquire basic knowledge of Buddhism (*XFZ*, 223). After graduation, some lay nuns remained in Xiamen, while others emigrated to Hong Kong, the Philippines, and the United States, establishing halls, medical clinics, and other social welfare organizations.

The ambiguous position of lay nuns enabled their continued existence in the PRC. Their status as Buddhists spared them from the state attack on sectarian religions and other secret societies during the Withdraw from Sects campaign (Tui dao yundong 退道運動) from 1951 to 1953. At the same time, they escaped persecution as Buddhist nuns because they were not ordained. Their numbers peaked in the early 1950s to 159 lay nuns in thirty-one halls (*XFZ*, 124). Some halls started textile factories to produce burlap bags and other products needed by the state during the Korean War. These enterprises gave lay nuns an income and favorable political status as members of the working class. But from the mid-1950s their population declined. Recruits dried up as state restrictions on population movement halted the migration of rural women to Xiamen, and the state began providing for orphans and the elderly. During the Cultural Revolution, some halls were confiscated by local governments, while others continued with members worshiping in secret.

In 1979, the lay nun tradition recovered along with Buddhism. Lay nuns reclaimed halls that the local government had requisitioned for public housing and restored them with funds from overseas Chinese, including lay nuns and monks who were their dharma masters. Lay nuns filled various roles resulting from the lack of ordained clerics, including managing temples reclaimed by the BAX. Nanputuo abbot Miaozhan regarded them highly and encouraged their community as part of the recovery of Buddhism. He permitted them to study in the BCM alongside ordained nuns and appointed some of the first graduates to teaching and administrative roles in the BCM, BAX, and Nanputuo Temple. The high point of the community's recovery was around 2000, with 113 lay nuns in twenty-six halls (XFZ, 124).

These growing numbers nevertheless masked the existential crises the lay nuns faced by the aging of their community. According to a BAX survey in the early 1990s, two-thirds were over age sixty-five, most being women who had left their halls during the Cultural Revolution and returned after 1979 (XFZ, 155). A major reason for the lack of young lay nuns was the introduction of the nuns' tradition in the early 1980s into Fujian (DeVido 2015) when the Fujian Buddhist Academy and BCM started admitting nuns. At first, lay nuns could enroll in the academies. Elderly lay nuns sent their young disciples to the BCM, expecting them to return to the halls after graduating. Upon enrolling, however, the young lay nuns saw the higher status of nuns in Buddhism, and many chose to be ordained. Then, in the 1990s, the two Buddhist academies stopped admitting lay nuns as part of the national standardization of Buddhist education (see chapter 6). They were now considered a local tradition with no place in Buddhist teachings. An additional reason for fewer young lay nuns was the declining practice of adopting orphan girls, which resulted from China's one-child policy and growing opportunities for women in the wealthier society. By the late 1990s, the lack of young lay nuns was becoming a crisis in halls as elderly ones passed away with no successors. By around 2010, the population had collapsed from its high point a decade earlier. The number of lay nuns fell by 78 percent to twenty-five persons, with thirteen under the age of forty. The number of halls plummeted by 81 percent to five persons, with many former halls becoming Buddhist temples for nuns.[31]

Transforming the Halls of Lay Nuns Into Temples for Nuns

Two cases illustrate the transformation of halls into nunneries for ordained nuns. The first highlights the issues of lineage succession and property ownership. Jinglian Hall 淨蓮堂 was founded in 1929 by two lay nuns affiliated with the Huangbo lineage and built during the following five years. One was a disciple of Hongding 宏定 (1878–1951), a lay nun ordained by Nanputuo Temple abbot Huiquan, and Xiamen's first ordained Buddhist nun (XFZ, 291). The lay nuns announced that their hall was ecumenical in a declaration engraved on the hall's stele, erected in 1933: "This vegetarian hall is publicly owned. No person is allowed to use it as their private property. . . . Only virtuous persons may reside here" (Jinglian tang 2018). Nanputuo clerics supported the temple as indicated by the names of Zhuanchen 轉塵 (1876–1961) and Xingyuan engraved on the stele as witnesses (XFZ, 94). In the 1940s, a new lay nun became the head. She was a disciple of Juebin 覺斌 (1896–1942), a monk of the Huangbo lineage, a disciple of Taixu, and the sixth abbot of Nanputuo Temple (XFZ, 270–271). The lay nuns continued living in the hall until the Cultural Revolution, when the government requisitioned it for a factory. The hall was recovered in 1983 and rebuilt with funds from a former resident who had moved to Singapore, and became an open religious activity site in 1992. That year, a new stele was erected that contradicted the declaration of ecumenicism in the 1933 stele. The new stele declared that the right of residence and leadership in the hall was based on religious kinship. "This entire restoration was entirely undertaken by the masters and disciples from our lineage. It is a place for our descendants and follows our rules of residence for pure cultivation. Those from another lineage do not have the right to occupy and live in it. Moreover, disciples and descendants of our lineage will forever inherit and manage it" (XFZ, 94).

In our view, the two stelae—emphasizing, respectively, the very different principles of ecumenicism and lineage in the lay nun hall—signify different historical contexts of the 1930s and the 1990s. The statement of ecumenicism in the 1930s, the high point of the modern reform movement of Buddhism, reflected the closeness of lay nuns with the monks at Nanputuo Temple, who were their masters. The expression of lineage ownership in the 1992 stele reflected the concerns of the lay nuns to maintain their halls during the recovery of Buddhism after the Cultural Revolution. A hall was legally a private residence and the property of its owner. When transferring legal ownership of the hall to a young successor, an elderly head lay nun wanted assurance that the successor would continue Buddhist worship at the hall and not secularize it into a private residence or commercial shop. Thus, the 1992 stele can be seen as an attempt to appoint a successor who could be trusted, which meant someone in the Huangbo lineage. The stele's forceful expression of lineage as the basis of ownership rights at Jinglian Hall could be related to the disruption of its lay nun community during the Cultural Revolution. After recovering her hall, the head lay nun sought to reconstitute her lay nun "family" by emphasizing the strong norms of master-disciple relations; this may have enhanced assurances for the inheritance of the property.

But the head lay nun lacked a successor, a common problem.[32] In such cases, head lay nuns had no choice but to give ownership of their halls to the BAX, which took responsibility for finding a successor. The BAX's solution was to assign young nuns who graduated from the BCM to live in the halls. When all lay nuns in a hall were deceased, the BAX recognized it as a nuns' temple. The halls remained sites of Buddhist worship, but probably not in the style preferred by elderly lay nuns. It was a difficult decision for the head lay nun of Jinglian Hall, who had lost it during political upheavals and then struggled to reclaim and rebuild it. The BAX officer met with her multiple times to persuade her before she finally gave up ownership. When we visited in 1999, the hall was a modern, U-shaped, two-story residence with a floor space of 389 square meters on a 217-square-meter plot of land. There were six elderly lay nuns and seven young nuns living in the hall. After the head lay nun died, a nun became prior. She rebuilt the hall as a five-story structure with six times the floor space and renamed it Jinglian Temple.[33] Notably, converting halls to nunneries enabled the BAX to find positions for the growing number of ordained nuns graduating from the BCM.[34]

The second case illuminates the social relations inside a hall during conversion to a temple for nuns. Miaoqing Temple 妙清寺 began in 1925 as a prayer room to worship Guanyin in the house of Chen Miaoliao 陳妙卿, a disciple of Juewu. In 1942, she founded Miaoqing Temple with five lay nuns in residence. In the 1950s, they started a cotton mill, gaining salaries and worker status. They continued living in the hall during the Cultural Revolution, but it fell into disrepair. Its restoration began in 1986 with funds from a former resident who lived in Los Angeles (XFZ, 57). The reopening ceremony was in 1989. The hall's new stele declared the purity of its Buddhism. "This temple is a place to propagate Buddhism. Only people of high talent and cultivation can reside here, purity must be kept, and it is not permitted to mix customs [不許習俗糊雜 buxu xisu huza]."[35]

When we visited in 1999, the head lay nun was the elderly Chen Ruiyi 陳瑞意, a disciple of Qingnian 清念 (1876–1957), the tonsure master of Yinshun (XFZ, 285–286). The rebuilt hall was a three-story modern building with 680 square meters of floor space on 253 square meters of land. The first floor housed a Guanyin statue, the second floor was the prayer hall (fo tang 佛堂), and the third floor was a shrine to the Amitabha Buddha and other bodhisattvas. Eleven lay nuns in their seventies and eighties resided there. They held morning and evening services attended by area residents and operated a clinic dispensing free medicine. They supported themselves by fees for on-demand rituals and their pensions as retired factory workers.[36] Additionally, four nuns lived there, all BCM graduates sent by the BAX in 1997 as successors to the elderly lay nuns.

The tensions between lay nuns and nuns who lived together in Miaoqing Temple and other halls were a result of the higher religious status that Buddhist doctrine gives to nuns.[37] The young nuns, including those who had only been ordained for a year, thought that they had more authority to chant than a lay nun with decades of experience, and the lay nuns found themselves sidelined during rituals in their own hall. The issue was especially difficult in temples where a young lay nun disciple was ordained as a nun, thereby becoming the religious superior of her lay nun master. She could not show deference to her master without creating discomfort in their relationship. For example, it was a New Year custom for disciples to bow to the head lay nun to show respect. But a nun could not bow to her lay nun master. Such status differences were marginalizing lay nuns within their halls. As an elderly lay nun explained to us: "It is difficult for the two [nuns and lay nuns] to be happy together."[38]

Furthermore, the nuns sent by the BAX were almost all from outside Fujian Province and did not understand the lay nun tradition. They relegated lay nuns to daily chores, such as cooking, laundry, and cleaning, greatly disappointing the lay nuns who had expected the much younger nuns to provide these services for them. There was also a communication gap because the nuns could not speak Minnan dialect, while elderly lay nuns spoke little or no Mandarin. With the passing of the last lay nun in the early 2000s, a nun became prior, and the BAX no longer considered Miaoqing Temple a lay nun hall. The situations of Jinglian Hall and Miaoqing Temple illustrate how, after the lay nuns had been recognized as ascetic and pious women and survived decades of political turmoil, their halls became nunneries, and younger lay nuns became nuns.

Moving to Buddhism as Culture

Some halls have survived by changing their shapes into sites of Buddhism as culture in the institutional and semiotic spaces. Two halls exemplify such transformations, but in different ways: one as an art center and the other as a heritage site. The first case is Qingfu Temple 慶福寺, a hall headed by a lay nun who ordained as a nun in order to adapt to the contemporary context. It was founded in 1790 by a cleric from Huxiyan Temple as a branch convent named Qingfu Court. After being destroyed by fire in the late nineteenth century, it was rebuilt in 1925 by a lay nun who renamed it Qingfu Hall 慶福堂. Since then, lay nuns have resided there, even during the Cultural Revolution, although a factory was built in its courtyard. Its recovery was led by its long-serving head, Zhiwen 智聞. In 1987 Zhiwen amassed funds to rebuild the temple from donations from overseas Chinese and local believers. In 1991 the hall was rebuilt as a modern structure next to the factory in its courtyard and renamed Qingfu Temple (XFZ, 93). The first floor was the shrine hall, the second floor was the prayer hall, and the third floor had residential quarters as well as a small room to worship the Western Trinity (Xifang sansheng 西方三聖). A fourth floor was subsequently added for sutra storage.

Zhiwen's disciple Xinliang 心量, who graduated from the BCM in 1991 and returned to the lay nun hall, expanded the image of the hall by transforming it into a salon for intellectuals. Then, after years as a devoted disciple, Xinliang succeeded her master Zhiwen to become the head of Qingfu in 1998. When we interviewed her the following year, Xinliang told us that the temple emphasized self-cultivation and propagated moral education for the correct behavior and positive perception of Buddhism as public service.[39] It held worship services on the first of each month and opened every Saturday to the public. In the early 2000s, she was ordained as a nun. In 2005, six lay nuns and three devotees (XFZ, 93) resided at Qingfu Temple. Xinliang did not permit other ordained nuns to live there, however, and the BAX continued to consider it a lay nun hall.[40]

Qingfu Temple was positioned in multiple niches and networks. It appealed broadly as a center for local art, embellished by the special character of a local Minnan tradition. Xinliang had founded the Buddha Calligraphy and Painting Society (Foguang shuhua she 佛光書畫社) in 1993 to display calligraphy and paintings by local artists, and the income from its exhibitions, as well as donations to the society, was redirected for temple expenses and charity. As a BCM graduate, she was respected by Buddhist clerics, officials, and artists and supported by Nanputuo abbot Miaozhan, who became honorary president of the Buddha Calligraphy and Painting Society. Drawing further on her Nanputuo ties, she invited artistic clerics who were BCM graduates to display their calligraphy and painting in the hall. The refashioning of Qingfu Temple as an art center fit new efforts by the local state administration to rebrand the city as a cultural industry center.

In the second case, a hall's closeness to the people involved it in early CPC history, eventually leading to its designation after its recovery as a site for patriotic religion. Miaofalin 妙法林, in downtown Xiamen, was founded in 1934 by Miaoyin 妙音, an overseas Chinese from Vietnam, and her disciple Zhiren 志忍, a disciple of Zhuanfeng who ecumenicized Nanputuo. Unlike other halls, it was built with southern-style Buddhist temple architecture. Zhuanfeng calligraphed its signboard, and the walls and pillars had inscriptions by Hongyi. Zhiren was the hall's first head and lived there with eight lay nuns. She was succeeded by Su Bifen 蘇碧芬. In 1959, the local government appropriated the hall for residential housing, and the lay nuns recovered it in 1982. In 1985, Su Bifen, who had moved to Singapore, paid to restore the hall (XFZ, 94–95). Its new head was Hubing 胡冰 (1916–2003), Zhiren's daughter and a CPC member.

When we visited Miaofalin in 1998, there were three lay nuns and three ordained nuns. One nun was a Minnan-speaking graduate of the BCM who had worked in the BAX. In 2003 she became the head of the hall, and four years later the XRAB recognized it as a religious activity site.

The state recognized value in the lay nun hall as a symbolic site of anti-Japanese and anti-ROC activities. In 1982 the Xiamen Municipal People's Government designated it as a "Revolutionary Cultural Relics Protection Unit" (Geming wenwu baohu danwei 革命文物保護單位) in recognition of its role as underground headquarters of the CPC in Xiamen from 1946 to 1949. After its recovery, political delegations and groups of school children often visited. The elderly lay nuns gave talks describing how they supported the CPC headquarters by hiding documents in baskets of fruits and chanting to mask the sounds of meetings. When we interviewed Hubing in 1999, she said that the many visitors prevented the lay nuns from doing on-demand rituals, so the hall lacked income despite its exalted status for patriotism.[41] This status was augmented in 2011 on the ninetieth anniversary of the CPC's founding when it was nationally honored as a "Patriotic Religion Education Base" (Zongjiao jie aiguozhuyi jiaoyu jidi 宗教界愛國主義教育基地).

Hubing's experiences show how lay nuns worked in society in ways difficult for nuns. She was born in Xiamen and studied at a girls' school in the Gulangyu international settlement and then at the BCM, under Hongyi and other clerics. In 1937, she joined the CPC to oppose the Japanese military occupation. After the fall of Xiamen, the CPC sent her to study journalism in Hong Kong and then, in 1941, to work in the transportation section of the People's Liberation Army in Jiangsu Province. In 1943, she returned to Xiamen and lived in Miaofalin. She married, but her husband was soon arrested for anti-ROC activities and died in prison. For her safety, the CPC sent her to Singapore and then to Hong Kong for party cadre training at the Ta Teh Institute (Dade xueyuan 香港達德學院).[42] After 1949, she was assigned to the United Front Work Department to handle overseas Chinese work, first in Beijing and then in Xiamen. During the Cultural Revolution, she was accused of being a traitor and spy for her Buddhism and overseas experiences. In 1983, she was cleared of these charges and retired two years later, becoming manager of Miaofalin. She said that she resided at the hall as a public servant and, even though very devout, would never be ordained. She saw Buddhism and

Communism as having similar aims, despite their ideological incompatibility, because the former saved sentient beings from suffering, and the latter benefitted the toiling masses (XFZ, 326–327). Miaofalin's prominence as a site of patriotic religion made it a shrine to CPC history while enabling it to remain a lay nun hall even when its new head was ordained as a nun.

Both Miaofalin and Qingfu Temple preserved the Minnan lay nun tradition by becoming sites of culture: Miaofalin as a CPC heritage site and Qingfu Temple as a local art venue with a national reach and an interest in preserving Minnan tradition. In the early twenty-first century, the leadership at these sites by ordained nuns with strong ties to Nanputuo Temple enabled their ongoing recognition as lay nun halls adapted to the contemporary situation. We next describe efforts to continue the lay nun tradition under the leadership of lay nuns.

Maintaining the Lay Nun Tradition

The successful efforts of two lay nuns to create a new hall in Xiamen illustrate not only the powerful semiotic space of lay nuns in the Minnan culture but also the local state flexibility in the institutional space of religion. Both these lay nuns were among the first graduates of Buddhist academies in the 1980s and were respected by Buddhists and society. Especially striking was their success in founding Ciguang Temple (pseudonym), which assumed the size and structure of a relatively large urban Buddhist temple. The overwhelming local support they received despite the local state ban on new temple construction testified to the deep local respect toward lay nuns as pious and celibate women devoted to Guanyin.

Lay Nun A (pseudonym) was born in Xiamen in the mid-1950s to a family of Buddhist believers. Her father worked in a government-owned retail store, and her mother was a housewife. As a child, she often visited an elderly lay nun next door to keep her company. In 1968, at age thirteen, she left her family to live in the hall. During the Cultural Revolution, the lay nuns worshiped in secret. "People came daily to worship because our temple was in the city center. The old lay nun was very acute in predicting the future, so the hall was well known. We burned incense brought to us by neighbors who hid it under their clothes. We never stopped morning and evening services. . . . We worshiped with believers hiding under mosquito nets so we could not be seen." Upon turning seventeen, she began working in a government factory where a fellow worker would become her dharma sister Lay Nun B (pseudonym). In 1983, the master of Lay Nun A's lay nun master, the monk Guang'an 廣安 (1924–1996), recommended Lay Nun A for entry into the Fujian Buddhist Academy.[43] While there she became aware that ordained nuns held a higher status in Buddhism, but Guang'an advised her not to ordain; in the 1980s, lay nun halls did not accommodate nuns, so ordainment could have prevented her from returning to her hall. Upon graduating in 1987, Miaozhan recruited her to supervise nuns studying in the BCM. She found it difficult to manage nuns from outside Minnan who were unfamiliar with the lay nun tradition, so she took a new job in 1989 managing the Nanputuo guesthouse for visiting clerics. That year, Lay Nun B graduated from the BCM to work at the BAX as a researcher for the *Gazetteer of Nanputuo Temple*.

The path to creating their lay nun hall started in 1989 when Guang'an bought a residential house in Xiamen as a shrine to his master Zhuanfeng (who ecumenicized Nanputuo Temple in 1924). The opening ceremony of Ciguang Hermitage (pseudonym) was attended by Miaozhan, Guang'an, and many devotees from Xiamen and Southeast Asia.[44] The city district government requisitioned the land, but in 1992, it compensated the lay nuns with several apartments in a new housing complex. The lay nuns considered it disrespectful to place a Buddha statue in an apartment, so they decided to build a Buddhist temple. They sold the apartments to raise money and resigned from their jobs to devote themselves full-time to the project. Their strong local networks helped them surmount local state rules prohibiting the establishment of new temples in Xiamen.

The lay nuns found supporters throughout the Xiamen Municipal People's Government. The officials were mainly from Minnan, so when the lay nuns visited government bureaus they were treated with understanding and respect. A friend in the public security bureau introduced them to the official in charge of razing buildings for new construction. This official requested the land planning bureau to allocate land for the temple, noting that its patron was a prominent overseas cleric. The bureau's director, also a family friend and Buddhist, was supportive. He permitted the lay nuns to select a piece of land on a ridge next to a residential area in the new downtown. They chose a 338-square-meter plot of land, and the bureau added more land for a garden and entrance. Their efforts to get the necessary permits from multiple government bureaus went smoothly. "When we went to each bureau," recounted Lay Nun B, "there was always someone we knew who could help us. They were sympathetic to us. They said, 'It's really something for you women to be coming out to do this.'"[45] A city vice mayor waived the permit fees by designating the temple as a public facility.

Monks at Nanputuo Temple provided much assistance. Nanputuo abbot Miaozhan paid attention to their careers and advised them. He helped the lay nuns assess the feng shui of their land by bringing in a Tibetan expert in geomancy. The monks then counseled the lay nuns on handling relations with the city bureaucracy when building the temple, suggesting that the lay nuns hire architects and a construction company recommended by the city government, rather than the more experienced Nanputuo Temple Construction Unit. Then, Miaozhan lent the architects the construction unit's blueprints for the temple roof and sent craftsmen to supervise its construction. The lay nuns' extensive personal ties of family, school, and work in Xiamen also provided much support. Of special note were their former "sister" factory workers from the Cultural Revolution who were employed by the local state administration or had married men who were. Some of their siblings were businesspersons who became patrons of the new temple.

When we visited Ciguang Temple in 1999, it was a five-story white building with 1,000 square meters of floor space under a saffron-colored roof. The structure resembled a cross between a large house and a temple. Nine lay nuns and a four-year-old orphan girl resided there (nuns were not permitted to reside at Ciguang Temple). Only a third of the lay nuns were elderly, which was unusual for a hall. Lay Nuns A and B were in their forties, while the others were in their twenties and early thirties. All had graduated from Buddhist academies, junior college, or middle school.

The temple's many activities were well attended. These consisted of daily morning and evening services, a half-day Medicine Buddha prayer assembly on the thirteenth of each month, and thousand-buddhas assemblies in February, June, and September. Clerics from Nanputuo Temple came to give dharma talks, and some BCM teachers used the opportunity to train students to give them. Attendees included devotees from Xiamen, believers living in the neighborhood, and the lay nuns' sister factory workers. In sum, the Ciguang Temple's situation demonstrates how lay nuns who graduated from Buddhist academies gained the self-confidence, religious recognition, and social networks to become vigorous leaders and advocates for the lay nun tradition.

Conclusion

The devotee and lay nun communities contributed to continuity in the space of religion. In the early twentieth century, devotees cooperated with monks to fit Buddhism into the modern context in a reform movement that included the recognition of lay nuns as Buddhists. In the 1980s, the shortage of clerics contributed to the crucial roles that the by-now elderly members of these communities played in Buddhism's recovery. Elderly devotees taught in the BCM, worked in the BAX, and revived the Xiamen Devotee Lodge, while lay nuns managed reclaimed temples and provided staff for the BAX and Nanputuo Temple. During the 1990s, the growing number of well-educated clerics, including many BCM graduates, reduced the need for devotees and lay nuns to work alongside clerics. The introduction of the nun tradition into Minnan and the standardization initiated by the central state constricted opportunities for young lay nuns. While these two communities increasingly struggled to adapt, new movements were visible in the semiotic space of religion, including the growing interest in Tibetan Buddhism and Buddhism as culture.

9

The Guanyin Festival: Being Buddhist the Chinese Way

THE GUANYIN FESTIVAL HAS BEEN the most significant event of Nanputuo Temple throughout its history. According to tradition, it is held three times a year on the nineteenth day of the second, sixth, and ninth months to celebrate the life cycle of Guanyin—birth (*chusheng* 出生), enlightenment (*chengdao* 成道), and renunciation of lay life (*chujia* 出家). On these days, the temple hosts the largest number of worshipers, and crowds are largest at midnight, because the magical efficacy of Guanyin was believed to reach its peak at the very start of the festival. The festival is the only occasion when the temple keeps its gates open overnight, physically connecting the temple to the people. Three times a year, as the crowds, excitement, and energy fill the temple, the temple fully functions as a space of religion.

Even during the Cultural Revolution, when the temple was shut, small groups came at night to worship in the hills behind the temple. It was rumored that monks were inside the temple softly chanting. When Nanputuo reopened in 1979, the temple gates remained shut during the night of the Guanyin festival, but thousands of people worshiped in front of them at midnight. From 1982, the gates remained open overnight three times a year, and attendance soared. The restarting of the festival greatly encouraged people, assuring them of the CPC's commitment to let religion exist.

Thus far the people we have discussed in this book have taken precepts—whether as clerics, devotees, or lay nuns—and belonged to recognized Buddhist communities in Xiamen. But tens of thousands of people who were neither ordained nor identified as Buddhists came to Nanputuo Temple during the festival. Many came only on festival days. They included local Xiamen residents who routinely went to local temples near their homes, where it was easier to talk to the clerics in the relaxed atmosphere than at Nanputuo, where monks seemed busy and there were many tourists. Despite this, Nanputuo Temple and Guanyin were centered in the mind of Xiamen residents. They may not have known the abbot's name, but they knew the dates of the festival and that Guanyin was in the Great Compassion Hall. By worshiping on these special days, people reactivated their bond with Guanyin. The festival made the temple an exceptional space for people, giving it a unique status and presence; if it were not held, Nanputuo Temple would be less distinguished. The Guanyin festival was a huge resource for the temple's vitality as a space of religion for people and communities.

In this chapter, we discuss the role and function of the Guanyin festival in making Nanputuo Temple and its meaning to the people. We first provide an overview of the festival that explains the origin and significance of Guanyin worship in China and describes the sequence of events for a single Guanyin festival, beginning to end. Then we draw on our survey of participants to examine who came and why.[1] And finally we consider the worship of the masses as the question of folk belief in the space of religion. We attended Guanyin festivals at least half a dozen times during our research, conducting interviews and recording our observations. In this chapter we draw mainly on our fieldwork at the 1999 festival, from July 30 to 31, through which we aimed to understand people's passions as they enjoyed the fully recovered temple, even more beautiful than before the Cultural Revolution. For further insight into changes over time, in the conclusion we juxtapose the data with another occurrence of the festival we observed ten years earlier (1989).

Overview and Sequence of the Festival

The festival is dedicated to the bodhisattva called Avalokiteśvara, known in Chinese as Guanyin. A bodhisattva is a person who does not seek self-enlightenment but rather the enlightenment of all living things (sentient beings). Avalokiteśvara, presented in the *Lotus Sutra*, was a compassionate being who could hear people's calls for help from anywhere in the world. When introduced into China a thousand years ago through such legends as Princess Miaoshan (the Chinese incarnation of Avalokiteśvara), the bodhisattva was transformed into a feminine form and given the name Guanyin; the full name for Guanyin, however, was Guanshiyin 觀世音, literally "the one who hears all laments in the world" (Yü 2001).

This image of a merciful being always ready to help or heal has made the belief in Guanyin extremely widespread in China. People with difficulties had only to utter her name while praying, and their problems would be solved or their suffering relieved. Therefore, Guanyin was viewed as a savior. Although her many worshipers were women, men also worshiped Guanyin because she was believed to help achieve success in education, work, and business. As we mentioned earlier, Nanputuo Temple had a very popular statue of Thousand-Handed and Thousand-Eyed Guanyin with eleven other heads on top of the main head. The eyes in the palms of the outward-radiating forty-eight arms enabled Guanyin to see and help people in trouble anywhere in the world.

The Guanyin festival revealed a deep distinction between Buddhism as defined by Buddhist monks and the CPC and the Buddhism practiced by the masses who came to the temple for the festival. This was evident in the double structure of the festival. Monks and devotees performed three special ceremonies: two were the morning and evening services held in the Great Buddha Hall, and third was a special ritual of offering food to Guanyin held in the Great Compassion Hall. Festival attendees did not participate in these rituals. Instead, they started coming on the evening of the eighteenth, carrying offerings of incense, food, and alms. They moved through the temple, stopping to worship here and there. Despite not partaking in the three special ceremonies, worshipers could hear the chanting of the monks while the monks felt the energy of the crowds.

The festival's double structure was also evident in the physical boundaries inside the temple that marked the space for the practices of monks as separate from the worship of the people. The monks blocked off the west compound that housed the BCM and their living quarters. People could worship in the central compound, visit the vegetarian restaurants in the east compound, relax by the Lotus Pond at the front ground, and wander the hills behind the temple. In this way, the space where people worshiped and enjoyed themselves was clearly delimited from the space for the practice and education of clerics.

In the rest of this section we describe the entire sequence of the festival we attended in July 1999. People began to arrive on July 30 in late afternoon. They entered the temple through the two mountain gates, passing by police officers stationed there. They relaxed by strolling alongside the lotus pond, leaning against its railing, sitting on stone benches, and walking clockwise around the Longevity Pagodas. Some visited the department store inside the East Mountain Gate, where they could buy temple souvenirs, such as bean cakes, and Xiamen mementos and other sundries. Some bought offerings, such as incense, prayer beads, and small Buddha statues, at a shop by the Heavenly Kings Hall. Plainclothes police officers mingled with the crowd to keep order, and BAX officers were on duty around the clock. A fire truck was parked next to the Nanputuo Temple Charity Foundation in case incense sticks sparked a fire.

The beating of the gong at 3:50 p.m. announced the start of the evening service, an hour earlier than usual, to accommodate the chanting service for Guanyin. Many monks began walking to the Great Buddha Hall for the evening service at 4:00. It had nine parts; four parts were the regular service, and five were special for the festival (see table 9.1). The abbot presided while the precentor led a dozen monks in chanting, and other monks played percussion instruments, striking at appropriate moments. The head donor, the layperson who financially sponsored the ceremony, participated. The temple had specially invited him to receive the great merit from being head donor. Experienced devotees also participated because Nanputuo Temple was ecumenical and open to them. Wearing black robes, they expressed piety by standing behind the monks while listening to the chanting.

As soon as the evening service began, people streamed into the temple bearing bags of incense and food. Worship on the festival eve was called "evening incense" (*wan xiang* 晚香). Those coming in the early evening were primarily the elderly and mothers with babies and small children. Everyone could hear the chanting of the monks suffusing the

TABLE 9.1 Rituals Performed by Monks on the Evening of July 30, 1999

Order	Name	Description
1	Hymn of praise 唱贊 chang zan	Chant for auspicious Guanyin festival (special for festival)
2	Amitābha Sutra (Skt.) 念誦彌陀經 niansong Mituo jing	Chanting Amitābha Sutra
3	Names of eighty-eight buddhas 八十八佛懺悔文 bashiba fo chanhui wen	Chant to remove karmic obstacles and draw out wisdom
4	Mengshan food bestowal 蒙山施食 meng shan shishi	Chant to give food to hungry ghosts
5	Circumambulation 繞念 rao nian	Monks circumambulate temple while chanting (special for festival)
6	Giving thanks 拜願 bai yuan	Pray for compassionate blessings of the Buddha and bodhisattvas
7	Three refuges 三皈依 san guiyi	Expressing devotion to the Buddha, dharma, and sangha
8	Great compassion incantation 大悲咒 dabei zhou	Praising Guanyin (special for festival)
9	Praising temple chant 伽藍贊 qielan zan	Chant for temple as representing cosmology and teaching of the Buddha (special for festival)

Source: Data obtained in interviews with Nanputuo clerics, Yoshiko Ashiwa and David Wank, August and September 1999

temple through loudspeakers, along with warnings to burn incense only at designated sites. The chanting gave voice to the Buddha's teachings, heard by all worshipers in the temple no matter where they were, purifying them and imparting merit. People could sense the temple "coming alive" because they were worshiping at the same time that monks were conducting rituals. Everyone proceeded counter-clockwise through the temple, stopping by incense urns in front of deities and in the courtyards, and worshiping at the Guanyin statue in the Great Compassion Hall, and at the Buddha Rock at the foot of Wulao Peak.

At 6:30 p.m., fifty BCM student monks took up positions at the entry to the halls and by the temple's eleven incense urns and nine incense tables where people stopped to worship.[2] They worked hard to enable the flow of worshipers through the temple. Ten monks standing at the Heavenly Kings Hall removed the burning sticks placed by worshipers in the incense urns and tables, dousing them in iron tubs of water. Their efforts kept the urns from filling up and catching fire. A dozen monks stood in the doorways of the Great Compassion Hall to protect the Thousand-Handed and Thousand-Eyed Guanyin statue from the crush of worshipers. Worshipers gave their offerings to these monks, who passed them over the altar to bless them and handed them back. Four monks stood by the Buddha Rock, where people burned spirit money.

As the evening deepened, the crowd grew, and its composition changed. It now consisted of families with older children; groups of young people, including high school students, many of them in high spirits to be on an outing with members of the other sex; and laborers from local factories and construction crews. The monks on duty were now busy gathering burning incense sticks from the urns; some were pushing wheelbarrows to collect the wet piles of sticks. Hazy light from small spotlights shone through the dense white incense smoke. At 10:10 the bell for monks to rest rang, followed twenty minutes later by the gong for lights out. These markers of temple routine were just formalities, as the festival was getting livelier.

Soon a swelling crowd of people jockeyed outside the Heavenly Kings Hall, straining to be the first to enter the compound just after midnight when the magical efficacy of worshiping the deities was believed to be greatest. The worshipers were now mostly young people in their teens to thirties. Many were white-collar employees and service workers on company outings who had come on buses displaying company logos. There were a few families with older children. At 12:30 a.m. on July 31, the second shift of fifty monks replaced the first shift that had been on duty for six hours. The large crowds moved slowly, bunching up in front of the incense urns and packing the cloisters along the sides of the compound. This was the time of greatest danger for people to get burned by incense sticks bobbing up and down in worshipers' hands. Visibility was limited now to a few meters because of the thick smoke. Some people wrapped scarfs around their mouths to keep from choking. Young monks worked feverishly to douse the incense sticks. The piles of wet sticks beside them grew because the wheelbarrows could not push through the crowds to collect the sticks.

By 3:00 a.m. on July 31, the crowd had thinned considerably, and the smoke dissipated. Worshipers were now primarily young men coming alone or in small groups. Elderly women devotees wearing loose-fitting gray and black clothing used brooms and bundles of straw to sweep up the incense wrappers, fruit peels, and other litter. The monks on duty were exhausted, their eyes bloodshot from the smoke, and their robes, arms, and faces blackened by soot. By 4:00 a.m., only a few worshipers remained as elderly devotees dozed, slumped on stools against the walls.

At 4:45 a.m., the wake-up gong sounded and was soon accompanied by the drumbeat announcing the morning service at 5:00. The ceremony started half an hour earlier than usual to accommodate five extra rituals for the Guanyin festival (see table 9.2).

During the morning service, the number of people coming to the temple rose again. They were mostly elderly people who lived nearby and walked over. At 6:30 a.m., the second shift of monks, exhausted from all-night duty, was replaced by the earlier shift that was now rested. Around 8:00, the flow of worshipers quickened as older people and young mothers with children began arriving by public bus. Soon, tour buses arrived

TABLE 9.2 Rituals Performed by Monks on the Morning of July 31, 1999

Order	Name	Description
1	Hymn of praise 唱贊 chang zan	Special chant for auspicious Guanyin festival
2	Śūraṅgama (Skt.) incantation 楞嚴咒 lengyan zhou	Chant
3	Universal Buddha 普佛 pu fo	Special chant for good fortune of head donor for the service
4	Guanyin eight-phrase hymn 觀音八句贊 guanyin ba ju zan	Hymn praising Guanyin chanted specially for festival
5	Invocation verse 祝願偈 zhuyuan ji	Chant praising the Buddha
6	Guanyin verse 觀音偈 Guanyin ji	Special chant for festival
7	Circumambulation 繞念 rao nian	Monks circumambulate temple while chanting (special for festival)
8	Giving thanks 拜願 bai yuan	Pray for compassionate blessings of the Buddha and bodhisattvas
9	Three refuges 三皈依 san guiyi	Expressing devotion to the Buddha, dharma, and sangha
10	Great Lakṣmī (Skt.) incantation 大吉祥天女咒 da jixiang tiannü zhou	Chant for wealth, happiness, and fertility
11	Weituo hymn 韋馱贊 weituo zan	Chant to praise Weituo, a heavenly king protecting the temple

Source: Data obtained in interviews with Nanputuo clerics, Yoshiko Ashiwa and David Wank, August and September 1999

to disgorge tourists from China, Taiwan, Hong Kong, and overseas directly in front of the Heavenly Kings Hall. Wearing baseball caps blazoned with the names of tour agencies, they followed guides carrying small colorful flags with agency logos. Curious worshipers trailed behind the tour groups, eager to catch the guides' explanations.

Tours started at the Heavenly Kings Hall. A guide whom we observed explained to her group that the staff held by the guardian king Weituo could point in different directions. A downward-pointing staff signaled that the temple was wealthy enough to give accommodations to wandering monks, but when held horizontally it indicated the opposite. When the tour group entered the central courtyard, she noted that its bell and drum towers harmoniously aligned with Wulao Peak. This indicated the temple was a miraculous place where the Buddhist cosmology fit the natural setting. Stopping by the Merit Pagoda in front of the Great Buddha Hall, she said that its height was a measure of the merit of the monks. She then recounted the legend of Buddha's birth. While his pregnant mother was returning home to give birth, she plucked a piece of fruit to eat. A child emerged from her armpit, and the mother died seven days later, indicating that god put Gautama Buddha into this world. Next, the tour guide stopped by the bodhi tree at the Great Compassion Hall. She explained that it was sacred, so birds did not build nests there, and incense ashes did not stick to it.

At 9:30 a.m., the gong rang to announce the final ceremony of the Guanyin festival, which was offerings to all buddhas and bodhisattvas. This hour-long ceremony occurred at the Great Compassion Hall housing the Thousand-Handed and Thousand-Eyed Guanyin statue. The hall's small size limited the number of participating monks. The ceremony had eight parts (see table 9.3).

By now, more families were coming with children. After worship, many climbed Wulao Peak or picnicked by the Lotus Pond. At 10:30 a.m., the ringing of the gong signaled both the end of the large offering to buddha ceremony and gratitude to the head donor. By noon, the intense sunlight had driven people out of the courtyard to seek shade. They lounged or napped on stone benches and mats under trees by the Lotus Pond as elderly women devotees rested in the compound's cloisters. With the coolness of late afternoon, there was a final rush of people, including the elderly, families, and employees who had been unable to come earlier. At

TABLE 9.3 Large Offering to Buddha Ceremony on Morning of July 31, 1999

Order	Name	Description (all rituals special festival)
1	Fragrance of burning incense hymn 爐香贊 lu xiang zan	Expresses praise to the Buddha and bodhisattva
2	Offering incantation 供養咒 gongyang zhou	Chanted three times
3	Food conversion mantra 變食真言 bianshi zhenyan	Chant to alleviate suffering of hungry ghosts.
4	Ambrosia mantra 甘露水真 ganlu shui zhen	Chant to purify temple
5	Verse 偈語 ji yu	Thanking the Buddha, feeding hungry ghosts
6	Universal offering mantra 普供養真言 pu gongyang zhenyan	Chant
7	Celestial offering hymn 天廚妙供贊 tian chu miao gong zan	Chant
8	Saṃghârāma (Skt.) hymn 伽藍贊 qielan zan	Chant in praise of divine protector of the temple

Source: Data obtained in interviews with Nanputuo clerics, Yoshiko Ashiwa, and David Wank, August and September 1999

5:00 p.m., the gong sounded for the regular evening service. The festival ended at 6:00, but the gates remained open although monks were not on duty. At 11:00, the gates shut.

Self-Recognition of Festivalgoers

To understand the body of people who came to the festival, we interviewed 103 attendees. We sought to understand their background, if they identified as Buddhists, and their reasons for coming. Even though Nanputuo Temple was a nationally important temple, the worshipers were overwhelmingly from Xiamen and the Minnan region. This showed the strong bond between the temple and Xiamen residents, who considered it their temple: 42 percent of respondents were from Xiamen; 38 percent came from elsewhere in Fujian, mainly the Minnan region; and 20 percent came from other provinces. The fact that the majority of the participants (62 percent) were not locals from Xiamen reflected the significance of Nanputuo Temple because no other temple in Xiamen attracted so many festival worshipers from outside the city. Therefore, we consider

Nanputuo Temple to be a locally embedded national temple. We found that those who attended each of the three annual festivals were mostly Xiamen residents. This indicates to us that the festival was implanted in their minds as part of the calendrical cycle of events of life in Xiamen. Concerning age, 43 percent were young (ages fifteen to thirty), 27 percent were middle-aged (ages thirty-one to fifty), and 31 percent were elderly (above the age of fifty). They worked in a diverse range of urban occupations (see table 9.4).

How did participants at the festival see Buddhism as a religion and regard their activities? How did they see themselves as persons worshiping Guanyin? What was their understanding of Buddhism? Unlike Christianity or Islam, a person does not convert to Buddhism to worship at a Buddhist temple, and a temple has no congregation to signify membership. Of course, a layperson could take the five precepts to be a devotee or even the eight precepts that indicated great piety. But very few worshipers, even those regularly attending festivals and other occasions at Buddhist temples, were devotees. Therefore, to what degree could it be said that the attendees at the Guanyin festival were Buddhists? To find out, we surveyed participants, starting with the question, "Are you a Buddhist? (*ni shi bushi fojiaotu* 你是不是佛教徒)." By analyzing their responses, we understood how they comprehended their participation in the festival.[3] We realized how specific criteria differentiated being a

TABLE 9.4 Occupations of Interviewees at 1999 Guanyin Festival*

Occupation	Number of persons
Factory worker/office worker	27
Retiree (workers and cadres)	19
Migrant laborer	15
Cadre/manager (with college degree)	10
Student	9
Small shop owner (peddler, taxi driver, etc.)	8
Businessman	2
Housewife	3
Farmer	1

*From the sample of 103 interviewees, 94 persons responded when asked their occupation.
Source: Survey data, Yoshiko Ashiwa and David Wank, July 30–31, 1999

Buddhist from not being a Buddhist in people's minds. These criteria gave insight into the Chinese way of Buddhism.

For each interview, a member of our research team approached a person, identified themself, and asked a series of open-ended questions in a conversational manner. To avoid alarming interviewees, we did not take notes during interviews. Upon completing an interview, the interviewer immediately wrote a summary that retained the interviewee's actual words and included observations on their background, behavior, and appearance. Interviews began on the eve of the festival and continued throughout the festival day. Most were conducted in the front yard, where people lingered before entering the temple, waited for others worshiping inside, or relaxed after worship. In this and the following sections, we paraphrase the interviewees' responses, retaining their phrasing to convey the nuances of their beliefs and ideas.

We categorized the survey respondents based on their degree of commitment to Buddhism. Ninety percent said that they were not Buddhist but said they believed in Buddha (*xin fo* 信佛) and came to the festival to worship (*bai* 拜), pray (*qiu* 求), or give offerings (*gong* 供) to Guanyin or the Buddha. These respondents indicated some commitment to Buddhism even though they denied being Buddhists (*fojiao tu* 佛教徒). We realized that seemingly ambiguous answers may have stemmed from the Chinese term for "Buddhist." It contains the character for "disciple" (*tu* 徒), which signifies a relationship with a master. Therefore, asking a person, "Are you a Buddhist?" is tantamount to asking, "Who is your master?" Similar questions, such as, "Are you a devotee?" and "Have you taken the Three Refuges and Five Precepts?," also imply that a person has a master. So, a negative response to our question "Are you a Buddhist?" enabled respondents to indicate that their commitment to Buddhism was less than a devotee following Buddhist precepts in daily life.

Based on the answers to our question "Are you a Buddhist?" we discerned four categories of respondents. We examine interviewees' responses in each category below.[4]

Buddhist

Five persons answered affirmatively to our question "Are you a Buddhist?" by saying, "Yes, I am a Buddhist (*wo shi fojiao tu* 我是佛教徒)" or

"You can say that I am a Buddhist (*keyi suan shi fojiao tu* 可以算是佛教徒)." Being a Buddhist meant observing such Buddhist practices as vegetarianism and morning and evening services. One person had taken the devotee precepts. She was a twenty-six-year-old graduate student at Xiamen University from North China. Her interest in Buddhism began when, depressed by work-related conflicts, she met a monk and felt better after talking to him. After deepening her understanding of Buddhism, she became a devotee. She very much believed in Buddhism and only offered incense at the festival because she felt that food was not as pure (interviewee 44).

Among the five participants who answered affirmatively, some were not devotees but intended to take the precepts after gaining more knowledge of Buddhism. Their plans showed their understanding of being a Buddhist as a process demarcated by the development of thought. A Xiamen woman in her thirties said she would take the devotee precepts after obtaining a sufficient understanding of Buddhist teachings. She had been attending the festival three times a year for over ten years and regularly burned incense at home. She also worshiped in a lay nun hall as she greatly respected the lay nun who helped solve her troubles (interviewee 2). For other participants, the development of thought reflected the amount of time spent in study and cultivation. One was a white-collar employee from Xiamen in his forties. His family had been Buddhist for generations, and his parents often took him to Nanputuo Temple as a child. Nowadays, he said, he was busy and only worshiped there when he was free, but he always made sure to come to every Guanyin festival. He wanted to take the devotee precepts but lacked time to commit to being a devotee (interviewee 5). Another person was a restaurant owner in her fifties from Xiamen who first came to the festival before the Cultural Revolution. Since it restarted in 1982, she came three times a year. She burned incense twice daily at her home altar and ate vegetarian on the first and fifteenth of each month. She had long wanted to take the precepts but was too busy. Now she was studying the dharma with lay nuns in preparation (interviewee 91).

The local women from Xiamen who were among the five people in the Buddhist category regularly interacted with lay nuns. For example, the parents of one housewife from Xiamen, who was now in her sixties, had brought her to the festival as a child. Since the early 1980s, she had come each year to all three festivals. She worshiped every morning and evening at her home altar and followed a vegetarian diet daily. She often went to Qingfu Temple to talk with its lay nuns and invite them to perform rituals in her home. She considered herself a devout believer in Buddha but not a lay nun because she had not left her family (interviewee 60). Clearly, this housewife considered herself especially pious because she frequently interacted with lay nuns.

These five persons considered themselves Buddhists not because they were devotees—only one had taken precepts—but because they followed Buddhist teachings in daily life by worshiping and eating vegetarian at least two days a month. Three wanted to take the precepts but were too busy to do so. They realized that observing the precepts while living with their families was difficult because vegetarianism did not easily fit into regular family life. They aspired to become devotees when they were older and free from childrearing and work.

Not Buddhist, but Believed and Worshiped

Fifty-five persons said they were not Buddhist but believed in Buddha and worshiped Buddha. We found the experience of a Xiamen woman in her fifties who worked in a hot sauce factory to be typical of such respondents. She said she was not a Buddhist because she was not a vegetarian. But she believed in Buddha and worshiped at her home altar on the first and fifteenth days of the month. She also came to the Guanyin festival three times a year to pray for security for her family (*qiu ping'an* 求平安), offering cookies, apples, and bananas, and donating small sums of money. Her use of vegetarianism as the criterion for distinguishing herself as a believer in Buddhism, but not a Buddhist (interviewee 27), revealed the necessary difficulty of applying and practicing Buddhist teachings to daily life. Keeping vegetarian while living with the family was difficult, as one had to cook separately from their family, except in the unlikely case that the entire family was vegetarian. Keeping vegetarian also required not eating garlic and scallions, which was difficult in Chinese cuisine. Therefore, vegetarianism was a straightforward way for this woman to explain her presence at the Guanyin festival without having to engage in religious and philosophical discussions.

Indeed, one quarter of the interviewees who said they were not Buddhist explained nonadherence to vegetarianism as the reason. Significantly, none of the interviewees attributed not being Buddhist to their lack of understanding the sutras. Respondents thus distinguished between being Buddhist—or not—by the criterion of practice, such as vegetarianism, rather than by knowledge of Buddhist teachings. A female shop employee from Xiamen who had been coming to the festival three times a year since 1995 and believed in Buddhism exemplified this view. Anyone coming to the temple to burn incense, she said, could be considered to believe in Buddha. She carried a large bundle of incense to worship at each bodhisattva (interviewee 4). For her, belief was reflected in the physical things a person did, such as traveling to the temple, bringing offerings, and burning incense. All respondents who said they believed in the Buddha also said they came to the festival to worship.

Because Guanyin was renowned for listening to and solving problems, people prayed for her help and support in their families, careers, and personal lives. For example, a high school student from Xiamen who believed in Buddha but was not Buddhist came to burn incense and pray for success in her studies and employment. She did not give alms because "sincerity when burning incense was sufficient (*chengxin shaoxiang jiu xing le* 誠信燒香就行了)" (interviewee 35). We also heard from a retired cadre in his sixties living in Xiamen. His parents and family all believed in Buddha, and he had worshiped at every festival since the early 1980s. He prayed for security and happiness, offering apples, biscuits, and alms of 60 yuan. But coming to the festival with a sincere heart was essential (interviewee 83). According to these persons, the likelihood of a prayer being answered depended on the sincerity of the worshiper.

Others told us they believed in the magical efficacy of the Buddha (*shenling* 神靈) to help them. A twenty-year-old company employee from Jiangxi Province working in Xiamen stressed that "worshiping the Buddha [at Nanputuo Temple] always brought some advantage, such as luck (*bai pusa zong hui you yidian hao chu, you yidian yunqi ba* 拜菩薩總會有一點好處, 有一點運氣吧)" (interviewee 97). A chauffeur in his thirties who had moved from elsewhere in Minnan to Xiamen held a similar view. He believed in the magical efficacy of the deities' power and worshiped at many temples in Minnan (interviewee 99). The comments of these two persons suggested some calculation in their beliefs. The company employee figured it was better to worship than not, while the chauffeur enhanced his prospects by worshiping at many temples.

Our respondents also spoke of their belief in luck (*yunqi* 運氣) or fate (*mingyun* 命運). A Minnan taxi driver in his thirties, for instance, prayed for peace and security for his family as well as for safe driving—though admittedly it was difficult to predict one's luck in an automobile. Nevertheless, he said that he "preferred to believe (*ningke xin* 寧可信)" because it was always better to have an extra layer of protection (interviewee 64). A company employee from Xiamen was not Buddhist but believed in fate. He said that he had been coming to the festival three times a year since it reopened to "make wishes and recompense for fulfilled wishes (*xuyuan huanyuan* 許願還願)." His prayers contained whatever he wanted to say to Guanyin at the moment (interviewee 75). This interviewee's comments were unusual because he did not worship to ask for things, unlike most other participants, but rather to communicate with Guanyin. While this made him feel better, he knew that fate decided his situation.

Some persons reflected views similar to CPC ideology in their talk about belief. A thirty-seven-year-old businessman from Xiamen said he pretty much believed in Buddha but was not a Buddhist because he was not vegetarian. He came to every festival to pray for wealth and security and sometimes felt the assistance of the deities. Although he knew that worship was merely psychological comfort, it was always better to believe than not (interviewee 24). This explanation was similar to the CPC view of religion as a crutch for the weak. We saw another reflection of CPC ideology in the response of a retired official from Xiamen who came to the festival once a year. He said that CPC members could not believe in religion, so he waited until retiring to attend the festival and was just accompanying his wife, who believed in Buddhism. He emphasized that he could not be considered a Buddhist because he only burned incense (interviewee 84).

Some participants said that they "only believed a little but not completely" (*you yidian xinfo, bu wanquan xin* 有一點信佛, 不完全信)." Such responses were only given by persons under fifty years old. They had been educated entirely in the PRC and exposed to ongoing antisuperstition and antireligion campaigns and propaganda. By saying that they only partially believe, they meant their belief was not blind but rather a matter of choice. For example, a tour guide from Minnan in her twenties working in Xiamen believed somewhat but not entirely in Buddha. When leading tour groups to temples, she always worshiped because "there was no harm in worshiping when going to a temple (*yiban jin miao dou hui qu baibai, meiyou huaichu* 一般進廟都會去拜拜, 沒有壞處)" (interviewee 53). Another example was a local man in his forties who declared that one should neither wholly believe in nor rely on Buddha. We consider that this man was not doubting Buddhism but instead saying that a person had to make efforts for prayers to be realized (interviewee 92). Another person, a shipping company employee in his forties from Xiamen, believed somewhat but not entirely in Buddha because he also believed in science. He had a Buddhist altar in his house and worshiped on the first and fifteenth of the month (interviewee 14). We think that he was expressing the need to avoid one-sided views. People should pray to Buddha but also have scientific thinking; to get better, a sick person can pray to Guanyin but should also take medicine.

Finally, some persons said that they only partially believed (*you yidian xin* 有一點信) to minimize their commitment to Buddhism. For example, a retired janitor from Xiamen in his sixties burned incense and prayed to Buddha at the festival but said he only partly believed because he worshiped for fun (*wan* 玩) (interviewee 1). This person's expression of commitment to Buddhism was among the weakest of those who said that they believed in and worshiped Buddha. But he still indicated some belief, unlike the respondents we consider next.

Neither Buddhist nor Believer, but Worshiped

Thirty-seven respondents said they were neither Buddhist nor believed in Buddha, but they nevertheless came to pray to Buddha (*qiu fo* 求佛) and Guanyin. A company employee from Xiamen in his late twenties was typical of this third category. He said that he could not be considered a Buddhist because he only "worshiped occasionally (*ou'er lai baiyibai* 偶爾來拜一拜)." But his wife believed and stood at length in front of the bodhisattva, asking for all sorts of protection. He just came to the festival to accompany his wife and prayed for security. He then disclosed that his parents, who had brought him to Nanputuo Temple since he was a child, worshiped a Buddha statue at home on the first and fifteenth of each month (interviewee 82). This person's response indicated that he did not believe in Buddhism, and his commitment to following Buddhist teachings was minimal. As we observed with many worshipers in this group, his denial of believing in Buddhism was indirect but unequivocally communicated by referencing other family members who did believe. Saying that his wife believed implied that he did not believe. At the same time, this response enabled him to avoid saying, "I do not believe in Buddha." This statement would have been extreme, tantamount to a declaration of being atheist, which he clearly was not because he was worshiping at the festival. So he qualified his worship by saying that he had not come for the express purpose of worship but rather from his love and duty to his wife, and that his worship was sporadic. This response indicated some clear commitment to Buddhism, as did the mention of accompanying his parents, who still worshiped at home, to visit Nanputuo as a child. He answered our question, "Are you a Buddhist?" by referring to the frequency of worship and contrasts with others, a response that did not demand any philosophical reflection or knowledge of Buddhist teachings.

Some respondents said they only worshiped when it did not require extra effort. A twenty-nine-year-old factory worker from Xiamen said she only "worshiped when she had some free time (*you kong lai baiyibai* 有空來拜一拜)," even though she came to the festival each time. She burned incense, prayed for her family's health, brought offerings of fruit, and donated 10 yuan. Her parents worshiped a Buddha statue at home on the first and fifteenth of the month. She characterized her worship as infrequent and irregular compared to her parents (interviewee 22). Another example was a retired factory worker from Xiamen who for several years had been coming "to Nanputuo to pray for luck and bring offerings only because it was conveniently located and required no extra effort (*dao nanputuo lai shaoxiang ye zhishi fangbian* 到南普陀來燒香也只是方便)." The fact that she came to worship showed some commitment on her part to Buddhism, tempered by concern about the commuting time (interviewee 98).

Other participants said they came to the Guanyin festival for a tourist-like experience, which had nothing to do with Buddhism. Four persons described having "fun" in its "hot and noisy" (*renao* 熱鬧) atmosphere. One was a laborer in his late teens from Putian. He had attended the festival several times and said that he was a "quasi-tourist" (*bange guanguang ke* 半個觀光客) who burned incense. Burning incense was fun and brought luck, so he prayed for health and security. He said, "Only good could come from this, and there is no harm (*zhi you haochu, buhui you shenma huaichu* 只有好處, 不會有什麼壞處)" (interviewee 102). The second was a retired worker in her fifties from Xiamen who lived near the temple. She came to see the excitement and burned incense, which required no additional effort. She said she was not a Buddhist and, therefore, no different from tourists who worshiped for peace of mind (interviewee 51). The third was a worker in his thirties from Minnan who had been coming annually to the festival since arriving in Xiamen six years ago. He liked to look around Nanputuo Temple because it was very lively. Usually he did not worship, but this time he brought his family to burn incense and pray for health. He did not consider himself a Buddhist (interviewee 48). The fourth was a male high school student from Xiamen who came with three classmates; it was their first time attending the festival without their parents. They came to have fun and pray to pass the college entrance exam (interviewee 94). While all of these persons worshiped, their reason for coming was to experience the heated festival atmosphere.

Some people mentioned education to explain why they were not Buddhists. They said they lacked sufficient knowledge of Buddhist teachings, as we heard in the response of a factory worker in his twenties from Minnan. This was his third time at the festival since coming to Xiamen three years ago. He said he was not a Buddhist because he had little understanding of Buddhism. He did not know how to worship the first time he came, so he imitated others. He burned incense; prayed for wealth, luck, and security; and gave 10 yuan (interviewee 81). Others said that they were not Buddhist because of their secular education. A retired official in his sixties from Xiamen was circumspect when expressing this view. Initially he told us that he had only come by himself for a walk, then allowed he had come with his family to worship, and finally admitted coming to every festival and even other times to pray. He said that his family members all believed in Buddhism and worshiped whenever there was a need, but he was well educated and so was not interested in believing (interviewee 6). This retired official typified the intellectuals who claimed not to believe but nevertheless practiced Buddhism by regularly worshiping at Nanputuo Temple.

Some respondents indicated political concerns. One such person was a man in his thirties from Xiamen, a local state official and CPC member. He was not a Buddhist, but his mother and grandmother were Buddhists who practiced vegetarianism. For the past six years, he had prayed at every festival for a successful career, security, and health but considered it too bothersome to bring offerings. He avoided saying that he believed in Buddhism because this violated rules for CPC members. He was one of the few interviewees who mentioned the anti–Falun Gong crackdown then underway and asked if our questions were related to it. Yet, despite his awareness of the campaign, he felt free to answer our questions (interviewee 43). Another person expressing political issues was a sixty-year-old retired factory worker. Before the Cultural Revolution, his family worshiped at the festival, and he now came three times a year. Neither he nor his family members were Buddhist, but he wished to worship Buddha and pray for peace and security. He said people should worship if they wanted to but not be forced to (interviewee 3). We consider his response to reflect the view of the state constitution and religious policy that religious belief is a voluntary decision by an individual. We further examine the relationship of such political concerns to the issue of belief in this chapter's conclusion.

In sum, the thirty-seven persons in the third category minimized their commitment to Buddhism because of humility, religious skepticism, or political ideology. But even as they professed not to believe in Buddhism or even mention belief, they worshiped at the Guanyin festival. Therefore we see the persons in this category as sharing a similarity to the fifty-five respondents in the second category who believed in and worshiped Buddha: persons in both categories denied being Buddhists, but they came to the Guanyin festival at Nanputuo Temple and worshiped.

Neither Buddhist nor Believer, and Did Not Worship

Six persons in our sample responded negatively to our question, "Are you a Buddhist?" These were men who said that they were neither Buddhists nor believed in Buddhism, or that they were atheists. Two were older officials with the typical attitude of CPC members at that time of being somewhat sympathetic to Buddhism but drawing a line between themselves and religion. One was a man in his seventies who had moved to

Xiamen after retirement to be near his children. He lived near Nanputuo Temple, coming daily with his wife to stroll around the Lotus Pond. He had joined the CPC in 1953 and did not believe in Buddhism. He said that no one believed in religion when Mao Zedong was alive, but that religion and worship had revived with the reform and opening-up policies because people now needed it in their lives. He was critical of monks living comfortably from donations but acknowledged that the bodhisattva had done many good things for the people. His wife used to believe in Buddhism, but he influenced her to stop (interviewee 13). Another official was a man in his fifties from Fuzhou. He came to Xiamen on a tour organized by his workplace. He did not know there was a festival at the temple and was taken aback by the crowds and activity. He was an atheist and did not worship. No one in his family believed in deities because his parents were from North China, where people were less superstitious, and his wife was from an intellectual family. But he said that people could believe whatever they wanted, that everyone believed in something, and that Buddhism had existed for many years (interviewee 56).

Three persons expressed indifference toward religion. A sailor in his forties from Jiangsu Province was not a Buddhist, did not believe in the Buddha, and did not worship. Instead, he came to Nanputuo Temple to get fresh air when his ship was in the harbor. He observed that belief differed by region. No one in his hometown believed, and people rarely went to temples. Each person decided on their own whether or not to believe (interviewee 25). A twenty-four-year-old worker from Xiamen was waiting in the temple yard. He said emphatically that he only came to accompany his girlfriend, who was worshiping. He did not worship the Buddha or burn incense even though his parents believed in the Buddha and took him to worship as a child. Worshiping the Buddha was for older people, whereas young people came to the festival for excitement (interviewee 34). A man in his early twenties from Minnan working in Xiamen as a sales agent was standing outside the temple. He was accompanying his girlfriend, who was inside worshiping. His family often worshiped at temples in his hometown, but he never did, as he did not believe in Buddha. He stressed that he had attended college (interviewee 26).

One participant was hostile toward Buddhism, calling it "feudal superstition (*fengjian mixin* 封建迷信)." He was a twenty-two-year-old technical school student from Jiangxi Province visiting his sister who worked in Xiamen. The festival was the occasion for his first visit to Nanputuo Temple, but he only came to look at the lively scene and had no intention of burning incense. He considered the festival to be useless feudal superstition. It only showed that people in Xiamen were rich enough to squander money on offerings and alms, he said. Such things did not occur in his hometown. Neither he nor his family believed in Buddha. He stressed that his sister and her husband were college graduates (interviewee 57). His final words indicated a common view that those with less education were more likely to believe in religion and be superstitious.

Notably, only one person in this category was from Xiamen, and half were from outside Fujian. The distribution is the obverse of the five persons in the first category who said they were Buddhists; all were from Xiamen except for one. We see this reflecting a greater attachment to Nanputuo Temple and Buddhist practice by locals rather than nonlocals. Furthermore, there was a similar ratio of locals to nonlocals between the second and third categories. The proportion of Xiamen locals in the second, those who believed and worshiped, was much larger than in the third, consisting of persons who worshiped but did not believe. This finding underscores our argument that Nanputuo Temple is a locally embedded national temple, and the Guanyin festival is vital for renewing ties between the temple and local people.

Reasons Festivalgoers Attend

Why did people come to the festival, and what did they do there? Our interviewees mentioned practical benefits, custom and tradition, social activity, and charms of the temple. Together, these constitute the Chinese way of being Buddhist for the mass laity.

Worship for This-Worldly Benefits

Practically everyone in our sample prayed for something, except for eight persons, including the six who did not believe in or worship Buddha. Notably, no one mentioned praying for ancestors or anything remotely connected to an afterlife and escaping from suffering. Instead, as the many heads and hands of Guanyin evoke the bodhisattva's purposeful devotion to saving people, worshipers saw the temple as full of Buddhist merit (*fo qi* 佛氣) and magical power to help them. They prayed (*qiqiu* 祈求, *qi* 祈, *qiu* 求) to Guanyin or the Buddha to protect living family members, solve their problems, gain material benefits, ensure their success, otherwise improve their lives, and augment this-worldly merit. Most prayed for multiple things.

The largest number of persons included prayers for security in their worship. Such requests applied to general well-being and health concerns, as the prayers of the following four participants reveal. A chauffeur prayed and hung a picture of the Buddha in his car to ensure safety for himself and his passengers (interviewee 64). A female company employee in her thirties prayed to Guanyin for family security, good fortune, and for all her wishes to come true (interviewee 2). A retired cadre in his sixties prayed for security and happiness in daily life (interviewee 83). A couple in their early thirties brought their sick child. The wife said she intensely believed in the Buddha and asked her husband, who did not believe and had never been to Nanputuo Temple, to worship with her to cast out the evil (*qu xie* 驅邪) from their child (interviewee 34).

Many prayed for wealth, with those in business praying for good fortune when things were not going well. A twenty-seven-year-old company employee from Jiangxi Province prayed for money to buy an apartment so his girlfriend could move to Xiamen (interviewee 86). An employee in her thirties prayed for the fortune of her company, damaged by the 1997 Asian financial crisis (interviewee 65). A taxi driver in his thirties who had wrecked his car prayed to save enough money to buy a new one (interviewee 69). A man in his thirties came with his wife. Ten years ago, they resigned their jobs in a city-run government department store to operate a privately owned clothing shop. The economy was bad, so he was worshiping to gauge his luck and look for an auspicious sign (interviewee 87).

Others prayed for success in their jobs, education, and relationships. A laborer in Xiamen from Minnan prayed for work to go smoothly and to earn much money (interviewee 11). A couple working in the financial sector felt pressured by the Asian financial crises. They prayed that the economic situation would improve so they could feel more secure (interviewee 88). A man in his forties had started worshiping at Nanputuo Temple two years earlier when his collective factory became a joint venture. He prayed that he would not be laid off (interviewee 79). A high school student prayed to pass the college entrance exam (interviewee 94). A young man in his twenties prayed to meet a beautiful girlfriend and achieve wealth (interviewee 67). A newlywed woman in her twenties gave thanks (*huanyuan* 還願) and prayed for wealth, security, and career success (interviewee 45). A young woman came with her boyfriend to pray for the stability of their relationship and that her work and life would flourish (interviewee 73). A high school student said her parents prayed for her to do well in school while she prayed for family security (interviewee 33).

Others prayed for a general improvement in their situations. A woman in her twenties prayed for Buddha's blessings in work and daily life (interviewee 12). A female laborer in her twenties from Minnan working in Xiamen "prayed for some improvement in her fate, as well as for more friends and wealth (*qiqiu mingyun hao yixie, duo yixie pengyou he caiqi* 祈求命運好一些, 多一些朋友和財氣)" (interviewee 47).

Custom and Tradition

Of the 103 respondents in our survey, 19 percent said that they came to Nanputuo Temple to worship at the Guanyin festival because it was a local tradition (*chuantong* 傳統) or custom (*xiguan* 習慣). A sixty-six-year-old retired elementary school teacher said he was not a Buddhist and only came to the festival because it was a Xiamen tradition that embodied a fine aspiration. He had come to every festival for more than a decade to pray for security (interviewee 18). A Zhangzhou woman working in Xiamen for two years said the festival was a Minnan custom. She emphasized that she was not a Buddhist because worship was only a custom, but her entire family believed in the Buddha, and she came twice a year to the festival (interviewee 95).

Some Xiamen residents linked the local custom of the festival to their family tradition of worshiping at Nanputuo Temple. A man in his forties from Xiamen said his parents had often brought him to the festival as a child. He felt that worshiping at the festival was customary for Xiamen residents and part of his routine. He prayed for Buddha's protection and security for his family (interviewee 92). A retired factory worker in his sixties said it was a Xiamen tradition to worship at Nanputuo Temple on the festival day. Before the Cultural Revolution, his family often attended, and he began coming again after the festival was revived (interviewee 3). An unemployed woman in her fifties from Xiamen had come to the festival three times a year since it restarted in 1982. She said that she was not a devout believer because she was not a vegetarian. But her family's belief in Buddha was passed down through generations of ancestors. She worshiped and prayed at each bodhisattva in the temple to protect her and her family (interviewee 28).

Others said they worshiped at Nanputuo Temple because of family traditions of belief and worship of Buddha. For example, a laborer from Minnan in his early twenties who was working in Xiamen happened to hear of the festival and came with three friends to have fun. As his parents believed in Buddha, he somewhat believed because the older generations always influenced the younger ones (interviewee 39). Many other interviewees mentioned family traditions of Buddhism by noting a mother, grandmother, or both parents who were pious Buddhists with a home altar, who ate vegetarian on the first and fifteenth of every month, visited many temples, and so forth.

Many nonlocals came to observe what they considered to be a local custom. A woman in her twenties from Minnan had attended almost every festival since she began working in Xiamen. Although she was not Buddhist, she came to worship because it was an ancient custom in Xiamen and also brought good fortune (interviewee 45). Other people used the phrase "when entering a country, follow the customs" (*ru xiang sui su* 入鄉隨俗), equivalent to the English axiom "When in Rome, do as the Romans." A man in his late twenties from Jiangxi Province was stationed in Xiamen as a soldier and then became a local taxi driver. He said Buddhism in his hometown was not as flourishing as Xiamen's. When he first came to Xiamen, he visited some temples but did not believe. After he started working as a taxi driver, he attached more importance to worshiping at a temple and came whenever he could. He saw this as a gradual process of "entering a country and following its customs" (interviewee 20). A twenty-eight-year-old man from Jiangxi Province working in Xiamen did not believe in the Buddha before coming to the city. But his Xiamen wife very much believed and came to the festival three times a year. At first, he just accompanied her, but now he attended to worship by himself, saying, "When entering a country, follow its customs" (interviewee 42).

Social Activity

Participation in the Guanyin festival was a social activity, as seen in the fact that 85 percent (n=90) of our interviewees came with others. Of these persons, 61 percent (n=55) came with friends and acquaintances, typically, high school classmates, teams of laborers, tour groups, colleagues on after-work company outings, military comrades-in-arms, and neighbor women. The remaining 39 percent (n=35) came with family or kin, typically, mothers with children, multigenerational families, and nonlocals working in Xiamen bringing visiting kin and friends. The social character was reflected in people's answers about why they came and what they did at the festival. They said that, in addition to worshiping, they would "play," "chat," or "look around" with those in their group.

Many came to the festival to enjoy time spent with their group. A bank employee from Xiamen in his fifties said he came to have fun with his wife, daughter-in-law, and grandson. When we interviewed him, he was relaxing on a ground cloth near the Releasing Life Pond, watching his grandson feed the fish while the women worshiped in the temple (interviewee 68). A twenty-seven-year-old man from Jiangxi Province working in a local company came with four colleagues. They would have a good time because it was the weekend and the festival was lively, while coming also brought luck (interviewee 86). An eighteen-year-old woman from Minnan living in Xiamen came with five classmates visiting from her hometown. She had been to Nanputuo Temple several times before, but this was her first visit with friends. They had a good time and burned incense (interviewee 37). A construction worker in his mid-twenties from Hubei Province came with his friends because they had mistakenly heard there was an opera performance (interviewee 17).

The festival was an opportunity to see friends and relatives. A laborer in his late teens from Minnan came with three cousins. It was his fourth visit to Nanputuo Temple but the first for his relatives. He brought them to give them a good time. He said it would be a waste for them to travel to Xiamen without seeing the temple at its liveliest. They intended to worship (interviewee 102). A woman in her twenties was sitting by the Lotus Pond with another woman and two men. They were coworkers who came to each festival to spend time together and sometimes worshiped (interviewee 10). We saw many young men and women who looked like students, laughing and talking excitedly as if on group dates.

Many parents brought their children. A man in his thirties from the Minnan region brought his two-year-old son to the festival to "dip him in the Buddha atmosphere (*zhanyizhan foqi* 沾一沾佛氣)" so that he would grow up healthy (interviewee 29). Coming as a family was a Xiamen tradition, as noted above. One person commented that the older people mobilized younger family members to worship at temples. By coming with parents, children learned how to worship (interviewee 41). During the 1999 festival, we observed parents showing their children how to hold the incense and bow before the statues to pray. One man who came with his wife told us sadly that his son had refused to come, but he was sure his son would better understand when he got older (interviewee 14).

Many nonlocals were also brought to the festival for the first time by others. Company employees from outside Xiamen were bused to the festival after work by their companies. Laborers newly arrived in Xiamen were taken by colleagues who knew about the festival and taught them how to worship. An example was a nonlocal man who was taken to the festival by a friend from Xiamen. He was not Buddhist and unsure what to do, but fortunately, his friend shared his incense and offerings. He gave alms after asking his friend the suitable amount (interviewee 9).

Another social aspect was including others in prayers. Inclusion occurred when people prayed for the health and security of the family, and the older generations prayed for the well-being and success of the younger ones. A laborer in his forties from Jiangxi Province working in Xiamen prayed for his son to get into college and for better days (interviewee 58). A forty-year-old tourist from Hangzhou prayed that her son could find a good job after graduation (interviewee 55). A sixty-four-year-old woman prayed that her son's work would go smoothly (interviewee 70). Some came to worship on behalf of those who could not attend. A woman in her fifties from Minnan had been asked by her aunt to come and worship in her stead (interviewee 96). A woman in her forties from Xiamen who regularly came to the festival was asked by a sick aunt to pray for her health (interviewee 72). Additionally, worshipers extended their merit of attending the festival to family members who did not attend by sharing food offerings. A newlywed woman brought cakes and fruit to the festival to be blessed at the Thousand-Handed and

Thousand-Eyed Guanyin statue in the Great Compassion Hall. She planned to take the offerings home to her family members to extend Buddha's merit to them when they ate the food (interviewee 45).

Charms of the Temple

Most participants mentioned the charms of Nanputuo Temple. A quarter of the sample (27 percent, n=28) were impressed by its size, using the words "big" and "most" when talking about it, as in most famous, largest size, and liveliest atmosphere. An oft-mentioned charm was the beauty of the temple. No other temple in the region had a Lotus Pond and two tall white pagodas. Its multihued roof eaves and red and gold characters engraved and painted on walls, pillars, and panels made it the most colorful temple in Xiamen. Some attributed the beauty to the temple's management, maintenance, or restoration. An official in the Xiamen municipal government said that the temple's environment had improved to the extent that a person could simultaneously get covered in merit and have fun (interviewee 43). A man in his twenties said the temple was beautiful enough to be a park, so he rarely went to other temples (interviewee 82). A man in his fifties who came with his grandchild said that the pleasant environment made children happy, and the elderly could stroll around (interviewee 84). A twenty-nine-year-old woman from Xiamen came with her husband and daughter because Nanputuo Temple was famous and her family could play (interviewee 22). A construction worker in his thirties said the environment made him happy, and often came to stroll around (interviewee 93). A retired local man in his sixties sitting by the Lotus Pond with three men had come the previous night to worship. Now he and his friends were back in the morning to enjoy the cool shade. They lived nearby and often came to relax (interviewee 100).

Others mentioned the temple's potent magical efficacy in assisting people. A twenty-eight-year-old man made it a point to worship at Nanputuo Temple because its great power let him avert misfortune (interviewee 63). A shop owner in his forties from Xiamen said that the temple's reputation for divine assistance was so tremendous that he rarely went to other temples (interviewee 8). A construction worker in his thirties from Minnan came because the temple had an excellent reputation and magical efficacy that relaxed him as he ambled around the grounds (interviewee

93). A couple in their sixties from Xiamen said that the temple was famous, was magically efficacious, and easily accessed by public transportation, so they did not go elsewhere for large festivals (interviewee 52). A worker in his twenties from Zhangzhou had attended every festival since coming to Xiamen two years earlier because it had the largest altar. Smaller temples were useless, he said (interviewee 19).

Many Xiamen residents said that they visited other local temples as well. For them, the charms of Nanputuo Temple did not extend to the clerics as they did not know any of the temple's monks and were hardpressed to name the abbot. Local women found it easier to cultivate relationships with Minnan-speaking lay nuns. They frequented lay nun halls and only came to the temple at the Guanyin festival. Other residents said local temples were more intimate and closer to their homes. A woman in her forties from Xiamen said that even though Nanputuo Temple had a lively and pleasant environment, she visited Puguang Temple, Hongshan Temple, and other temples for rituals (interviewee 80). A sixty-three-year-old man regularly worshiped at Riguangyan Temple 日光岩寺 near his home, coming to Nanputuo Temple only on special occasions because it was famous and most magically efficacious (interviewee 52).

Nonlocals worshiped at Nanputuo Temple in place of going to temples in their hometowns. For example, a company employee in her twenties from Sichuan Province had previously worshiped at a hometown temple during the Guanyin festival. Since moving to Xiamen three years earlier, she often came to Nanputuo Temple to pray for security and health but did not visit local temples in Xiamen (interviewee 40). A young factory worker from Minnan worshiped at Nanputuo Temple because it was the most famous temple. She did not go to other local temples, she said, but in her hometown she worshiped at the Mazu Temple (interviewee 12). These two persons were typical of nonlocal persons because, unlike locals, they did not visit other temples in Xiamen. Additionally, they worshiped at Daoist and deity temples, such as Mazu, Zushigong, and Baosheng Dadi, located in their hometowns.

A few people, however, commented negatively. Two men waiting in the front yard for family members said Nanputuo Temple was too crowded and noisy. One young woman from Xiamen complained that the crowds made it difficult to carry offerings, so she only brought incense (interviewee 33). Another young woman could not stand the smoke and crowds, so she left the temple to wait in the yard for her boyfriend, who was worshiping (interview 73). Also, many people commented on the need to buy tickets to enter the temple for the festival. We understood this as simultaneously expressing criticism of the monks for charging a fee to attend the festival and respecting their ability to earn money to maintain the temple.

In sum, most participants at the Guanyin festival came to worship even though they did not self-identify as Buddhists. They gave many reasons for attending, including praying for various things, having a good time with friends and family, and enjoying the charms of the temple. If the festival were held once a year, such as at Christmas, it would come and go with much less impact on people's minds. But its occurrence three times a year meant that as soon as one festival ended, people anticipated the next. For many, the festival was the only time they came to Nanputuo Temple. The large number of participants who attended multiple times a year showed the significance of the temple and its festival in people's lives.

The Practice of Folk Religion at Nanputuo Temple

Many beliefs and practices of those attending the Guanyin festival were neither part of orthodox Buddhism nor fit the CPC view of modern religion. Of course, monks and local state officials were aware of this discrepancy. Yet the temple door was open to all without clarifying who among the attendees were Buddhist. Buddhism makes no demands on those visiting a temple to be devotees, as all are considered purified by Buddha's teachings upon entering a temple. Participants could thus feel some purpose in coming to the festival, even those who neither believed in Buddhism nor came to worship.

The temple became an especially sacred space for people during the Guanyin festival. Their styles and awareness of worship included folk beliefs such as the magical efficacy of deities to render assistance and the prayer that resulted in this-worldly benefit. People's beliefs were expressed in actions like entering the temple at midnight (when the magical efficacy of the temple was thought to be greatest) and worshiping at the Buddha Rock. We now examine the Guanyin festival to understand how the temple reproduced semiotic space as a living religion in contemporary society.

Popular Belief

We have juxtaposed our survey findings from the 1999 festival with survey findings from another occurrence of the festival we observed on July 20 and 21, 1989; from that comparison we were able to analyze how the belief of the masses at the Guanyin festival reproduced over time.[5] The values and practices that people communicated to us in interviews at both festivals were the same, with responses to our question, "Are you a Buddhist?," showing similar distributions (see table 9.5). People at both festivals prayed for the same benefits of health, family security, wealth, and success in schools and careers. These similarities over a decade suggest the stability of folk belief.

But the comparison of data reveals notable differences in people's behavior and ways of speaking at the two Guanyin festivals. These differences indicate changes in the relationship between people, state, and temple over the decade. One change was people's confidence in attending the festival. Both festivals we observed occurred during national political crises. In 1989, the festival was held a month after the Tiananmen Square protests. The 40,000 attendees numbered about half of those who typically came in the preceding few years.[6] This steep decline reflected people's fears that the political tension could again lead to state suppression of religion. In 1999, the festival was held a week after the start of the massive campaign to suppress Falun Gong. Nevertheless, 100,000 people attended; the number was similar to festivals in the few years prior, according to a BAX officer.[7] People were keenly aware of the campaign;

TABLE 9.5 Responses to Question "Are You a Buddhist?" at 1989 and 1999 Guanyin Festivals

Response	1989	1999
Buddhist	3 (8%)	5 (5%)
Not Buddhist, but believed and worshiped	20 (50%)	55 (54%)
Neither Buddhist nor believer but worshiped	13 (33%)	37 (36%)
Neither Buddhist nor believer, and did not worship	3 (8%)	6 (6%)
Unclear	1 (3%)	
Total	40	103

Percentage amounts have been rounded; the total thus exceeds 100.
Source: Survey data, Yoshiko Ashiwa and David Wank, July 20–21, 1989, and July 30–31, 1999

some even asked if our interview questions were related.[8] But almost everyone we approached spoke comfortably with us, an indication that they did not link their participation in the festival with the campaign. The state media was not attacking Falun Gong as superstition but rather as illegal, and at the same time emphasizing Buddhism as a religion and worship as legal. As a result, people did not have to worry about whether their beliefs and practices could be deemed superstitious. They felt confident and secure while worshiping in a Buddhist temple.

We noticed a second change in the level of articulation when people discussed beliefs. In 1989, they described their beliefs, as well as their actions at the festival, more briefly than in 1999. Notably, the 1989 participants did not acknowledge degrees of commitment to Buddhism, such as vegetarianism, as a criterion for distinguishing between Buddhists and Buddhist believers. In contrast, the 1999 participants clearly expressed specific degrees of commitment, and they did so in greater detail. For example, many people used such criteria as keeping vegetarian and the frequency of worship to distinguish between those who both believed in Buddhism and worshiped at the temple from those who only came to worship. Their use of such criteria reflected the existence of acceptable discourses by 1999 for people to talk about their beliefs, even with strangers in public places.

A third change was the confidence of people to talk with us about religion and their beliefs. In 1989, about half the people we approached declined to be interviewed, while those who agreed appeared nervous and anxious to end the interviews. Their unease was probably because the suppression of religion during the Cultural Revolution was relatively recent. They still regarded religion as linked to politics, a view reinforced by the political tension of the Tiananmen Square protest a month earlier. In contrast, attendees in 1999 were much more willing to talk to us about their beliefs and worship activities at the festival. This willingness was partly because of the greater historical distance from the Cultural Revolution and the political climate of religious tolerance cultivated over two decades. However, it was also due to the efforts of the state media to clearly distinguish belief and worship in Buddhism from the state crackdown on Falun Gong.

A fourth change consisted of the kinds of connections that people drew between religion and other phenomena. In 1989, some participants equated belief with politics. For example, a man in his forties from Xiamen who had believed in Buddhism since childhood, even worshiping secretly during the Cultural Revolution, told us that Buddhism was the same as communism because both were faiths that asked people to behave ethically (*zuoren* 做人) to make a better future. And when we asked a student at Xiamen University if she was a Buddhist, she said she believed in everything, including Marxism and Leninism. Her response may have indicated anger at the CPC for killing students during the Tiananmen Square protest. Such comments indicated a residual uncertainty about attending the festival after the Tiananmen Square protest, a time when religion and politics were still linked in people's minds. But in 1999, no one said communism and religion were interchangeable beliefs. Instead, people drew parallels regarding how their Buddhist beliefs reflected and addressed their own needs, and no one made any link to politics. This was especially visible among young people in their twenties and thirties. They talked about worship as a form of mental support (*jingshen anwei* 精神安慰) and a new experience (*xin jingyan* 新經驗). Some even said they were seeking to understand the world through Buddhism. One Xiamen University student, for example, said that she worshiped to deepen her understanding and experience of the Buddha. In 1999, participants no longer connected religion to politics but rather to their own needs. Interestingly, this link of worship and participation in the Guanyin Festival to oneself was congruent with the state discourse of religion as "individual belief."

Collaboration of Monks and Officials

The opening of Nanputuo Temple to crowds of people during the Guanyin festival would have been impossible without the collaboration of the monks and local state officials. They were all aware that the beliefs and practices of the people conformed to neither "orthodox" Buddhism nor the CPC's image of religion. But monks and officials also knew they could not prevent the people's passion, which was so strong that many believers had braved persecution during the Cultural Revolution to secretly worship at midnight behind the temple.

The older monks understood the festival's significance for the people, even though younger students at the BCM from North China were shocked by such passion and beliefs, which they did not consider part of Buddhism. For example, one young monk told us that he had never seen anything like the festival in his hometown and found it altogether rather frightening. He said the people burning spirit money did not know how to worship the Buddha. A genuine believer in Buddhism would know that making three bows to the Buddha was better than burning a thousand pieces of paper spirit money for dead souls. Although the festival was a Minnan custom, he was sure the Buddha would be surprised to see it. Despite such concerns, he and his fellow monks worked hard to help the people worship by gathering their incense sticks and passing their offerings over the Guanyin altar. The monks realized that the festival was a time when people renewed their commitment to the temple. It was the basis of the temple's popularity. The monks understood that they could not stop the people's passion and that the passion helped make Nanputuo Temple extraordinary.

The monks nevertheless made efforts to preserve the space of Buddhism in the temple as they practiced it, such as preventing people from entering the Great Buddha Hall, where monks held services to celebrate the festival. Further efforts were visible in changes between the 1989 and 1999 festivals to separate the semiotic space of the Buddhism practiced by the monks from practices related to Buddhism by the people. In 1989, people could bring spirit money inside the temple to give to monks to burn and freely wander in its side compounds. But in 1999, they were prohibited from doing so. Instead, they had to burn the money at a furnace outside the west wall of the temple compound and could no longer enter the monastery section of the west compound where monks lived and studied.

Officials in the Xiamen Municipal People's Government worked to enable the Guanyin festival. As long as the festival occurred inside the temple, it could be considered "religion" regardless of what people actually believed. The local state supported the festival by running more public buses to bring people to and from Nanputuo Temple and providing police to direct traffic; they even sent a fire truck in case spirit money or incense burning got out of hand. The support of local officials also reflected, no doubt, their awareness that the Guanyin festival enhanced the tourist appeal of Nanputuo Temple.

Yet at the same time, the local state administration increasingly sought to temper the festival's exuberant sociability. This concern was seen in changes in administrative actions. In 1989, the festival had a tumultuous "hot and noisy" atmosphere evocative of a rural temple fair (Chau 2008, 147–168; Cooper 2013). Dozens of stalls and hawkers selling incense, spirit money for dead souls, fruit and cake for offerings, as well as snacks of soda, candy, and ice cream lined the paths from the mountain gates to the Heavenly Kings Hall. Groups of uniformed policemen sat around on piles of construction materials chatting with worshipers, several fights broke out between young men, and people wandered freely in the temple. In 1999, the fair was more orderly with a subdued atmosphere even though there were twice as many worshipers. Peddling was not permitted, plainclothes police mingled with the crowds to keep order, and the west compound with the BCM and clerics' dormitories was closed to the public. Another difference was the temple's openness to popular folk belief practices. As we noted above, people at the 1989 festival could bring spirit money to burn inside the temple, but in 1999 the practice was banned. Although such prohibitions were made in the name of public safety rather than suppressing superstition, they caused some confrontations and affected the semiotic experience for worshipers. For example, one man who used to burn spirit money at the temple remarked to us in 1999 that this practice was now banned. He said that burning incense on its own was not that meaningful, but he was getting used to it.

The festival was the largest occasion to reproduce the semiotic space of Nanputuo Temple as a center for Guanyin worship, through which people could seek help in their lives. At this time, popular imagination of the semiotic space was most potent and actively revitalized. Attendees experienced a tumultuous, other-worldly atmosphere of smoke, fire, incense, sweat, packed bodies, and a shared recognition of others as gathering to communicate their deepest desires and problems to Guanyin. These practices were not part of any Buddhist teachings, but they gave Nanputuo Temple its distinct character as a Buddhist temple, and the emotion and other-worldly atmosphere contributed to its popularity. For the people it was a time when new possibilities were palpable, which created fears of social order for the state. While the monks and officials worked hard to delimit and control folk belief inside the temple, the people's enormous passion and energy made it clear that the temple belonged to the crowds during the Guanyin festival.

Conclusion

As a fervent expression of folk beliefs inside a major Buddhist temple, the Guanyin festival is part of the century-long process of positioning folk beliefs linked to Buddhism within the administrative system of modern Chinese states. After 1979, the CPC realized the futility of trying to eliminate widespread beliefs among the people, even if they did not accord with its image of religion. In the case of the Guanyin festival, the expressions of folk beliefs became "Buddhist" because they took place inside a Buddhist temple. The festival's occurrence three times a year created the most significant and essential character of Nanputuo Temple, a Buddhist temple dedicated to Guanyin. During this time, the semiotic, physical, and institutional spaces worked together to activate the temple for the largest number of people. It was a time for all to renew their connections with Guanyin and Nanputuo Temple and for the temple to renew its distinct character as a popular place for worship of Guanyin.

The mountain gate of Bailudong Temple. The temple is built into a cave on a hillside in the middle of the city. Its prior in the 1990s emphasized Minnan local culture and used the local dialect as the temple's daily language. (photo 2017)

Huxiyan Temple has a high status in the Chan Buddhist tradition because of its preserved dharma lineage transmission. Yinyuan, the founder of Japan's Ōbaku sect in the seventeenth century, stayed here for a while before departing to Nagasaki (Japan). This photo (2017) shows the restored oldest part of the temple, which houses a Thousand-Handed and Thousand-Eyed Guanyin statue.

Hongshan Temple sits atop a hill in downtown Xiamen surrounded by a public park. The temple has become a center for intellectuals, artists, and youth because of its location next to the park and the surrounding new residential development, as seen in the newly built tall buildings behind the recently constructed Heavenly Kings Hall. (photo 2017)

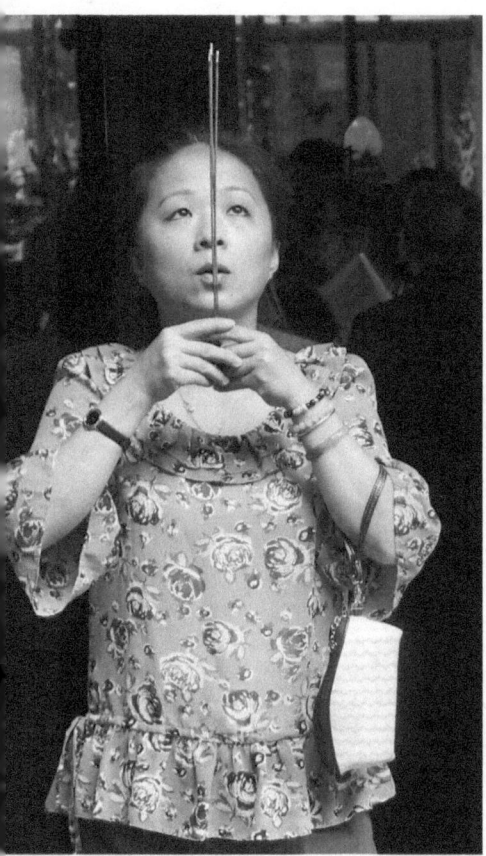 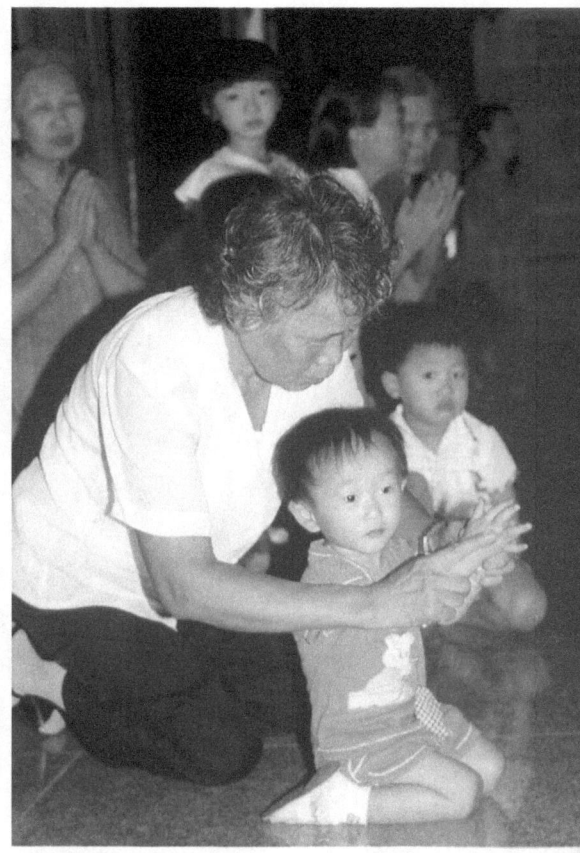

(*left*) A woman worshiping Guanyin. Nanputuo Temple attracts many people like her, including local entrepreneurs. (photo 1999)

(*right*) A timeless scene of a grandmother teaching her grandchild how to worship. (photo 1999)

Local believers at a thousand-buddhas assembly circumambulate inside Nanputuo Temple in winter 1990. At that time, these monthly services were held in the main square between the Heavenly Kings Hall and the Great Buddha Hall. They were later stopped because of the increasing number of tourists.

Devotees and believers worshiping in the Great Buddha Hall of Nanputuo Temple in 1989. The service was led by monks in the front row. The participants were mostly middle-aged and elderly women from Xiamen. At that time, the temple held these services on the first and fifteenth of the month.

People who take the devotee precepts wear black robes at services and chant in front of other lay believers directly behind the monks. The devotees in this photograph held the *Buddhist Cultivation Handbook* compiled by the Xiamen devotee Liu Zhengsong, which was used for self-cultivation (see page 271). The scene is in the Great Buddha Hall, Nanputuo Temple, 1989.

Worshipers could burn spirit money by the Buddha Rock behind Nanputuo Temple at the foot of Wulao Peak until the late 1990s. After that, it was only allowed at a new furnace outside the west compound, near the columbarium. (photo 1999)

Midnight scene in front of the Great Buddha Hall, Nanputuo Temple, during the Guanyin birthday festival on July 30–31, 1999. People, mostly younger, jostled to offer incense just after midnight when Guanyin's birthday began. To prevent people from accidentally burning others or starting fires, they were only allowed one incense stick, so they brought a thick one. Still, some brought many sticks.

Monks and workers immediately removed the incense sticks people placed in the urns and doused them in water buckets. The temple became full of smoke, and it was chaotic. Nowadays, people are given a single stick of incense to burn outside the temple's main square in front of the Heavenly Kings Hall and can only bring flowers inside as offerings to Guanyin.

Xuefeng Temple 雪峰寺, lay nun hall in downtown Xiamen, under construction in 2017. To the right is the main hall and on the left is a wing for the dormitory and classrooms. Building the hall was a long-term effort facilitated by two lay nuns. The local government gave special permission for its construction on land not previously designated for religion.

A service at a lay nun hall. The three women in front are lay nuns. Behind them are devotees, followed by believers wearing regular lay clothing. The participants are all women, and they performed the chanting without clerics. (photo 1999)

Yangzhen Temple, dedicated to Baosheng Dadi, is the headquarters of the Xiamen Devotee Lodge. It lies just off the main street of the old commercial center in an alley surrounded by shops, apartments, and houses. Behind it is Nengren Temple, built in the late 1990s to turn the folk belief temple into a Buddhist site. (photo 2000)

Gazing southward from the front of Nanputuo Temple in 2017. Local people believed that the newly constructed twin towers between the temple and the sea disturbed the feng shui of the temple. Some people said this was why the windows at the top of the towers kept breaking.

The celebration of the ninetieth anniversary of the Buddhist College of Minnan in 2015 brought together over a thousand alumni, students, and teachers from around China and overseas at a large conference hall in Xiamen. The clerics chanted in front of a digital image of the altar from the Great Buddha Hall of Nanputuo Temple.

A copy of the spiritual message that Miaozhan wrote on his deathbed in 1995, which says: "Do not forget the many suffering people in the world." It was displayed at the ninetieth anniversary of the Buddhist College of Minnan as Miaozhan's message to all attendees.

Conclusion

IN *THE SPACE OF RELIGION* we have explained the transformations and changes that have occurred during China's past century—in Buddhism as a religion, in the state's perceptions of religion, in the positioning of Buddhism in the state system, and in the lives of the people—as observed through Nanputuo Temple. We describe how this one temple, a popular site of Guanyin worship in Xiamen, and a center of modern Buddhism in China, operated to the extent that was possible throughout modern China, especially within the recent delimitations of state policies. The temple sought more autonomy as a religious place, operating in various stances of cooperation, conflict, and competition, while it adjusted to changes in state policy. And the modern state, during its process of formation, searched for an acceptable and favorable position for Buddhism. There is considerable flexibility in the delimitations of state policies depending on the power relations among actors and the needs of implementing and improvising policy interpretations by multiple layers of state agencies. Through these manifold and interconnected processes, we observed how the temple, the state, and Buddhism have been mutually making the space of "religion," frequently adjusting their shapes by various means.

By taking an overview of the past century, we see the transformation of Buddhism itself, and the state's attitudes toward religion in policies

CONCLUSION

and administrative systems, occurring in two periods during which significant concepts, practices, organizations, and power alignments were formed. From 1912 to 1949 in the Republic of China, the state distinguished religion from superstition to establish the legitimacy of the new state as "modern." At the same time, reformist Buddhist devotees and clergies endeavored to make Buddhism more relevant as a modern religion for its followers, emphasizing scriptural study and focusing on living people and their needs, not on dead ancestors. They founded seminaries to educate clerics, supported young devotees and women, and created associations and overseas networks to survive the political turmoil and waves of modernization. In this manner, Buddhism sustained itself through changing political regimes to avoid catastrophe after the founding of the PRC in 1949, although the emigration of clerics and state restrictions severely diminished Buddhist activity. These efforts were crushed by the Cultural Revolution, which destroyed temples, small and large, and chased clerics all over the country.

From 1979, after the Cultural Revolution, the CPC was less concerned with the "modernity" of religion than its obedience to the state. This concern was expressed in Document 19 through the discourse of "love country, love religion" that placed loyalty to China, socialism, and the CPC over religion. Initially, the CPC expected Buddhism to encourage economic investment by promoting tourism, encouraging overseas Chinese investment, and burnishing the global credibility of the PRC as a modern state that acknowledged and protected religion. Gradually, the CPC recognized additional uses for Buddhism and tightened institutional control. It demanded that Buddhists and other religions adapt internal practices and teachings to meet CPC expectations. At the same time, Buddhists changed Buddhism to emphasize such state-driven projects as charity, diplomacy, and national standardization and to respond to the needs of the increasingly wealthy society. Therefore, the relationship between religion and the state has been transformed from efforts by the state to destroy religion to increasingly supporting it in ways the CPC deems suitable for the PRC.

In concluding this book, we first summarize our conceptual argument developed for researching, analyzing, and explaining the transformation of religion and the state system as seen through the recovery of one temple, from the end of the Cultural Revolution until 2004. That year marked the acceleration of far-reaching state control of Buddhism, seen in new political uses of such discourses as "Buddhist culture" (*fojiao wenhua* 佛教文化) and "Sinicized Buddhism" (*zhongguohua fojiao* 中國化佛教). Also, that was the final year of service for the temple's second abbot since the Cultural Revolution, who played a significant role in deepening Buddhism's adaptation to state needs and aligning Nanputuo Temple more firmly with the expectations of the CPC and central state. The new abbot, Zewu, pursued these newly emphasized political discourses in projects that prepared Nanputuo Temple and Buddhism to meet changing CPC expectations for the wealthier and more globally powerful country.

Space, Networks, Episodes

We have viewed this transformation from 1979 as Nanputuo Temple recovered from the suppression of religion during the Cultural Revolution, through the concepts of space, network, and episode. The concept of space enabled us to develop a theoretical approach toward religion for our overall argument. We have examined the layers of the physical, institutional, and semiotic spaces of religion as seen at the temple to discern how they have been created, functioned, and transformed. Religion is, in a sense, predominantly the semiotic space of cosmology and ideas for understanding a world of sentient and divine beings. It expands, acquiring physical space as sacred areas and meeting places, and institutional space as an organization with rules and regulations. To exist in a modern, secular state, the semiotic, physical, and institutional spaces of Buddhism need to be mutually constituted with the state through processes of adjustment and contestation, especially in the context of the PRC, which is governed by a communist party.

From 1979, the CPC enabled Buddhism's recovery by reopening the space of religion in its ideology. Buddhism, which had been existing in a semiotic space "hidden" in people's minds, gained legitimacy to openly reveal its semiotic space through the recovery of temples, expanding the physical space of Buddhism. At first, the institutional space was rudimentary and vague, leading to much conflict. The state's assertion of a more detailed institutional space of religion affected the semiotic space of Buddhist teaching and practice and the semiotic understanding of

CONCLUSION

religion in CPC ideology, while tourism deeply affected the physical space of temples. Our observations in this book, made over three decades, have enabled us to discern the alignments of the three spaces during the recovery process of one Buddhist temple. We have described this process up to 2004, at which point we argue that Buddhism had recovered much of what had been lost earlier and was expanding in new directions. This point is a premonition of an entirely new phase in the mutually constitutive transformation of Buddhism and the state, in other words, the metamorphosis of Chinese Buddhism.

The recovery of the semiotic space among Buddhists and the physical space of the temples proceeded smoothly, although not without difficulties. To comprehend the activation of the space of religion, we researched networks and multilayered interactions among individuals, organizations, and the state, domestically and globally connected to Nanputuo Temple. The recovery reflected the different experiences, understandings, and aspirations regarding Buddhism of networked actors, which created overlaps of the spaces. Ideas, resources, and power in the networks continually shifted and realigned among multilayered, local, and translocal individuals and Buddhism, the state, and broader society.

Critical matrices involved two abbots, Miaozhan and Shenghui, during the first two decades of the revival of Buddhism as the state power reconstituted its center and expanded to locales. The temple's recovery reflected their different understandings and aspirations of Buddhism before the founding of the PRC in 1949 and under the CPC since the 1980s. Miaozhan's understanding inhered in monastic life before 1949 that in subsequent decades continued to exist in lineages and transnational networks of Chinese Buddhist clergies, devotees, and believers who left China due to political turmoil. Miaozhan did not hesitate to confront the local state administration to preserve the autonomy of Buddhism as he understood it. Shenghui, born and educated in the PRC, knew how to cooperate with the administrative authority, moving the temple closer to the central state. These different ideas and networks activated the space in the temple, transforming interactions with the local communities of Buddhism, including overseas Chinese, and state officials.

For this book we chose multiple episodes to describe and analyze the interactions and shifts affecting the transformation of religious space. Each episode was constituted by many stories and cuts in a specific context or issue of Buddhism involving Buddhist communities and state agencies, locally and globally, as seen from the perspective of Nanputuo Temple. The episodes showed processes of reconstituting Buddhist teachings, administration, responses to national political events, abbot selection, local party and state interests, central state expectations, clerics' transnational movements, and the people's passion that was most palpable at the Guanyin festival. Each episode illustrated some aspect of transforming values and systems through cooperation, competition, conflict, and coexistence of systems and values. Over the course of an episode, the relations between Buddhism, its communities, and the state were rearranged. The changes, be they drastic or slight, visible or invisible, recognized or unrecognized by communities and agencies, affected values concerning religion and the state system of religious administration on a large scale. The chain of episodes over time and space that we observed is the alteration of the actualities and awareness of Buddhism among the people in China.

Buddhism as Culture

By the early 2000s, Buddhism, more stabilized in the state system, was moving in new directions under CPC promotion as Chinese "culture," mainly for Han Chinese. The term "Buddhist culture," which had mostly referred to such aspects of Buddhism as architecture, painting, and music in temples and among clerics, was increasingly emphasized politically as practices spreading broadly in society. This change reflects critical events. The enormous state capacity used in the campaign against Falun Gong from 1999 led the CPC to rethink its approach to controlling the people's passions in folk beliefs. The party moved away from labeling ancestor worship and other popular folk beliefs and practices as superstition to seeing them as cultural practices of Chinese Buddhism (Zhongguo fojiao 中國佛教). The Buddhist Association of China has increasingly emphasized the historical origins of Buddhist sects and traditions in China, not as transmissions from India, but as mixing with Chinese Confucianism and Daoism to fuse into Chinese Buddhism that subsequently spread to other countries in Asia. This view has been significantly furthered under Xi Jinping 習近平, who sees Buddhism as one of the vital historical foundations of Chinese civilization. Since around 2015, he has

CONCLUSION

placed Buddhism at the center of state-supported efforts to spread Buddhism globally, not to enhance it as a religion, but to support PRC geopolitical and economic strategies centered on the Belt and Road Initiative.

Following this CPC direction, Buddhist temples and clerics have increasingly promoted aspects linked to Buddhism as practices of Buddhist culture in society. These events are promoted in temples and other venues in society, including social media. Efforts have coincided with an emerging quest among the increasingly wealthy young middle class for a Chinese "neotraditional" lifestyle that is not imitative of Western ones. Buddhism as cultural practice derives authenticity from Buddhism, even though it requires no knowledge of Buddhist teachings or even awareness of the links to Buddhism. The practices appeal to people and the state as Chinese culture rather than religion. Once criticized by the CPC as a bourgeois indulgence, tea culture is now linked to Chan Buddhist teaching as embodying purity, tranquility, and freedom from worldly worries. Martial arts are being taught as forms of bodily and mental conditioning. Meditation is promoted as a technique for mental stability for those exhausted working in the market economy and to sharpen children's concentration for study. Their spread is creating new practices in temples, such as short-term monasticism, and even outside temples in large private halls, company headquarters, and scenic tourist sites. Some Chinese temples have even set up branch temples abroad to promote Chinese Buddhism. The CPC has encouraged this spread. The aim is not to further belief in Buddhism as a religion but rather to add a cultural dimension that the party can discursively control to further domestic cultural integration and support its global economic and political aspirations.

These trends have transformed the space of religion in Nanputuo Temple. Zewu, its young abbot since 2005, has promoted Buddhism as culture to reconnect the temple to people. When we met him in 2014, he said Buddhism reflects the national culture and is a pillar of the country's social peace and stability. For him, Buddhist culture spans a wide array of aesthetic and contemplative components, including architecture, meditation, tea, Buddhist counseling, vegetarian food, calligraphy, and painting. Under his leadership, the temple's physical, institutional, and semiotic spaces have taken new forms to fit the CPC's expectations of Buddhism as culture. One was the consecration in 2009 of a statue for Hongyi, a pioneer a century earlier in the New Culture Movement (Xin wenhua yundong 新文化運動) through contributions to Buddhist art. The figure of Hongyi has become a significant capital for the temple, just as Taixu had been before him. Another form was rebuilding the temple with the highest quality materials and artisanship. Their exquisite details and bright colors of the halls, quite different from the earthier colors of the previous restoration under Miaozhan, have imparted a theme park–like atmosphere to the main compound. Zewu has furthered ancestor worship by building a large columbarium in 2010, and the sale of funerary urns has become the temple's primary income. This increased the temple's wealth, enabling Zewu to eliminate the temple's entrance fee, one of the first major temples to do so. Through all of these efforts, Buddhist culture was made more accessible to people.

The BCM, under its rector Shenghui, the former abbot, has aligned with new expectations by promoting the globalization of Chinese Buddhism. In 2015, The BCM formalized its transnational ties by founding alumni associations in Malaysia, Singapore, and Indonesia. In 2017, the BCM opened an International English Buddhist Studies Department to train students who could be active along the routes of the Belt and Road Initiative. It began taking graduating BCM students on transnational tours in a program called Retracing the Maritime Silk Road (Chong zou haishang sichou zhi lu 重走海上絲綢之路). The tours traverse the sea routes that brought Buddhism to China via Fujian Province in the Tang dynasty. Only now, the direction is reversed in outflows of culture, wealth, and power along the Belt and Road Initiative.

The semiotic space of paintings and epigraphs has been transforming. This change was visible in the stories on the side of the Great Buddha Hall that were repainted during Zewu's renovation of the temple. During a visit in 2015, we noticed some stories had been altered from those we recorded in 1999. The story "Plucking Flowers to Offer to the Buddha" was replaced with "Offering Flowers to the Buddha." We asked monks to explain the reason for the change but could not get a satisfactory response. So, we offer our own. The original story told how poor people who were obligated to gather flowers for the king were so impressed by the Buddha that they gave him the flowers instead. The new story simply told of people buying flowers to offer the Buddha. We think the monks removed the king from the new story in case the advice to work for the Buddha, not the ruler, was interpreted as undermining the state.

CONCLUSION

Interestingly, the new story was not in *Stories of the Buddha's Life*, which likely supports its recent provenance. Another change was replacing the story "Four Kings Offering Begging Bowl" with "Regret of the Ferryman." The first story taught that wealthy kings and nobles should show respect for the Buddha by giving him simple offerings with a pious mind, such as a begging bowl, rather than expensive and extravagant things. The new story, which is included in *Stories of the Buddha's Life,* told of a miserly ferryman who made the Buddha pay him for a ride. Afterward, the ferryman regretted it, and the king decreed that the Buddha and his disciples forever be transported for free. The original story may have been changed because it communicated to people that the temple did not want valuable donations and offerings. The changes in the two stories likely reflected the concerns of the clerics to avoid politics and encourage modest donations befitting Buddhist values.

Changes at Nanputuo Temple affected other Buddhist communities in Xiamen. In 2009, the temple established a volunteers department (*yigong bu* 義工部) to encourage people to associate with the temple if they were interested in Buddhist culture but not wanting (or ready) to take the devotee vows. This organization had thousands of members, mostly middle-aged retired women in their forties to sixties, who could attend dharma talks and provide free labor for the temple's maintenance and tour guide services. The new department extended control over believers who came to the temple while providing leisure activities for the rapidly aging population. It brought the lay believers under the direct supervision of the clerics, unlike the Xiamen Devotee Lodge, which existed outside the temple and whose members prided their independence from clerics, even while respecting their authority as Buddhist masters. Regarding lay nuns, Nanputuo clerics and BAX officers sought to preserve their dwindling numbers. They worked with local officials to harmonize local regulations that permitted lay nuns to remain in their halls despite new national regulations issued in 2007 establishing that only ordained clerics could live in religious activity sites. BAX officers used the language of cultural preservation by referring to the lay nuns as a valued Minnan heritage, thus justifying their tremendous efforts to allow a small number of lay nuns to continue residing in their halls. But their efforts at cultural protection did not change the fundamental circumstances for the lay nuns' decline, namely, the lack of access to

Buddhist education in the BCM. This displayed the disjuncture between preserving the lay nun tradition as a unique Minnan culture while not protecting its reproduction as a religious community.

The Question of Belief

If Buddhism is spreading among people as a part of Chinese culture, and not just as religion, what is happening to the belief of the people? The promotion of Buddhism as culture has affected beliefs by blurring boundaries between being and not being Buddhist to a much greater degree. Buddhism, or rather the cultural aspects of Buddhism and culture linked to Buddhism, is now entering people's experiences as lifestyles. They can listen to sutra-based fusion music for yoga or relaxation, enjoy Buddhist-inspired clothing resembling costumes in historical dramas, decorate home interiors with Buddhist-related colors and calligraphy, and eat organic vegetarian food, all without serious devotion to Buddhism. People may even lack awareness of the link between these enjoyments and Buddhism as religion and experience no discomfort for not taking the precepts, not holding morning and evening services at home, or not worshiping at temples on major festivals.

As seen at the Guanyin festival, Buddhism can be for everyone. Most temples open their doors, to the extent possible, to all visitors without concern for who has received precepts or not. In the 1990s, worshipers at the Guanyin festival were concerned with distinguishing between real Buddhist devotees and persons like themselves with less commitment—people who only worshiped at Nanputuo Temple on festivals, perhaps, or prayed when they felt the need for good luck. They answered our question, "Are you a Buddhist?," by saying that they were not, and then citing the reason: they were not vegetarians. But in the twenty-first century, many people enjoying Buddhism as culture through tea ceremony and meditation or pursuing a neotraditional lifestyle related to Buddhism as culture are less aware of demarcating who is Buddhist and who is not. This was evident during our visit in 2016 to a vast Buddhist products and crafts trade exhibition in Xiamen that had started up a decade earlier. Although we did not conduct a formal survey, in our many conversations over three days at the fair, no one even mentioned Buddhism as a religion or indicated their position regarding belief.

CONCLUSION

We see the CPC's greater emphasis on Buddhism as Chinese culture as linked to declining emotional commitment among people to Buddhism at Nanputuo Temple. Until the late 1990s, people were passionate about coming to the temple to practice qigong, participating in sutra chanting groups led by monks, and worshiping at the Guanyin festival to receive merit and divine assistance. But we noted a substantial change in the temple at a Guanyin festival we attended in 2015. It was far quieter than the one we observed in 1999 (see chapter 9) with only 50,000 attendees—half that of the earlier festival—and many seemed to be tourists. The temple was further subdued by new practices of "civilized rituals" (*wenming jisi* 文明祭祀) that banned the burning of incense in the temple's main square and prompted worshipers to offer flowers rather than food to the Thousand-Handed and Thousand-Eyed Guanyin statue. Consequently, there was no thick, fragrant incense smoke that had contributed to the heat and noise of the festival. People could no longer expect to embody the magical power of Guanyin by eating and sharing food that the bodhisattva had semiotically consumed. These changes accord with our observation in chapters 6 and 7 that as Nanputuo Temple aligned with CPC projects, people shifted their worship to local temples that paid more attention to their needs.

These circumstances are accompanied by several trends among the communities of Buddhism in Xiamen. Some clerics go along with promoting Buddhism as Chinese culture, presenting Buddhist ideas and philosophy through tea ceremony, and meditation for health. This form of Buddhism as culture is more open and accessible to the people who now expect to benefit from experiences of Buddhism despite offering less serious engagement with Buddhist teachings. In the meantime, other clerics concentrate on Buddhist teachings and religious practices to deepen their spiritual understandings. They emphasize strict observance of the precepts, scholarly study of the sutras, and self-cultivation, paying little attention to the propagation of Buddhism as religion among people. For devotees serious about attaining a higher stage of Buddhism, "Buddhism as culture" has little appeal. They increasingly search outside the temple for a more "genuine" Buddhism to find a spiritual commitment to Buddhist teachings. Many organize Buddhist activities and study groups through social media and are not affiliated with any organization or cleric. Although largely invisible in society, their numbers are said to be

CONCLUSION

increasing among young people under Xi Jinping. Some young people leave their jobs for a year or two to travel to Buddhist sites in China and Asia. Others migrate abroad, where they consider Buddhism freer and more "authentic," to study Buddhism and get ordained. It is unpredictable how serious devotees of Buddhism as religion will keep their activities less visible and for how long. Throughout history, when devotees and believers lost respect for Buddhism as practiced by clerics in temples, they organized independent groups to study and practice it. It will be interesting to observe the effects of the new generation of pious devotees on Buddhism.

In 2018, as we were completing this book, there was news of a momentous transformation occurring in the state system. The dual state system of party and government administration of religion established half a century earlier was abolished. The State Administration for Religious Affairs, previously a government bureau, was absorbed into the CPC's Central United Front Work Department, along with the bureau that handled overseas Chinese and other affairs. This arrangement enhanced the capacity of the CPC to promote a China-centered Buddhism with a global reach. Buddhism, already elevated by the state as Chinese culture to be actively promoted, will undoubtedly undergo an unprecedented metamorphosis in the new state system as China aspires to be a global superpower under a communist party-state. We finish this book by quoting the words of a long-time CPC member in Xiamen who was devoted to supporting the abbot Miaozhan in his struggle for the recovery of Nanputuo Temple and the autonomy of Buddhism. He said, "I need to live a long life to see who is right at the end of the day, Marx or the Buddha."

Appendix 1

Leaders of Nanputuo Temple, 1684–

Years of Leadership	Name (birth and death)	Position and Term[1]	Accomplishments as Leader
1684–1708	慧日 Huiri (n.d.–1708)	Prior	First leader of Nanputuo Temple.
1723–1758	如淵 Ruyuan (n.d.–1758)	Prior	Repaired and expanded temple.
1759–1775, 1796–1803	景峰 Jingfeng (n.d.)	Prior	Renovated temple.
1823–1850	省己 Shengji (n.d.)	Prior	Rebuilt Great Buddha Hall.
1851–1874	有情 Youqing (n.d.)	Prior	Rebuilt monks' dormitory (then rebuilt Nanshan Temple).
1872–1874, 1885–1894	佛乘 Focheng (1834–1899)	Acting prior, prior	
1895–1911	喜參 Xican (1848–1911)	Prior	Rebuilt temple; made Releasing Life Pond.
1911–1912	佛化 Fohua (1833–1912)	Prior	Led temple in transition from Qing dynasty to ROC.
1913–1919	轉道 Zhuandao (1872–1943)	Prior	Raised funds in Singapore to renovate temple; started school for clerics at temple.
1920–1924	轉逢 Zhuanfeng (1979–1952)	Prior	Led effort to ecumenicize temple.
1924–1927, 1935–1937	會泉 Huiquan (1874–1943)	Abbot, 1st & 5th	First abbot of ecumenicized temple; founded BCM.
1927–1933	太虛 Taixu (1889–1947)	Abbot, 2nd & 3rd	Served as BCM rector; made temple nationally prominent.
1933–1934	常惺 Changxing (1897–1939)	Abbot, 4th	
1934–1936	轉塵 Zhuanchen (n.d.)	Acting abbot[2]	Rectified BCM.
1936–1937	性願 Xingyuan (1889–1962)	Acting abbot	Served one year, then went to the Philippines.
1938–1942	覺斌 Juebin (1897–1942)	Abbot, 6th	Tried to revive BCM during WW II.
1942–1943	塊然 Kuairan (n.d.)	Acting abbot	Resigned after one year due to difficult political situation.

(*continued next page*)

APPENDIX 1

(continued from previous page)

Years of Leadership	Name (birth and death)	Position and Term[1]	Accomplishments as Leader
1943–1945	會覺 Huijue (n.d.)	Acting abbot	Unsuccessful in reviving BCM.
1946–1952	廣心 Guangxin (1900–1967)	Abbot, 7th	Led temple during the civil war and first years of PRC; established BAX; opened elementary school.
1952–1956	慈舟 Cizhou (1877–1957)	Acting abbot	Well-known Buddhist educator; unsuccessful in reviving BCM.
1956–1957	二埋 Ermai (n.d.)	Acting abbot	Led temple for a year until death.
1989–1995[3]	Miaozhan (1910–1995)	Abbot, 8th	Came to temple in 1957; led its recovery from 1979; reactivated transnational networks; renovated and expanded temple; revived BCM and opened nuns campus; founded Nanputuo Temple Charity Foundation; built Meditation Hall; made temple accessible to devotees.
1997–2005	聖輝 Shenghui (1951–)	Abbot, 9th–11th	Sent by Buddhist Association of China; tightened discipline, upgraded BCM; engaged in state's Buddhist diplomacy and anti–Falun Gong campaign; remained BCM dean after retirement.
2005–	則悟 Zewu (1974–)	Abbot, 12th–15th	Emphasized Buddhist culture; rebuilt temple compound, eliminated entrance fee; founded devotee volunteers association; built large Merit Hall.

Data from *NSZ*, 20–22

Appendix 2

Nanputuo Temple, a Millennium of Construction and Renewal

Time	Benefactor	Construction	Source
Ca. 10th century	Qinghao	Built Sizhou Temple.	QGN, 1
Ca. 11th century	Wencui	Rebuilt temple and renamed it Wujinyan (Boundless Crag 無盡岩).	QGN, 1
1341		Temple is destroyed.	QGN, 1
1368	Jueguang	Rebuilt temple and named it Puzhao Temple (Infinite Illumination Temple 普照寺).	QGN, 1
1628		Temple destroyed in fighting at end of Ming dynasty.	QGN, 1
1684	Admiral Shi Lang	Rebuilt temple, named it Nanputuo Temple, and dedicated it to Guanyin by building Great Compassion Hall.	QGN, 1, 51; NSZ, vol. 1, 12; Xiamen nanputuo si 1995, 9
Early 18th century		Built Huiri Pagoda 慧日塔 on east side of temple. Huiri was first prior of Nanputuo Temple (1684–1708).	NSZ, vol. 1, 56
1764	Ruyuan	Restored Great Buddha Hall, Great Compassion Hall; constructed Dragon King Temple on west side of Great Buddha Hall.	NSZ, vol. 1, 35
1788		Yubei Pavilion 御碑亭 built on Wulao Peak.	NSZ, vol. 1, 49–50
Mid-19th century		Black Dragon Temple relocated to Xiamen harbor.	NSZ, vol. 1, 35
1833	Shengji	Built terrace around Great Compassion Hall; added second floor to Bell Tower and Drum Tower.	QGN, 3
1866	Zhenhui	Engraved the Buddha 佛 character on rock at foot of Wulao Peak.	QGN, 67
1895	Xican	Renovated temple.	NSZ, vol. 1, 35
1904		Dug Releasing Life Pond.	NSZ, vol. 1, 48
1924	Zhuanfeng	Rebuilt Mountain Gate, built east and west arhat arcades, bell towers.	NSZ, vol. 1, 35; QGN, 17–18, 32, 68
1925	Huichuan	Started the BCM, and presumably then built a dormitory and classroom in west courtyard.	QGN, 4

(continued next page)

APPENDIX 2

(continued from previous page)

Time	Benefactor	Construction	Source
1930	Taixu	Rebuilt Great Compassion Hall after destruction by fire.	QGN, 51
1936	Zhuanfeng	Rebuilt Great Buddha Hall using granite in Minnan style.	QGN, 37
1936		Constructed building for Dharma Hall (first floor) and Sutra Library (second floor).	QGN, 61
1936	Hongyi	Furbished Jingyelüdong (cave) on Wulao Peak.	NSZ, vol. 1, 52
1948	Xingyuan	Lightly repaired temple.	NSZ, vol. 1, 36
1950	Government	Rebuilt all halls.	NSZ, vol. 1, 36
1952		During land reform, 65 mu (4.3 ha) of temple land given to Farmers' Association.	NSZ, vol. 1, 26
1954–1957	Guangjing	Built Zhuanfeng stupa.	QGN, 75; NSZ, vol. 1, 26
1959		Restored Great Buddha Hall.	NSZ, vol. 1, 27
1959		Rebuilt Great Compassion Hall with concrete roof after typhoon damage.	NSZ, vol. 1, 27
1962–1963		Built Huiquan stupa.	QGN, 77; NSZ, vol. 1, 28
	Daxing	Built Taixu Memorial Pavilion.	QGN, 69
1963		Repaired Great Compassion Hall and raised base one meter.	QGN, 51
1966	Red Guards	Smashed statues of Four Heavenly Kings and Eighteen Arhats and burnt ancestor tables in Merit Hall.	NSZ, vol. 1. 28; Wu 2014, vol. 7, book 1, 39
1980		Built stone pavilion on Wulao Peak.	Wu 2014, vol. 7, book 1, 39
1980		Temple land given to Xiamen University for faculty housing.	Wu 2014, vol. 7, book 1, 23
1980		Constructed mountain gates.	NSZ, vol. 1. 47
1980		Built three-story Haihuilou Restaurant in east compound.	Wu 2014, vol. 7, book 1, 46–47
1981	Miaozhan	Restored Heavenly Kings Hall.	Wu 2014, vol. 7, book 1, 54
1981	Miaozhan	Repaired second floors of Bell and Drum Towers.	Wu 2014, vol. 7, book 1, 48
1982		Built pavilion on Wulao Peak.	Wu 2014, vol. 7, book 1, 48
1982	Miaozhan	Constructed three-story dormitory for resident clerics in east compound.	Wu 2014, vol. 7, book 1, 58
1982	Miaozhan	Rebuilt Great Buddha Hall and Great Compassion Hall.	Wu 2014, vol. 7, book 1, 126, 140

APPENDIX 2

Time	Benefactor	Construction	Source
1983	Miaozhan	Rebuilt Tushita Hall.	Wu 2014, vol. 7, book 1, 126, 140
1983	Miaozhan	Dug water well next to Releasing Life Pond.	Wu 2014, vol. 7, book 1, 141
1983		Built student dormitories for Buddhist Instruction School in west compound.	Wu 2014, vol. 7, book 1, 163–164
1985	Miaozhan	Renovated BCM facilities and added two stories to student dormitories.	QGN, 93; Wu 2014, vol. 7, book 1, 164
1985	Xiamen City Government	Constructed Puzhaolou Restaurant.	QGN, 95
1989		Built guesthouse and Zhengming Building.	Wu 2014, vol. 7, book 2, 106
1990		Constructed buildings for BCM and Taixu Memorial Library.	NSZ, vol. 1, 35
1992		Built two-story office and department store inside East Mountain Gate.	Wu 2014, vol. 7, book 4, 12
1993		Built Seven Past Buddhas pagodas alongside Releasing Life Pond.	NSZ, vol. 1, 48
1994	Nan Huaijin and disciple	Built Meditation Hall in west compound.	Xiamen nanputuo si 1995, 29; NSZ, vol. 1. 34, 38
1994	Miaozhan	Constructed four-story Nanputuo Temple Charity Foundation building along front of west compound.	QGN, 99; Wu 2014, vol. 7, book 3, 210
1994	Believer	Built 30-meter-tall Longevity Pagodas on both sides of the Releasing Life Pond.	QGN. 14; NSZ, vol. 1, 39; Wu 2014, vol. 7, book 3, 50
1995	Miaozhan	Opened free clinic on first floor of Nanputuo Temple Charity Foundation.	QGN, 100
1995		Built temple administrative annex.	NSZ, vol. 1, 40
1996	Singapore real estate company	Opened campus for BCM nuns section in Zizhulin Temple with seven buildings (for classroom, dormitories, administration).	NSZ, vol. 1, 41
1997		Constructed Miaozhan stupa.	Wu 2014, vol. 7, book 4, 24
1998	Singapore real estate company	Built library for BCM women's section at Zizhulin campus.	NSZ, vol. 1, 43
2006	Zewu	Repaired Heavenly Kings Hall.	QGN, 62
2006	Zewu	Rebuilt Great Buddha Hall using Burmese teak to prevent termites.	NSZ, vol. 1. 62; QGN, 37–38
2007	Zewu	Added exquisite wood carvings of scenes from *Buddhist Stories* on walls of Great Buddha Hall.	NSZ, vol. 1, 38

(continued next page)

APPENDIX 2

(continued from previous page)

Time	Benefactor	Construction	Source
2007	則悟	Built large Merit Hall, five-story guest house, and parking lot to west of temple compound.	*NSZ*, vol. 1, 46, 63
2008	則悟	Replenished greenery on Wulao Peak.	*NSZ*, vol. 1, 71
2010	則悟	Reconstructed the Dharma Hall.	*QGN*, 61

Appendix 3
Buddhist College of Minnan Curriculum, 1989

Program	Time	Curriculum
Remedial course (three months)		Chinese 語言, Calligraphy 書法, Physical Fitness 體育
Preparatory program (two years)	1st year	An Inspiration to Give Rise to the Bodhi Mind 勸發菩提心文, Novice Precepts 沙彌律, Explanation of Morning and Evening Rituals 二課合解, Introduction to Buddhism 佛學概論, Amitābha Sutra 阿弥陀經, Three Legacies of the Teaching of the Buddha 佛遺教三經, Three Character Sutras in Buddhism 佛教三字經, Concise History of Buddhism in India 印度佛教簡史, Four Books 四書, Chinese 語文, Foreign Languages 外語, Physical Fitness 體育, Calligraphy 書法, Politics 政治
	2nd year	Way to Buddhahood 成佛之道, Introduction to Buddhism 佛學概論, Biographies of Eminent Monks 高僧傳, Verses Delineating the Eight Consciousnesses 八識規矩頌, Discussions on the Garden of Law 法苑談叢, Five Theories on the Great Vehicle 大乘五蘊論, Clear Introduction to Hundred Dharmas Treatise 百法明門論, Concise History of Buddhism in China 中國佛教簡史, Treasured Teaching of Chan 禪林寶訓, Sutra of Great Treasure Collection 寶積經, Four Books 四書, Chinese 語文, Calligraphy 書法, Foreign Languages 外語, Politics 政治, Physical Fitness 體育
Undergraduate program (four years)	1st year	History of Buddhism in India 印度佛教史, Thirty Verses on Consciousness-Only 唯識三十論, Awakening Faith in the Mahayana Treatise 大乘起信論, Essentials of Buddhist Śīla and Vinaya 戒律學綱要, Dharma Analysis Treasury 俱舍論, Twenty Verses on Consciousness-Only 唯識二十頌, Sutra of Perfect Enlightenment 圓覺經, Five Sutras of the Pure Land School 淨土五經, Calming (śamatha) and Insight (vipaśyanā) Meditation 童蒙止觀, Writing 寫作, Calligraphy 書法, Classical Chinese 古代漢語, Foreign Language 外語, History of China 中國通史, History of Chinese Philosophy 中國哲學史, Politics 政治, Physical Fitness 體育
	2nd year	History of Buddhism in India 印度佛教史, Compendium of the Great Vehicle 攝大乘論, Twelve Gates Treatise 十二門論, One Hundred Verse Treatise 百論, History of Zen in China and India 中印禪宗史, Regulations for the Four Departments 四寮規約, Dharma Analysis Treasury 俱舍論, History of Pure Land Teachings 淨土教理史, Writing 寫作, Calligraphy 書法, Classical Chinese 古代漢語, Foreign Language 外語, History of China 中國通史, History of Chinese Philosophy 中國哲學史, Politics 政治, Physical Fitness 體育

(continued next page)

APPENDIX 3

(continued from previous page)

Program	Time	Curriculum
	3rd year	History of Chinese Buddhism 中國佛教史, Sutra of the Explanation of Profound Secrets 解深密經, Middle Way Treatise 中論, Śūraṅgama Sutra 楞嚴經, Forest of Gems in the Garden of the Dharma 法苑珠林, Vimalakīrti Sutra 維摩詰經, Evidential Study of Introduction to Logic 因明入正 理門論, Brief Exposition of the Bohdi Path 菩提道次第略論, Platform Sutra of Sixth Patriarch 六祖壇經, Five Treatises on Avatamsaka School Teachings 賢首五教儀, Ten Essentials of Pure Land 淨土十要, Seng-Chao Treatise 肇論, Essence of Teaching and Practice 教觀網宗, Golden Lion in the Flower Adornment Sutra 華嚴經金獅子章, Brahmajala Sutra 梵网經, Four-Part Vinaya (Vinaya Piṭaka) 四分律, Selected Readings of Masterpieces of Chinese Classical Literature 中國歷代文學作品選, Foreign Language 外語, Calligraphy 書法, History of Western Philosophy 西方哲學史, Physical Fitness 體育
	4th year	History of Chinese Buddhism 中國佛教史, Differentiation of Middle Way from the Extremes 辯中邊論, Outline of School of Three Treatises 三論宗綱要, Sutra on Entering the Country of Lanka (Laṅkāvatāra Sutra) 楞伽经, Four Teachings of Tiantai 天台四教義, Selected Readings of the Flower Adornment Sutra 華嚴經選讀, Obscure Meaning of the Three Treatises 三論玄義, Diamond Sutra 金剛經, Rules and Codes of Buddhist Monasteries 百丈清規, History of Scientific Thought 科學思想史, Selected Readings of the Masterpieces of Chinese Classical Literature 中國歷代文學作品選, Foreign Language 外語, Calligraphy 書法, Physical Fitness 體育

Source: Curriculum sheet received from BCM instructor, Nanputuo Temple, 1990

Appendix 4

Ordination Ceremony Schedule, October 13–29, 1989, Guanghua Temple

Day	Dawn Activities	Morning Activities	Afternoon Activities	Evening Activities
1	報到 Registration 早課 Morning service	進堂 Enter temple 引禮師見面 Meet instructors 帶新戒挂搭 Ordinands reside at temple	禮佛 Worship the Buddha[1]	
2	早課 Morning service 下啟 Invite teachers 教用餐事宜 Learn dining etiquette[2]	唱界淨壇上供 Chant to purify the boundaries and make offerings[3] 念規約交香板 Learn rules of ceremony	教穿衣袍事宜 Teach the proper way to wear robes	禮佛 Worship the Buddha
3	早課 Morning service	念規約交香板 Learn rules of ceremony	教四威儀問答 Teach etiquette and answers[4]	禮佛 Worship the Buddha
4	早課 Morning service	授五戒 Receive the five precepts	請二師 Invite two teachers[5]	禮佛 Worship the Buddha
5	早課 Morning service	二師開示 Two teachers elucidate teachings	剃頭沐浴 Shave heads and wash	禮通宵 Worship all night
6	早課 Morning service 下啟 Invite teachers	授沙彌戒 Receive ten novice precepts 分沙彌律本 Receive novice Vinaya treatise	學沙弥律 Study novice precepts	禮佛 Worship the Buddha
7	早課 Morning service	講沙彌律 Lecture on novice Vinaya	晚課巡寮看单 Visit dormitories	禮佛 Worship the Buddha
8	早課 Morning service	請和尚開示 Master elucidates teachings	開示 Elucidate teachings	禮佛 Worship the Buddha
9	早課 Morning service	學問答 Study questions and answers[6]	問答 Questions and answers	禮佛 Worship the Buddha
10	早課 Morning service	乞授具足戒 Ask to receive full precepts 請七尊証 Invite the seven witnesses	問遮難 Questions and responses	禮通宵 Worship all night
11	早課 Morning service	授比丘戒 Receive biqiu (bhikṣu) precepts	授比丘戒 Receive biqiu (bhikṣu) precepts	禮佛 Worship the Buddha
12	早課 Morning service	授比丘戒 Receive biqiu (bhikṣu) precepts	授比丘戒 Receive biqiu (bhikṣu) precepts	禮佛 Worship the Buddha

(continued next page)

357

APPENDIX 4

(continued from previous page)

Day	Dawn Activities	Morning Activities	Afternoon Activities	Evening Activities
13	早課 Morning service	授比丘戒 Receive *biqiu (bhikṣu)* precepts	授比丘戒 Receive *biqiu (bhikṣu)* precepts	禮佛 Worship the Buddha
14	早課 Morning service 禮祖 Worship ancestors	乞菩薩戒 Request bodhisattva precepts	詞四分戒 Read Dharmaguptaka Vinaya 巡寮看单 Inspect dormitory[7]	禮通宵 Worship all night
15	早課 Morning service 禮祖巡寮 Worship ancestors and inspect dormitories[8] 下啟 Invite teachers	留影 Take photographs 發戒牒 Issue ordination certificates	謝引禮師和执事師 Thank ordination master and deacon	教掛單問答 Learn ceremonial questions and answers for seeking short-term stay at temple
16	早課 Morning service			
17	出堂 Departure			

Source: Ordination schedule obtained at Guanghua Temple, 1989

NOTES

1. Themes and Concepts of the Study

1. Generally speaking, a Buddhist temple is a place for worshiping Buddha, and a monastery is a residence for Buddhist clerics. A third kind of building in Buddhism is the stupa, a bell-shaped structure modeled on ancient Indian burial grounds that contains a sacred relic (Ch. *shali* 舍利, Skt. *śarīra*), the cremated ashes of a Buddhist master. A relic is the most important symbol of a temple and object of worship in Theravada Buddhism. In East Asia, however, stupas became layered pagodas with relatively less significance.

2. For discussions regarding fieldwork studies of Mahayana Buddhism see Nichols (2019). For views of Chinese scholars on fieldwork studies of world religions in the PRC see Cao (2018) and Liang (2016). Several edited volumes contain discussions of social science methodologies and theories, as well as fieldwork studies of religion in the contemporary PRC (Yang and Lang 2011; Yang et al. 2015a, 2015b).

3. For fieldwork-based studies on other state-recognized religions in the PRC see: Catholicism (Lozada 2002; Madsen 1998), Daoism (Chau 2008; Dean 1995; Jones 2017; Palmer 2017), Protestantism (Cao 2010; Hunter and Chan 1993; Lim 2012; Ma and Li 2017; Vala 2017; White 2018; Yang et al. 2017), and Islam (Erie 2016; Gillette 2002; Gladney 1991, 2004; Ho 2015; Jaschok and Shui 2000; Kaltman 2007; Rudelson 1997; Stewart 2016; Wang 2004).

4. For essays in edited volumes on specific topics in contemporary Buddhism in the PRC, including leadership, education, charities, Buddhist tourism, and lay practices, see: Ji, Tian, and Wang 2016; Ji, Fisher, and Laliberté 2019; Kiely and Jessup 2016; Lu and He 2014; Shi 2009.

5. Unpublished doctoral dissertations on contemporary Buddhist temples and communities include: Emei Shan (Qin 2000), Mount Putuo (Bruntz 2014), and devotees (Gao 2010; Jones 2010).

1. THEMES AND CONCEPTS OF THE STUDY

6. The term "city" refers to the urban districts on Xiamen Island, where we conducted most of our fieldwork, and not to Xiamen Municipality, a prefectural-level administrative unit encompassing the island's urban districts and some suburban and rural districts on the mainland.

7. The campaign's full name was "Shatter the Four Olds and Cultivate the Four News" 破四舊立四新. These categories were not defined, so Red Guards destroyed whatever they considered "old," including religious sites and museums, along with antiques and genealogical records (Ho 2006; Ho 2011).

8. Juzan taught at the BCM in 1937 (Lingyin Temple n.d.).

9. This chapter's historical sketch of Nanputuo Temple draws on gazetteers and histories of the temple (*NFZ*, *QGN*, *XFZ*), the unpublished memoir of a BAX official (Wu 2014), and interviews with BAX officials and Nanputuo clerics.

10. Potalaka, a mythical octagon-shaped mountain in the oceans south of India, is said to be the home of the bodhisattva Guanyin. But in China, an actual octagon-shaped island named Putuoshan (Mount Putuo) off the coast of Zhejiang Province 浙江省, became a center of Guanyin worship. Other Chinese phonetic transliterations of the Sanskrit name Potalaka are Putuoluojia 普陀洛伽 and Butuoluojia 補陀洛迦.

11. The Heyun lineage, in the Linji school, began in the Ming dynasty in Nanshan Temple, Zhangzhou. Clerics in the lineage went to Xiamen and Quanzhou, and overseas to Taiwan, Singapore, and the Philippines (*XFZ*, 133).

12. Zhuanfeng was born in Quanzhou and ordained at Nanputuo Temple in 1900. In addition to ecumenicizing the temple, he propagated Buddhism among overseas Chinese communities in Southeast Asia (*XFZ*, 282–284).

13. The *shifang conglin* system was instituted in the Song dynasty (Buswell and Lopez 2013, 804). Temples operating by the system were considered the common property of all clerics residing there rather than belonging to clerics of a certain lineage. Their strict observance of the monastic rules made them exemplars of Buddhist monasticism (Welch 1967, 4).

14. For the *shifang conglin* rules at Nanputuo Temple see *XFZ*, 546–547.

15. In the early eighteenth century, Huxiyan was rebuilt and Yuanfei 元飛 (n.d.) became prior. He was a disciple of Yinyuan 隱元 (1592–1673), founder of the Huangbo lineage (*XFZ*, 78).

16. Taixu established five Buddhist schools to promote ecumenicism among the three traditions of Buddhism. Three schools focused on Mahayana Buddhism, or rather Taixu's interpretation of it. They were: the Wuchang Buddhist Academy (1922–1926, 1929–1949, 1994–2007) at Baotong Temple 寶通禪寺, in Wuchang, Hubei Province 湖北省武漢市; the Bolin Academy 柏林寺教理院 at Bolin Temple in Beijing (1930–1931); and the BCM (1927–1937, 1985–) in Xiamen. For Tibetan Buddhism, he established the Sino-Tibetan Buddhist Institute (1932–1949) in Chongqing, Sichuan Province 四川省重慶市, which taught Tibetan language and Buddhism to Chinese monks. For Theravada Buddhism, he founded the Pali Tripitaka Institute 巴利三藏院 at Daxing Temple 大興寺 in Xi'an, Shaanxi 陝西省西安市, which functioned briefly in 1945. The BCM was the longest running of Taixu's academies.

17. The name of the school is translated as "Buddhist Spiritual Nurturing School" on the Nanputuo Temple website (*Nanputuo si* n.d.)

1. THEMES AND CONCEPTS OF THE STUDY

18. This incident is described in Ken Ling's memoir of his time as a Red Guard in Xiamen. Sixteen Red Guards from Xiamen University tied ropes around the four statues of the heavenly kings in the Heavenly Kings Hall, toppling one until chased away by monks. This desecration angered Xiamen residents, and local factory workers entered the university to punish the students, who fled (Ling 1972, 56). We also heard from informants about the toppling of the statue, as well as the burning of ancestor tablets, while the destruction of arhat statues is noted in the *Nanputuo Temple Gazetteer* (*NSZ*, vol. 1, 28).

19. During the Cultural Revolution, local state governance in China was conducted by revolutionary committees consisting of representatives of the CPC, military, and the people. They were disbanded in 1978 when regular state administration resumed.

20. This occurred during the Up to the Mountains and Down to the Villages Campaign 上山下鄉運動, a state policy from the late 1950s until 1978. Millions of high school graduates had to give up their relatively privileged urban lifestyles to reside for years in rural villages to learn from the workers and farmers.

21. Space has become a conceptual approach in religious studies that enables investigation of a religious phenomenon without positing an underlying conceptualization or definition of religion itself (Chidester 2016). Knott (2005, 12) argues that the idea of space proposed by Henri Lefebvre enables an analytic approach to the "material, ideological, and social forms of religion and their embeddedness in broader networks of social and cultural relations" that are irrespective of the underlying conceptualization of "religion" itself. See Lefebvre 2009a and 2009b.

22. The term "space" often appears in scholarship on religion, and social phenomena more generally, with no discussion of its meaning or use. Therefore, our elaboration of the concept may be useful for such studies.

23. Our earlier research has examined transnational networks of temples and clerics linked to Nanputuo Temple (Ashiwa 1991, 2000; Ashiwa and Wank 2005, 2016). Other scholars have examined the global networks of Fo Guang Shan (Chandler 2004; Reinke 2021), Ciji Gongdehui (Huang 2005), Huayan Buddhism (Hammerstrom 2020), and the transnational mobilities to Southeast Asia (Chia 2020) and historical networks (Bingenheimer 2018). Additionally, some scholars use related concepts of exchange, interaction, and influence, as seen in the essays in *Buddhism after Mao* (Ji, Fisher, and Laliberté 2019) regarding dharma transmission (Campo 2018), state administration of temples (Huang 2019; Vidal 2019), and communication among devotees and worshippers (Fisher 2019; Travagnin 2019).

24. Latour's ideas have influenced some scholars of religion. Lassander and Ingman (2012) see them as inspiration for a non-essentialized study of religion, a view close to ours. Other scholars draw on Latour's actor-network theory (ANT) as a methodology to explain religions as assemblages of human and nonhuman actors. Such studies downplay social agency to emphasize the materiality of religion, including its spaces (Day 2009; Finch 2012), and in China (Chambon 2017, 2020; Wang 2019). For discussion of the multiple scholarly interpretations of Latour's ideas see Law and Hassard (1999).

25. Our use of Luhmann's ideas is limited to the concept of episode in social change. For a fuller application of his ideas of communication and systems to Buddhism, see Schwieger's study of Tibetan Buddhism (Schwieger 2021).

2. Physical and Semiotic Spaces of Nanputuo Temple

1. The physical site of Nanputuo Temple that we describe throughout its recovery is the result of renovations that were undertaken by artisans whose skills in the art and crafts of Buddhist and folk belief temples had been transmitted over many family generations in their rural villages. Stonemasons came from Hui'an County 惠安縣 in Minnan, and carpenters and painters from Xianyou County 仙游縣 in Putian. After the restoration of the temple compound, several artisans remained to maintain the paintings and engravings, which faded, peeled, and cracked in a few years. Maintenance proceeded one building at a time in a continuous cycle to uphold the beauty of the temple as a visible sign that Buddhist teachings were flourishing in it. For the revival of handicraft production see Cooper and Jiang's study of villages in Zhejiang Province (Cooper and Jiang 1998).

2. A temple layout represents the mandala, the visual form of the essence of Buddhist teachings, and cosmology constituted by deities and the previous, current, and future Buddhas, and bodhisattvas. The southern orientation of the halls on a north-south axis ensures the flow of the freshest air (*qi* 氣) from the mountain through the temple to the ocean and the world. A temple conforming to this layout is called a "seven-hall structure" (*qitang qielan* 七堂伽藍). According to popular belief, a temple structure conforms to the human body with the seven halls being the top of the head, nose, mouth, two ears, and two feet (Okimoto 2013). In Chinese history, this ideal has developed various versions, merging with the concept of feng shui for the geographic position of halls (Robson 2010). For the structure of Chinese Buddhist temples see also Prip-Møller (1967) and Scott (2020).

3. One hectare equals 2.5 acres.

4. Ticket sales generated income for the temple's repair and upkeep during its recovery.

5. The Seven Past Buddhas are Gautama Buddha, Vipaśyin Buddha (Ch. Piposhi fo 毗婆尸佛), Śikhin Buddha (Ch. Shiqi fo 屍棄佛), Viśvabhu Buddha (Ch. Pishepo fo 毘舍婆佛), Krakucchaṃda Buddha (Ch. Juliusun 拘留孫), Kanakamuni Buddha (Ch. Junahanmo 拘那含牟), and Kāśyapa Buddha (Ch. Jiaye 迦葉).

6. Adam Chau argues that the concept of magical efficacy, or *ling*, is at the core of widespread folk beliefs and popular religion. Magical efficacy is thought to be a deity's miraculous response (*lingying* 靈應) to a worshiper's request for divine assistance in handling matters. Matters typically concern health, wealth, and other personal matters of the worshiper and their loved ones (Chau 2008, 2). At Nanputuo Temple, worshipers sought divine assistance from the Buddha, Guanyin, and other bodhisattvas, whom they referred to as deities (*shen* 神). The most common forms of worship were direct prayer or making offerings of food, incense, and alms. Some worshipers engaged in divination, such as tossing two coins in front of statues to discern answers in how they fell, a practice mimicking the use of divination blocks (*jiao bei* 筊杯). The people's experience of the semiotic space of Nanputuo Temple is described in chapter 9 on the Guanyin festival.

7. For a related discussion in the context of Chinese Buddhist temples see Robson (2010).

3. INSTITUTIONAL SPACE AND HISTORICAL CAPITAL

8. Couplets are paired and concise lines of poetry in classical Chinese containing auspicious thoughts. Each line is an independent thought that relates to the other line. The two lines share the same number of characters and adhere to rules of correspondence regarding lexical meanings and pronunciation of the characters. A couplet is enigmatic due to the allegorical and metaphorical style through multiple meanings of the characters. In a temple, couplets are located in doorways with the first line on the right side of the door and the second line on the left. Couplets are also engraved on opposing walls or symmetrically placed pillars.

9. Many engravings indicated their authors and creation dates. These names engraved in smaller characters were less visible to people walking past, while most authors were obscure. Therefore, they are not pertinent to our discussion of the semiotic space of the temple and are not discussed in detail in this book.

10. Luojia is a shortened form of Putuoluojia 普陀洛伽, which is the Chinese transliteration of the Sanskrit name Potalaka (see chap. 1, n. 10).

11. From the fifth to the ninth centuries, three emperors persecuted Buddhists for becoming rich and powerful enough to oppose them. These persecutions are called the "Three Disasters of Wu" 三武之禍 because the emperors' posthumous names contained the character 武 (wu).

12. For the naming of clerics, see Welch (1967, 279–281).

13. Versions of these stories have been compiled throughout history, including the *Genealogy of the Buddha* (*Shijia pu* 釋迦譜) by the monk Sengyou 僧祐 (445–518), and *Record of the Enlightenment of Buddha Tathagata* (*Shijia rulai chengdao ji* 釋迦如來成道記) by the literati Wangbo 王勃 in the Tang dynasty. Many stories were similar to the *jataka* tales in Theravada Buddhism recounting stories of previous Buddhas and their reincarnations. In this book, we refer to a widely used contemporary version originally edited in the Ming dynasty and revised in the Qing dynasty into an illustrated collection of 208 stories titled *Stories of the Buddha's Deeds in Past Lives*. It was printed in 1939 by the Shanghai Buddhist Publishing House 上海佛學書局 accompanied with new illustrations and then reissued in 1999 with vernacular translations of the stories. The stories were edited to reflect the life of Gautama Buddha from his birth to death, similar to the New Testament of the Christian Bible. The penultimate story, "Great Dharma Reaches the East" (Dafa dong lai 大法東來), describes the coming of Buddhism to China. The stories have been translated, distributed, and retold with slight variations in Korea, Vietnam, Japan, and Taiwan (Komine 2008).

3. Institutional Space and Nanputuo Temple's Historical Capital

1. The concept of freedom of belief as encompassing both belief and its opposite, nonbelief, is contained in the PRC Constitutions of 1975 (People's Republic of China 1975, 39, art. 28), 1978, and 1982 but not the constitution of 1954. This formulation resembles, and may have been inspired by, the 1936 USSR Constitution article that states, "Freedom of religious worship and antireligious propaganda is recognized for all citizens" (Union of Soviet Socialist Republics 1936, art. 124)

3. INSTITUTIONAL SPACE AND HISTORICAL CAPITAL

2. This "narrow" view of rights in the 1982 PRC Constitution can be traced back to the 1912 ROC Constitution and even earlier to the 1871 Constitution of the German Empire. The German Constitution sought a place for the emperor in a modern state by establishing a constitutional monarchy with delimited rights for individuals and is sometimes called an "imperial constitution"; in contrast, the liberal constitutions of revolutionary states in the United States and France sought to protect citizens from arbitrary state power. Efforts to draft a constitution in China beginning in 1908 at the end of the Qing dynasty sought to preserve a role for the emperor. The drafters were directly inspired by the 1889 Japanese Meiji Constitution that rejected the U.S. Constitution as too liberal to draw on the German Constitution as a model (Chiu 1993, 1; Cohen 1979, 59). A main concern of drafters of the 1912 Republic of China Constitution was effective governance rather than circumscribing state power to protect individual rights (see Chen 2017, 3–4; see also Suami et al. 2019). For discussion of constitutionalism in China in the late Qing dynasty see Zarrow (2006).

3. Travagnin (2015) sees this CPC demand for patriotic religion after 1979 as continuous with aspects of with Chiang Kai-shek's Three Principles of the People (Sanmin zhuyi 三民主義), first expressed in 1905, and Taixu's Buddhism for the Human Realm.

4. The political sociologist Xueliang Ding argues that the CPC emphasis on patriotism after the Cultural Revolution reflected the leadership's fears that communism and Marxism had lost legitimacy among the people. The CPC began to use patriotism to bolster support for the state. In 1982, it began a long-running patriotic campaign called the "Three Loves" for country, party, and socialism (*re'ai zuguo, re'ai gongchandang, re'ai shehui zhuyi* 熱愛祖國, 熱愛共產黨, 熱愛社會主義) that included flag raising and singing the national anthem in schools (Ding 1994, 143–145). Zhao (2004, 28) links the CPC view of patriotism to Lenin's idea of "socialist patriotism," as devotion to country through commitment to communism rather than nationalism.

5. The expectation for religions to be patriotic in Document 19 applied to all the five state-recognized religions. This appeared to differ from the CPC demand for patriotic religion in the 1950s that was mostly directed at Catholics and Protestants whose loyalty was suspect due to their foreign origins and ties (Wickeri 1988, 94–101).

6. One exception to the delimitation was small-scale activities "customarily" held in people's homes. In Xiamen, the XRAB permitted Buddhist sutra chanting and Christian prayer gatherings if participants were few and limited to family and friends.

7. When founded in 1954, the bureau's name was the State Council Religious Affairs Bureau (Guowuyuan zongjiao shiwu ju 國務院宗教事務局), the State Council being the highest authority of the government. In 1998, the bureau's name was changed to State Administration of Religious Affairs in recognition of its heightened importance, especially in regard to folk beliefs and popular religious movements. To avoid confusing name changes in this book we use the current name "State Administration of Religious Affairs" to refer to the national agency headquartered in Beijing from 1954 to the present. The term "religious affairs bureau" is used for provincial and county-level bureaus.

8. In local governments, religious and ethnic affairs were typically administered by the same bureau. Thus, in Xiamen, the official name of the XRAB was Xiamen Municipal Ethnic and Religious Affairs Bureau. But it mostly handled religious affairs because there were few ethnic minorities in Xiamen.

3. INSTITUTIONAL SPACE AND HISTORICAL CAPITAL

9. There are five national religious associations in the PRC, one for each state-recognized religion: Buddhist Association of China, Chinese Daoist Association, Islamic Association of China, Three-Self Patriotic Movement (Protestant), and Chinese Patriotic Catholic Association.

10. Political elites had been concerned about maintaining a distinction in political and religious authority since the onset of modern state formation in China. Rebecca Nedostup's study of the state and religion in the ROC from 1928 to 1937 shows the efforts to observe this distinction in the state administration of religion as well as the difficulties of doing so (Nedostup 2009, 43–46).

11. Congresses have been held in 1953, 1957, 1962, 1980, 1987, 1993, 2002, 2010, 2015, and 2020.

12. Interview with BAX officer by Yoshiko Ashiwa and David Wank, Xiamen, September 1999.

13. Decentralization led to the *tiaokuai* (跳塊) system, a quasi-federalized state structure with vertical and horizontal lines of authority. Vertical lines in functional areas of state administration, such as religion, policing, or commerce, imposed standard policy models from a national ministry onto provincial and local levels. Horizontal lines operated through coordination among bureaus within a local state's territorial jurisdiction to help adapt central policies to local conditions (Lieberthal and Lampton 1992; Montinola et al. 1995).

14. Interview with BAX officer by Yoshiko Ashiwa and David Wank, Xiamen, August 1999.

15. The Zhanshan Buddhist Academy was founded in 1935, shut down in the 1940s, and reopened in 2004 (*Sina* 2004).

16. *Yunyou* is a stage in a cleric's career that entails visiting many places to study under eminent clerics. The experience of traveling severed attachments to place and security.

17. Interview with female devotee by Yoshiko Ashiwa and David Wank, Singapore, 2000.

18. Of the twelve clerics at the temple in 1979, half had laicized.

19. They had come to visit Huxiyan Temple 虎溪岩, which is connected to the Ōbaku school. See n. 43.

20. Interview with XRAB official serving in the early 1980s by Yoshiko Ashiwa and David Wank, Xiamen, December 1998.

21. In dharma transmission, a cleric passed down to another cleric an understanding of the teaching of Buddhism that had been passed down through a generational lineage of master and disciples said to extend back to the Buddha. This created a strong master-disciple bond between the two clerics to perpetuate a Buddhist lineage. A dharma transmission occurred in a private ceremony witnessed by other clerics of the lineage during which the dharma receiver's name was inscribed into the generational scroll of the dharma giver (Campo 2019; Welch 1967, 163–164).

22. Some of these BAX officers were CPC members who did not say that they were Buddhists because party rules prohibited members from believing in religion.

23. There were other important clerics at Nanputuo from the 1920s to the 1940s, most notably Hongyi, but during the 1980s and 1990s, Taixu's image was the most

365

prominent asset contributing to the CPC view of Nanputuo Temple. In the 2000s, Hongyi was increasingly recognized, as we describe in this book's conclusion.

24. Deng saw Singapore as a development model for the PRC because of its dynamic market economy with an international orientation driven by persons of Chinese descent and governed by a one-party state (Khong 1999, 114).

25. The Buddhist Association of China ran the Buddhist Academy of China (Zhongguo foxue yuan) 中國佛學院 reopened in 1980 along with two branch academies, the Mount Lingyan Buddhist Branch Academy of China (Zhongguo foxue yuan lingyanshan fenyuan 中國佛學院靈岩山分院) in Suzhou, and the Qixia Mountain Buddhist Branch Academy of China (Zhongguo foxueyuan qixiashan fenyuan 中國佛學院棲霞山分院), opened in 1982 in Nanjing. The Buddhist Association of Fujian ran the Fujian Buddhist Academy, which opened in 1983 with a monks' campus at Guanghua Temple in Putian and a nuns' campus at Chongfu Temple 崇福寺 in Quanzhou.

26. Gatha names indicate generations of a lineage on its dharma scroll (Welch 1963).

27. Interviews with Singapore Devotee Lodge president Lee Bock Guan (Li Muyuan 李木源) by Yoshiko Ashiwa and David Wank, Singapore, August 2000.

28. Interview with Ruijin by Yoshiko Ashiwa and David Wank, Manila, March 2000.

29. In 1995 Singapore also became a base for the training of clerics from the PRC in the use of modern broadcast media for propagating Buddhism. This occurred through the Dharma Training Course (Jiang jing peixun ban 講經培訓班) established by Jingkong 淨空 (1927–2022) at the Singapore Devotee Lodge. Every day, monks from China listened to Jingkong's lectures on the sutras and studied computer and internet skills and the scientific study of religion. The students were sent by temples or self-nominated. The first class had ten clerics, and that number tripled as the Singapore government became more supportive (fieldwork by David Wank and Yoshiko Ashiwa, Singapore Devotee Lodge, August 2000). Jingkong was from Anhui Province 安徽省 and went to Taiwan after 1949, where he was ordained. He worked closely with devotees, although unassociated with any temple, and pioneered modern media to propagate Buddhist teachings (Sun 2017).

30. Interviews with BAX officials by Yoshiko Ashiwa and David Wank, Xiamen, 1989, 1990, 1999.

31. Interview with tour company president by Yoshiko Ashiwa and David Wank, Singapore, August 2000.

32. The statistics in this paragraph are from an interview with a Fujian Religious Affairs Bureau official conducted by Yoshiko Ashiwa and David Wank, Fuzhou, August, 2000. The numbers for the 1990s generally accord with those given by the Buddhist Association of China in an edition of *Fayin* featuring Buddhism in Fujian (Benxing 2000).

33. Interviews with a BAX officer by Yoshiko Ashiwa and David Wank, Xiamen, 1990, 1999; Fujian Religious Affairs Bureau official, Fuzhou, 1999.

34. Interview with Fujian Religious Affairs Bureau official by Yoshiko Ashiwa and David Wank, Fuzhou, August 1999.

35. Interview with Fujian Religious Affair Bureau official, Yoshiko Ashiwa and David Wank, Fuzhou, August 1999.

36. The distrust partly stemmed from the experiences of returned overseas Chinese. In the 1950s and 1960s, a million overseas Chinese from Indonesia, Malaysia, Burma, and other Southeast Asian countries moved to the PRC. They were motivated by patriotism toward China and anti-Chinese policies in their countries. In the PRC, many experienced hardships because they were suspected of being foreign "spies" and assigned to live and work in state farms where conditions were difficult (Godley 2002, Godley and Coppel 1990). Some fled to Hong Kong and Macao as refugees, and their plight became widely known among overseas Chinese. This created distrust toward the CPC that lingered even after the late 1970s when overseas Chinese were again welcomed in the PRC (Wang 2009).

37. These interviews were conducted from 1988 to 1990 by David Wank as part of his doctoral research on the revival of privately owned business in Xiamen (Wank 1999).

38. Interview with XRAB official by Yoshiko Ashiwa and David Wank, Xiamen, March 1990.

39. Interview with Xiamen Bureau of Industry and Commerce official by David Wank, Xiamen, March 1989. For a related study of religion in ties of overseas Chinese to ancestral villages in Minnan see Kuah-Pearce (2011).

40. Interview with Nan'an Religious Affairs Bureau official by Yoshiko Ashiwa and David Wank, Quanzhou, October 1989.

41. The 3 temples were among the 142 temples designated in 1983 by the state as of national historical and cultural significance; 14 temples in Fujian Province, among the most in any province, were so designated: Yongquan Temple, Xichan Temple 西禪寺, Linyang Temple 林陽寺, Dizang Temple 地藏寺, Chongsheng Temple 崇聖寺, Nanputuo Temple, Guanghua Temple, Cishou Temple 慈壽寺, Guangxiao Temple 光孝寺, Wanfu Temple, Kaiyuan Temple, Longshan Temple 龍山寺, Nanshan Temple, and Zhiti Huayan Temple 支提華嚴寺 (Guowuyuan 1983).

42. The precocious timing of Nanputuo Temple's recovery compared to other temples around the country was confirmed in an interview with Dao Shuren, vice president of the Buddhist Association of China (interview by Yoshiko Ashiwa and David Wank, Beijing, January 1990), and in other surveys of temples in the 1980s (Luo 1991, 170–182; MacInnis 1989, 135).

43. The founder of the Ōbaku sect in the seventeenth century was Yinyuan 隱元 (1592–1673) (Jp. Ingen), abbot of Wanfu Temple of the Linji school in Fujian. In 1651, Japanese Buddhists invited him to Japan, where he remained due to China's political unrest. His Japanese followers created the Ōbaku sect (Wu 2015). Ōbaku became the smallest Zen (Chan) Buddhist sect in Japan and has retained more of its Chinese character (Baroni 2000; Wu 2015).

4. Revival of Buddhist Practice and Education, 1982–1989

1. Xi Zhongxun was the father of Xi Jinping, PRC leader since 2012. He visited Nanputuo Temple on February 17, 1983 (Wu 2014, vol. 7, book 1, 151).

4. REVIVAL OF BUDDHIST PRACTICE, 1982-1989

2. Mengcan was from Northeast China and a disciple of Tanxu. He was ordained in 1931, studied under Tanxu, Xuyun, Hongyi, and Cizhou 慈舟 (1877–1958), and then traveled to Lhasa in the 1940s to study Tibetan Buddhism. In the 1950s, he was imprisoned for refusing to laicize and his sentence was subsequently extended for propagating Buddhism in jail. Upon release in 1982 at age sixty-nine, he taught the Vinaya at the Chinese Buddhist Academy, served as dean of the revived BCM, propagated Buddhism in North America, and gathered funds to restore temples in China (Hu 2014).

3. Interview with BCM dean by Yoshiko Ashiwa and David Wank, Nanputuo Temple, January 1990; multiple interviews with BCM teachers by Yoshiko Ashiwa and David Wank, Xiamen, 1989 and 1990.

4. The Tripitaka consists of sutras (*jingzang* 經藏), said to be words spoken by the Buddha; the Vinaya (*lücang* 律藏), which were the rules of conduct and behavior for novices, clerics, and monastic life; and treatises (*luncang* 論藏), which were exegeses written by clerics on aspects of Buddhism.

5. Interview with Dingmiao by Yoshiko Ashiwa and David Wank, Nanputuo Temple, October 1990.

6. Interview with presiding monk by Yoshiko Ashiwa and David Wank, Guanghua Temple, January 1990. In 1983, the Buddhist Association of China banned the practice on the grounds that it was not part of Buddhism and impaired the health of clerics (Zhongguo fojiao xiehui 1983).

7. According to tradition, an appointment to office in the temple administration is for six months, from the fifteenth day of the first month of the lunar year to the fifteenth day of the seventh month.

8. Interview with senior guest prefect by Yoshiko Ashiwa and David Wank, Nanputuo Temple, November 1989.

9. Rules regulating the daily life of temples vary with the rules of a specific temple, indicating much about its character.

10. For a perspective on visitor management at temples at Mount Putuo see Wong, McIntosh, and Ryan (2016).

11. The pamphlet was likely a publication of Guanyin Famen 觀音法門, a meditation movement founded in the late 1980s in Taiwan by Ching Hai (Qing hai 青海), a former Buddhist nun of Vietnamese-Chinese background. The movement soon spread in the PRC where it was banned in 1995.

12. Interview with the sacristan by Yoshiko Ashiwa and David Wank, Nanputuo Temple, February 1990.

13. Interview with the precentor by Yoshiko Ashiwa and David Wank, Nanputuo Temple, February 1990.

14. Interview with the ritual specialist by Yoshiko Ashiwa and David Wank, Nanputuo Temple, March 1990.

15. For a more recent list of rituals at Nanputuo Temple see Gildow (2014).

16. On-demand rituals were expensive and mostly commissioned by wealthier business persons and overseas Chinese.

17. The terms "service" and "enterprise" were standard administrative terms in the PRC. A service unit was a government (public-sector) unit providing a service to society but has no administrative function or profit-orientation, such as a school, hospital, or

utility. An enterprise unit was an industrial or commercial enterprise attached to a state agency (Foster 2002) or a business venture loosely affiliated with one agency (Duckett 1996). The use of enterprise units for private gain was targeted by administration reforms in the 1990s.

18. The breakdown of the income was: ritual fees and donations (780,000 yuan), alms (500,000 yuan), gate receipts (100,000 yuan), and scripture sales (20,000 yuan). Interview with BAX official by Yoshiko Ashiwa and David Wank, Xiamen, February 1990.

19. The *Gazetteer of Xiamen Buddhism*, published in 2006, indicates that the figures are from 1986. But the same figures appear in the 1993 draft manuscript of the gazetteer, which suggests that they cover the period from 1986 to 1992.

20. Hu Yaobang was CPC general secretary from 1982 until forced to resign in 1987 for not dealing firmly with student protests at that time. A week after his death in April 1989, tens of thousands of students marched in Tiananmen Square to urge the CPC to restore his name.

21. For the student protests in Xiamen, see Erbaugh and Kraus (1990) and Wank (1995).

22. Interview with BAX officer by Yoshiko Ashiwa and David Wank, Xiamen, 1990.

23. Interview with senior monk by Yoshiko Ashiwa and David Wank, Nanputuo Temple, September 1989.

24. Interviews with monks by Yoshiko Ashiwa and David Wank, Xiamen, June through August 1989.

5. Expansion and Conflict in the Space of Religion, 1989–1995

1. We observed the entirety of Miaozhan's abbatial ascension ceremony, participated in its events, and discussed the ceremony with clerics, devotees, BAX officers, and others during and after the ceremony. The words spoken by Miaozhan during the ceremony come from a script given to us by a cleric involved in planning the ceremony, as well as our own recordings.

2. Interview with BAX officer by Yoshiko Ashiwa and David Wank, Xiamen, 1989.

3. The Longhua Assembly (Longhua Hui 龍華會) refers to the Maitreya Buddha's assembly under the dragon-flower tree, the site for preaching the Buddha-truth.

4. Miaozhan was referring to the lack of a middle-aged cohort of clerics between the young (green) cohort in their twenties and thirties, and the elderly (yellow) cohort in their sixties and seventies.

5. Our description of the meeting on July 18, 1990, draws on an unpublished report by the Buddhist Association of China titled "Venerable Master Miaozhan Reported to the State Council State Administration of Religious Affairs Bureau on Existing Structural Problems at Nanputuo Temple" (妙湛老法師到國務院宗教局匯報南普陀寺存在體制問題的一些情況) (Zhongguo fojiao xiehui 1990).

6. Contracting and leasing were practices instituted after 1979 that gave a private person the management and income rights for a collective enterprise or some of its operations.

5. EXPANSION AND CONFLICT, 1989–1995

7. Our account of the meeting on November 21, 1990, draws on a transcript of the discussion made by the BAX titled "Recording of the Discussion of Zhao Puchu and Others on the Temple Structure" (趙樸初等討論寺體錄音紀錄) (Xiamen fojiao xiehui 1990).

8. The policy that the XRAB deputy director referred to was "Pilot Plan for the Management of Han Buddhist Temples in China" (全國漢傳佛教寺院管理試行辦法) issued by the Buddhist Association of China in 1987.

9. This agreement was recorded in a document drafted by the XRAB in 1990 and titled "Opinion on Strengthening and Improving the Management of Nanputuo Temple" 關於加強和完善南普陀寺管理的意見.) (Xiamen shi zongjiao ju 1990).

10. Description of the detachment of the enterprise draws on a report sent by Miaozhan to Zhao Puchu at the Buddhist Association of China in 1994 describing the history of the conflict. It was titled "Strengthening the Self-Construction of Nanputuo Temple, and Safeguarding the Clerics' Independent Management of the Temple and Sovereignty" (加強南普陀寺自身建設, 維護僧人自主管理寺廟和主權) (Miaozhan 1994).

11. The account of the resistance of the monks draws on several sources: interviews with a BAX official by Yoshiko Ashiwa and David Wank in Xiamen in 1999 and 2000; and a report sent by the BAX on September 10, 1994, to Zhao Puchu describing the conflict, which was titled "Request for Further Rationalizing the Structure of Nanputuo Temple, Xiamen" (關於請求協助進一步理順廈門市南普陀寺體制的請示報告) (Xiamen fojiao xiehui 1994).

12. The summary of the July 22, 1994 meeting is contained in minutes compiled by the XRAB (Xiamen shi zongjiao ju 1994).

13. BAX report (Xiamen fojiao xiehui 1994).

14. BAX report (Xiamen fojiao xiehui 1994).

15. Our account of the clerics' uprising draws on several sources: interviews with a BAX official conducted by Yoshiko Ashiwa and David Wank in Xiamen, 1999 and 2000; and a letter dated May 25, 1995, sent by the Nanputuo monks to the Xiamen Municipal People's Government protesting the XRAB's actions, which was titled "Opinions on 'The Notice from the Xiamen Municipal People's Government on Strengthening Management Work at Nanputuo Temple'" (關於 "針對廈門市人民政府關於加強南普陀寺管理工作的通知" 的若干意見.) (Nanputuo si 1995).

16. A copy of the plan was supposedly taken by a Taiwan monk visiting Nanputuo Temple who saw it lying on an office desk. When he left China, the document was found in a search of his luggage at the airport.

17. The new system was announced in a document titled "Notice of the Xiamen Municipal People's Government on Strengthening the Management of Nanputuo Temple" (廈門市人民政府關於加強南普陀寺管理工作的通知) (Xiamen shi renmin zhengfu 1995).

18. Large character posters (*dazi bao* 大字報) expressing grievances against government officials are often hung on walls in public places to gain attention and support.

19. Nanputuo si (1995).

20. Nanputuo si (1995).

21. Buddhist charities inspired by Taixu's teachings had been established in Taiwan, Hong Kong, and overseas Chinese communities several decades earlier.

22. Interview with nun by Yoshiko Ashiwa and David Wank, Nanputuo Temple, August 1999.

23. The old revolutionary base was on the border of Jiangxi and Fujian Provinces.
24. Forty-eight grants appear to be operating funds for the free clinic run by the Nanputuo Temple Charity Foundation, while the remaining seventy-one were external grants.
25. Interview with dean of BCM nuns section by Yoshiko Ashiwa and David Wank, Zizhulin, August 2000.
26. Interview with donor by Yoshiko Ashiwa and David Wank, Singapore, July 2000.
27. Interviews with BAX officer by Yoshiko Ashiwa and David Wank, Xiamen, August and September 1999.
28. Interview with BAX officer by Yoshiko Ashiwa and David Wank, Xiamen, August 1999.
29. Interview with Monk A by Yoshiko Ashiwa and David Wank, Singapore, August 2000.
30. Interview with Monk B by Yoshiko Ashiwa and David Wank, Manila, April 2000.
31. It was relatively easy for a cleric to get a passport to leave the PRC because all Han Chinese clerics are surnamed 釋 (*shi*), the first character of the Chinese translation of Shakya (Ch. Shijia 釋迦, Skt. Śākya), the clan name of Gautama Buddha. Therefore, the government considered a cleric in the PRC to be a family member of the overseas sponsoring cleric.
32. The data regarding these three clerics comes from our interviews and conversations over the years in New York, Los Angeles, and Toronto between 2002 and 2017.
33. It was named after a temple in Tianjin City 天津市 where Tanxu resided.
34. The first Young Men's Buddhist Association was created in Sri Lanka in 1898 to give Buddhist youth an alternative to the Young Men's Christian Association.
35. In the 1970s, Ledu invited Xingkong 性空 and Chengxiang 誠祥 to North America. They settled in Toronto and founded the Cham Sham Temple.
36. The description of Miaozhan's funeral comes from interviews with clerics and BAX officers conducted by Yoshiko Ashiwa and David Wank in Xiamen in 1999, and the memorial volume for Miaozhan (*Miaozhan heshang jinian ji* 1997).

6. Aligning with the Central State, 1996–2004

1. During the 1990s many grassroots groups (*shetuan* 社團) were created spontaneously by people, such as hobby clubs, professional associations, and qigong groups, that lacked institutional recognition by the state (White et al. 1996). So they paid public enterprises and state agencies "management fees" to gain institutional status as a subsidiary unit, thereby safeguarding their existence. An example of one such group is Falun Gong (Otehode 2009). The state increasingly viewed these groups as corrupting officials and promoting societal disorder.

2. Key policies were: "Regulations Regarding the Management of Religious Activity Sites" (宗教活動場所管理條例), issued January 1994; "Provisions on the Administration of Religious Activities of Foreigners in the People's Republic of China" (中華人民共和國境內外國人宗教活動管理規定) (1994); "Registration Procedures for Religious Activity Sites"

6. ALIGNING WITH THE CENTRAL STATE, 1996-2004

(宗教活動場所登記辦法) (1994); "Method for the Annual Inspection of Religious Activity Sites" (宗教活動場所年度檢查辦法) (1996); and "Measures for Employing Foreign Professionals in Religious Schools" (宗教院校聘用外籍專業人員辦法) (1994).

3. This sacristan was the successor to the one described in chapter 4.

4. Shenghui's other positions were Buddhist Association of China executive board member, China Buddhist Academy instructor, Mount Jiuhua Buddhist Academy vice rector, abbot of Ganlu Temple 甘露寺 at Mount Jiuhua, and vice president of the Buddhist Association of Changsha 長沙, Hunan Province.

5. The views of the two abbots are based on interviews with devotees, BAX officers, and clerics by Yoshiko Ashiwa and David Wank, Xiamen, July and August 1999 and 2000.

6. Interview with nun by Yoshiko Ashiwa and David Wank, Nanputuo Temple, August 1999.

7. Interview with monk by Yoshiko Ashiwa and David Wank, Singapore, August 2000.

8. The tradition began when Taixu served concurrently as abbot of Nanputuo Temple and president of the China Buddhist Association Xiamen Branch 中國佛教會廈門分會, established in 1931 (*XFZ*, 176).

9. Interview with Miaozhan by Yoshiko Ashiwa and David Wank, Nanputuo Temple, February 1990.

10. Large ecumenical temples in wealthy regions were often controlled by monks from an adjacent poorer region (Welch 1967, 405).

11. The campaign started in 1995. The Three Priorities were "study" 講學習, "politics" 講政, and "righteousness" 講正氣. After July 1999, the Three Priorities Education merged with the anti–Falun Gong campaign because many officials participated in Falun Gong.

12. Our account of upgrading education draws on two sources: the *Buddhist College of Minnan Comprehensive Report* 閩南佛學院總結報告 issued in 1999 (Minnan foxue yuan 1999); and interviews with the BCM dean and instructors conducted by Yoshiko Ashiwa and David Wank, Nanputuo Temple, 1999 and 2000.

13. Interview with Fujian Religious Affairs Bureau official by Yoshiko Ashiwa and David Wank, Fuqing, August 1999.

14. Interview with Nanputuo Temple Charity Foundation deputy director by Yoshiko Ashiwa and David Wank, Nanputuo Temple, August 1999.

15. The first relic tour was to Burma in 1955, accompanied by monks from the PRC (Welch 1972, 181).

16. Between 1952 and 1966, thirty-six foreign Buddhist delegations visited China, and eleven Chinese delegations traveled abroad. They sought to impress foreign Buddhists with the CPC's handling of Buddhism in the PRC (Welch 1972, 185).

17. Interview with a monk who participated on the goodwill tour to Australia by Yoshiko Ashiwa and David Wank, Xiamen, August 1999.

18. Many new qigong masters paid management fees to state-sponsored qigong associations to obtain institutional recognition (Palmer 2007, 169). The boards of directors of these associations were composed of officials from more established associations, such as the All-China Federation of Trade Unions (Otehode 2009, 236). (See n. 1 above).

19. The White Lotus Society was a millenarian movement mixing folk beliefs and Buddhist teachings that emerged in the thirteenth century and led several rebellions in imperial China (see Dai 2019; Ter Haar 1992).

20. Interview with monk by Yoshiko Ashiwa and David Wank, Nanputuo Temple, July 1999.

21. Interview with devotee by Yoshiko Ashiwa and David Wank, Xiamen, July 1999.

22. Interview with devotee by Yoshiko Ashiwa and David Wank, Xiamen, July 1999.

23. Interview with devotee by Yoshiko Ashiwa and David Wank, Xiamen, July 1999.

24. Interview with devotee by Yoshiko Ashiwa and David Wank, Xiamen, July 1999.

25. Interviews with BAX officers by Yoshiko Ashiwa and David Wank, Xiamen, August 1999; interview with Fujian Religious Affairs Bureau official by Yoshiko Ashiwa and David Wank, Xiamen, August 1999.

26. For a preliminary discussion of "Buddhism as culture" both as changes to meet shifting popular demands and as a strategy of state accommodation see Ji (2011, 33–37).

7. Dynamism of Local Temples

1. The number of temples refers only to the numbers for the city on Xiamen Island, in the 2000s. There were also many more folk belief temples, mostly devoted to Mazu and Baosheng Daodi, as well as Wang Ye 王爺 (池王爺), Earth God, Zushi, Guanyin, Xuantang Shangdi 玄天上帝, Fo Zu 佛祖, and Wang Gong 王公 (also called *wangniang* 王娘). Lian (2010) estimates there were two thousand folk belief temples in all of Xiamen municipality (including districts on the mainland).

2. Miaohua was born in northern Fujian Province and went to Vietnam in 1945. Among the temples he helped build were Wanfo Temple 萬佛寺 in Ho Chi Minh City, Dizang Temple 地藏寺 in Taipei City, and Miaohui Temple 妙慧寺 in California.

3. Interview with Fayun by Yoshiko Ashiwa and David Wank, Hongshan Temple, September 1999.

4. Masters located overseas can designate clerics in China to perform the tonsure in their place. Then, the new disciple's name is written under that of the master in the generational scroll and they are considered master and disciple, even if they have not met. Their relationship is similar to that of a parent and child. Masters assume responsibility for their disciples, including financially supporting their study at the BCM. Interview with Nanputuo Temple ritual specialist by Yoshiko Ashiwa and David Wank, Nanputuo Temple, March 1990.

5. Interview with Anjing by Yoshiko Ashiwa and David Wank, Puguang Temple, July 1999.

6. Interview with Anjing by Yoshiko Ashiwa and David Wank, Puguang Temple, July 1999.

7. The Marco Polo Bridge Incident, which occurred on July 7, 1937, was a military clash between Japanese and Chinese troops that is considered the first shot of the Second Sino-Japanese War (1937–1945).

7. DYNAMISM OF LOCAL TEMPLES

8. We heard from several people that his crime was to conceal the temple's money from the occupying Nationalist soldiers. When the soldiers discovered the money, they took it and imprisoned Ruizhi for financial crimes.

9. Interview with Anjing by Yoshiko Ashiwa and David Wank, Puguang Temple, July 1999.

10. This effort by the XRAB occurred during the shifting local politics when Shenghui became abbot of Nanputuo Temple and declined to lead the BAX (see chapter 6). The XRAB used this as an opening to develop commercial partnerships with the BAX.

11. Interview with BAX officer by Yoshiko Ashiwa and David Wank, Xiamen, August 2000.

12. Interview with devotee by Yoshiko Ashiwa and David Wank, Xiamen, September 1999; interview with BAX officer by Yoshiko Ashiwa and David Wank, Xiamen, August 2000.

13. Yuanguo had resided at Chongfu Temple in Quanzhou before 1949 and served as its abbot in the 1980s, before moving to Hong Kong.

14. Interviews with Changqin by Yoshiko Ashiwa and David Wank, Bailudong Temple, August and September 1999.

15. In the early stages of temple recovery there were few clerics, and some people may have served in administrative positions without being fully ordained. Because Changqin had already been tonsured, Yuanguo likely considered that sufficient to make him prior at Chongfu.

16. Interview with BAX officer by Yoshiko Ashiwa and David Wank, Xiamen, August 1999.

17. Born Lin Yuanyang 林鴛鴦 in Anxi County 安溪縣, she left her family at age thirteen to reside in Foxin Temple 佛心寺, Tongan County. A few days before her death in 2016, she was ordained as a nun. Her memorial service was attended by many clerics and officials from the Xiamen Municipal People's Government (*Fojiao xinwen wang* 2016).

18. The website was no longer accessible as of December 2021, but some of its content is included in the temple's description in the *Gazetteer of Xiamen Buddhism* (XFZ, 58–60).

19. Multiple interviews with three BAX officers by Yoshiko Ashiwa and David Wank, Xiamen, 1999, 2000, and 2015.

20. Interview with prior by Yoshiko Ashiwa and David Wank, Xiamen, September 1999.

21. Interview with president of the Xiamen Devotee Lodge by Yoshiko Ashiwa and David Wank, Xiamen, September 2014.

22. Interviews with officers of the BAX and Xiamen Devotee Lodge by Yoshiko Ashiwa and David Wank, Xiamen, August and September 1999.

8. Devotees and Lay Nuns

1. These categories of clerics have two subgroups, male novice (Ch. *shami* 沙彌, Skt. *śrāmaṇer*) and female novice (Ch. *shamini* 沙彌尼, Skt. *śrāmaṇerī*).

8. DEVOTEES AND LAY NUNS

2. Lay nun communities also existed in Taiwan, and parts of Southeast Asia with large overseas Chinese populations of Minnan ancestry. For more detailed discussion on the lay nuns see Ashiwa and Wank (2019)

3. Some scholars writing in English refer to such a woman as "vegetarian nun" (i.e., Chang 2007), but we prefer the term "lay nun" used by Marjorie Topley (1956, 126). They are not simply vegetarians but lead a lifestyle similar to Buddhist nuns except that they neither ordain nor shave their heads. The seemingly contradictory term "lay nun" expresses their ambiguous position between female devotee and ordained nun.

4. During our conversation with Lin Ziqing in Beijing in January 1990, he mentioned that he had studied at a Buddhist college in Kyoto. We think that it was Otani University (Jp. Ōtani daigaku 大谷大学).

5. The yearbook appears to have been published by the Shanghai Fojiao Shuju 上海佛教書局 sometime after Hongyi's death in 1942. The collection of Hongyi's works was first published in 1992 by the Fujian Renmin Chubanshe 福建人民出版社.

6. The 1993 draft of the *Gazetteer of Xiamen Buddhism* defended Cai at greater length. "When speaking at the society's public activities, he only expressed positions he had advocated all along on the Buddhist thought of true belief, opposing superstition, and building a Buddhist family. He never parroted the Japanese Buddhist propaganda of 'same race, same culture, same belief' [to emphasize the unity of Asians]" (*XFZ*, 59).

7. Interview with Cai Jitang by Yoshiko Ashiwa and David Wank, Xiamen, August 1989.

8. Interview with Cai Jitang by Yoshiko Ashiwa and David Wank, Xiamen, August 1989.

9. Interview with Cai Jitang by Yoshiko Ashiwa and David Wank, Xiamen, December 1989.

10. Interview with Cai Jitang by Yoshiko Ashiwa and David Wank, Xiamen, August 1989.

11. Interviews with Zheng Mengxing by Yoshiko Ashiwa and David Wank, Xiamen, 1999 and 2000.

12. Fieldwork by Yoshiko Ashiwa and David Wank, Xiamen, July 2000.

13. Interview with Xiamen Devotee Lodge secretary by Yoshiko Ashiwa and David Wank, Xiamen, July 1999.

14. Interview with Liu Zhengsong by Yoshiko Ashiwa and David Wank, Xiamen, February 1990.

15. When we visited the temple in 1999 there were eight monks in residence, all from North China. The prior was a cleric in his twenties from Xian, the capital of Shaanxi Province, and a BCM graduate. He said that the temple had the most earnings from incense sales of any temple in Xiamen and funded a free clinic. We then learned that in the 2000s the clerics moved out because they considered the temple unsuitable for their Buddhist cultivation. When we visited again in 2015, the clerics had moved back in (see related discussion in chapter 7 on Tianzhuyan Temple).

16. Interview with Xiamen Devotee Lodge secretary by Yoshiko Ashiwa and David Wank, Xiamen, September 1999.

17. Interview with Xiamen Devotee Lodge secretary by Yoshiko Ashiwa and David Wank, Xiamen, September 1999.

8. DEVOTEES AND LAY NUNS

18. Interview with Liu Zhengsong by Yoshiko Ashiwa and David Wank, Xiamen, February 1990.

19. Reprints occurred in 1960 (香港佛教雜誌社); 1977, 1993 (新文鳳出版社); 1991, 1998, 2001, 2014 (上海佛學書局).

20. Interview with Liu Zhengsong by Yoshiko Ashiwa and David Wank, Xiamen, September 1999.

21. Interview with Liu Zhengsong by Yoshiko Ashiwa and David Wank, Xiamen, September 1999.

22. Interview with Liu Zhengsong by Yoshiko Ashiwa and David Wank, Xiamen, September 1999.

23. Interview with Liu Zhengsong by Yoshiko Ashiwa and David Wank, Xiamen, September 1999.

24. Interview with Youth Chan Society founder by Yoshiko Ashiwa and David Wank, Xiamen, August 1999.

25. Interview with Youth Chan Society founder by Yoshiko Ashiwa and David Wank, Xiamen, August 1999.

26. Interview with Xiamen Youth Buddhist Book Club founder by Yoshiko Ashiwa and David Wank, Xiamen, August 1999.

27. Interviews with former Youth Chan Society member by Yoshiko Ashiwa and David Wank, Xiamen, August 1999.

28. Interview with former Youth Chan Society member by Yoshiko Ashiwa and David Wank, Xiamen, August 1999.

29. For females there was the additional status of *shichamona* (式叉摩那, Skt. *śikuṣamānā*), a two-year transitional position for studying the dharma between the positions of female novice and ordained nun. In Chinese, it was called "dharma studying female" (*zhengxue nü* 正學女). There was no place in this classification, however, for a lay nun. A lay nun cannot be a *shichamona* because being a lay nun is for a lifetime, not just for two years.

30. During the historical process by which Buddhism was Sinicized, the original nongendered image of Guanyin transformed into a female-like Guanyin, creating kinship between Guanyin and local deities that fused with local legends and myths (Yü 2001). This process created the legend of a woman named Miaoshan 妙善, the etymological story of Thousand-Handed and Thousand-Eyed Guanyin, that told of a strong, independent, and celibate woman who blinds herself and cuts off her hands to help others. The story has been told and retold in Chinese opera, novels, and paintings, enabling it to continually circulate among the people. It merges with the figure of the Thousand-Handed and Thousand-Eyed Guanyin, each hand having an eye to see people in trouble and help them if they call her. The well-known legend of Miaoshan, who transformed into Guanyin, hints to people that the lay nuns they see in everyday life are the mercy of Guanyin. This has given strong popular recognition and power to the lay nun tradition (Ashiwa and Wank 2019).

31. Interview with BAX secretary by Yoshiko Ashiwa and David Wank, Xiamen City, September 2014.

32. Interview with BAX officer by Yoshiko Ashiwa and David Wank, Xiamen, August 1999.

33. Interviews with lay nuns by Yoshiko Ashiwa and David Wank, Jinglian Temple, September 1999.

34. Interview with BAX secretary by Yoshiko Ashiwa and David Wank, Xiamen, September 2014.

35. Miaoqing Temple stele erected in 1987.

36. Interview with lay nuns by Yoshiko Ashiwa and David Wank, Miaoqing Temple, August 1999.

37. Interviews with lay nuns by Yoshiko Ashiwa and David Wank, Xiamen, 1999, 2000, and 2015.

38. Interview with Hubing by Yoshiko Ashiwa and David Wank, Miaofalin, September 1999.

39. Interview with Xinliang by Yoshiko Ashiwa and David Wank, Qingfu Temple, September 1999.

40. Interview with BAX secretary by Yoshiko Ashiwa and David Wank, Xiamen, September 2014.

41. Interview with Hubing by Yoshiko Ashiwa and David Wank, Miaofalin, September 1999.

42. The Ta Teh Institute was a full-time arts college established in Hong Kong by the Guangdong CPC branch that operated from 1946 to 1949. Its teaching staff of well-known artists and scholars taught an estimated 800 students who served as CPC cadres (Hung 2016).

43. Guang'an was born in Quanzhou, became a monk at age thirteen, and lived at Kaiyuan Temple, before emigrating to Singapore after the Cultural Revolution (*NSZ*, 194–196). Lay Nun A's lay nun master was also from Quanzhou and close to Guang'an.

44. Guang'an's lay disciples were connected with Singapore's Longshan Temple and Manila's Xinyuan Temple. These two temples had been founded by, respectively, Guangyi 廣義 (1914–1995) and Xingyuan, who paid much attention to the lay nuns and helped establish the Juehua Women's Buddhist Academy in 1948 to teach them literacy and Buddhist teachings (*XFZ*, 223).

45. Interviews with lay nuns by Yoshiko Ashiwa and David Wank, Ciguang Temple, August 1999.

9. The Guanyin Festival: Being Buddhist the Chinese Way

1. Our survey sought to understand who the attendees were, their reasons for coming to the festival, and their activities inside the temple. It was conducted with the research assistance of Xiamen University students in the anthropology and journalism departments. The assistants were organized into two-person teams. Some teams focused on observations. They waited outside the temple to select a person or group to follow into the temple and observe their worship activities. Their task was to document people's routes, noting where they stopped to worship and what they did in each place, and then, at the end, approach them for an interview. Other teams focused only on interviewing. They mingled with diverse persons lounging in the temple's front yard by the

9. THE GUANYIN FESTIVAL

Lotus Pond, engaging them in conversations about their backgrounds, impressions of Nanputuo Temple, and so on. At the start of an interview, all teams introduced themselves to interviewees as students of Xiamen University conducting research on culture in Xiamen. Interviews were a sequence of open-ended questions and typically lasted from three to ten minutes. After each interview, researchers wrote down verbatim as much of the conversation as they could recall. Shifts of teams maintained the research for the entire cycle of the festival starting on its eve and continuing throughout the festival day until the evening.

2. Two groups of monks worked in four shifts to ensure public safety, support the activities of worshipers, and protect temple property. Their shifts times were: Group A, 6:30 p.m.–12:30 a.m.; Group B, 12:00 a.m.–6:40 a.m.; Group A, 6:20 a.m.–12:00 p.m.; Group B, 11:30 a.m.–6:20 p.m.

3. In his study of lay Buddhists, Welch (1967, 357) notes that the question "Are you a Buddhist?" is not a useful way to understand who is a "lay Buddhist." It would likely generate a negative response because of the strong connotations of the term "Buddhist." But Welch's purpose was to identify those with a strong commitment to Buddhism—devotees—whereas ours was to understand the varying commitments of the mass body of attendees at the Guanyin festival. Therefore, we found the question "Are you a Buddhist?" to be a useful opening question for people to talk about their beliefs and practices, and reasons for attending the Guanyin festival.

4. The distribution of responses is consistent with other findings that the number of people identifying with Buddhism or who practice Buddhism is far greater than those taking devotee precepts. For example, the *Spiritual Life Study of Chinese Residents* conducted in 2007 shows that 18 percent of the population identified as a Buddhist, but only 2 percent had "formally converted" (Leamaster and Hu 2014, 237, ftn. 3).

5. In the 1989 survey we interviewed forty-one persons, using the same questions as in the 1999 survey.

6. Interview with BAX officer by Yoshiko Ashiwa and David Wank, Xiamen, September 1989.

7. Interview with BAX officer by Yoshiko Ashiwa and David Wank, Xiamen, August 1999.

8. Four interviewees asked if our questions were related to Falun Gong. Of these, three interviewees seemingly asked from curiosity. One interviewee was an eighteen-year-old high school student who had come with her classmates. She said she was a believer, but then asked if we were investigating Falun Gong. In another case, as we were interviewing a company employee in his thirties from Xiamen, one of his friends asked if our survey was related to Falun Gong. In both cases, we explained that our research was not related, and the interviews proceeded. A third interviewee was a woman from Anhui Province visiting her son in Xiamen. She stopped the interview by asking, "Are you investigating religion because of the Falun Gong affair?" A fourth interviewee, a local state official in his thirties, was initially happy to explain that he was not Buddhist but regularly worshiped at Nanputuo Temple. Then, he asked if our questions were related to Falun Gong and became more guarded in talking to us. Additionally, three people who declined to be interviewed may have been concerned about Falun Gong. One instance involved a couple in their twenties with a young child. When we

asked the husband if they planned to burn incense at the temple, he said warily, "I don't want to talk about this. Go ask the people over there." Similarly, a woman with a young child said, "I'm sorry. Please find somebody else."

Appendix 1. Leaders of Nanputuo Temple, 1684–

1. The term of an abbot at Nanputuo Temple was for three years. An abbot can serve multiple terms.
2. An acting abbot (*daili fangzhang* 代理方丈) is a cleric who serves out the term of an elected abbot unable to continue in office.
3. Miaozhan's abbatial ascension ceremony occurred in 1989, but many Buddhists considered him the leader of Nanputuo Temple from 1957, when the previous abbot died, until Miaozhan's death in 1995. In the *Gazetteer of Xiamen Buddhism*, he is listed as the eighth-term abbot.

Appendix 4. Ordination Ceremony Schedule, October 13–29, 1989, Guanghua Temple

1. Everyone goes to the Great Buddha Hall to worship the Buddha.
2. Ordinands are taught dining etiquette for clerics, including the placement of rice and food bowls, holding chopsticks, sitting with one foot in front and one in back, eating silently, signaling for more food, and waiting until all have finished eating before leaving the dining hall.
3. Ordinands are led around the temple perimeter to see the physical boundaries of the ceremony. They chant at each place where ceremony activities will occur, eat in the dining hall, and chant in the Great Buddha Hall. After this, they cannot leave the temple until the ceremony ends.
4. Ordinands are taught the proper way for a cleric to walk, stand, and sit; examples are not crossing legs when sitting, not running in clerical robes, and sleeping on the right side. They are also taught how to answer questions they will be asked at the ordination ceremony.
5. The ordination instructor and confessor are invited to the ceremony.
6. Ordinands are taught answers to the questions posed by the three masters and seven witnesses, including, "Do your parents approve of your renunciation of lay life?"
7. The three masters and seven witnesses go to the dormitories to see if ordinands have sufficient blankets and quilts.
8. Ordinands go to Merit Hall to worship the temple's ancestral monks and the dormitory to roust any lazy ordinands who may be resting there.

REFERENCES

Primary Sources

Benxing 本性. 2000. "Fujian fojiao gaikuang" 福建佛教概況 [Overview of Buddhism in Fujian], *Fayin* 法音 185, no. 1: 6–9.

Chen Xingqiao 陳星橋. 2002. "Zhongguo fan xiejiao xiehui diwuci baogao hui ji xueshu taolunhui zai Xiamen Nanputuo si longzhong juxing" 中國反邪教協會第五次報告會暨學術討論會在廈門南普陀寺隆重舉行 [The fifth report meeting and academic symposium of the China Anti-Cult Association held at Nanputuo Temple]. *Fayin* 法音 5, no. 13: 46.

China Post. 2002 (March 4). "Jubilant Celebrations as Buddha Finger Relic Reaches Kaohsiung." No longer accessible online, www.chinapost.com.tw/news/2002/03/04/23841/Jubilant-celebrations.htm.

Cishan 慈善 [Charity]. 1995a. "Cishan yulu pushi youmiao" 慈善雨露普施幼苗 [Charitable rain and dew promotes seedlings]. 27.

———. 1995b. "Zhenzai shi women de benfenshi" 震災是我們的本份事 [Responding to earthquake disasters is our duty]. 19.

———. 1998. "Xiamen Nanputuo si cishan shiye jijin hui zhangcheng" 廈門南普陀寺慈善事業基金會章程 [Xiamen Nanputuo Temple Charity Foundation Charter]. No. 4, 7.

———. 2000. "Gongde fangming" 功德芳名 [Merit donors] and "Ku wei shi" 庫為事 [Foundation activities]. No. 2: 3.

Fojiao shuji wang 佛教書籍網. n.d. "Lin Ziqing jushi" 林子青居士 [Devotee Lin Ziqing]. Accessed December 15, 2021, http://wap.fjzjg.com/wapbook-2847-17123/.

Fojiao xinwen wang 佛教新聞網. 2016 (March 8). "Xiamen Wanshilian si jüxing Kaiyin nishi zhuisi tupi fahui" 廈門萬石蓮寺舉行開因尼師追思荼毗法會 [Dharma memorial service for the cremation of Nun Kaiyin at Wanshilian Temple, Xiamen]. www.china777.org/html/fwzt/2016030811853.html.

REFERENCES

Guojia zongjiao shiwu ju 國家宗教事務局 [State Administration of Religious Affairs]. 1980. *Guanyu luoshi zongjiao tuanti fangchan zhengce wenti de baogao* 關於落實宗教團體房產政策問題的報告 [Report on implementing policy for real estate of religious groups]. Putuoshan 普陀山. Accessed February 11, 2022, https://www.putuo.org.cn/article/zcfg/4657.shtml.

Guowuyuan 國務院 [State Council]. 1983. "Guowuyuan pizhuan guowuyuan zongjiao shiwu ju guanyu queding Hanzu diqu fu daojiao quanguo zhongdian siguan de baogao de tongzhi" 國務院批轉國務院宗教事務局關於確定漢族地區佛道教全國重點寺觀的報告的通知 [State council circular approving and transmitting the report of the state administration of religious affairs bureau on confirming the national key temples and views of Buddhism and Daoism in Han ethnic areas]. Baidu 百度. Accessed February 11, 2022, https://x.gd/tRE8f.

———. 1998. "Shehui tuanti dengji guanli tiaoli" 社會團體登記管理條例 [Regulations on administration and registration of social organizations]. No longer accessible online, http://mjzx.mca.gov.cn/article/zcfg/201304/20130400437175.html.

Hongchuan fashi jinian tekan 宏船法師紀念特刊 [Master Hongchuan memorial issue]. 1993. Singapore: Kong Meng San Phor Kark See Temple.

Hongyi 弘一. 2010 [1933]. "Fanxing qingxin nü jiangxi hui yuanqi" 梵行清信女講習會緣起 [Opening remarks for lectures to ascetic and pious women]. In *Hongyi dashi quanji* 弘一大師全集. Ed. Lin Ziqing 林子清. Vol. 7, 626. Fuzhou: Fujian renmin chuban she.

Hu Ranyue 胡冉月. 2014 (December 8). "Mengcan zhanglao: ruyu sanshisan nian 'zuomeng' zhu wo sheqi jueming niantou" 夢參長老: 入獄三十三年 "做夢" 助我捨棄絕命念頭 [Elder Mencan: 'dreaming' gave me the strength to let go of thoughts of utter hopelessness during my thirty-three years of imprisonment]. *Dagong wang* 大公. Accessed January 30, 2022, http://bodhi.takungpao.com/sspt/sramana/2014-12/2851666.html.

Huiran 慧然 et al. 1998. "Xiamen Nanputuo si—dianshi zhuanti pian jieshuoci" 南普陀寺-電視專題片解說詞 [Nanputuo Temple—commentary on television feature film]. Nanputuo si. Accessed January 30, 2022, http://1999.fosss.org:82/202.102.14.2/xiyuan/jcls/gscq/npts.htm.

Jiang Zemin 江澤民. 1993 (November 7). "Gaodu zhongshi minzu gongzuo he zongjiao gongzuo" 高度重視民族工作和宗教工作 [Attach great importance to ethnic work and religious work]. Zhongguo gaige xinxi ku 中國改革信息庫. Accessed January 30, 2022, http://www.reformdata.org/1993/1107/4263.shtml.

"Jinglian tang" 淨蓮堂 [Jinglian hall]. 2018. Xiamen shi Siming qu renmin zhengfu 廈門市思明區人民政府. No longer accessible online, www.siming.gov.cn.

Jiqun 濟群. 2000. "Fujian conglin shenghuo mantan: yi wo zai Fujian chujia shenghuo wei xiansuo" 福建叢林生活漫談—以我在福建出家生活為線索 [Discussing Fujian's *conglin* life: using my life in Fujian as a monk for insight]. *Fayin* 法音 185, no. 1: 36–43.

Li Zhanhua. 李湛華. 1995. "Taiguo renmin longzhong yingqing Zhongguo fo zhi sheli" 泰國人民隆重迎請中國佛指舍利 [Thai people give grand welcome to Chinese Buddha finger relic]. *Fayin* 法音 125, no. 1: 34.

Lingguang si 靈光寺 [Lingguang Temple]. n.d. "Foya sheli fu Xianggang tebie xingzheng qu xunli gongfeng" 佛牙舍利赴香港特別行政區巡禮供奉—1999年5月20日至5月29日 [Buddha tooth relic went to Hong Kong Special Administration Region for veneration from May 20 to May 29, 1999]. Accessed February 16, 2017, www.lingguangsi.com/index.php/Article/view/id/252.

Lingyin Temple. n.d. "Master Juzan." Accessed August 8, 2019, http://en.lingyinsi.org/list_337.html.

Miaozhan 妙湛. 1989a. "Seng jiaoyu de xin gousi" 僧教育的新構思 (New ideas for education). *Minnan foxue yuan xuebao* 閩南佛學院學報 2: 1–3.

———. 1989b (October 1). "Guanyu Xiamen Nanputuo si huifu shifang conglin zhidu de yijian" 關於廈門南普陀寺恢復十方叢林制度的意見 [Opinion on restoring the *shifang conglin* temple structure at Nanputuo Temple, Xiamen]. Report sent by Miaozhan to Zhao Puchu. Unpublished, in the authors' possession.

———. 1994. "Jiaqiang Nanputuo si zishen jianshe, weihu sengren zizhu guanli simiao he zhuquan" 加強南普陀寺自身建設, 維護僧人自主管理寺廟和主權 [Strengthening the self-construction of Nanputuo Temple, and safeguarding the clerics' independent management of the temple and sovereignty]. Report sent by Miaozhan to Zhao Puchu. Unpublished, in the authors' possession.

———. 1995. "Kuayue shiji de chuandeng shiye" 跨越世紀的傳燈事業 [A century of transmitting the light]. *Fayin* 法音 130, no. 6: 20–22.

Miaozhan heshang jinian ji 妙湛和尚紀念集 [Master Miaozhan memorial volume]. 1997. Xiamen: Xiamen chuangxian caiyin zhiba youxian gongsi.

Minnan foxue yuan 閩南佛學院 [BCM]. 1999. *Minnan foxue yuan zongjie baogao* 閩南佛學院總結報告 [Buddhist College of Minnan comprehensive report]. Xiamen: Nanputuo si.

Nanputuo si 南普陀寺 [Nanputuo Temple]. 1995. "Guanyu zhendui 'Xiamen shi renmin zhengfu guanyu jiaqiang Nanputuo si guanli gongzuo de tongzhi' de ruogan yijian" 關於針對"廈門市人民政府關於加強南普陀寺管理工作的通知"的若干意見 [Several opinions on the "notice from the Xiamen Municipal People's Government on strengthening management work at Nanputuo Temple"]. Letter by the clerics of Nanputuo Temple to the Xiamen Municipal People's Government on May 25. Unpublished, in the authors' possession.

———. 1999. "Zhongguo fojiao zhongzhen: Nanputuo si" 中國佛教重鎮—南普陀寺 [An important center of Chinese Buddhism: Nanputuo Temple]. Public announcement in Nanputuo Temple (June 4).

———. n.d. "The Founding of the Buddhist Spiritual Nurturing School." Accessed January 31, 2022, https://en.nanputuo.com/colleage/Introducedetails.aspx?channel_id=73.

Nanputuo si guizhang zhidu 南普陀寺規章制度 [Nanputuo Temple rules and regulations]. 1996. Xiamen: Nanputuo si.

Nanputuo si zhi 南普陀寺誌 [Gazetteer of Nanputuo Temple]. 2011. 2 vols. Shanghai: Shanghai cishu chubanshe.

National Bureau of Statistics of China. n.d. Accessed August 15, 2017, no longer available online, http://data.stats.gov.cn/english.

People's Republic of China. 1954. *The Constitution of the People's Republic of China*. Beida fabao 北大法寶. Accessed February 1, 2022, http://en.pkulaw.cn/display.aspx?cgid=52993&lib=law.

———. 1975. *The Constitution of the People's Republic of China*. Accessed January 10, 2022, https://china.usc.edu/sites/default/files/article/attachments/peoples-republic-of-china-constitution-1975.pdf.

REFERENCES

People's Republic of China. 1978. *The Constitution of the People's Republic of China.* Accessed January 10, 2022, https://china.usc.edu/sites/default/files/article/attachments/peoples-republic-of-china-constitution-1978.pdf.

———. 1982. *The Constitution of the People's Republic of China.* Accessed January 10, 2022, https://china.usc.edu/constitution-peoples-republic-china-1982#chap3.

Qiannian gusha Nanputuo 千年古剎南普陀 [A thousand years of ancient Nanputuo]. 2013. Beijing. Zhongguo wenhua chubanshe.

Qiming 啟明. 1995. "Zhong Tai liang guo fojiao jie de kuanggu shengshi" 中泰兩國佛教界的曠古盛事 [An ancient event in Buddhist circles of China and Thailand] 中泰兩國佛教界的曠古盛事. *Fayin* 法音 127, no. 3: 1–2.

Shenghui 聖輝. 2001a. "Zhongguo fojiao daibiao tuan jitiao fayan" 中國佛教代表團基調發言 [Keynote speech by the Chinese Buddhist delegation]. *Fayin* 法音 207, no. 11: 2.

———. 2001b. "Poxie yangshan re'ai heping weihu renquan—zai Rineiwa lianheguo renquan weiyuanhui di 57 jie huiyi shang de fayan" 破邪揚善, 熱愛和平維護人權—在日內瓦聯合國人權委員會第57屆會議上的發言 [Smashing evil and promoting good, loving peace and protecting human rights—speech at the 57th session of the United Nations Commission on Human Rights in Geneva]. *Fayin* 法音201, no. 5: 1.

———. 2001c. "Chu e fan xie qu wei kuangzheng" 除惡反邪去偽匡正 [Eliminate evil and counter evil to rectify falsehoods]. *Fayin* 法音 1999, no. 3: 2.

Sina. 2004. "Shandong Zhanshan foxue yuan chengli" 山東湛山佛學院成立 [Establishment of the Shandong Zhanshan Buddhist Academy]. Accessed January 30, 2022, http://news.sina.com.cn/o/2004-10-24/11054020136s.shtml.

Taiwan haixia shibao 台灣海峽時報 [Taiwan strait news]. 2002 (February 23). "Xiamen Nanputuo si fangzhang Shenghui daheshang tan fo zhi sheli fu Tai" 廈門南普陀寺方丈聖輝大和尚談佛指舍利赴台 [Xiamen Nanputuo Temple abbot master Sheng Hui talked about the Buddha's finger relic going to Taiwan].

Union of Soviet Socialist Republics. 1936. *Constitution (Fundamental Law) of the Union of Soviet Socialist Republics.* Accessed February 6, 2022, www.marxists.org/reference/archive/stalin/works/1936/12/05.htm.

Wu Shaoren 吳昭仁. 2014. *Tianchang dijiu: hiuyilü* 天長地久: 回憶錄 [As enduring as heaven and earth: a memoir]. 10 vols. Privately published and distributed.

Xiamen fojiao xiehui 廈門佛教協會 [Buddhist association of Xiamen]. 1990. "Zhao Puchu deng taolun si ti luyin ji" 趙樸初等討論寺體錄音紀錄 [Recording of the discussion of Zhao Puchu and others on the temple structure]. Transcript of audio recording of a meeting on July 18 at Nanputuo Temple. Unpublished, in the authors' possession.

———. 1994. "Guanyu qingqiu xiezhu jinyibu lishun Xiamen shi Nanputuo si tizhi de qingshi baogao" 關於請求協助進一步理順廈門市南普陀寺體制的請示報告 [Request on instructions to further rationalize the system of Nanputuo Temple, Xiamen]. Document dated September 10. Unpublished, in the authors' possession.

Xiamen fojiao zhi 廈門佛教誌 [Gazetteer of Xiamen Buddhism]. 1993. First draft of "*Xiamen fojiao zhi.*" Unpublished, in the authors' possession.

———. 2006. Xiamen: Xiamen daxue chubanshe.

Xiamen Nanputuo si 廈門南普陀寺 [Xiamen Nanputuo Temple]. 1995. Xiamen: Minnan ren chubanshe.

Xiamen ribao 廈門日報 [Xiamen evening news]. 1999 (July 23). "Zhonghua renmin gongheguo minzheng bu guanyu qudi falun dafa yanjiuhui de jueding" 中華人民共和國民政部關於取締法輪大法研究會的決定 [Decision of the Ministry of Civil Affairs of the People's Republic of China on banning the Falun Dafa Research Association], 1.

Xiamen shi renmin zhengfu 廈門市人民政府 [Xiamen Municipal People's Government]. 1995. "Xiamen shi renmin zhengfu guanyu jiaqiang Nanputuo si guanli gongzuo de tongzhi" 廈門市人民政府關於加強南普陀寺管理工作的通知 [Notice of the Xiamen Municipal People's Government on strengthening the management of Nanputuo Temple]. Unpublished report, in the authors' possession.

Xiamen shi zongjiao ju 廈門市宗教局 [Xiamen Municipal Religious Affairs Bureau]. 1990. "Guanyu jiaqiang he wanshan Nanputuo si guanli de yijian" 關於加強和完善南普陀寺管理的意見 [Opinion on strengthening and improving the management of Nanputuo Temple]. Unpublished, in the authors' possession.

———. 1994 (July 2). "Minutes of religious affairs bureau meeting with Nanputuo abbot Miaozhan." Unpublished, in the authors' possession.

Xiamen wanbao 廈門晚報 [Xiamen evening news]. 1999 (July 23). "Li Hongzhi qi ren qi shi" 李洪志其人其事 [The person and deeds of Li Hongzhi].

Xiao Xianfa 肖賢法. 1980. "Zai Zhongguo fojiao xiehui di si ci quanguo daibiao huiyi shang de jianghua (gaiyao)" 在中國佛教協會第四次全國代表會議上的講話(概要) [Speech at Buddhist Association of China fourth national congress (abstract)]. Zhongguo fojiao xiehui. Accessed January 22, 2022, https://www.chinabuddhism.com.cn/60zn/lcfdh/4/2013-06-20/3041.html.

Zhao Puchu 趙樸初. 1995 (June 16). "Letter to the Fujian Province Religious Affairs Bureau." Unpublished, in the authors' possession.

Zheng Lixin 鄭立新. 2002. "Shenqie huainian lin ziqing xiansheng" 深切懷念林子青先生 [Heartfelt remembrances of Mr. Lin Ziqing]. *Fayin* 法音 2002, no. 11: 34–36.

Zhonggong zhongyang 中共中央 [CPC Central Committee]. 1991. "Zhonggong zhongyang guowuyuan guanyu jinyibu zuo hao zongjiao gongzuo ruogan wenti de tongzhi" 中共中央國務院關於進一步做好宗教工作若干問題的通知 [Circular of the CPC Central Committee and the State Council on several issues in regard to further improvement of religious work]. Accessed February 10, 2023, https://x.gd/4Dnoc.

Zhongguo fojiao xiehui 中國佛教協會 [Buddhist Association of China]. 1983. "Guanyu Han chuan fojiao simiao tidu chuanjie wenti de jueyi" 關於漢傳佛教寺廟剃度傳戒問題的決議 [Resolution on issues regarding ordinations in Han Buddhist temples].

———. 1990. "Miaozhan lao fashi dao guowuyuan zongjiao ju huibao Nanputuo si cunzai tizhi wenti de yixie qingkuang" 妙湛老法師到國務院宗教局匯報南普陀寺存在體制問題的一些情況 [Venerable Master Miaozhan reported to the State Administration of Religious Affairs on existing structural problems at Nanputuo Temple]. Unpublished, in authors' posession.

Zhonghua renmin gongheguo 中華人民共和國 [People's Republic of China]. 1994 (November 6). "Zhongguo renmin gongheguo zhengfu he tai wangguo zhengfu guanyu Zhongguo fo zhi sheli fu Taiguo gongfeng de xieyi" 中華人民共和國政府和泰王國政府關於中國佛指舍利赴泰國供奉的協議 [Agreement between the People's Republic of China and the Royal Thai Government concerning the Chinese Buddhist finger relic to be worshiped in Thailand]. Accessed March 3, 2016, www.law-lib.com/lawhtm/1994/77621.htm.

Secondary Sources

Asad, Talal. 2003. *Formations of the Secular: Christianity, Islam, Modernity*. Stanford, CA: Stanford University Press.

Ashiwa, Yoshiko 足羽與志子. 1991. "Buddhist Revival and Economic Reform in Post-Mao China: A Field Report from Xiamen City." *Kōbe yamate joshi tanki daigaku kiyō* 神戸山手女子短期大学紀要 33: 1-23.

———. 2000. "Chūgoku nanbu ni okeru bukkyō fukkō no dōtai: kokka-shakai-toransunashonarizumu" 中国南部における仏教復興の動態—国家・社会・トランスナショナリズム [Dynamics of the Buddhist revival in southern China: state, society, transnationalism]. In *Gendai chūgoku no kōzō hendō: shakai-kokka to no kyōsei kankei* (5) 現代中国の構造変動:社会−国家との共棲関係 (5). Ed. Hishida Masaharu 菱田雅治, 239-274. Tokyo: Tokyo daigaku shuppan-kai.

———. 2001. "Chūgoku no darumapāra: ajia no kindai to bukkyō fukkō" 中国のダルマパラ—アジアの近代と仏教復興 [Dharmapala in China: Modern Buddhist reconstruction in Asia]. *Ajia Yūgaku* アジア遊学, 24: 101-112.

———. 2009. "Positioning Religion in Modernity: State and Buddhism in China." In *Making Religion, Making the State: The Politics of Religion in Modern China*. Ed. Yoshiko Ashiwa and David L. Wank, 43-73. Stanford, CA: Stanford University Press.

Ashiwa, Yoshiko, and David L. Wank. 2005. "The Globalization of Chinese Buddhism: Clergy and Devotee Networks in the Twentieth Century." *International Journal of Asian Studies* 2, no. 2: 217-237.

———. 2006. "The Politics of a Reviving Buddhist Temple: State, Association, and Temple in Southeast China." *Journal of Asian Studies* 65, no. 2: 337-359.

———. 2009a. "Making Religion, Making the State: An Introductory Essay." In *Making Religion, Making the State: The Politics of Religion in Modern China*. Ed. Yoshiko Ashiwa and David L. Wank, 1-21. Stanford, CA: Stanford University Press.

———. eds. 2009b. *Making of Religion in Modern China*. Stanford, CA: Stanford University Press.

———. 2016. "Xiandai zhongguo fojiao de kuaguo sengsu wangluo: kuayue minzu guojia de hezuo moshi yu ziyuan liutong" 現代中國佛教的跨國僧俗網路: 跨越民族國家的合作模式與資源流通 [Transnational networks of clergy and laity in modern Chinese Buddhism: cooperation and resource circulation across borders]. In *Ershi shiji Zhongguo fojiao de liangci fuxing* 二十世紀中國佛教的兩次復興 [The two revivals of Buddhism in twentieth-century China]. Ed. Tian Shuijing 田水晶, Ji Zhe 汲喆, and Wang Qiyuan 王啟元, 109-132. Shanghai: Fudan daxue chubanshe.

———. 2019. "A Study of Laynuns in Minnan, 1920s-2010s: Buddhism, State Institutions, and Popular Culture." In *Buddhism After Mao: Negotiations, Continuities, and Reinventions*. Ed. Ji Zhe, Gareth Fisher, and André Laliberté, 210-248. Honolulu: University of Hawai'i Press.

Bao, Jiemin. 2015. *Creating a Buddhist Community: A Thai Temple in Silicon Valley*. Philadelphia: Temple University Press.
Baroni, Helen J. 2000. *Obaku Zen: The Emergence of the Third Sect of Zen in Tokugawa Japan*. Honolulu: University of Hawai'i Press.
Barstow, Geoffrey. 2017. *Food of Sinful Demons: Meat, Vegetarianism, and the Limits of Buddhism in Tibet*. New York: Columbia University Press.
Belting, Hans. 2011. *An Anthropology of Images: Picture, Medium, Body*. Princeton, NJ: Princeton University Press.
Berstein, Anya. 2013. *Religious Bodies Politic: Rituals of Sovereignty in Buryat Buddhism*. Chicago: University of Chicago Press.
Bianchi, Ester. 2001. *The Iron Statue Monastery: "Tiexiangsi," a Buddhist Nunnery of the Tibetan Tradition in Contemporary China* [in Italian]. Florence: Olschki.
Bingenheimer, Marcus. 2018. "Who Was 'Central' for Chinese Buddhist History? A Social Network Approach." *International Journal of Buddhist Thought and Culture* 28, no. 2: 45–67.
Blackburn, Anne M. 2010. *Locations of Buddhism: Colonialism and Modernity in Sri Lanka*. Chicago: University of Chicago Press.
Bond, George. 1988. *The Buddhist Revival in Sri Lanka: Religious Tradition, Reinterpretation, and Response*. Columbia: University of South Carolina Press.
Borchert, Thomas, A. 2017. *Educating Monks: Minority Buddhism on China's Southwest Border*. Honolulu: University of Hawai'i Press.
Brook, Timothy. 1994. *Praying for Power: Buddhism and the Formation of Gentry Society in Late-Ming China*. Cambridge, MA: Harvard University Press.
Bruntz, Courtney. 2014. "Commodifying Mount Putuo: State Nationalism, Religious Tourism, and Buddhist Revival." PhD dissertation, Graduate Theological Union.
Buffetrille, Katia. 2012. *Revisiting Rituals in a Changing Tibetan World*. Leiden: Brill Publishers.
Buswell, Robert, E., Jr. 1992. *The Zen Monastic Experience: Buddhist Practice in Contemporary Korea*. Princeton, NJ: Princeton University Press.
Buswell, Robert E., Jr., and Donald S. Lopez Jr. 2013. *The Princeton Dictionary of Buddhism*. Princeton, NJ: Princeton University Press.
Campo, Daniela. 2019. "Bridging the Gap: Chan and Tiantai Dharma Lineages from Republican to Post-Mao China." In *Buddhism After Mao: Chinese Modes of Religious Production*. Ed. Ji Zhe, André Laliberté, and Gareth Fisher, 123–151. Honolulu: University of Hawai'i Press.
Cao, Nanlai. 2010. *Constructing China's Jerusalem: Christians, Power, and Place in Contemporary Wenzhou*. Stanford, CA: Stanford University Press.
———. 2018. "The Rise of Field Studies in Religious Research in the People's Republic of China." *China Review* 18, no. 1: 137–164.
Carter, James. 2010. *Heart of Buddha, Heart of China: The Life of Tanxu, a Twentieth-Century Monk*. Oxford: Oxford University Press.
Chambon, Michael. 2017. "The Action of Christian Buildings on their Chinese Environment." *Studies in World Christianity* 23, no. 2: 100–121.
———. 2020. *Making Christ Present in China: Actor-Network Theory and the Anthropology of Christianity*. Cham, Switzerland: Palgrave-Macmillan.

Chandler, Stuart. 2004. *Establishing a Pure Land on Earth: The Foguang Buddhist Perspective on Modernization and Globalization*. Honolulu: University of Hawai'i Press.

Chang, Chi-p'eng. 1983. "The CCP's Policy Toward Religion." *Issues & Studies* 19, no. 5: 55–70.

Chang, Chia-lan. 2007. "The Modern Legend of Miaoshan: The Development of the Sangha of Vegetarian Nuns in China." In *The Constant and Changing Faces of the Goddess: Goddess Traditions of Asia*. Ed. Deepak Shimkhada and Phyllis K. Herman, 246–272. Newcastle upon Tyne: Cambridge Scholars Publishing.

Chau, Adam Yuet. 2008. *Miraculous Response: Doing Popular Religion in Contemporary China*. Stanford, CA: Stanford University Press.

Chen, Albert H. Y. 2017. "Constitutions, Constitutionalism and the Case of Modern China." University of Hong Kong Faculty of Law Research Paper 2017/023. https://ssrn.com/abstract=3027562.

Chia, Jack Meng-Tat. 2008. "Buddhism in Singapore-China Relations: Venerable Hongchuan and His Visits 1982–1990." *The China Quarterly* 196: 864–883.

———. 2020. *Monks in Motion: Buddhism and Modernity Across the South China Sea*. New York: Oxford University Press.

Chidester, David. 2016. "Space." In *The Oxford Handbook of the Study of Religion*. Ed. Michael Stausberg and Steven Engler, 329–340. Oxford: Oxford University Press.

Chinese Academy of Social Sciences. 2010. *Blue Book on Religion*. Beijing: Chinese Academy of Social Sciences.

Chiu, Hungdah. 1993. "Constitutional Development and Reform in the Republic of China on Taiwan." Occasional Papers/Reprints Series in Contemporary Asian Studies 2, no. 115. http://digitalcommons.law.umaryland.edu/cgi/viewcontent.cgi?article=1114&context=mscas.

Clark, Hugh R. 2002. *Community, Trade, and Networks: Southern Fujian Province from the Third to the Thirteenth Century*. Cambridge: Cambridge University Press.

Cohen, Jerome Alan. 1979. "China's Changing Constitution." *Northwestern Journal of International Law and Business* 1, no. 1: 57–121.

Cooper, Eugene, with Jiang Yinhuo. 1998. *The Artisans and Entrepreneurs of Dongyang County: Economic Reform and Flexible Production in China*. Armonk, NY: M. E. Sharpe.

Cooper, Gene. 2013. *The Market and Temple Fairs of Rural China: Red Fire*. Abingdon: Routledge.

Coppel, Charles A. 2002. *Studying Ethnic Chinese in Indonesia*. Singapore: Singapore Society of Asian Studies.

Dai, Yingcong. 2019. *The White Lotus War: Rebellion and Suppression in Late Imperial China*. Seattle: University of Washington Press.

Day, Matthew. 2009. "Constructing Religion without the Social: Durkheim, Latour, and Extended Cognition." *Zygon: Journal of Religion and Science* 44, no. 3: 719–737.

Dean, Kenneth. 1995. *Taoist Ritual and Popular Cults of Southeast China*. Princeton, NJ: Princeton University Press.

———. 1998. *Lord of the Three in One: The Spread of a Cult in Southeast China*. Princeton, NJ: Princeton University Press.

DeVido, Elise A. 2015. "Networks and Bridges: Nuns in the Making of Modern Chinese Buddhism." *The Chinese Historical Review* 22, no. 1: 72–93.

Ding, Xueliang. 1994. *The Decline of Communism in China: Legitimacy Crises, 1977–1989.* Cambridge: Cambridge University Press.

Duara, Prasenjit. 1995. *Rescuing History from the Nation: Questioning Narratives of Modern China.* Chicago: University of Chicago Press.

Duckett, Jane. 1996. "The Emergence of the Entrepreneurial State in Contemporary China." *Pacific Review* 9, no. 2: 180–198.

Dy, Ari C., SJ. 2013. "Chinese Buddhist Temples of the Philippines." *Tulay: Fortnightly Chinese-Filipino Digest* 26, no. 4. https://tulay.ph/2021/09/14/chinese-buddhist-temples-of-the-philippines-29/.

Erbaugh, Mary S., and Richard Curt Kraus. 1990. "The 1989 Democracy Movement in Fujian and Its Aftermath." *Australian Journal of Chinese Affairs* 23 (January): 145–160.

Erie, Matthew S. 2016. *China and Islam: The Party, the Prophet, and Law.* New York: Cambridge University Press.

Esler, Joshua. 2020. *Tibetan Buddhism Among Han Chinese: Mediation and Superscription of the Tibetan Tradition in Contemporary Chinese Society.* London: Lexington Books.

Finch, Martha. 2012. "Rehabilitating Materiality: Bodies, Gods, and Religion." *Religion* 42, no. 4: 625–631.

Fisher, Gareth. 2014. *From Comrades to Bodhisattvas: Moral Dimensions of Lay Buddhist Practice in Contemporary China.* Honolulu: University of Hawai'i Press.

———. 2019. "Places of Their Own: Exploring the Dynamics of Religious Diversity in the Public Buddhist Temple Space." In *Buddhism After Mao.* Ed. Ji Zhe, André Laliberté, and Gareth Fisher, 271–289. Honolulu: University of Hawai'i Press.

Foster, Kenneth W. 2002. "Embedded within the Bureaucracy: Business Associations in Yantai." *The China Journal* 47 (January): 41–65.

Gao Hong 高虹 2010. "Fojiao xinyang zai dangdai shehui de shijian fangshi" 佛教信仰在當代社會的實踐方式 [The practice of Buddhist belief in contemporary society]. PhD dissertation, Shanghai University.

Garrett, Shirley S. 1970. *Social Reformers in Urban China: The Chinese Y.M.C.A., 1895–1926.* Cambridge, MA: Harvard University Press.

Geary, David. 2017. *The Rebirth of Bohd Gaya: Buddhism and the Making of a World Heritage Site.* Seattle: University of Washington Press.

Gernet, Jacques. 1998. *Buddhism in Chinese Society: An Economic History from the Fifth to the Tenth Century.* New York: Columbia University Press.

Gildow, Douglas M. 2014. "The Chinese Buddhist Ritual Field: Common Public Rituals in PRC Monasteries Today." *Journal of Chinese Buddhist Studies* 27: 59–127.

Gillette, Maris Boyd. 2002. *Between Mecca and Beijing: Modernization and Consumption Among Urban Chinese Muslims.* Stanford, CA: Stanford University Press.

Gladney, Dru. 1991. *Muslim Chinese: Ethnic Nationalism in the People's Republic.* Cambridge, MA: Harvard University Press.

———. 2004. *Dislocating China: Muslims, Minorities, and Other Subaltern Subjects.* Chicago: University of Chicago Press.

Godley, Michael R., and Charles A. Coppel. 1990. "The Pied Piper and the Prodigal Children: Report on the Indonesian-Chinese Studies who went to Mao's China." *Archipel* 39, no. 1: 179–198.

Goldstein, Melvyn C., and Matthew T. Kapstein, ed. 1998. *Buddhism in Contemporary Tibet: Religious Revival and Cultural Identity*. Berkeley: University of California Press.

Gombrich, Richard F. 1971. *Precept and Practice: Traditional Buddhism in the Rural Highlands of Ceylon*. Oxford: Clarendon Press.

Gombrich, Richard F., and Gananath Obeyesekere. 1988. *Buddhism Transformed: Religious Change in Sri Lanka*. Princeton, NJ: Princeton University Press.

Goossaert, Vincent, and David A. Palmer. 2012. *The Religious Question in Modern China*. Chicago: University of Chicago Press.

Groot, Gerry. 2004. *Managing Transitions: The Chinese Communist Party, United Front Work, Corporatism and Hegemony*. New York: Routledge.

Hammerstrom, Erik J. 2020. *The Huayan University Network: The Teaching and Practice of Avataṃsaka Buddhism in Twentieth-Century China*. New York: Columbia University Press.

Harrison, Henrietta. 2000. *The Making of the Republican Citizen: Ceremonies and Symbols in China, 1911–1929*. Oxford: Oxford University Press.

Ho, Daphon David. 2006. "To Protect and Preserve: Resisting the Destroy the Four Olds Campaign, 1966–1967." In *The Chinese Cultural Revolution as History*. Ed. Joseph W. Esherick, Paul G. Pickowicz, and Andrew G. Walder, 64–97. Stanford, CA: Stanford University Press.

Ho, Denise Y. 2011. "Revolutionizing Antiquity: The Shanghai Cultural Bureaucracy in the Cultural Revolution, 1966–1968." *The China Quarterly* 207 (September): 687–705.

Ho, Wai-Yip. 2015. *Islam and China's Hong Kong: Ethnic Identity, Muslim Networks and the New Silk Road*. Abingdon: Routledge.

Huang, C. Julia. 2005. "The Compassion Relief Diaspora." In *Buddhist Missionaries in the Era of Globalization*. Ed. Linda Learman, 185–209. Honolulu: University of Hawai'i Press.

Huang, Weishan. 2019. "Urban Restructuring and Temple Agency—A Case Study of the Jing'an Temple." In *Buddhism After Mao*. Ed. Ji Zhe, André Laliberté, and Gareth Fisher, 151–270. Honolulu: University of Hawai'i Press.

Humphrey, Caroline, and Hürelbaatar Ujeed. 2013. *A Monastery in Time: The Making of Mongolian Buddhism*. Chicago: University of Chicago Press.

Hung, Steven Chung Fun. 2016. "Analysis of the Establishment and Closure of the Ta Teh Institute in British Hong Kong during the Chinese Civil War." *Cambridge Journal of China Studies* 11, no. 2: 34–54. https://doi.org/10.17863/CAM.1644.

Hunter, Alan, and Kim-Kwong Chan. 1993. *Protestantism in Contemporary China*. New York: Cambridge University Press.

Jaschok, Maria, and Shui Jingjun. 2000. *The History of Women's Mosques in Chinese Islam: A Mosque of Their Own*. Richmond, Surrey: Curzon Press.

Ji Zhe. 2004. "Buddhism and the State: The New Relationship." *China Perspectives* 55 (September–October): 3.

———. 2008. "Secularization as Religious Restructuring: Statist Institutionalization of Chinese Buddhism and Its Paradoxes." In *Chinese Religiosities: Afflictions of Modernity and State Formation.* Ed. Mayfair Mui-Hui Yang, 233–260. Berkeley: University of California Press.

———. 2011. "Buddhism in the Reform Era: A Secularized Revival?" *Religion in Contemporary China: Revitalization and Innovation.* Ed. Adam Yuet Chau, 32–52. London: Routledge.

———. 2013. "Zhao Puchu and His Renjian Buddhism." *The Eastern Buddhist* 44, no. 2: 35–58.

———. 2017. "Comrade Zhao Puchu: Bodhisattva Under the Red Flag." In *Making Saints in Modern China.* Ed. David Ownby, Vincent Goosaert, and Ji Zhe, 312–348. New York: Oxford University Press.

Ji Zhe, Gareth Fisher, and André Laliberté, eds. 2019. *Buddhism After Mao: Negotiations, Continuities, and Reinventions.* Honolulu: University of Hawai'i Press.

Ji Zhe 汲喆, Tian Shuijing 田水晶, and Wang Qiyuan 王啟元, eds. 2016. *Er shi shiji Zhongguo fojiao de liangci fuxing* 二十世紀中國佛教的兩次復興 [The two revivals of Buddhism in twentieth-century China]. Shanghai: Fudan daxue chubanshe.

Jones, Allison Denton. 2010. "A Modern Religion? The State, the People, and the Remaking of Buddhism in Urban China Today." PhD dissertation, Harvard University.

Jones, Charles. 1999. *Buddhism in Taiwan: Religion and the State, 1660–1990.* Honolulu: University of Hawai'i Press.

———. 2021. *Taixu's On the Establishment of the Pure Land in the Human Realm: A Translation and Study.* London: Bloomsbury.

Jones, Stephen. 2017. *In Search of the Folk Daoists of North China.* Abingdon: Routledge.

Kaltman, Blaine. 2007. *Under the Heel of the Dragon: Islam, Racism, Crime, and the Uighur in China.* Athens: Ohio University Press.

Khong, Yuen Foong. 1999. "Singapore: A Time for Economic and Political Engagement." In *Engaging China: The Management of an Emerging Power.* Ed. Alastair Iain Johnston and Robert S. Ross, 111–131. Abingdon: Routledge.

Kiely, Jan, and J. Brooks Jessup, eds. 2016. *Recovering Buddhism in Modern China.* New York: Columbia University Press.

Kieschnick, John. 2003. *The Impact of Buddhism on Chinese Material Culture.* Princeton, NJ: Princeton University Press.

Knott, Kim. 2005. *The Location of Religion: A Spatial Analysis.* London: Equinox.

Kojima, Takahiro. 2012. "Tai Buddhist Practices in Dehong Prefecture, Yunan, China." *Southeast Asian Studies* 1, no. 3: 395–430.

Komine, Kazuaki 小峰和明. 2008. "'Shaka no honji' no e to monogatari wo yomu" 釈迦の本地』の絵と物語を読む [Reading pictures and stories of Buddha's homeland]. *Ajia Yūgaku* アジア遊学 109: 32–43.

Kuah-Pearce, Khun Eng. 2003. *State, Society and Religious Engineering: Towards a Reformist Buddhism in Singapore.* Singapore: Eastern Universities Press.

———. 2011. *Rebuilding the Ancestral Village: Singaporeans in China.* Hong Kong: Hong Kong University Press.

REFERENCES

Lam, Willy Wo-Lap. 1994. "Locking Up the Floodgates: Striking a Balance Between Reform and Repression." In *China Review 1994*. Ed. Maurice Brosseau and Lo Chi Kin, 2.1–2.52. Hong Kong: Chinese University Press.

Lassander, Mika, and Peik Ingman. 2012. "Exploring the Social without a Separate Domain for Religion: On Actor-Network Theory and Religion." In *Post-Secular Religious Practices*. Ed. Tore Ahlbäck, 201–217. Turku, Finland: Donner Institute for Research in Religious and Cultural History.

Latour, Bruno. 2007. *Reassembling the Social: An Introduction to Actor-Network-Theory*. Oxford: Oxford University Press.

Law, John, and John Hassard, eds. 1999. *Actor-Network Theory and After*. Hoboken, NJ: Wiley-Blackwell.

Leamaster, Reid J., and Anning Hu. 2014. "Popular Buddhists: The Relationship between Popular Religious Involvement and Buddhist Identity in Contemporary China." *Sociology of Religion* 75: 234–259.

Learman, Linda, ed. 2005. *Buddhist Missionaries in the Era of Globalization*. Honolulu: University of Hawai'i Press.

Lefebvre, Henri. 1991 [1974]. *The Production of Space*. Trans. Donald Nicholson-Smith. Oxford: Basil Blackwell.

———. 2009a [1978]. "Space and the State." In *State, Space, World*. Ed. Neil Brenner and Stuart Elder, trans. Gerald Moore, Neil Brenner, and Stuart Elden, 223–253. Minneapolis: University of Minnesota Press.

———. 2009b [1979]. "Space: Social Product and Use Value." In *State, Space, World: Selected Essays*. Ed. Neil Brenner and Stuart Elder, trans. Gerald Moore, Neil Brenner, and Stuart Elden, 185–195. Minneapolis: University of Minnesota Press.

LeVine, Sarah, and David N. Gellner. 2007. *Rebuilding Buddhism: The Theravada Movement in Twentieth-Century Nepal*. Cambridge, MA: Harvard University Press.

Li, Xianping. 2017. "Increased Production and Education—The New Modern Buddhist Thought and Practice of the Monk Juzan." *Studies in Chinese Religions* 3, no. 1: 83–100.

Lian Xinhao 連心豪. 2010. "Xiamen shi minjian xinyang gongmiao xianzhuang kaocha" 廈門市民間信仰宮廟現狀考察 [Investigation on the current situation of folk belief temples in Xiamen]. *Mintai wenhua jiaoliu* 閩台文化交流 24, no. 10: 84–89.

Liang, Yongjia. 2016. "The Anthropological Study of Religion in China: Contexts, Collaborations, Debates, and Trends." Asia Research Institute Working Paper Series, 250, National University of Singapore.

———. 2018. *Religion and Ethnic Revival in a Chinese Minority: The Bai People of Southwest China*. Abingdon: Routledge.

Lieberthal, Kenneth, and David M. Lampton. ed. 1992. *Bureaucracy, Politics, and Decision Making in Post-Mao China*. Berkeley: University of California Press.

Lim, Francis Khek Gee. 2012. *Christianity in Contemporary China: Sociocultural Perspectives*. Abingdon: Routledge.

Lin, Yu-ju. 2015. "Trade, Public Affairs and the Formation of Merchant Associations in Taiwan in the Eighteenth Century." In *Merchant Communities in Asia: 1600–1980*. Ed. Lin Yu-ju and Madeleine Zelin, 11–27. London: Pickering and Chatto.

Ling, Ken. 1972. *Red Guard: From Schoolboy to "Little General" in Mao's China*. London: MacDonald.
Liu Peng. 1996. "Church and State Relations in China: Characteristics and Trends." *Journal of Contemporary China* 5, no. 11: 69–79.
Lozada, Eriberto, Jr. 2002. *God Above Ground: Catholic Church, Postsocialist State, and Transnational Processes in a Chinese Village*. Stanford, CA: Stanford University Press.
Lü Daji and Gong Xuezeng, eds. 2014. *Marxism and Religion*. Trans. Chi Zhen. Leiden: Brill.
Lu Yunfeng 盧雲峰 and He Yuan 和園. 2014. "Shanqiao fangbian: Dangdai fojiao tuanti zai zhongguo chengshi de fazhan" 善巧方便：當代佛教團體在中國城市的發展 [Skill in means: The development of contemporary Buddhist groups in Chinese cities]. *Xuehai* 學海 2: 26–34.
Luhmann, Niklas. 1995 [1984]. *Social Systems*. Trans. John Bednarz Jr. and Dirk Baeker. Stanford, CA: Stanford University Press.
Luo, Zhufeng, ed. 1991. *Religion Under Socialism*. Trans. Donald E. MacInnis and Zheng Xi'an. Armonk, NY: M. E. Sharpe.
Ma, Li, and Jin Li. 2017. *Surviving the State, Remaking the Church: A Sociological Portrait of Christians in Mainland China*. Eugene, OR: Pickwick Publications.
MacInnis, Donald E. 1989. *Religion in China Today: Policy and Practice*. Maryknoll, NY: Orbis Books.
Madsen, Richard. 1998. *China's Catholics: Tragedy and Hope in an Emerging Civil Society*. Berkeley: University of California Press.
———. 2000. "Editor's Introduction." *Chinese Law and Government* 33, no. 3: 5–11.
McLaughlin, Levi. 2019. *Soka Gakkai's Human Revolution: The Rise of a Mimetic Nation*. Honolulu: University of Hawai'i Press.
Mertha, Andrew C. 2009. "'Fragmented Authoritarianism 2.0': Pluralization in the Chinese Policy Process." *The China Quarterly* 2000: 995–1012.
Meyer, John W., John Boli, and George M. Thomas. 1987. "Ontology and Rationalization in the Western Cultural Account." *Institutional Structure: Constituting State, Society, and Individual*. Ed. George M. Thomas et al., 2–37. London: Sage Publications.
Montinola, Gabriella, Yingyi Qian, and Barry R. Weingast. 1995. "Federalism, Chinese Style: The Political Basis for Economic Success in China." *World Politics* 5, no. 3: 50–81.
Morrison, Peter. 2008. "Religious Policy in China and its Implementation in the Light of Document no. 19." *Religion in Communist Lands* 12, no. 3: 244–255.
Nedostup, Rebecca. 2009. *Superstitious Regimes: Religion and the Politics of Chinese Modernity*. Cambridge, MA: Harvard University Press.
Ng, Chin-Keong. 1983. *Trade and Society: The Amoy Network on the China Coast, 1683–1735*. Singapore: National University of Singapore Press.
Nichols, Brian J. 2019. "Advancing the Ethnographic Study of Chan Buddhism." In *Concepts and Methods for the Study of Chinese Religions I: State of the Field and Disciplinary Approaches*. Ed. André Laliberté and Stefania Travagnin, 139–162. Berlin: De Gruyter.

Nichols, Brian J. 2022. *Lotus Blossoms and Purple Clouds: Monastic Buddhism in Post-Mao China*. Honolulu: University of Hawaii's Press.

Okimoto Masanori 沖本正憲. 2013. "Nihon no zenshū jiin: shichidōgaran to jintai-hyō aizu" 日本の禅宗寺院: 七堂伽藍と人体表相図 [Zen Buddhist temples in Japan: The seven-hall compound and human body diagram]. *Yuki no oto* 雪の音 117: 16-19.

Otehode, Utiraruto. 2009. "The Creation and Reemergence of Qigong in China." In *Making Religion, Making the State*. Ed. Yoshiko Ashiwa and David L. Wank, 241-265. Stanford, CA. Stanford University Press.

Ownby, David. 2008. *Falun Gong and the Future of China*. Oxford: Oxford University Press.

Palmer, David. A. 2007. *Qigong Fever: Body, Science, and Utopia in China*. New York: Columbia University Press.

———. 2009. "China's Religious *Danwei*: Institutionalizing Religion in the People's Republic." *China Perspectives* 4: 17-30.

———. 2017. *Dream Trippers: Global Daoism and the Predicament of Modern Spirituality*. Chicago: University of Chicago Press.

Penny, Benjamin. 2003. "The Life and Times of Li Hongzhi: Falun Gong and Religious Biography." *The China Quarterly* 175 (September): 643-661.

Pew-Templeton Foundation. 2012. *The Global Religious Landscape: A Report on the Size and Distribution of the World's Major Religious Groups as of 2010*. Washington, DC: Pew Research Center.

Pittman, Don. 2001. *Towards a Modern Chinese Buddhism: Taixu's Reforms*. Honolulu: University of Hawai'i Press.

Potter, Pitman. 2003. "Belief in Control: Regulation of Religion in China." *The China Quarterly* 174 (June): 317-337.

Powers, John. 2016. *The Buddha Party: How the People's Republic of China Works to Define and Control Tibetan Buddhism*. Oxford: Oxford University Press.

Prip-Møller, Johannes. 1967 [1937]. *Chinese Buddhist Monasteries: Their Plan and Its Function as a Setting for Buddhist Monastic Life*. Hong Kong: Hong Kong University Press.

Qin, Wenjie. 2000. "The Buddhist Revival in Post-Mao China: Women Reconstruct Buddhism on Mt. Emei." PhD dissertation, Harvard University.

Reinke, Jens. 2021. *Mapping Modern Mahayana: Chinese Buddhism and Migration in the Age of Global Modernity*. Berlin: De Gruyter.

Ritzinger, Justin. 2017. *Anarchy in the Pure Land: Reinventing the Cult of Maitreya in Modern Chinese Buddhism*. Oxford: Oxford University Press.

Robson, James. 2010. "Monastic Spaces and Sacred Traces: Facets of Chinese Buddhist Monastic Records." In *Buddhist Monasticism in East Asia: Places of Practice*. Ed. James A. Benn, Lori Meeks, and James Robson, 43-64. London: Routledge.

Rogaski, Ruth. 2014. *Hygienic Modernity: Meanings of Health and Disease in Treaty-Port China*. Berkeley: University of California Press.

Rong, Xinjiang. 2004. "Land Route or Sea Route? Commentary on the Study of the Paths of Transmission and Area in which Buddhism Was Disseminated during the Han Period." Trans. Xiuqin Zhou. *Sino-Platonic Papers*, 144 (July): 2-32. http://sino-platonic.org/complete/spp144_han_dynasty_buddhism.pdf.

Rudelson, Justin. 1997. *Oasis Identities: Uyghur Nationalism Along China's Silk Road.* New York: Columbia University Press.

Schlutter, Morten. 2010. *How Zen Became Zen: The Dispute Over Enlightenment and the Formation of Chan Buddhism in Song-Dynasty China.* Honolulu: University of Hawai'i Press.

Schottenhammer, Angela, ed. 2001. *The Emporium of the World: Maritime Quanzhou 1000–1400.* Leiden: Brill.

Schottenhammer, Angela. 2007. "The East Asian Maritime World 1400–1800: Its Fabrics of Power and Dynamics of Exchanges—China and Her Neighbors." In *The East Asian Maritime World 1400–1800: Its Fabrics of Power and Dynamics of Exchanges.* Ed. Angela Schottenhammer, 1–86. Wiesbaden: Harrassowitz Verlag.

Schwieger, Peter. 2021. *Conflict in a Buddhist Society: Tibet Under the Dalai Lamas.* Honolulu: University of Hawai'i Press.

Scott, Gregory Adam. 2020. *Building the Buddhist Revival: Reconstructing Monasteries in Modern China.* Oxford: Oxford University Press.

Shi, Fangfang. 2009. "Evaluation of Visitor Experience at Chinese Buddhist Sites: The Case of Wutai Mountain." *Tourism in China: Destination, Cultures and Communities.* Ed. Chris Ryan and Huimin Gu, 197–212. Abingdon: Routledge.

Shore, Cris, and Susan Wright. 1997. "Policy: A New Field of Anthropology." *Anthropology of Policy: Critical Perspectives on Governance and Power.* Ed. Cris Shore and Susan Wright, 3–30. Abingdon: Routledge.

Southwold, Martin. 1983. *Buddhism in Life: The Anthropological Study of Buddhism and the Sinhalese Practice of Buddhism.* Manchester: Manchester University Press.

Spiro, Meldford E. 1982. *Buddhism and Society: A Great Tradition and Its Burmese Vicissitudes.* Berkeley: University of California Press.

Stewart, Alexander. 2016. *Chinese Muslims and the Global Ummah: Islamic Revival and Ethnic Identity Among the Hui of Qinghai Province.* Abingdon: Routledge.

Suami, Takao, Anne Peters, Dimitri Vanoverbeke, and Mattias Kumm. 2019. *Global Constitutionalism from European and East Asian Perspectives.* Cambridge: Cambridge University Press.

Sun, Yanfei. 2017. "Jingkong: From Universal Saint to Sectarian Saint." In *Making Saints in Modern China.* Ed. David Ownby, Vincent Goosaert, and Ji Zhe, 394–418. New York: Oxford University Press.

Tan Leshan 譚樂山. 2005. *Nan chuan shangzuobu fojiao yu daizu cun she jingji: dui Zhongguo xinan xishuang banna de bijiao yanjiu* 南傳上座部佛教與傣族村社經濟: 對中國西南西雙版納的比較研究 [Theravada Buddhism and Dai village society and economy: A comparative study of Xishuangbanna, southwest China]. Kunming: Kunming daxue chubanshe.

Ter Haar, Barend J. 1992. *The White Lotus Teachings in Chinese Religious History.* Leiden: Brill.

Topley, Marjorie. 1956. "Chinese Religion and Religious Institutions in Singapore." In *Cantonese Society in Hong Kong and Singapore: Gender, Religion, Medicine and Money.* Ed. Jean De Bernardi, 125–174. Hong Kong: Hong Kong University Press.

Travagnin, Stefania. 2015. "Political Adjusting(s) in the Minnan Buddhist Institute: *Sanmin* 三民主義 and *aiguozhuyi* 愛國主義 in the Sangha Education Context." *Review of Religion and Chinese Society* 2, no. 1: 21–50.

———. 2019. "Cyberactivites and 'Civilized' Worship: Assessing Contexts and Modalities of Online Ritual Practices." In *Buddhism After Mao*. Ed. Ji Zhe, André Laliberté, and Gareth Fisher, 290–311. Honolulu: University of Hawai'i Press.

Tymick, Kenneth J. 2014. "Chan in Communist China: Justifying Buddhism's Turn to Practical Labor Under the Chinese Communist Party." *Constructing the Past* 15, no. 1, 9.

Vala, Carsten. 2017. *The Politics of Protestant Churches and the Party-State in China: God Above Party*. Abingdon: Routledge.

Van der Veer, Peter. 2001. *Imperial Encounters: Religion and Modernity in India and Britain*. Princeton, NJ: Princeton University Press.

Van Slyke, Lyman P. 1967. *Enemies and Friends: The United Front in Chinese Communist History*. Stanford, CA: Stanford University Press.

Vidal, Claire. 2019. "Administering Bodhisattva Guanyin's Island: The Monasteries, Political Entities, and Power Holders of Putuoshan." In *Buddhism After Mao*. Ed. Ji Zhe, André Laliberté, and Gareth Fisher, 45–76. Honolulu: University of Hawai'i Press.

Walsh, Michael J. 2010. *Sacred Economies: Buddhist Monasticism and Territoriality in Medieval China*. New York: Columbia University Press.

Wang, Canbai. 2009. "Guiqiao: Returnees as a Policy Subject in China." *The Newsletter*, 50 (International Institute for Asian Studies IIAS).

Wang, Jianxin. 2004. *Uyghur Education and Social Order: The Role of Islamic Leadership in the Turpan Basin*. Tokyo: Research Institute for Languages and Cultures of Asia and Africa, Tokyo University of Foreign Studies.

Wang, Xing. 2019. "The Stone of Mount Tai: *Shigangdang* Worship in Northern China and the Power of Symbols." *The Journal of Objects, Art and Belief* 15, no. 1: 54–81.

Wank, David L. 1995. "Civil Society in Communist China? Private Business and Political Alliance, 1989." In *Civil Society: Theory, History, Comparison*. Ed. John A. Hall, 56–79. Cambridge: Polity Press.

———. 1999. *Commodifying Communism: Business, Trust, and Politics in a Chinese City*. New York: Cambridge University Press.

———. 2000. "Bukkyō fukkō no seijigaku: kyōgō suru kikō to seitōsei" 仏教復興の政治学: 競合する機構と正当性 [The politics of the Buddhist revival in China: competing institutions and legitimacy]. In *Gendai chūgoku ni okeru kokka to shakai* 現代中国における国家と社会 [State and society in contemporary China]. Ed. Hishida Masaharu 菱田雅晴, 275–304. Tokyo: Tokyo daigaku shuppan-kai.

———. 2009. "Institutionalizing Modern 'Religion' in China's Buddhism: Political Phases of a Local Revival." *Making Religion, Making the State*. Ed. Yoshiko Ashiwa and David L. Wank, 126–150. Stanford, CA: Stanford University Press.

Welch, Holmes. 1963. "Dharma Scrolls and the Succession of Abbots in Chinese Monasteries." *T'oung Pao*, 50, nos. 1–3: 93–149.

———. 1967. *The Practice of Chinese Buddhism, 1900–1950*. Cambridge, MA: Harvard University Press.

———. 1968. *The Buddhist Revival in China*. Cambridge, MA: Harvard University Press.

———. 1972. *Buddhism Under Mao*. Cambridge, MA: Harvard University Press.

Wen Jinyu 溫金玉. 2012. "1949–1993 nian fojiao sengjia zhidu jianshe huigu" 1949–1993 年佛教僧伽制度建設回顧 [Retrospective on the construction of Buddhist monastic system: 1949–1993]. *Shijie zongjiao wenhua* 世界宗教文化 5: 66–72.

White, Chris, ed. 2018. *Protestantism in Xiamen: Then and Now*. Basingstoke: Palgrave Macmillan.

White, Gordon, Jude A. Howell, and Shang Xiaoyuan. 1996. *In Search of Civil Society: Market Reform and Social Change in Contemporary China*. Oxford: Clarendon Press.

Wickeri, Philip L. 1988. *Seeking the Common Ground: Protestant Christianity, the Three-Self Movement, and China's United Front*. Maryknoll, NY: Orbis Books.

Wilson, Jeff. 2012. *Dixie Dharma: Inside a Buddhist Temple in the American South*. Chapel Hill: University of North Carolina Press.

Wong, Cora Un In, Alison McIntosh, and Chris Ryan. 2016. "Visitor Management at a Buddhist Sacred Site." *Journal of Travel Research* 55, no. 5: 675–687.

Wu, Jiang. 2015. *Leaving for the Rising Sun: Chinese Zen Master Yinyuan and the Authenticity Crises in Early Modern East Asia*. Oxford: Oxford University Press.

Xue Yu 學愚. 2015a. *Zhongguo fojiao de shehui zhuyi gaizao* 中國佛教的社會主義改造 [The socialist transformation of Chinese Buddhism]. Hong Kong: Xianggang zhongwen daxue.

———. 2015b. "Buddhism and the State in Modern and Contemporary China." In *Modern Chinese Religion II: 1850–2015*. Ed. Jan Kiely, Vincent Goossaert, and John Lagerwey, 259–301.

Yang Fenggang 楊鳳崗, Gao Shining 高師寧, and Li Xiangping 李向平. 2015a. *Tianye guilai (shang) Zhongguo zongjiao yu shehui yanjiu: Lilun yu shiji* 田野歸來（上）中國宗教與社會研究：理論與實際 [Returning from fieldwork (1): Research on Chinese religion and society—theory and practice]. Taipei: Taiwan jidujiao wenyi.

———. 2015b. *Tianye guilai (zhong) Zhongguo zongjiao yu shehuixue yanjiu: chuanbo yu liudong* 田野歸來（中）中國宗教與社會研究：傳播與流動 [Returning from fieldwork: research on Chinese religion and society (2)—communication and mobility]. Taipei: Taiwan jidujiao wenyi.

Yang, Fenggang, and Graeme Lang, ed. 2011. *Social Scientific Studies of Religion in China: Methodology, Theories, and Findings*. Leiden: Brill.

Yang, Fenggang, Joy K. C. Tong, and Allan H. Anderson, ed. 2017. *Global Chinese Pentecostal and Charismatic Christianity*. Leiden: Brill.

Yang, Mayfair Mei-Hui, ed. 2008. *Chinese Religiosities: Afflictions of Modernity and State Formation*. Berkeley: University of California Press.

Yü, Chun-fang. 2001. *Kuan-yin: The Chinese Transformation of Avalokiteśvara*. New York: Columbia University Press.

Yü, Dan Smyer. 2014. *The Spread of Tibetan Buddhism in China: Charisma, Money, Enlightenment*. London: Routledge.

Yu Lingbo 于凌波. 1997. *Zhongguo fojiao haiwai hongfa renwu zhi* 中國佛教海外弘法人物誌 [Overseas Propagators of Chinese Buddhism Gazetteer]. Taipei: Huiju chubanshe.

Zarrow, Peter. 2006. "Constitutionalism and the Imagination of the State: Official Views of Political Reform in the Late Qing." In *Creating Chinese Modernity: Knowledge and Everyday Life, 1900–1940*. Ed. Peter Zarrow, 51–82. Bern: Peter Lang.

REFERENCES

Zhao, Suisheng. 2004. *A Nation-State by Construction: Dynamics of Modern Chinese Nationalism*. Stanford, CA: Stanford University Press.

Zhuo Xinping. 2015. "Religious Policy and the Concept of Religion in China." In *Religion in China: Major Concepts and Minority Positions*. Ed. Max Deeg and Bernhard Scheid, 51–64. Vienna: Austrian Academy of Sciences Press.

INDEX

actor-network theory (ANT), 37, 361n24
All-Seeing King (Guangmu tianwang), 56
All Souls' Festival, 133–134
ancestor rituals, 50, 85, 130, 134, 135, 207, 227, 245
ancestor tablet storage, 50, 246, 254, 343
Anjing (prior of Puguang Temple), 245, 246, 248–249
Anti-Rightest Campaign, 24
Australia, 215–216
Avalokiteśvara Bodhisattva, 291–292. *See also* Guanyin worship

Bailudong Temple, 252–255, *325*, 374n15
Baosheng Dadi (Life Protection Emperor), 239, 270, *333*, 373n1
Baotong Temple, 360n16
BAX (Buddhist Association of Xiamen Municipality) (Xiamen shi fojiao xiehui): abbot selection and, 200, 372n8; authority over local Xiamen temples, 79, 202, 237, 245, 249, 250, 251, 252; BCM and, 203; Cai Jitang and, 265; coordination (*xietiao*) and, 76, 78, 80; devotees and, 266, 276; dharma transmission temples and, 245; establishment of, 76; Falun Gong campaign and, 220; Guanyin festival and, 293; Guanyin Temple and, 258; Hongshan Temple and, 242; lay nun halls and, 239, 281, 284; lay nuns and, 120, 239, 279, 287; Miaozhan and, 84, 85; Miaozhan's funeral and, 191; Nanputuo Temple expansion and, 183–184; overseas Chinese clerics and, 90; popular religious practices and, 202, 246; religious activity sites and, 79; Tiananmen Square protest and, 144; Tianzhuyan Temple and, 259; Xiamen Devotee Lodge and, 269; XRAB cooperation, 201–203; XRAB-Nanputuo Temple conflicts and, 166, 169, 198, 374n10
BCM. *See* Buddhist College of Minnan
Beow Heong Lim Temple (Miaoxianglin si), 90
Bolin Academy, 360n16
Buddha Calligraphy and Painting Society (Foguang shuhua she), 284

399

INDEX

Buddha Rock (Nanputuo Temple), 28, 47–48; Guanyin festival and, 294, 295; magical efficacy (*ling*) and, 48, *106*, 318; semiotic space and, 68; spirit money burning and, *330*

Buddhism: introduction to China, 7; precepts, 43, 208, 262, 278; structure of, 19; teachings as semiotic space, 36, 46, 55–56. *See also* Chinese Buddhism; modern reform movement; semiotic space

Buddhism Forum, 264

Buddhism for the Human Realm (Renjian fojiao), 25, 30, 85, 86, 268, 364*n*3. *See also* modern reform movement

Buddhism Under Mao (Welch), 21

Buddhist Academy of China (Zhongguo foxue yuan): BCM and, 115; Buddhist Association of China and, 366*n*25; Jiqun and, 272; Lin Ziqing and, 264; Mengcan and, 112; Miaozhan and, 140; ordination and, 121; recovery from Cultural Revolution and, 70; religious activity sites and, 78–79; Shenghui and, 198, 372*n*4

Buddhist Association of China: BCM and, 205; Buddhist Academy of China and, 366*n*25; Buddhist culture discourse and, 341; devotees and, 75, 264, 265, 266; establishment of, 26, 75, 85, 365*n*9; Falun Gong campaign and, 217, 218, 220, 222; journal published by, 117; Juzan and, 85; Miaozhan and, 83, 84–85, 140; Miaozhan's abbatial ascension ceremony and, 150; Miaozhan's funeral and, 191–192; Nanputuo Temple abbots and, 75–76; Nanputuo Temple recovery and, 87–88; national congresses, 78, 365*n*11; ordination and, 121, 368*n*6; overseas Chinese communities and, 87; religious activity sites and, 78–79; semiotic space of Nanputuo Temple and, 53; Shenghui and, 32–33, 198, 199, 200, 372*n*4; state Buddhist diplomacy and, 211, 214, 215–216; XRAB-Nanputuo Temple conflicts and, 164, 165, 173, 370*n*8; Yuanzhuo and, 96

Buddhist Association of Fujian, 120, 265, 266

Buddhist Association of Xiamen Municipality. *See* BAX

Buddhist belief variations, 4; Buddhist culture discourse and, 345–346; Guanyin festival attendees and, 298, 299–310, 319–321, *319*, 345, 378–379*nn*3–4, 8; Nanputuo Temple volunteers department and, 344

Buddhist College of Minnan (BCM), 112–120; admissions, 117–119, *119*, *179*; Anjing and, 249; BAX and, 203; Buddhist Culture Seminar and, 272, 273; Cai Jitang and, 265; campus for nuns, 32, 179–181; cleric emigration and, 185, 187, 188; curriculum, 112–113, 116–117, 143–145, *355–356*; devotees as instructors, 114–115, 264, 265, 266, 276; Falun Gong campaign and, 221; founding of, 29, 360*n*16; globalization and, 343; graduates of, 119–120, *120*; Hongshan Temple and, 242; Juzan and, 360*n*8; lay nun admission to, 85, 113, 206, 279, 284, 285, 287; lay nun exclusion from, 206–207, 279, 344–345; local Xiamen temples and, 250, 257, 260; Mengcan and, 112; Miaozhan and, 84, 85, 86, 112–113, 114, 117, 118; Miaozhan's abbatial ascension ceremony and, 151, 159; Miaozhan's funeral and, 189, 193; ninetieth anniversary celebration (2015), *335*, *336*; nuns at, 113–114, 118–119, 257, 281; ordination and, 120, 125; organization of, 114–116, *116*; overseas Chinese clerics and, 86, 88, 114, 118; physical space and, 48; recovery from Cultural Revolution and, 32; religious activity sites and, 79; rituals and, 132, 134; Shenghui's reforms, 205–207; state Buddhist diplomacy and, 213; Taixu

400

INDEX

and, 86, 112–113; temple bureaucracy and, 126; Tiananmen Square protest and, 143, 144, 145; XRAB-Nanputuo Temple conflicts and, 173; Zewu and, 33
Buddhist Cultivation Handbook (*Fojiao xiuxue yaodian*), 271–272, 329
Buddhist culture discourse (*fojiao wenhua*), 4, 24, 339, 341–346; Buddhist belief variations and, 345–346; Buddhist practices and, 342; globalization and, 4, 341–342, 343, 347; lay nun halls and, 283–286, 344; local relationships with Nanputuo Temple and, 33; Nanputuo Temple and, 342–344; popular religious practices and, 225, 341
Buddhist Culture Research Institute (Zhongguo fojiao wenhua yanjiu suo), 264
Buddhist Culture Seminar (Fojiao wenhua yantao ban), 272, 273–274
Buddhist Instruction School (Yangzheng yuan), 29, 32, 112, 114, 132, 134, 141, 360n17
burning mouths release ritual, 62, 85, 134, 135, 207, 208

Cai Jitang, 265–266, 269, 276
Caodong school, 241, 252
Cham Sham Temple (Zhanshan jingshe), 187, 371n35
Chan Buddhism: Buddhist Association of China and, 86; meditation and, 181; physical space of Nanputuo Temple and, 43; semiotic space of Nanputuo Temple and, 59, 65, 161–162; Wanfu Temple and, 96. *See also* Linji school
Changqin (prior of Bailudong Temple), 252–254, 255, 374n15
Chaozhou Buddhist Association, 161
Chau, Adam, 362n6
Chengtian Temple, 88
Chengxiang, 371n35
Chen Jiageng, 256
Chiang Kai-shek, 364n3

China Buddhist Association (Zhongguo fojiao xiehui), 26, 264
China-Korea-Japan Buddhist Goodwill Congress (Zhong han ri sanguo fojiao youhao jiaoliu huiyi), 214–215
China Qigong Science Society (Zhongguo qigong kexue yanjiu), 217
Chinese Buddhism: Buddhist culture discourse and, 341–342; introduction of, 7; persecution of (Three Disasters of Wu), 55, 363n11; popular forms of, 218, 219; population of, 4; scholarship on, 20–21
Chinese Buddhism (*Zhongguo zongjiao*), 117
Chinese civil war (1945–49), 9, 26, 31, 249, 285, 374n8, 377n42
Chinese Dream (Zhongguo meng), 4
Chinese People's Consultative Political Conference (Zhongguo remin zhengzhi xieshang huiyi), 76
Ching Hai, 368n11
Chongfu Temple, 120, *233*, 254, 374n13
Christianity, 8, 9, 25, 266
Chung Tian Temple (Zhongtian si), 215
Cihang Prayer Hall, 188
Cishan (*Charity*), 177
civil war. *See* Chinese civil war
clerical self-management (*shifang conglin*): abbot selection and, 197; Document 19 on, 79, 136, 137, 211; ecumenicization and, 29; Nanputuo Temple Charity Foundation and, 211; Song dynasty origins, 360n13; XRAB-Nanputuo Temple conflicts and, 136, 137, 163, 164–165, 166, 370n8
clerics (*biqiu/biqiuni*): converted temples and, 260–261; Cultural Revolution and, 9, 24, 27, 71, 82, 115, 121, 122–123, 124, 125, 365n18, 368n2; devotees and, 269; dharma transmissions and, 244–245, 251, 256–257, 365n21, 373n4; discipline and, 203–205; early PRC period decline, 31; gatha names, 88, 366n26; graves of, 50; Guanyin festival and,

401

INDEX

clerics (*biqiu/biqiuni*) (*continued*)
292, 293, 294, 295, 296, 296, 321–322; Japanese occupation and, 30–31; local Xiamen temples and, 250; meal practice, 47, 379n2; missing cohort of, 114, 369n4; modern reform movement and, 25, 29; monasteries as residences for, 19, 359n1; precepts and, 43; Putian vs. Wenzhou origins, 201–202, 372n10; retirement home for, 50–51; semiotic space and, 36; Six Priorities Activities (Liu jiang huodong) campaign, 204–205; surnames of, 371n31; terms for, 262, 374n1; XRAB-Nanputuo Temple conflicts and, 138–139, 141–142; *yunyou* (wandering), 82, 365n16. *See also* clerical self-management; clerics, education for; ordination; overseas Chinese clerics

clerics, education for: Buddhist Instruction School, 29, 32, 112, 114, 132, 134, 141, 360n17; Huiquan and, 256; internet access to, 366n29; Miaozhan on, 49, 84; Taixu and, 9, 25, 29, 84, 86, 112–113, 117, 360n16; Tiananmen Square protest and, 143–144. *See also* Buddhist Academy of China; Buddhist College of Minnan; ritual knowledge

Compassion Relief Tzu Chi Foundation (Ci ji gongde hui), 86

CPC (Communist Party of China): Nanputuo Temple expansion and, 181; overseas Chinese communities and, 90, 91; Project Hope, 178–179; Three Loves campaign, 364n4; Three Priorities Education (San jiang jiaoyu) campaign, 204, 372n11; Tiananmen Square protest and, 147; Tiananmen Square protest impact on, 147; united front policies, 23, 75, 76. *See also* Chinese civil war; CPC Central United Front Work Department; CPC ideology on religion; Falun Gong campaign; state Buddhist diplomacy; Tiananmen Square protest

CPC Central United Front Work Department (Zhonggong zhongyang tongyi zhanxian gongzuo bu), 75, 87, 111, 347

CPC ideology on religion, 3; Buddhist belief variations and, 308; Buddhist Culture Seminar and, 274; Cultural Revolution and, 27; Cultural Revolution remnants and, 70–71; Document 6 on, 148; Document 19 on, 72–74, 364nn3–5; early CPC period, 26, 31; Falun Gong campaign and, 224–225; Four Modernizations and, 24, 71; freedom of belief, 3, 23–24, 71–72, 363n1; freedom of belief and, 23–24; globalization and, 4, 341–342, 343, 347; grassroots groups (*shetuan*) and, 196, 371n1; Guanyin festival and, 321; increased hostility, 26–27; institutional space and, 35; Juzan and, 26; Miaozhan and, 85; modern reform movement and, 86, 364n3; network methodology on, 37–38; party discipline and, 76, 304, 365n22; patriotism and, 73–74, 80, 143–144, 145–146, 364nn3–5; PRC constitutions and, 71–72, 363n1, 364n2; security concerns and, 24; Shenghui and, 199, 200, 201, 204–205; Sinicized Buddhism discourse (*zhongguohua fojiao*), 339; Six Priorities campaign, 204–205; state religious bureaucracy and, 24, 75, 76, 78, 339–340; Tiananmen Square protest and, 143–144, 148–149; transformations of, 337–338; two civilizations and, 241. *See also* Buddhist culture discourse; Cultural Revolution

Cultural Revolution: ancestor hall destruction and, 130, 246; Anjing and, 248–249; clerics and, 9, 24, 27, 71, 82, 115, 121, 122–123, 124, 125, 365n18, 368n2; destruction of ritual knowledge, 89, 113, 135; devotees and, 24, 27, 31, 46, 264, 265–266; Dingmiao and, 122; education for clerics and, 144; Guanghua Temple and, 95; Guanyin festival attendees and, 320; Guanyin

402

festival during, 290; Hongshan Temple and, 240-241; Huxiyan Temple and, 249; impact of, 9, 27; lay nuns and, 125, 278-279, 280, 283, 285, 286-287, 288; local state religious administration during, 361*n*19; local Xiamen temples and, 31, 237, 252; Mengcan and, 368*n*2; Miaozhan and, 82, 83, 84; Shatter the Four Olds campaign, 24, 31, 360*n*7, 361*n*18; State Administration for Religious Affairs and, 75; Up to the Mountains and Down to the Villages Campaign, 31, 48, 361*n*20; Xiamen Devotee Lodge and, 268; XRAB-Nanputuo Temple conflicts and, 171

Cultural Revolution, Buddhist recovery from, 2, 10, 24; devotees and, 266; Fujian, 92-97, 367*n*41; Huxiyan Temple, 249-250; lay nuns and, 93, 279, 280, 281, 284; local Xiamen temples, 93, 237, 241, 242, 243-244, 245, 256, 265; opening up-policies and, 3-4; ordination ceremonies and, 121; semiotic space and, 339-340. *See also* Nanputuo Temple recovery

Dajue Buddhist Studies Society (Dajue foxue she), 256
Dajue Temple, 187, 188, 371*n*33
Danxia Temple, 270
Daoist temples, 239, 255, 260, 270, 276
Daxing Temple, 360*n*16
Deng Xiaoping, 87, 91, 147, 241, 366*n*24
devotees (*jushi*), 263-277; as BCM instructors, 114-115, 264, 265, 266, 276; Buddhist Association of China and, 75, 264, 265, 266; *Buddhist Cultivation Handbook* and, 271-272, 329; Buddhist Culture Seminar and, 272-273; Cultural Revolution and, 24, 27, 31, 46, 264, 265-266; Falun Gong campaign and, 219-220; Guanyin festival and, 293, 295-296, 301; increased numbers of, 346-347; independence of, 263, 268, 269, 271; lay nuns and, 267-268, 287, 332;

leaders of, 263-268, 271; local Xiamen temples and, 250, 260; marginalization of, 276-277; Miaozhan and, 85, 207-208, 275, 276; Miaozhan's abbatial ascension ceremony and, 151; Minnan language/culture and, 50, 51, 207-208, 268, 269; modern reform movement and, 25, 30, 266; overseas Chinese, 91, 183, 287, 377*n*44; overseas Chinese clerics and, 366*n*29; popular religious practices and, 269, 270, 272, 276-277, *333*; precepts (*wujie*) and, 208, 262, 278; Puzhao Temple and, *107*; retired clerics and, 51; Shenghui and, 207-208, 276; Tibetan Buddhism and, 275-276, 277; tourism and, 91, 270; worship at Nanputuo Temple and, 45, 46, 50, 207-208, *329*; Xiamen Devotee Lodge, 250, 260, 267, 268-272, 276-277, *333*, 344. *See also* local relationships with Nanputuo Temple

Dharma Drum Mountain, 264-265
Dharmapala, Anagarika, 25
Dharma Training Course (Jiang jing peixun ban), 366*n*29
dharma transmissions, 244-245, 251, 256-257, 365*n*21, 373*n*4
Diamond Sutra (*Jingang jing*), 66-67
Dingmiao, 122, 135, 227, *228*
Ding, Xueliang, 364*n*4
Dizang Bodhisattva, 207
Dizang Hall, 154
Document 6, 148
Document 19: on clerical self-management, 79, 136, 137, 211; discursive values in, 72-74, 364*nn*3-5; Falun Gong campaign and, 224-225; impact of, 111; on local state religious administration, 80, 137; local Xiamen temples and, 247-248; overseas Chinese communities and, 139-140; on religious activity sites, 74, 78, 79, 364*n*6; on state religious bureaucracy, 75; on temple revenue, 138; XRAB-Nanputuo Temple conflicts and, 138, 175
Dragon King (Long wang), 28

INDEX

Earth God, 259, 260, 373n1
Eighteen Arhats (Shiba luohan), 45
episodic approach, 38–39, 340–341
Eternal Life Buddha (Amituofo; Amitābha), 44, 103

Falun Gong campaign, 216–225; Buddhist culture discourse and, 341; CPC ideology on religion and, 224–225; devotees and, 268, 274; Falun Gong as grassroots group and, 371n1; Guanyin festival attendees and, 308, 319–320, 378–379n8; local state religious administration and, 218–221, 254; Shenghui and, 215, 216, 218–219, 221–225; state religious bureaucracy and, 221–225
Famen Temple, 212
Fang Litian, 205
Fawang Temple, 187
Faxian, 7–8
Fayin (*Voice of Dharma*), 264
Fayuan Temple, 79
Fayun (prior of Hongshan Temple), 241–242, 243
Feng Zikai, 66
five precepts (*wujie*), 208, 262, 278. See also devotees; lay nuns
Fo Guang Shan, 86, 213, 215–216
Four Modernizations (Sige xiandaihua), 24, 71
freedom of belief, 3, 23–24, 71–72, 363n1
Fujian: introduction of Buddhism to, 7–8; recovery from Cultural Revolution, 92–97, 367n41. See also Xiamen
Fujian Buddhist Academy (Fujian foxue yuan), 85, 95, 115, 125, 180, 279, 287
Fujian Buddhist Association, 117
Fujian Religion (*Fujian zongjiao*), 117
Fujian Religious Affairs Bureau, 93, 94, 143, 166, 186, 220–221

gaige kaifang (opening-up policies), 3–4, 27, 147
Ganlu Temple, 372n4

Gaomin Temple, 82, 181
Garland Sutra (*Huayan jing*), 161–162
Gazetteer of Xiamen Buddhism, 267, 287, 379n3
Genealogy of the Buddha (*Shijia pu*) (Sengyou), 363n13
Great Buddha Hall (Daxiong bao dian) (Nanputuo Temple): Buddhist culture discourse and, 343–344; Guanyin festival and, 2, 292, 293, 322; Miaozhan's abbatial ascension ceremony and, 154; renovations of, 30, 31, 32; semiotic space and, 44, 57–63, 61, 343–344; statues in, 44, 45, 46, 103; stories of Buddha's lives in, 60–63, 61, 343–344; worship in, 45, 134, 329
Great Compassion Hall (Dabei dian) (Nanputuo Temple), 104; construction of, 28; Guanyin festival and, 63, 292, 294, 295, 297; layout of, 45; Miaozhan's abbatial ascension ceremony and, 154–155; renovations of, 30, 31, 32; semiotic space and, 46, 63–65; statues in, 28, 45, 105, 295, 297; visiting ritual, 46; worship in, 46, 63, 96
Great Leap Forward (Da yuejin) (1958–62), 24
Guandi, 239, 269, 270
Guang'an, 278, 287, 377nn43–44
Guanghua Temple: abbatial ascension ceremony, 150; Miaozhan's funeral and, 193–194; ordination ceremonies at, 120, 121–122, 125, 230, 254, 357–358, 379nn1–8; recovery from Cultural Revolution, 95–96; religious status of, 28; ritual knowledge and, 135. See also Yuanzhuo
Guangjing (prior of Longshan Temple), 185, 186, 241
Guangji Temple, 70, 79, 121, 215
Guan Gong, 44
Guangshu (prior of Puguang Temple), 245
Guangyi, 267, 377n44
Guangyu, 245, 248
Guanyin Famen, 368n11

404

INDEX

Guanyin festival (Guanyin jie), 133, 290–324, *331*; attendee belief variations, 298, 299–310, 319–321, *319*, 345, 378–379nn3–4, 8; attendee changes over time, 319–321; attendee motivations, 310–318, *319*; attendee occupations, *299*; double structure of, 292–293, 322; during Cultural Revolution, 290; Great Buddha Hall and, 2, 292, 293, 322; Great Compassion Hall and, 63, 292, 294, 295, 297; local relationships with Nanputuo Temple and, 298–299, 310, 312–313; local state religious administration and, 322–323; magical efficacy (*ling*) and, 2, 295, 303–304, 310–312, 316–317, 318, 346; Nanputuo Temple recovery and, 2–3, 290; popular religious practices and, 207, 295, 318–321, 322, 323–324, *330*; recent changes in, 346; sequence of, 293–298, *294, 296, 298,* 378n2; tourism and, 306–307, 322

Guanyin Temple, 257–258, *259*

Guanyin worship: devotees and, 30, 269; Hongshan Temple and, 243; Huxiyan Temple and, *326*; lay nuns and, 277, 286, 376n30; local relationships with Nanputuo Temple and, 28, 30; local Xiamen temples and, 243, 373n1; Miaoshan and, 64, 292, 376n30; modern reform movement and, 30; at Nanputuo Temple, 96, *327*; Nanputuo Temple consecration and, 28; popularity of, 292; popular religious practices and, 376n30; Putuoshan and, 28, 55, 360n10, 363n10; semiotic space of Nanputuo Temple and, 55, 67; statues and, 28, 44, 45, 96, *103, 105, 108,* 292, 295, 297. *See also* Great Compassion Hall; Guanyin festival

Gulangyu, 8–9

Guo Moruo, 66

Gushan Temple, 134

Haihui Pagoda, 51

Healing Sutra (*Yaoshi jing*), 273

Heavenly Kings Hall (Nanputuo Temple), 99, *101*; Cultural Revolution impact on, 31, 361n18; Guanyin festival and, 297; Miaozhan's abbatial ascension ceremony and, 152–153; renovations of, 32; semiotic space and, 54–57; statues in, 43–44, 56, 57, 152; worship in, 42

Heilongjiang Buddhist Association, 162

Heyun lineage (Linji school), 28, 59, 240, 360n11

History of Scientific Thought (*Kexue sixiang shi*) (Taixu), 117

Hongchuan (abbot of Kong Meng San Phor Kark See Temple), 84, 86, 89, 90, 94, 249, 256

Hongding, 280

Honghui, 252

Hong Kong, 213. *See also* overseas Chinese communities

Hong Kong Buddhist Association, 252

Hongshan Temple, 120, 240–244, 317, 326

Hongyi: Buddhist culture discourse and, 342–343; devotees and, 265, 267; education for clerics and, 29, 112; lay nuns and, 85, 239, 256, 278, 285; Miaofalin and, 284; recognition of, 365–366n23; scholarship on, 264, 375n5; Wulao Peak retreat, 30

Hsing Yun (Xingyun), 86, 213, 215, 216

Hua Guofeng, 87

Huangbo lineage (Linji school), 29, 59, 280, 281, 360n15. *See also* Ōbaku sect

Hubing, 284, 285

Huiquan (prior of Huxiyan Temple; abbot of Nanputuo Temple): education for clerics and, 249; Hongchuan and, 90; lay nuns and, 280; memorial stupa for, 31, 48; Miaozhan and, 84; Nanputuo Temple abbotship of, 29; overseas Chinese clerics and, 89; semiotic space of Nanputuo Temple and, 56–57, 58, 59; Wanshilian Temple and, 256

Huiyuan, 58–59

405

INDEX

Huxiyan Temple, 249–252, *326*; devotees and, 250; early history of, *326*, 360*n*15; Huiquan and, 29, 58, 59, 249; Kaizheng as prior, 250, 251–252, 255; lay nun halls and, 283; local state religious administration and, 250–251, 254–255; ordination ceremonies at, 29; recovery from Cultural Revolution, 249–250
Hu Yaobang, 142, 369*n*20

Ingman, Peik, 361*n*24
institutional space, 34; defined, 35; devotee marginalization in, 276–277; Nanputuo Temple Charity Foundation and, 177; physical space and, 36; religious activity sites and, 19, 74, 364*n*6; split in, 175; Tibetan Buddhism and, 276, 277. *See also* CPC ideology on religion; Document 19; local state religious administration; state religious bureaucracy; *specific organizations and policies*

Japanese occupation (1937–45), 9, 26; Cai Jitang and, 265, 375*n*6; Lin Ziqing and, 264; local Xiamen temples and, 240, 247, 248; Marco Polo Bridge Incident, 373*n*7; Miaozhan and, 82; Nanputuo Temple clerics and, 30–31; state Buddhist diplomacy and, 211; united front policies and, 23; Wanshilian Temple and, 256
jataka tales, 363*n*13
Jetavana Hermitage (Qiyuan jingshe), 25
Jiang Zemin, 148, 169
Jing'an Buddhist Academy (Jing'an foxue yuan), 264
Jingfeng Buddhist School, 29
Jingkong, 366*n*29
Jinglian Hall, 280–281
Jinta Tourism, 91
Jiqun, 205, 272–273, 274
Journal of the Buddhist College of Minnan (Minnan foxue yuan xuebao), 86

Jüehua Women's Buddhist Academy (Jue hua nüzi foxue yuan), 278, 377*n*44
Juewu (abbot of Nanputuo Temple), 280
Juzan, 26, 85, 360*n*8

Kaiyin, 256, 374*n*17
Kaiyuan (Tang emperor), 58
Kaiyuan Temple, 88
Kaiyuan Zhenguo Chan Temple, 161
Kaizheng (prior of Huxiyan Temple), 250, 251–252, 255
Knott, Kim, 361*n*21
Kong Meng San Phor Kark See Temple (Guangmingshan pujue si), 89, 90
Korean War, 278
Kwan Ying Buddhist Temple (Guanyin si), 188

Laiguo, 82, 181
Lassander, Mika, 361*n*24
Latour, Bruno, 37, 361*n*24
lay nun halls (*zhu caigu de si*): as BCM dormitories, 257; Buddhist culture discourse and, 283–286, 344; conversion for nuns, 239, 280–283; Cultural Revolution and, 286–287; local attendance, 302; new construction, 286–289, *332*; priors as BAX members, 76; religious activity sites and, 285, 344; tourism and, 285; worship at, *332*
lay nuns (*caigu*), 277–289, *332*; aging population, 279–280; BAX employment, 120; BCM admission, 85, 113, 206, 279, 284, 285, 287; BCM exclusion, 206–207, 279, 344–345; Chinese civil war and, 285; Cultural Revolution and, 125, 278–279, 280, 283, 285, 286–287, 288; devotees and, 267–268, 287, *332*; education for, 253, 279, 377*n*44; Guanyin worship and, 277, 286, 376*n*30; Hongshan Temple and, 240; local respect for, 286–288, 301–302, 317; local Xiamen temples and, 240, 256;

Miaozhan and, 85, 113, 206, 279, 287, 288; Minnan language/culture and, 206, 262, 283, 286, 287, 317, 344; Nanputuo Temple and, 278, 281, 288; overseas Chinese communities and, 278, 279, 285, 375*n*2; recovery from Cultural Revolution and, 93, 279, 280, 281, 284; Shenghui and, 206–207; status of, 239, 262–263, 277, 278, 375*n*3, 376*n*29. *See also* lay nun halls
layout. *See* physical space
Ledu, 186–187, 188, 371*n*35
Lefebvre, Henri, 34, 361*n*21
Lenin, V. I., 364*n*4
Li Hongzhi, 216, 217, 219, 223–224. *See also* Falun Gong campaign
Lingyanshan Temple, 83
Linji school, 27, 58, 241; Heyun lineage, 28, 59, 240, 360*n*11. *See also* Ōbaku sect
Lin Ziqing, 244, 247, 263–265
Li Peng, 212
Liu Zhengsong, 271–272, *329*
local relationships with Nanputuo Temple: Buddhist culture discourse and, 33; detachment under Shenghui, 207–208; Guanyin festival and, 298–299, 310, 312–313; Guanyin worship and, 28, 30; semiotic space and, 65; vegetarian restaurants and, 51, 136. *See also* devotees; popular religious practices
local state religious administration, 78–81, 128–129, 365*n*13; coordination (*xietiao*) and, 76, 77, 78, 80; Daoist temples and, 270, 276; during Cultural Revolution, 361*n*19; Falun Gong campaign and, 218–221, 254; Guanyin festival and, 322–323; lay nun halls and, 287–289, *332*; local Xiamen temples and, 250–251, 254–255; Miaozhan and, 84; Miaozhan's abbatial ascension ceremony and, 150; new temple construction restrictions, 79, 202, 257, 286, *332*; ordination and, 121; political/religious authority distinction and, 76, 365*n*10; XRAB-BAX cooperation, 201–203. *See also* BAX; XRAB; XRAB-Nanputuo Temple conflicts
local Xiamen temples, 237–261; Bailudong Temple, 252–255, *325*, 374*n*15; BAX authority over, 79, 202, 237, 245, 249, 250, 251, 252; Cultural Revolution and, 31, 237, 252; dharma transmissions and, 84, 244–245, 256; Guanyin Temple, 257–258, *259*; Hongshan Temple, 120, 240–244, 317, *326*; local state religious administration and, 250–251, 254–255, 374*n*10; Minnan language/culture and, 252–255, *325*; priors as BAX members, 76, 78; Puguang Temple, 132, 245–249, 317; recovery from Cultural Revolution, 93, 237, 241, 242, 243–244, 245, 256, 265; semiotic space and, 237; Tianzhuyan Temple, 259–261; tourism and, 250–251, 374*n*10; types of, 238–239, *238*, *240*; Wanshilian Temple, 114, 120, 255–257. *See also* Huxiyan Temple
Longhua Assembly (Longhua Hui), 369*n*3
Long March, 23
Longshan Temple (Singapore), 185, 186, 241, 377*n*44
Lotus Sutra (*Fahua jing*), 64, 273, 292
Luhmann, Niklas, 38
Luojia Mountain, 54, 363*n*10
Lu Xiujing, 58–59

Mahayana Buddhism, 360*n*16
Manila Buddha Temple, 186
Mao Zedong, 309
Marco Polo Bridge Incident (1937), 373*n*7
Marxism/Maoism, 3, 23, 71, 115, 117
May Fourth Movement (Wu si yundong), 25, 30
Mazu (Sea Goddess), 239, 269, 270, 373*n*1
Medicine Buddha (Yaoshifo; Bhaiṣajyaguru), 44, *103*

INDEX

Mengcan, 112, 368n2
Miaofalin, 284–286
Miaofeng, 186–188
Miaohua, 241, 373n2
Miaoshan, 64, 292, 376n30. *See also* Guanyin worship
Miaoshi Temple, 202–203
Miaoyin, 284
Miaozhan (abbot of Nanputuo Temple), 32, 48, 81–85, 228, 229, 340; BCM and, 84, 85, 86, 112–113, 114, 117, 118; Buddha Calligraphy and Painting Society and, 284; Buddhist Association of China and, 83, 84–85, 140; *Buddhist Cultivation Handbook* and, 271; Buddhist Culture Seminar and, 273; clerical self-management and, 163, 164–165, 166; cleric emigration and, 186–187; death and funeral of, 189–194; devotees and, 85, 207–208, 275, 276; dharma transmissions and, 84, 245, 257; on education for clerics, 49, 84; final saying of, 176, 189, *336*; Hongshan Temple and, 241; lay nuns and, 85, 113, 206, 279, 287, 288; local Xiamen temples and, 245, 251, 256, 257; Nanputuo Temple Charity Foundation and, 176, 177; Nanputuo Temple expansion and, 175, 180, 181, 182, 183, 184, 199; ordinations and, 121; overseas Chinese clerics and, 81, 84, 150, 200–201; overseas Chinese communities and, 82; personality of, 200–201; popular religious practices and, 85; rituals and, 132; state Buddhist diplomacy and, 212, 214; successor selection and, 197, 199; temple bureaucracy and, 126, 130–131; Tiananmen Square protest and, 142, 143, 145; XRAB-Nanputuo Temple conflicts and, 138, 139, 163, 164, 170, 171, 173, 184. *See also* Miaozhan's abbatial ascension ceremony
Miaozhan's abbatial ascension ceremony (1989), 149–163, 228, 229, 369nn3–4;

attendees, 150–151; semiotic space and, 159–163; sequence of, 151, 152–159; timing of, 149–150, 379n3
Mile (Maitreya), 43, 57, 152–153, 269
Ming dynasty, 8, 27
Mingyang (abbot of Lingyingshan Temple), 150, 160, 162, 229
Minnan language/culture: Bailudong Temple and, 252; devotees and, 50, 51, 207–208, 268, 269; Dingmiao and, 122; Guanyin festival and, 322; Guanyin worship and, 243; lay nuns and, 206, 262, 283, 286, 287, 317, 344; local Xiamen temples and, 252–255, *325*; Miaozhan's respect for, 85, 206; Nanputuo Temple abbot selection and, 197, 199; Nanputuo Temple rituals and, 132, 134; overseas Chinese clerics and, 89, 186, 188; Protestant missionaries and, 8; state Buddhist diplomacy and, 216; XRAB-BAX cooperation and, 202
modern reform movement, 3; charities and, 370n21; CPC ideology on religion and, 86, 364n3; devotees and, 25, 30, 266; ecumenicization and, 281, 360n16; local Xiamen temples and, 240, 243, 249; May Fourth Movement and, 30; Miaozhan and, 201; Nanputuo Temple as center for, 28–30; ordination ceremonies and, 29–30; origins of, 25–26; overseas Chinese clerics and, 88–89; popular religious practices and, 25; state Buddhist diplomacy and, 216. *See also* Hongyi; Huiquan; Taixu
modern state formation, 22–24
monasteries, function of, 19, 359n1
monks. *See* clerics
Mount Putuo (Putuoshan), 28, 46, 54, 55, 64, 65, 269, 360n10, 363n10
Mount Taiwu, 54–55, 58
Mount Wutai, 132

Nan Huaijin, 177, 181–182, 183
Nanputuo Temple, 99, *100*, *101*; abbot selection, 197–201, 372n2; abbots'

408

positions in Buddhist Association of China, 75–76; Ancestor Hall, 153–154; BAX location at, 79; beauty of, 316; Bell Tower, 32, 44, 99; Buddha Calligraphy and Painting Society and, 284; Buddhist culture discourse and, 342–344; Buddhist Culture Seminar and, 273; as center for modern reform movement, 28–30; cloisters, 65–66; Cultural Revolution impact on, 27, 31, 82, 361n18; devotees and, 30, 270, 275, 276, *329*; Dharma Hall, 30, 46–47, 66–67, 151, 155–161, 189–191; Dizang Hall, 44, 152, 153; Drum Tower, 32, 99; ecumenicization, 29, 58–59, 240, 281, 360n12; guest department, 47; history of, 27–33, 58, 59, 65, *351–354*; Hongshan Temple and, 242; lay nuns and, 278, 281, 288; leaders of, 32–33, 75–76, *349–350*, 379nn1–2; local Xiamen temples and, 249, 250, 253; Longevity Pagodas (Wanshou ta), 32, 42, *100*, 181, 182, 183–185, 293; Lotus Pond, 32, 42, *100*, 183, 297; main square, 43; Meditation Hall, 32, 49, 181–183; Merit Hall, 31, 50; Mind Purifying Pond, 67; monastery, 48, 49; mountain gates, 52–54, *102*, 152; name tablet, *99*; nuns and, 279; ordination ceremonies at, 29–30; overseas Chinese cleric networks, 89–91; as public park, 31, 135; Qielan Hall, 44, 153; Releasing Life Pond, 28, 32, 42; revenue, 137–139, 140, 175–176, 343, 362n4, 368–369nn17–18; Sutra Chanting Hall, 30, 50; Sutra Library, 46; Taixu Library, 49, 86, 205–206; Tiananmen Square protest and, 142–146; Tushita Hall, 30; vegetarian restaurants, 32, 51, 66, 136, 138, 140, 250; volunteers department (*yigong bu*), 344; Xiamen as treaty port and, 9; Zhengming Building, 50–51. *See also* Buddha Rock; Great Buddha Hall; Great Compassion Hall; Heavenly Kings Hall; local relationships with Nanputuo Temple; Miaozhan's abbatial ascension ceremony; Nanputuo Temple bureaucracy; Nanputuo Temple recovery; physical space of Nanputuo Temple; semiotic space of Nanputuo Temple; Wulao Peak; XRAB-Nanputuo Temple conflicts

Nanputuo Temple bureaucracy, 125–135; guest department, 128–130, 368n11; management department, 32, 47, 126–128, 135; overview, 126; rituals and, 131–135, *133*; sacristy, 130–131; terms of office, 126, 368n7

Nanputuo Temple Charity Foundation, 32, 49, 175–179, *178*, 199, 204, 210–211, 371nn23–24

Nanputuo Temple expansion, 175–185; BCM campus for nuns, 32, 179–181; Longevity Pagodas, 182, 183–185; Meditation Hall construction, 32, 181–183; Nanputuo Temple Charity Foundation, 175–179, *178*, 199

Nanputuo Temple recovery, 1, 10, 32; Guanyin festival and, 2–3, 290; income for, 362n4; Lin Ziqing and, 265; Miaozhan and, 81–85; overseas Chinese clerics and, 86–87, 89–91; overseas Chinese communities and, 10, 150; space and, 37; state support and, 87–88; Taixu and, 5, 85–88, 96, 365–366n23; Xiamen special economic zone and, 135–136. *See also* Miaozhan's abbatial ascension ceremony; XRAB-Nanputuo Temple conflicts

Nanputuo Temple Regulations for Permanent Residence (*Nanputuo si changzhu guiyue*), 128

Nanputuo Temple Rules and Regulations (*Nanputuo si guizhang zhidu*), 204

Nanshan Temple, 28, 88, 185–186, 264

Nan Tien Temple (Nantian si), 215

National Anti-cult Association (Quanguo fan xiejiao xiehui), 221

National People's Congress (Quanguo remin daibiao dahui), 78

INDEX

Nedostup, Rebecca, 365*n*10
Neiwu Temple, 270
Nengren Temple, 270, *333*, 375*n*15
network methodology, 37–38
New Buddhist Youth Association, 243
New Culture Movement (Xin wenhua yundong), 342–343
New Street Church (Xinjie libaitang), 8
North America, 186–187, 371*nn*33–35. *See also* overseas Chinese communities
Northern Song dynasty, 27
nuns (*biqiuni*): at BCM, 113–114, 118–119, 257, 281; BCM campus for, 32, 179–181; emigration of, 188; lay nun hall conversion for, 239, 280–283; ordination of, 120, 123–124, 125, *233*; *shichamona* status, 376*n*29. *See also* clerics; lay nuns

Ōbaku sect, 83, 96, 97, 249, *326*, 365*n*19, 367*n*43. *See also* Huangbo lineage
opening up-policies (*gaige kaifang*), 3–4, 9, 27, 79, 147. *See also* Cultural Revolution, Buddhist recovery from
Opium War (1839–1842), 8
ordination, 120–125; applications for, 120–121; Buddhist Association of China and, 121, 368*n*6; Guanghua Temple ceremonies, 120, 121–122, 125, 230, 254, *357–358*, 379*nn*1–8; Huxiyan Temple and, 29; meal practice and, *231*, 379*n*2; modern reform movement and, 29–30; of nuns, 120, 123–124, 125, *233*; ordinand backgrounds, 122–125, *123*, *124*, *232*; overseas Chinese communities and, 121

overseas Chinese clerics: BCM and, 86, 88, 114, 118; Buddhist Association of China and, 87; dharma transmissions and, 244–245, 373*n*4; emigration of, 185–188, 360*n*11, 371*nn*31, 33–35; Guanghua Temple and, 95; Heyun lineage and, 360*n*11; internet education for Chinese clerics and, 366*n*29; Lin Ziqing and, 264; local Xiamen temples and, 256, 258; Miaozhan and, 81, 84, 150, 200–201; Miaozhan's abbatial ascension ceremony and, 150; modern reform movement and, 88–89; Nanputuo Temple networks, 89–91; Nanputuo Temple recovery and, 86–87, 89–91; ritual knowledge and, 89–90, 91, 135; Taixu and, 88

overseas Chinese communities: *Buddhist Cultivation Handbook* and, 271; Chinese economic development and, 9–10, 93–94, 211; cleric emigration and, 187–188; devotees in, 91, 183, 287, 377*n*44; early CPC period Nanputuo Temple funding, 31; early establishment, 7; Guanghua Temple and, 95; lay nuns and, 179, 279, 285, 375*n*2; local state religious administration and, 76, 80, 139–140; local Xiamen temples and, 244, 250, 252; Miaozhan and, 82; Miaozhan's abbatial ascension ceremony and, 150; Nanputuo Temple expansion and, 183; Nanputuo Temple recovery and, 10, 150; Nanputuo Temple rituals and, 368*n*16; ordination and, 121; Protestant missionaries in, 8; return experiences, 94, 367*n*36; Singapore as development model and, 87, 366*n*24; state Buddhist diplomacy and, 211, 215; Taixu and, 86, 370*n*21; Tiananmen Square protest and, 146; united front policies and, 76; worship tours, 91; XRAB-Nanputuo Temple conflicts and, 137–138, 139; Zhuanfeng and, 360*n*12. *See also* overseas Chinese clerics

Pali Tripitaka Institute, 360*n*16
People's Republic of China (PRC): Belt and Road Initiative, 342, 343; early period (1949–66), 26–27, 31; economic development, 9–10, 81, 93–94, 211; founding of, 23, 26; one-child policy, 279; overseas Chinese distrust of, 94, 367*n*36; relations with Singapore,

90–91. *See also* CPC ideology on religion; state religious bureaucracy
Philippines, 89, 186
physical space, 34–35, 36, 260, 340. *See also* physical space of Nanputuo Temple
physical space of Nanputuo Temple, *xviii, xix*, 40–51; Buddhist culture discourse and, 343; central compound, 42–48; east compound, 50–51; feng shui and, 40, *334*, 362n2; Guanyin festival and, 292–293, 322; history of, *351–354*; layout overview, 41–42; location, 1, 40; Miaozhan's abbatial ascension ceremony and, 151, 152, 159; rural artisans and, 361n1; semiotic space and, 362n2; seven-hall structure (*qitang qielan*) and, 362n2; west compound, 48–50
plenary mass ritual, 207
popular religious practices: ancestor rituals, 50, 85, 130, 134, 135, 207, 227, 245; ancestor tablet storage, 50, 246, 254, 343; Buddhist culture discourse and, 225, 341; burning mouths release ritual, 62, 85, 134, 135, 207, 208; devotees and, 269, 270, 272, 276–277, *333*; vs. Falun Gong, 219–220; Guanyin festival and, 207, 295, 318–321, 322, 323–324, *330*; Guanyin worship and, 376n30; lay nuns and, 239; local temples for, 28, 239, 259–260, 373n1; local Xiamen temples and, 237, 246; magical efficacy (*ling*) and, 239, 259, 318, 362n6; Miaozhan and, 85; modern reform movement and, 25; semiotic space of Nanputuo Temple and, 362n6; Shenghui's banning of, 207, 208, 237, 323; state religious bureaucracy and, 364n7. *See also* spirit money burning ritual; worship at Nanputuo Temple
Potalaka. *See* Putuoshan
precepts, 43, 208, 262, 278
Project Hope (*xiwang gongcheng*), 178–179
Puguang Temple, 132, 245–249, 317

Pure Land Buddhism, 59, 245
Pure Rules of Baizhang (Baizhang qinggui), 125
Putuoshan (Mount Putuo), 28, 46, 54, 55, 64, 65, 269, 360n10, 363n10
Putuo Temple (Manila), 186
Puzhao Temple, 27, 99, *107*

Qian Qichen, 212
qigong, 273, 372n18. *See also* Falun Gong campaign
Qing dynasty, 3, 8, 27–28, 59, 364n2
Qingfu Temple, 283–284, 302
Quanzhou Buddhist Academy (Quanzhou foxue yuan), 253

Realm Upholding King (Chiguo tianwang), 56
Record of the Enlightenment of Buddha Tathagata (Shijia rulai chengdao ji) (Wangbo), 363n13
relics, 48, 211, 212–214, 359n1, 372n15
Religion and Overseas Chinese Group (Zongjiao huaqiao zu), 80–81
religious activity sites (*zongjiao huodong changsuo*), 19, 74, 78–79, 258, 285, 364n6
Religious Protection Section, 80
Republic of China (ROC): constitution of, 364n2; modern reform movement and, 25–26; political/religious authority distinction and, 365n10; state religious bureaucracy, 3, 22–23; Taixu and, 86. *See also* Chinese civil war
research methods, 10–14, 21
Riguangyan Temple, 317
ritual knowledge: Chinese clerics and on, 89–90, 91, 135; Cultural Revolution destruction of, 89, 113, 135; Nanputuo Temple ritualist and, 134–135, 227. *See also* clerics, education for
Ruijin, 89
Ruizhi (prior of Puguang Temple), 247–248, 374n8
Ruman, 186

411

INDEX

Sakyamuni Buddha (Shijiamoni), 44, 46, 103
Sandalwood Academy, 29
Second Sino-Japanese War. *See* Japanese occupation
self-management. *See* clerical self-management
semiotic space, 34, 35–37; Buddhist recovery from Cultural Revolution and, 339–340; local Xiamen temples and, 237. *See also* semiotic space of Nanputuo Temple
semiotic space of Nanputuo Temple, 40, 51–69; authors/creation dates and, 53, 363n9; Buddhist cosmology and, 43, 297, 362n2; Buddhist culture discourse and, 343–344; Buddhist teachings and, 46, 55–56; cloisters, 65–66; couplet format and, 363n8; Dharma Hall, 66–67, 159–160, 189–191; ecumenicization and, 58–59; Great Buddha Hall, 44, 57–63, *61*; Great Compassion Hall, 46, 63–65; Guanyin festival and, 322, 323–324; Heavenly Kings Hall, 54–57; Miaozhan's abbatial ascension ceremony and, 159–163; mountain gates, 52–54; Nanputuo Temple expansion and, 175; popular religious practices and, 362n6; pure land (*jingtu*) and, 52; state religious bureaucracy and, 162–163; stories of Buddha's lives and, 60–63, *61*, *102*, 297; Wulao Peak, 40, 52, 64, 67–69, *107*
Seng Guan Temple (Xinyuan si), 89
Sengyou, 363n13
seven Buddhas, 42, 362n5
seven-hall structure (*qitang qielan*), 362n2
Shatter the Four Olds campaign, 24, 31, 360n7, 361n18
Shenghui (abbot of Nanputuo Temple), 6, 32–33, 196–197, 340; background of, 198–199, 372n4; BCM reforms, 205–207; Buddhist Culture Seminar and, 274; devotees and, 207–208, 276; Falun Gong campaign and, 215, 216, 218–219, 221–225; Fayun and, 241; lay nuns and, 206–207; local Xiamen temples and, 251; personality of, 200; political connections of, 199–200; popular religious practice banning, 207, 208, 237, 323; selection of, 198–201; state Buddhist diplomacy and, 213–214, 215; temple standardization and, 203–211, 279; XRAB-Nanputuo Temple conflicts and, 208–210

Shengji (prior of Nanputuo Temple), 65
Shengyan, 265
shifang conglin. *See* clerical self-management
Shi Lang, 27–28, 59, 255
Sichuan Buddhist Institute for Nuns (Sichuan nizhong foxue yuan), 179
Singapore, 87, 89, 90–91, 186, 366nn24, 29
Singapore Devotee Lodge, 269
Sinicized Buddhism discourse (*zhongguohua fojiao*), 339
Sino-Tibetan Buddhist Institute, 360n16
Sizhou Yard, 27
Song dynasty, 360n13
Southeast Asia, 89, 185–186. *See also* overseas Chinese communities
space: analysis framework and, 33–34, 361n21; dimensions of, 34–37, 339; Miaozhan's abbatial ascension ceremony and, 149
spirit money burning ritual: BAX revenue and, 202; Buddha Rock and, *330*; Guanyin festival and, 2, 295, 322, 323, *330*; local Xiamen temples and, 246; Miaozhan and, 85; modern reform movement and, 25; physical space of Nanputuo Temple and, 50; Shenghui's banning of, 207, 209, 323
State Administration for Religious Affairs (Guojia shiwu zongjiao ju): absorption of, 347; 1990s standardization policies,

196, 371–372n2; popular religious practices and, 364n7; state religious bureaucracy structure and, 75; Tiananmen Square protest and, 143; XRAB-Nanputuo Temple conflicts and, 165–166

state Buddhist diplomacy, 211–216; Fo Guang Shan and, 213, 215–216; foreign delegations and, 211, 372n16; relic tours, 211, 212–214, 372n15

state religious bureaucracy: Buddhist Association of China national congresses and, 78, 365n11; coordination (*xietiao*) and, 76, 77, 78, 80; CPC dominance and, 74–75; creation of, 24; devotees and, 274, 277; Falun Gong campaign and, 221–225; flexibility of, 337; institutional space and, 35; Miaozhan's funeral and, 191–192; Nanputuo Temple Charity Foundation and, 176; Nanputuo Temple guest department and, 129, 368n11; national religious associations, 365n9; network methodology on, 37–38; 1990s standardization policies, 196, 217, 371–372n2; popular religious practices and, 364n7; qigong and, 372n18; recovery from Cultural Revolution and, 87–88, 92–94; religious activity sites and, 19, 74, 78–79, 258, 285, 364n6; Republic of China, 3, 22–23; semiotic space and, 162–163; structure of, 75–76; Withdraw from Sects campaign, 278; XRAB-Nanputuo Temple conflicts and, 164–166, 369n6. *See also* Buddhist Association of China; Buddhist culture discourse; Cultural Revolution; Document 19; Falun Gong campaign; local state religious administration; State Administration for Religious Affairs; state religious bureaucracy

Stories of the Buddha's Deeds in Past Lives (*Shijia rulai ying hua siji*), 60–63, 61, 344, 363n13

stupas, 31, 48, 68, 359n1
Su Bifen, 284

Taiping Rebellion, 243
Taiwan, 213, 214. *See also* overseas Chinese communities
Taiwan Straits crisis, 252
Taiwu (emperor), 58
Taixu (abbot of Nanputuo Temple): Buddhism for the Human Realm, 25, 30, 85, 86, 268, 364n3; Buddhist Association of China and, 76, 86; cleric emigration and, 185; critics of, 199; devotees and, 265; education for clerics and, 9, 25, 29, 84, 86, 112–113, 117, 360n16; memorial stupa for, 31, 48; Miaoshi Temple and, 202; modern reform movement origins and, 25–26; as Nanputuo Temple abbot, 9, 29; Nanputuo Temple Charity Foundation and, 176; Nanputuo Temple recovery and, 5, 85–88, 96, 365–366n23; overseas Chinese clerics and, 88; overseas Chinese communities and, 86, 370n21; state Buddhist diplomacy and, 211; Wulao Peak retreat, 30. *See also* modern reform movement
Tang dynasty, 58, 363n13
Tanxu, 82, 84, 187, 368n2
Tao Yuanming, 58–59
Ta Teh Institute (Dade xueyuan), 285, 377n42
temples: function of, 19, 359n1; institutional space and, 35; network methodology on, 38; physical space and, 35; as religious activity sites, 19, 74, 78; semiotic space and, 35–36. *See also specific temples*
Thailand, 90, 212–213. *See also* overseas Chinese communities
Thaksin Shinawatra, 212
Theravada Buddhism, 360n16, 363n13
"Three Laughing Persons at Tiger Creek" (Huxi san xiao), 58

Ti'an, 241
Tiananmen Square protest (1989), 142–146; Buddhist belief variations and, 218, 321; cleric emigration and, 186, 187; CPC ideology on religion and, 143–144, 148–149; devotees and, 218, 272; Guanyin festival and, 319; Guanyin festival attendees and, 2, 320, 321; Hu Yaobang and, 142, 369n20; Miaozhan's abbatial ascension ceremony and, 150; Nanputuo Temple and, 142–146; Nanputuo Temple expansion and, 175, 181, 182; overseas clerics and, 131; Project Hope and, 178
Tiantong Temple, 122, 132, 249
Tianzhuyan Temple, 259–261
tiaokuai system, 365n13
Tibetan Buddhism, 275–276, 277, 360n16
Tiexiang Temple, 179
Topley, Marjorie, 375n3
tourism: devotees and, 91, 270; Guanyin festival and, 306–307, 322; lay nun halls and, 285; local Xiamen temples and, 250–251, 374n10; physical space and, 340; vegetarian restaurants and, 136; worship at Nanputuo Temple and, 328; XRAB-Nanputuo Temple conflicts and, 135–137, 138, 139, 172, 176, 181, 209
Tripitaka, 116–117, 368n4
Tzu Chi Buddhist Compassionate Mercy Foundation, 186

UN Human Rights Commission, 222
Up to the Mountains and Down to the Villages Campaign, 31, 48, 361n20

Vimalakirti Sutra (*Weimo jiejing*), 273

Wanfu Temple, 95, 96–97, 367n43
Wangbo, 363n13
Wang Gong, 373n1
Wang Ye, 373n1
Wanshi Buddhist Research Society (Wanshi foxue yanjiu she), 256
Wanshilian Temple, 114, 120, 255–257

The Way to Buddhahood (*Cheng fo zhi dao*), 117
Weituo (Skanda), 43–44, 57, 297
Welch, Holmes, 21, 378n3
Wen Tianxiang, 144
Western Trinity (Xifang sansheng), 283
White Lotus Society, 218, 263, 373n19
Withdraw from Sects campaign (Tui dao yundong), 278
women. *See* devotees; nuns
World New Youth Buddhist Propagation Troupe (Fo hua xin qingnian shijie xuanchuan dui), 265
World War I, 9
worship at Nanputuo Temple: *Buddhist Cultivation Handbook* and, 271, 329; chanting services, 2, 45, 134, *328*; devotees and, 45, 46, 50, 207–208, *329*; during Cultural Revolution, 31, 321; Great Buddha Hall, 45, 134, *329*; Great Compassion Hall and, 46, 63, 96; Guanyin and, 96, *327*; magical efficacy (*ling*) and, 47, 48, 295, 303–304, 316–317, 318, 362n6; rituals, 50, 130, 131–135, *133*, 368n16; spirit money burning, *330*; travelers and, 68–69; Wulao Peak slopes and, 31, 47, *107*. *See also* Buddha Rock; Guanyin festival; popular religious practices
Wuchang Buddhist Studies Academy (Wuchang foxue yuan), 26, 29, 360n16
Wujin Crag, 27
Wulao Peak: Guanyin festival and, 297; magical efficacy (*ling*) and, 47; retreats on, 30, 48, 86; semiotic space and, 40, 52, 64, 67–69, *107*; statue grotto on, 48, *108*; worship during Cultural Revolution, 31. *See also* Buddha Rock

Xiamen: city defined, 360n6; history of, 8–10; map, *xxii*; as special economic zone, 1–2, 9–10, 80, 93–94, 132, 135–136
Xiamen Civil Affairs Bureau, 176, 177, 211
Xiamen Devotee Lodge, 250, 260, 267, 268–272, 276–277, *333*, 344

INDEX

Xiamen Mahayana Buddhist Society (Xiamen dasheng fojiao hui), 265
Xiamen Municipal Public Security Bureau (Xiamen shi gong'an ju), 80
Xiamen National Security Bureau (Xiamen shi anquan ju), 80
Xiamen Parks and Forestry Bureau, 135, 180
Xiamen United Front Work Department, 76, 78, 80–81, 82, 139–140, 258, 266
Xiamen University: BCM and, 115; Buddhist Culture Seminar and, 272–273, 274; devotees and, 268; Nanputuo Temple expansion and, 183; Tiananmen Square protest and, 143, 144
Xiamen Youth Buddhist Book Club (Xiamen qingnian foxue shushe), 274
Xiang Nan, 92
Xiao Xianfa, 78
Xican (prior of Nanputuo Temple), 65, 240, 243
Xichan Temple, 186
Xi Jinping, 4, 341, 367n1
Xingkong, 371n35
Xingyuan, 88, 89, 186, 256, 271, 278, 280, 377n44
Xingyun (Hsing Yun), 86, 213, 215, 216
Xinliang, 283–284
Xinyuan Temple (Manila), 377n44
Xiyuan Temple, 83
Xi Zhongxun, 111, 367n1
XRAB-Nanputuo Temple conflicts, 6, 135–142, 163–175; abbot selection and, 197, 198, 200, 374n10; clerical self-management and, 136, 137, 163, 164–165, 166, 370n8; cleric resistance and, 169–171; cleric uprising and, 172–175, 370n16; disrespect and, 138–139, 165; local Xiamen temples and, 374n10; Miaozhan's abbatial ascension ceremony and, 150; Miaozhan's funeral and, 192–194, 209; Nanputuo Temple Charity Foundation and, 176; Nanputuo Temple Enterprise separation and, 167–169; overseas Chinese donations and, 137–138, 139; secularization and, 140–141; Shenghui and, 208–210; state religious bureaucracy intervention, 164–166, 369n6; temple expansion and, 181, 182, 183–184; temple reopening and, 135; temple revenue and, 137–138, 140, 368–369nn17–18; tourism and, 135–137, 138, 139, 172, 176, 181, 209; young clerics and, 141–142

XRAB (Xiamen Municipal Ethnic and Religious Affairs Bureau; Xiamen shi zongjiao shiwu ju): BAX cooperation, 201–203; BCM and, 117; coordination (xietiao) and, 76, 78, 80; Daoist temples and, 276; Fayun and, 241; lay nun halls and, 285; local Xiamen temples and, 250–251, 252, 253, 257, 374n10; Miaozhan and, 83, 85; name of, 364n8; Religion and Overseas Chinese Group and, 81; state religious bureaucracy structure and, 75, 79–80; temple guest department and, 128; Tiananmen Square protest and, 144, 145–146; Xiamen Devotee Lodge and, 269. *See also* XRAB-Nanputuo Temple conflicts
Xuantang Shangdi, 373n1
Xuecheng, 96
Xuefeng Temple, *332*
Xuyun, 29, 187

Yang Wenhui, 25
Yangzhen Temple, 270, *333*
Yanpei, 86
Ye Xiaowen, 189
Yijing, 7–8
Yinguang, 265
Yinshun, 86, 117, 187, 213, 256, 264
Yinyuan, 249, *326*, 360n15, 367n43
Yongquan Temple, 85, 114
Young Men's Buddhist Association (Fojiao qingnian hui), 131, 187, 371n34
Youth Chan Society (Qingnian chanxue she), 273, 274, 275, 277

INDEX

Yuanchan, 95
Yuanfei (prior of Huxiyan Temple), 249, 360n15
Yuanguo, 252, 254, 374nn13, 15
Yuanying, 29
Yuanzhuo (abbot of Guanghua Temple), 95–96, 150–151, 154, 155, 189, 194, 229
Yue Fei, 144
Yufuo Temple, 83

Zen Buddhism, 83, 365n19, 367n43
Zewu (abbot of Nanputuo Temple), 33, 213, 339, 342–343
Zhaist groups, 263
Zhanru, 273
Zhanshan Buddhist Academy (Zhanshan foxue yuan), 82, 365n15
Zhanshan Buddhist Seminary, 187
Zhao Puchu: background of, 75; calligraphy by, 53, *102*; dharma transmissions and, 257; Miaozhan and, 83, 84, 140; Miaozhan's abbatial ascension ceremony and, 161; Miaozhan's funeral and, 189, 191–192; Nanputuo Temple abbot selection and, 198; recovery from Cultural Revolution and, 87; Singapore visit, 91; state Buddhist diplomacy and, 213, 214, 215; Taixu and, 86; Xiang Nan and, 92; XRAB-Nanputuo Temple conflicts and, 164, 165, 166, 171, 173, 174–175
Zhengguo, 121
Zheng Mengxing, 266–268
Zhengyan, 86
Zhiren, 284
Zhiwen, 283
Zhuanchen, 280
Zhuandao, 245
Zhuanfeng (prior of Nanputuo Temple), 29, 31, 48, 88, 284, 287, 360n12
Zhumo, 86
Zizhulin Temple, 32, 257
Zushi, 373n1
Zushi Gong, 269

THE SHENG YEN SERIES IN CHINESE BUDDHIST STUDIES
Edited by Daniel B. Stevenson and Jimmy Yu

Huaiyu Chen, *In the Land of Tigers and Snakes: Living with Animals in Medieval Chinese Religions*

John Kieschnick, *Buddhist Historiography in China*

Chün-fang Yü, *The Renewal of Buddhism in China: Zhuhong and the Late Ming Synthesis*, Fortieth Anniversary Edition

Erik J. Hammerstrom, *The Huayan University Network: The Teaching and Practice of Avataṃsaka Buddhism in Twentieth-Century China*

Dewei Zhang, *Thriving in Crisis: Buddhism and Political Disruption in China, 1522–1620*

Geoffrey C. Goble, *Chinese Esoteric Buddhism: Amoghavajra, the Ruling Elite, and the Emergence of a Tradition*

Jan Kiely and J. Brooks Jessup, editors, *Recovering Buddhism in Modern China*

Jiang Wu and Lucille Chia, editors, *Spreading Buddha's Word in East Asia: The Formation and Transformation of the Chinese Buddhist Canon*

Erik J. Hammerstrom, *The Science of Chinese Buddhism: Early Twentieth-Century Engagements*

N. Harry Rothschild, *Emperor Wu Zhao and Her Pantheon of Devis, Divinities, and Dynastic Mothers*

Paul Copp, *The Body Incantatory: Spells and the Ritual Imagination in Medieval Chinese Buddhism*

Beverley Foulks McGuire, *Living Karma: The Religious Practices of Ouyi Zhixu (1599–1655)*

Koichi Shinohara, *Spells, Images, and Maṇḍalas: Tracing the Evolution of Esoteric Buddhist Rituals*

Michael J. Walsh, *Sacred Economies: Buddhist Business and Religiosity in Medieval China*

GPSR Authorized Representative: Easy Access System Europe, Mustamäe tee 50, 10621 Tallinn, Estonia, gpsr.requests@easproject.com